The Soul of Doubt

THE SOUL OF DOUBT

The Religious Roots of Unbelief from Luther to Marx

DOMINIC ERDOZAIN

OXFORD
UNIVERSITY PRESS

OXFORD
UNIVERSITY PRESS

Oxford University Press is a department of the University of Oxford. It furthers the University's objective of excellence in research, scholarship, and education by publishing worldwide.

Oxford New York
Auckland Cape Town Dar es Salaam Hong Kong Karachi
Kuala Lumpur Madrid Melbourne Mexico City Nairobi
New Delhi Shanghai Taipei Toronto

With offices in
Argentina Austria Brazil Chile Czech Republic France Greece
Guatemala Hungary Italy Japan Poland Portugal Singapore
South Korea Switzerland Thailand Turkey Ukraine Vietnam

Published in the United States of America by
Oxford University Press
198 Madison Avenue, New York, NY 10016

Library of Congress Cataloging-in-Publication Data
Erdozain, Dominic.
The soul of doubt : the religious roots of unbelief from Luther to Marx / Dominic Erdozain.
pages cm
ISBN 978–0–19–984461–6 (cloth : alk. paper)
1. Conscience—Religious aspects—Christianity—History of doctrines.
2. Faith—History of doctrines. I. Title.
BJ1278.C66E73 2016
234'.23—dc23
2015004453

1 3 5 7 9 8 6 4 2
Printed in the United States of America
on acid-free paper

To Connie, George, and Emma

So far, all that has given color to existence still lacks a history. Where could you find a history of love, of avarice, of envy, of conscience, of piety, of cruelty?

—NIETZSCHE, *The Gay Science*

Minds are not conquered by force, but by love and generosity.

—SPINOZA, *The Ethics*

Contents

Acknowledgments

HUGH TREVOR-ROPER ONCE said that the best history is written by amateurs—honest campaigners, richer in enthusiasm than the protocols of academic discourse. I hope he is right. This study began when I was invited to give a lecture at Cambridge University in 2009 on "The making of a secular outlook in modern Britain." I called my paper "Christianity without the Mumbo-Jumbo," based on a phrase of Clement Attlee's. Asked whether he was a Christian, shortly before his death, the ex-Prime Minister and architect of Britain's welfare state had replied tersely: "Believe in the ethics of Christianity. Can't believe in the mumbo-jumbo." To the enquiry, "Is there an after-life, do you think?" Attlee responded: "Possibly." This struck me as a perfect summary of what some scholars have termed "diffusive Christianity" and I presented it as a stoutly British phenomenon—what Nietzsche mockingly termed "the English consistency"; the faith that outlives faith; the Christian ethic that somehow judges Christian belief. I knew there were parallels with Kantian philosophy but my lecture emphasized the organic quality of British doubt against the intellectual bravura of Continental secularism, with humorous examples to prove it.

But as I prepared the piece for publication, I started to wonder whether the contrast with Europe was overstated. Was the French Enlightenment remotely the "intellectual *coup d'état*" (in one scholar's phrase), or the "rise of modern paganism" (in another formulation), that I had taken it to be? I began to dig around in Voltaire and Pierre Bayle, one of the guiding lights of the *philosophes*, and the results—to my untrained eye—were astonishing. Far from an alternative to my concept of "Christianity without the mumbo-jumbo," I felt that I was staring at the shining exhibit. I will never forget my first encounter with Bayle's *Philosophical Commentary*, one of the bombshells of the early Enlightenment, and the startling discovery that I was dealing not with philosophy, as I then understood it, but with a Bible study—and no ordinary one at that. Finding similar themes in Ludwig Feuerbach and Baruch Spinoza—a figure I had hardly envisaged reading, let alone writing about—I sensed that a project was in the making. That it has survived the journey from idea to reality is thanks to the support and inspiration of many people.

It was my old schoolteacher and friend, Bernard Green, who first supplied the Attlee quotation and inspired me to think more deeply about the "implicit" Christianity of which I had been so skeptical in my doctoral work. Bernard died before I could complete this book, but it was a joy to catch up with him in Oxford in May 2012, to discuss my imminent move to America, and to assure him that I was still living off his intellectual capital. I still am. Among my colleagues at King's College London, special thanks are due to Clare Carlisle for sharing precious material on Spinoza and for generous comments on some draft material, and to Paul Janz, Susannah Ticciati, Ben Quash, Markus Vinzent, and Maria Rosa Antognazza for encouragement and insight along the way. An Early Career Fellowship from the Arts and Humanities Research Council provided a major boost, and I am especially indebted to three anonymous reviewers who assessed the proposal, forcing me to clarify what I meant by "conscience" as a unifying thread, and helping me to believe in the integrity of the argument. I am grateful to Cynthia Read and everyone at OUP for taking on the project and for seeing it through with enthusiasm and precision.

Although most of the book was written after I left my post at King's, I have been more grateful than ever for the wider fellowship of the academic community as I have attempted to turn an abstract noun into a tangible thesis. Yvonne Maria Werner invited me to speak at Lund University, in Sweden, where I enjoyed wonderful hospitality and clarified some thoughts on the thorny issue of "secularization." Frances Knight invited me to present a paper at the theology and religious studies seminar at the University of Nottingham, which gave me great encouragement and led to some helpful conversations on Spinoza. John Stackhouse invited me back to teach and give a public lecture at Regent College Vancouver during a glorious week in July 2014. The resulting conversations, in and outside of the classroom, have been invaluable to me. I would also like to thank Cristian Romocea for inviting me to join a British delegation to the Bible and Culture seminar at the Shanghai Academy of Social Sciences in October 2014, where I spoke about Christianity and Western individualism, during another memorable week. Cheng Zuming's comment about Christian conscience being "externalized" as human rights and other legal frameworks provided a vital insight at a late stage of this project. Finally, I would like to thank Ian McFarland, Ed Phillips, Jonathan Strom, and Brooks Holifield for welcoming me so warmly as a visiting scholar at Emory University, these past two years, and Myron McGhee for wonderful assistance at the Pitts Theology Library. Jonathan and Brooks both read draft chapters and shared important insights, while patiently briefing me on the politics of the South.

Thanks are also due to David Bebbington and Hugh McLeod for comments on individual chapters, and to James Orr for encouraging feedback on the first five chapters. John Coffey offered a wealth of insight on the first four chapters, and I am enormously grateful to Timothy Larsen for kind and vigorous reflections on the whole book. Peter Webster, George Gross, and Carole Irwin each helped me trim the final product. If I may be permitted to quote Feuerbach, one last time: "However faulty a man may be, it is a proof that there is a germ of good in him if he has such people for his friends." The titles of chapters 1 and 6 are borrowed from Isaac Deutscher's biography of Trotsky, and Richard Crossman's study of six intellectuals who lost their faith in Communism, respectively. I have not quoted either in the text but the phrases seemed to set the tone better than any of my own, so I leave them as the ghost of studies past.

Special thanks are due to my wife, Meara, for taking everything in her stride as we have left the known unknowns of London for the unknown unknowns of Atlanta, and for giving me the opportunity to write while she does what might be described as a proper job. But my biggest thanks are for my children, whose cheerful enquiries about "which chapter" I am working on have provided the purest stimulus to complete this task, and whose frustrations with the process have taken ever more inventive forms. I will not forget the occasion when their efforts to distract me from reading Samuel Butler's *The Way of All Flesh* one afternoon resulted in all-out war, with repeated attempts to seize the book from my hands, followed by a flow of menacing handwritten notes, passed silently under my nose. My resistance was finally broken with a note bearing the immortal words: "JUST PLAY WITH US!" I know whose side Butler would have been on. To three irrepressible characters, whose boundless humor has been a continual antidote to the grind of scholarship, I dedicate this book.

D.E.

Atlanta, Georgia, March 2015

Abbreviations

CH Sebastian Castellio, *Concerning Heretics; Whether They Are to Be Persecuted and How They Are to Be Treated; a Collection of the Opinions of Learned Men, Both Ancient and Modern; an Anonymous Work Attributed to Sebastian Castellio, together with Excerpts from Other Works of Sebastian Castellio and David Joris on Religious Liberty*, edited by Roland H. Bainton, Records of Civilization, Sources and Studies, no. 22 (New York: Columbia University Press, 1935).

ODNB *Oxford Dictionary of National Biography*, edited by H. C. G. Matthew and Brian Harrison (Oxford: Oxford University Press, 2004). Online edn., edited by Lawrence Goldman, October 2009, http://www.oxforddnb.com/.

TTP Benedict de Spinoza, *Theological-Political Treatise*, edited by Jonathan I. Israel, translated by Michael Silverthorne and Jonathan I. Israel (Cambridge: Cambridge University Press, 2007).

WV Voltaire, *The Works of Voltaire: A Contemporary Version*, a critique and biography by John Morley, notes by Tobias Smollett, translated by William F. Fleming, 21 vols. (New York: E. R. DuMont, 1901).

The Soul of Doubt

Introduction

DESECULARIZING DOUBT

WHEN THE "JIM Crow" laws of the American South died a slow and undignified death in the 1960s, the cry went up against "secular humanism." When the Equal Rights Amendment of 1972 proposed a brave stance of female equality, the complaint was of the erosion of "Judeo-Christian values."[1] When the long delayed integration of the public schools started to become a reality, many responded by sending their children to a cluster of newly established "Christian Schools." The number of students enrolled in these nearly-all-white institutions increased by 95% in the 1970s. "The ostensible reason for their establishment was the perceived secularization of the public schools," writes one scholar, "but hostility to the forced integration was also a major factor."[2] Indeed "secularization" was often a code for unwelcome cultural change. As reactions to civil rights and feminism helped to create the "two nations" of modern America, resistance mobilized around the challenge of "secular humanism." Supported by the preacher and broadcaster, Pat Robertson, and Governor George Wallace, more than six hundred families sued the state of Alabama in 1986 for promoting "secular humanism" in public school textbooks.[3] Pressure was finally brought to bear in Washington, where a clause against the secular contagion was inserted in a bill earmarking funds for schools undertaking desegregation. It was only after the bill became law that the mysterious "Prohibition" was subject to vexed scrutiny. "I have no idea what secular humanism is," commented one senator. "No one knows."[4]

The specter of secular humanism became a unifying focus of the Religious Right, marshaled by the theologian and cultural critic, Francis

Schaeffer, who traced a dark history of spiritual decline in film and print.[5] Definitions lagged behind indignation, however, as Schaeffer switched between attributing the secular menace to an Enlightenment humanism that made "Man the measure of all things" and a Darwinian philosophy that reduced life to chance. As Schaeffer warned in an influential lecture: "The world view that the final reality is only material or energy shaped by pure chance, inevitably, (that's the next word I would bring to you) mathematically—with mathematical certainty—brings forth all these other results which are in our country and in our society which have led to the breakdown in the country."[6] A comparable preoccupation with Darwin among prominent atheists has deepened the perception of religion and unbelief as alien "worldviews," locked in mortal combat.

One of the claims of this book is that such a dichotomy between "religious" and "secular" thought is unsustainable. Fierce Christian apologists, and even fiercer "new atheists," share a common root system. Indeed the ferocity directed against religion in public life is to no small degree a product of it: a pointed and articulated fury that bears little resemblance to any hard-wired "process of secularization." Part of my challenge is that the narrative of secularization—whether a song of vindication for triumphant unbelief, or a song of lament for embattled cultures of faith—is a concept that distorts historical reality, both in the age of Enlightenment and in the era mistakenly attributed to Darwin. It turns the subjective materials of doubt and alienation into a fixed and objective phenomenon. After many years of staring at the sources, I am yet to find evidence of this implacable historical reaper, invoked so habitually in the academic literature. A telling comment came from Schaeffer's son, Frank, who had been in the frontline of the culture wars before a dramatic change of heart. He and his father, he later reflected, made careers attacking a "secular America" of which they "really knew *nothing*." Their "jaundiced" worldview was an untested demonology, conjured from fundamentalist polemics and a set of enduring prejudices about "the evils of liberals." Secularization was sectarianism minus the shooting. "I had no context, no sense of proportion, no hands-on experience," he ruefully recalled.[7] The fallacies Schaeffer detected in his father's reasoning are not confined to popular apologetics. Narratives of religious decline have been defined too narrowly by religious traditions themselves, inviting scholars to interpret heterodoxy and dissent as the signs of a fated secularity.[8] Modernity cannot be thus contained.

The context in which a book is written should not determine its argument, but it would be difficult to move to the home of Martin Luther King Jr. without perceiving some of the ironies of "secularization." As King urged in his "Letter from Birmingham Jail" (1963), religious cultures often embody the secular values that they profess to deny. Indeed, he argued, it is often those who insist on a strict separation of the "sacred" and the "secular" who align Christianity most emphatically with the secular order. A soul-centered theology, which either ignores or postpones questions of justice, King suggested, creates "merely a thermometer" religion, which rises and falls with "the principles of public opinion." It fosters an inert piety, "silent behind the anesthetizing security of stained glass windows." "Far from being disturbed by the presence of the church," he continued, "the power structure of the average community is consoled by the church's silent and often vocal sanction of things as they are." King had been criticized for dragging "social issues" into the pulpit, but he threw the charge back at his accusers. Silence was the greatest secularism of all. A religious culture that functions as the "archdefender of the status quo" is the real motor of disenchantment. "Every day," he wrote, "I meet young people whose disappointment with the church has turned into outright disgust."[9]

King's brutal analysis of a theology of pious resignation, which conceives the church as an island of purity surrounded by profane and threatening seas, may be one of the most penetrating comments on secularization ever written. With the contention that a church which is "inextricably bound to the status quo" is *ipso facto* a secular one, he turns the conventional narrative on its head. And by exposing the inherent secularity of a "lofty," "other worldly," and "heavenward" piety, King was at one with two of the most radical critics of religion in the modern era: Ludwig Feuerbach and Karl Marx. The atheist humanists of the nineteenth century, and the Christian civil rights leader of the twentieth, leveled many of the same criticisms at the religious establishments of their time. Both raised the problem of a theological timescale that pushes freedom and justice into heavenly abstraction; both observed the irony of a secular/sacred divide that preaches holiness from the best seats in the house; and both employed biblical language of the "imago Dei"—the idea of humankind made in the image of God—against theological systems that would reduce people to objects. The suggestion of a leading evangelist that King would do well "to put on the brakes a little bit" in his struggle for justice, and the priestly admonition that, "Only when Christ comes again will little white children of Alabama walk hand in hand with little Black children," would not have startled the nineteenth-century humanists.[10] Christians like King, and ex-Christians like Feuerbach, were fighting similar battles. The claim of this study is that such parallels are not accidental. The "secular" critique of Christianity was a burning product of the religion it dared to appraise.

Secularization, however, is a concept so instinctive to conversations about religion in the modern age that even critics seem to submit to its subtle, steering logic. Ever since the great sociologist, Max Weber, offered his influential reflections on "rationalization and intellectualization" as the "fate of our times," in the early twentieth century, the notion of secularization as a process and a destiny has dominated the interpretation of religion and modernity.[11] Even when the clean lines of the thesis are disturbed by the humble toil of history, or the subtle erudition of philosophy, a normative contrast between a "religious" past and a "secular" present endures. And this stern, often moralized, contrast obscures one of the engines of modern thought and consciousness: religious conviction itself. The certainty that "we," in the twenty-first century, are less religious than our forebears provides the starting point for an enquiry that knows the answer in advance. The comfortable certainty of a secular outcome disciplines the sources and corrupts the pursuit of causation. As an English historian gently warned, "the story looks different when you know, or think you know, how it ended."[12]

The Canadian philosopher, Charles Taylor, has made a major contribution to this field of scholarship with his masterful account of a "secular age" delivered from the hands of religious thought and practice.[13] For Taylor, secularization does not happen to Christendom: it emerges from it. Religious discipline creates a secular order. Yet Taylor's concern for the "conditions" of belief, rather than belief itself, serves to reproduce some of the fatalism of the older, Weberian analysis that he so eloquently critiques. It elevates the context of religious faith over its content, so that the fate of religion in any period seems to turn on the hospitality of the circumstances. It may indeed be harder to believe in 2000 than it was in 1500, but the risk of an emphasis on conditions is the muzzling of those rogue agents of history: human decisions. Even in a study as sophisticated as Taylor's, the guiding assumption of a secular modernity seems to flatten the drama of personal motivation. The urge to explain how we "got here" conditions the material, turning the discordant voices of Enlightenment and "Counter-Enlightenment" into the "stages" of a complex but ultimately known journey.

Taylor's narrative carries a kind of gravitational momentum, which rides too briskly over the coveted ground of causation. Ideas become movements. Novas become supernovas. It is not always clear why. Taylor shows, for example, how "Deism" provided a link between a theological outlook and an "anthropocentric," or humanistic one. But he says little about the anguish that might push someone from one to the other. The process is mapped rather than explained. Although I remain in Taylor's debt, my suspicion is that *A Secular Age* represents a version of what has been termed the "intellectualist" fallacy: a tendency to privilege the clean logic of ideas above the raw fuel of human experience among the forces of historical change.[14] When all has been said about "social imaginaries," "buffered selves," and "immanent frame[s]," the more prosaic truth may be that people are repelled by a religion that threatens to diminish them. It is that inner history of alienation, rather than an outer history of cooling conditions, that this study seeks to provide.

My canvas is smaller than Taylor's. It concerns aggressive and articulate unbelief, rather than the wider ecology of doubt. But it aims to supply some of the motive power that intellectual genealogies often lack: an elusive, dynamic force that I will term "conscience." The claim is that assaults on religious orthodoxy are seldom motivated by rigorous questions of intellectual plausibility. Rather, they are typically prompted by moral or spiritual anxieties, to which philosophical reasoning may or may not be subsequently added. Such anxieties, far from representing a pagan or secular distaste for Christian faith, have consistently emerged from a set of Christian assumptions and expectations. A visceral sense of right and wrong, rather than a scientific or historical suspicion of supernatural truth claims, has served as the primary solvent of orthodoxy in the West. Christianity has generated its own critique—the process consistently overlooked by a historical perspective that reads the cause from the outcome, locating the origins of unbelief in a rational scientific consciousness that is somehow taken for the reality of the present.

A history of conscience does not come at the expense of science or philosophy, however. Chapters on Spinoza, Darwin, and Marx show that sophisticated philosophical systems can emerge from initially ethical dissent. The claim is that the ferocity of such systems remains traceable to religious values. The fiercest religious cultures have produced the fiercest philosophical dissent. The Bible continues to justify its critics.

Clearly, in a movement such as Marxism, there is a repudiation of religious sources, often violent. But repudiation cannot always be taken for separation. Indeed it is in the molten energies of European socialism that the presumptive diagnosis of secularization is arguably most precarious. Socialism embodied a complaint central to all of the major traditions of dissent: that Christendom is not Christian enough. The possibility that secularization is not so much a misstatement as an inversion of historical reality is one that at least deserves consideration.

As the French scholar, Jean Delumeau, has urged: before we can talk about "de-Christianization" we have to know what we mean by "Christianization," and he was far from sure. His haunting account of a religious culture paralyzed by "magic, Manichaeism and fear" delivered a rebuke to the simplistic association of early modern Christendom with vibrant Christian piety. It challenged a theological demonology of the Enlightenment as some sort of pagan assault on a settled Christian consensus. The truth, Delumeau suggested, may be the other way round. He hinted at such an interpretation of Voltaire.[15] An American historian has offered a similarly robust challenge, arguing that the brute fact of persecution alone ought to be enough to confuse the before-and-after model of religious decline. "Medieval Christians knew that faith was not axiomatic," he dryly comments, "if only because so many needed to be killed to make it so."[16]

My concern is not the theological question of what Christendom was or claimed to be. It is fair analysis of the critics, heretics, and troublemakers, whose motives in rattling what has passed at various times for religious orthodoxy have been as consistently misrepresented by their admirers as their enemies. Voltaire is a case in point; Spinoza is the supreme example. Very few of the skeptics encountered in these pages were atheists, and those that were continued to measure religion by Christian standards. Conscience outlived conscious belief. One of my claims is that modernity has been characterized by the internalization of religious ideas, not their disintegration. And if such inner pilgrimages have been followed by externalization—as the piercing spirit takes up residence in "rights," causes, and revolutions—such migrations continue to elude the heavy shepherding of secularization. The influence of a religion cannot be limited to the rational currency of belief. All of the figures explored here served to weaken the historic coordinates of Christian orthodoxy. All reduced the status and prestige of theology. And each hastened the demise of that "fifteen-hundred-year-old adventure" of Christendom.[17] Yet every one of them was motivated by impulses native to the Christian faith. It is on such a paradox that this study turns.

The "religious roots" that I consider fundamental to modern cultures of unbelief are twofold: the positive content of dissent, including conscience, Bible and Christian ethics, and the negative stimulus of dogma, persecution, and theologically induced fear. This binary contribution of the Christian culture to its own critique is developed in the opening chapter, on Martin Luther. Here, I show how Luther energized and expanded the claims of the Christian conscience, against papal authority and religious tradition, before diminishing it in relation to his master principle of "justification by faith alone" and the theocratic muscle of the state. Luther is thus the prophet of conscience and the architect of an emerging era of "confessionalization," in which orthodoxy becomes the measure of the Christian. He sets in motion a conflict between conscience and creed that will run, in various forms, into the late modern era.

Tension between the younger Luther's message of freedom and the older Luther's passion for order is explored in chapter 2, where themes of doubt and theological skepticism surface as the survival mechanisms of radical Protestants such as Sebastian Franck and Sebastian Castellio. The chapter shows how Castellio's dispute with John Calvin over the punishment of heretics provoked more than a vigorous debate on religious toleration: it prompted eloquent appeals for the suspension of theological certainty in favor of a simplified religion of conscience. The foundations of the Enlightenment settlement were established by men of intense but bruised Christian convictions—in the sixteenth century.

Chapter 3 charts a similar transition from a heart-centered Protestantism to a kind of spiritual rationalism in the seminal contexts of the English civil war and the newly liberated Dutch Republic. I show that Spinoza was not only familiar with the dissolvent thought-world of radical Protestantism but intimately connected to it, developing both his biblical criticism and his much-feared metaphysics as a reaction to the overbearing Calvinism of the Dutch Reformed Church. Far from seeking to destroy Christianity, I argue that Spinoza was trying to restore its original emphasis on love and mercy. The central figure of the Radical Enlightenment was a man of fervent piety, challenging confessional authority from a stance of intensified, not attenuated, spirituality.

Chapter 4 pursues similar themes in the central Enlightenment figure of Voltaire. I show how Voltaire's hostility to the Catholic orthodoxy of his time centered on what he regarded as the twin evils of persecution and the divisive, neo-Augustinian theology of Jansenism. The chapter explores, first, Voltaire's debts to Christian philosophers such as Pierre Bayle in his defense of conscience and salutary doubt, and, second, the striking emphasis of his writing on mercy and forgiveness. While the search for a theology of mercy and a "Father" God was initially pursued with a degree of distance from Christian sources, Voltaire came to an increasingly explicit affirmation of what he regarded as the "right" kind of Christianity. The leading critic of organized religion in the modern era emerges as a profoundly Christian thinker, attempting to steer a violent orthodoxy back to peaceable origins.

Chapter 5 explores the nineteenth-century "crisis of faith" that continues to be associated with Darwin and natural selection. I show that the Victorian religious public in fact absorbed evolution relatively painlessly, arguing that the "warfare" between science and religion revolved around ethical and professional concerns rather than religious knowledge as such. It was a revolt against theological control rather than theology itself. I argue that it was, in many ways, an extension of the Enlightenment's conflict between conscience and "clericalism," and it led few into atheism or philosophical "materialism." I show that the real solvent of faith in the nineteenth century was the evangelical conscience, reacting with force and penetration to harsh renderings of Christian orthodoxy. The chapter concludes with a discussion of the aesthetic revolt against Victorian earnestness, presaging the more emotive unbelief of the twentieth century.

The sixth chapter returns to the subject of the first: Luther's radical doctrine of faith and its contribution to what Ludwig Feuerbach considered an amoral and authoritarian Protestant culture. I show that Feuerbach's intuition that humans create a God in their own image springs from an essentially moral critique of the "egoism" of faith. The chapter shows how this moral, even theological, critique lays the foundation of the Marxist analysis of religion as "ideology," oiling the wheels of power and privilege. The ferocious challenge of atheist materialism thus emerges from a Christian sensitivity to the fallacy of a selfish religion. Although Marx's "conscience" differs substantially from Feuerbach's, his critique of both religion and religiously sanctioned capitalism remains theological: it is the enduring charge of "idolatry." Communism was a millenarian revolt against a heavenly yet all-too-earthly theology of gain.

If my suspicion of secularization carries its own air of dogma, I can only plead a historian's immunity. The religious intensity of my army of critics has constantly amazed me. I expected this study to be footnotes on Kant, the high priest of "autonomy," not Spinoza, the unrepentant mystic. But to be conquered by the sources is not the joy of history: it is the reason for it.

I

The Prophets Armed

LUTHER AND THE MAKING AND BREAKING OF CONSCIENCE

He that is spiritual judges all things, yet he himself is judged of no man.

—1 CORINTHIANS 2:15

IT WAS JULY 2, 1505, and Martin Luther was doing what any sensible 25-year-old with a Master's degree would do: he was going back to university to study the law. His father was relieved, and it would have been impossible for the earnest graduate not to think of the security that lay ahead. Nothing had prepared him for the storm that sprang from the horizon like a holy ambush: a mass of divine fury that appeared to have his name on it. Thrown from his horse, Luther did not dare to address the God who seemed to be tormenting him: "Help, St. Anne, I will become a monk," he called out in terror. Two weeks later, to the amazement of friends and the disappointment of his father, he entered the Augustinian monastery at Erfurt with words of pious resignation: "You see me today and never again."[1] It was not long, however, before Luther was inspiring meteorological metaphors himself, as he hammered his way out of a medieval thought world with an intensity that would remold the European landscape. Finding that the monastery was anything but the refuge he was looking for, Luther inched his way toward a revolutionary theology of freedom. His theory that faith, and faith alone, opens the gates of divine mercy was that rare thing in history: an idea that creates an era.

There was, however, a restless ambiguity at the heart of the revolutionary formula. Luther was, on the one hand, the prophet of the free conscience, the champion of an arresting and sacred individualism. No one advocated the rights of the "inner man" with greater force or eloquence.

On the other hand, no one, apart from John Calvin, made a bolder attempt to control and discipline the liberated conscience. It was from this tension between freedom and discipline that powerful currents of skepticism would emerge. Luther began the revolution as a fiery mystic, cleaving to conscience against theology, Church, and world; he ended up an unrepentant dogmatist, holding conscience in the iron grip of doctrine. The story of Protestant radicalism, and the religious skepticism it unleashed, is the story of Luther's conscience turning on Luther's Reformation. From the creedless spiritualists of the 1520s to the pious atheism of Ludwig Feuerbach in the 1840s, the culture of unbelief was leavened, indeed driven, by sentiments traceable to Luther. Luther is equally the parent of Calvin and Kant: the era of hard confessional orthodoxy and the righteous liberation of Enlightenment.

Luther's Burning Conscience

Nietzsche once complained that everything "that has given color to existence still lacks a history." You can read about kings, empires, and ideas. But, he wondered, "Where could you find a history of love, of avarice, of envy, of conscience, of piety, [or] of cruelty?" Enlightenment philosophers treated such things as fixed and timeless phenomena, stable in their burden upon the human psyche, but any historical thinker knew that they were moveable feasts, subject to time and chance.[2] Of Nietzsche's mysterious nouns, conscience is especially ripe for scrutiny. Advocates of conscience as the supreme arbiter of moral truth emphasized its primal, eternal qualities against the ephemera of creed and tradition. The truths of conscience were etched into the fabric of creation, hard and irreversible. But even at its leanest and least articulate, conscience was a child of culture and tradition. Inner truths were always in dialogue with habit and social expectation. A mental faculty that was often identified with the very voice of God was as historical as any other.

Luther's conscience was sensitive and volatile from the start. But as he wrestled with his sins in the appraisive chamber of the monastery, he also revealed the power of a deep and richly sedimented culture of "guilt" and "fear."[3] The hunched ordinand, pouring out his transgressions over six-hour visits to the confessional, was every bit the Augustinian monk. Luther's revolution began with a great expansion of this inherited sensorium, before moving to an emphasis on liberation and exoneration. If

Luther's doctrine of faith ultimately served to subdue the restless conscience, he owed the triumphant clarity of his theology to his long struggles with guilt, fear, and looming judgment. One of the motors of the Reformation was a collision between a lively, convulsive conscience and a liberating doctrine of grace—both inherited from Augustine.

If Western Christianity developed an interiority complex, Augustine of Hippo (354–430) was perhaps its original neurotic, translating biblical categories of "law" and "grace" into an internal drama of the soul.[4] Augustine's *Confessions* all but invented the art of self-scrutiny, inspiring generations to interpret the tremors of conscience as the echoes of Sinai, the witness of a holy God. Medieval theology had not silenced Augustine's conscience, but it offered a menu of negotiation, contrition, and penance. By Luther's time, the fierce, occasionally suicidal terrors to which he was prone were relatively rare. Part of his critique of academic theology (scholasticism) centered on a tendency to gloss over the terrors of the anxious conscience, to proclaim peace where there was no peace. Luther found no comfort in the rhythms of penance and absolution. His originality as a theologian lay in the perception that both schools of medieval theology had succumbed to the same folly of trying to appease a holy God.

Luther had been trained in the "nominalist" tradition, which emphasized the power and inscrutability of the divine character to a frightening degree. The nominalist God was untethered by human logic, free to do as he wished. He was, in William of Ockham's haunting phrase, "no man's debtor." Such theology underpinned Luther's contempt for the rival tradition of Thomas Aquinas, which presumed to place God and humankind on a shared matrix of values. Yet Luther began to fear that the nominalist theologians, who trained him, were guilty of the same urge to negotiate terms with the deity, to build stairways to heaven. He sensed arrogance in the injunction to do your best and trust God for the rest. Luther's experience among the spiritual athletes of the monastery was one of sobering failure. The best is not enough. In fact, it is in the urge to impress and cajole the deity that the malignancy of sin resides.

Luther's theology thus began with a magnification of the claims of conscience against doctrines of compromise and self-flattery: what he would later term a "theology of glory." His resentment of Aristotle as an interloping influence on Christian thought derived in part from the philosopher's trivialization of conscience as practical reason: a moral compass that assists in ethical decisions, rather than a divine force appraising the whole person. He found in Augustine, and a range of mystical sources, a deeper, more emotive account of conscience, which provided resonance if not relief. Luther's enduring complaint against scholasticism was that it substituted intellectual reasoning for spiritual experience. Drunk on syllogism and deduction, academic theology served as an anesthetic to the soul, masking the effects of sin and dimming the spiritual senses. Luther turned instead to mystical writers who wrote with disconcerting vividness and immediacy, offering a theology of experience, will, and affection. It was here that he discovered an authentic grammar of theological reflection. "By living, indeed by dying and being damned, one becomes a theologian," he wrote in 1520, "not by thinking and reading and speculating."[5] The Reformation was medieval before it was modern.

Scholars have written of a "democratization of mysticism" in the late medieval period, a broad and diffusive reaction to the sterile precision of scholasticism.[6] This included the "Modern Devotion," associated with the Brothers of the Common Life in the Low Countries, and the classic devotional work, *The Imitation of Christ*. "I had rather feel contrition than be skillful in the definition thereof," urged the author of this much admired text.[7] Luther was taught by the Brethren, but he seems to have drawn greater sustenance from an anthology of mystical writing known as the *German Theology*. Luther published three editions of this text between 1516 and 1518, listing it behind only the Bible and the works of Augustine among his greatest influences. He praised the book as a reminder that "God speaks only in and through the weak, declaring his glory from the mouth of babes," rather than those who are "rationally gifted and clever."[8] Luther also imbibed the insights of Jean Gerson, a French devotional writer and a leading advocate of "conciliarism," as well as Johannes Tauler, a disciple of Meister Eckhart and the primary influence on the *German Theology*. Conciliarism was the principle of balancing the authority of popes with the wisdom of church "councils." Luther's decision to name the anthology the "German" Theology suggested a similar congruence of spirituality and dissidence. But it was the spiritual power of mysticism that appealed to Luther in 1515, when he scribbled an admiring comment in the margin of one of Tauler's sermons: "This whole sermon evolves from mystical theology which draws its knowledge from experience [*sapientia experimentalis*] and not from doctrine."[9] Central to a theology of experience was a dynamic, almost physical account of conscience.

Writers like Gerson and Tauler followed Augustine in characterizing conscience as a vital "spark" of divinity in an otherwise fallen nature.[10] The *German Theology* elaborated Meister Eckhart's belief that "this spark has more truth within it than everything man can learn"—a sentiment also attributed to Augustine.[11] Others spoke of a divine "seed," buried in the ground of the soul. Still more evocative was Jerome's image of the conscience as an unresting "eagle," pursuing virtue and hunting out evil in the service of its Maker. Sometimes it was identified with Christ himself: the "pre-incarnate" Word who was in the world before taking on human flesh. It was an idea that threatened to dispense with the whole machinery of sacrament and penance. Truth was within.

In 1509, Luther commented on Augustine's discussion of John 1:4, which refers to "the divine light which shines in all human beings" as a foreshadowing of the incarnate Christ. "It appears," he wrote, "that this light is our *synteresis*." This was a medieval term for conscience, implying more than a moral compass or a branch of reason. It was a remnant of God in the soul, preserving life and exposing sin. This holy witness, Luther wrote in agreement with Tauler, proved that "God is closer to the soul than it is to itself."[12] The mystical "*synteresis*"—literally a "co-knowing" with God—was central to Luther's escape from the word play of medieval theology. Although Luther's emphasis on the atoning work of Christ would soon pull the drama of salvation away from the internal movements of the heart, conscience remained the site, if not the source, of salvation. Mysticism helped Luther to shift theology from intellect and discourse to heart and experience—which was why his own attempts to reformulate salvation as doctrine would excite such dismayed suspicion. But that was a problem for the future. The early years of the Reformation set conscience and faith in dynamic synergy, as Luther turned the gravity of the accusing conscience into the thunderous joy of liberating faith. You could not have one without the other.

"The Spiritual Man Relies on Faith": Luther as Liberator

Luther's struggles did not hinder him from either ordination (1507) or receiving his doctorate in theology (1512). He caught the eye of Johannes von Staupitz, the head of the Augustinian monasteries in Saxony, who appointed him as his successor to the chair of biblical literature at Wittenberg in 1512. It was Staupitz who urged Luther to turn his mind to Christ, rather than speculate on the hidden God, and to focus on the written text of the Bible rather than the forest of medieval commentary.[13] This was the humanist method, the warm breeze of free enquiry, though it led Luther into fresh uncertainties. One of the casualties of his enquiries was the esteem in which he had held the mystical conscience.

Luther did not deny that conscience was the voice of God in the soul, but as he inched through the Psalms (1513–15) and sighed and trembled his way through Romans (1515–16), he came to see it as the announcement of law, not grace. The conscience was not God's final offer: it was a beginning. Luther continued to praise the "*synteresis*" in sermons and his lectures on the Psalms, where he argued that we would "crawl upon the earth" if there were no "vestiges of God" "in our wings." In his commentary on Romans 3:10, Luther argued that sin had not wiped out the image of God: "For we are not so completely inclined to evil that a portion does not still remain which is inclined toward good, as is evident in the *synteresis*."[14] But he also wrote of the *synteresis* with a degree of terror, describing the "fiercely accusing conscience" as a source of crushing anxiety, even a "bed of grief."[15] Luther had experienced all the "groaning" and none of the "rapture" of the mystical conscience. Scrutiny only increased his troubles, which included the fear that he had been predestined to damnation.[16] Around 1515 Luther scribbled a short phrase on one of Tauler's sermons, signaling a change of direction: "The spiritual man relies on faith."[17]

In his ruminations on Paul's letter to the Romans, Luther came to a new understanding of the concept of "righteousness," suddenly perceiving it as a gift not a demand. He began to see the whole Bible in a new light, marveling at passages that had once terrified him. Luther's conversion to the doctrine of justification by faith alone (*sola fide*) was a moment of joyous liberation. That simple phrase of the apostle, "The just person lives by faith," Luther recalled, "was for me the true gate to paradise."[18] The trembling conscience began to breathe freely. The experience was molded by the terrors that preceded it, but faith, even more than love, was to keep no record of the past. A healthy conscience was one in which fear turned into hope, and faith did the talking.

Luther's ecstasies might have remained private had they not collided with the Church's most brazen manifestation of a "theology of glory": the sale of "indulgences." Selling salvation was not a new idea, but the latest scheme, designed to finance the building of St. Peter's basilica in Rome, promote the interests of an unusually ambitious archbishop, and release souls from purgatory, by the simple mechanism of cash payment, was a reckless provocation. "As soon as a coin in the coffer rings," went the infamous marketing couplet, "the soul from purgatory springs." When Luther penned his iconic protest in October 1517, the issue quickly transcended the finer points of theology. Brushed aside as clerical insubordination, Luther's attempt to discuss the Church's theology of salvation turned at once into a debate about the Church itself. Luther was initially confident that "if the Pope knew" the extent of the indulgence scandal, "he would rather that St. Peter's church should go to ashes, than that it should be built up with the skin, flesh and bones of his sheep."[19] Two years later, he was not so sure.

Between the posting of the Ninety-Five Theses and the imperial ban that followed his appearance at the Diet of Worms in 1521 events moved quickly. Luther defended his theology at three high-profile disputations, he was excommunicated by his religious order and then by the Pope, and he found time to write so many books that few could believe that the mountain of literature presented to him at Worms was the work of a single man. Luther was radicalized by the conflict. He wrote with an accelerating certainty of the truth of his theology and the folly of an all-knowing Church. He may have been half-joking the first time he suggested the pope was an imposter, put in place by the devil. By the summer of 1520, he was coldly certain that the pope was indeed "the Antichrist," waging war on Christendom.[20] The nervous monk had become a warrior of faith.

Luther's meeting with Cardinal Cajetan at Augsburg (1518) and his debate with Johan Eck at Leipzig (1519) sealed the transition from critic to heretic. Luther was disheartened by Cajetan's aloofness but emboldened by Eck's gloating arrogance. Eck thought that he had nailed Luther to the ultimate vessel of destruction when he drew him into sympathetic statements about John Huss, the notorious heretic who was burnt at the Council of Constance in 1415. But Luther, who had previously condemned Huss in soberingly graphic terms, changed his mind. The Church had been wrong. Huss's beliefs were "truly Christian and evangelical." The Church had burned a disciple. "I said [at Leipzig] that the Council of Constance condemned some propositions of Huss that were truly Christian," he declared in 1520. "I retract. All his propositions were Christian, and in condemning him the Pope has condemned the Gospel."[21] It was not the humanist or the scholar who rejected the Papacy: it was the believer. With parting words of melancholy disdain, Luther rose to the part of righteous exile: "Farewell, unhappy, hopeless, blasphemous Rome!"[22]

Luther discovered a genius for polemical writing, setting out his "evangelical" theology with biting eloquence. His three pamphlets of 1520 combined soaring expressions of spiritual freedom with rugged criticism of religious "bondage." In holding his ground before Emperor Charles V at the Diet of Worms in 1521 Luther cemented a prophetic status. He traveled to Worms under an imperial order of safe conduct knowing precisely what such an assurance had meant for Huss a hundred years earlier. In the event, the discussion was brief and prosaic. But Luther's response to the question, "Do you wish to defend all of your books?" would outlive him. "If then, I revoke these books, all I shall achieve is to add strength to tyranny," he reasoned, with ponderous gravity. "I am bound by the Scriptures I have quoted and my conscience is captive to the Word of God. I cannot and I will not retract anything, since it is neither safe nor right to go against conscience."[23] The words that followed were the conceit of a publisher—"Here I stand; I can do no other"—but they captured the drama of the moment. This solemn if apocryphal phrase opens the modern era.

Worms offered the exemplary drama of a disgraced monk standing before the most powerful man in the known world and declaring his own conscience the higher authority. Luther, of course, would claim that he was going back to the age of the apostles, not forward to the age of me, myself, and I, but the notion of a conscience "captive" to scripture should not obscure the novelty of the stance. The Bible was subject to personal, private conviction—however theological it happened to be. Luther's *Address to the Christian Nobility* (1520) was a blistering assertion of the rights of ordinary believers against clerical power and a fierce defense of the inwardness of faith. His ambition was to "overcome" the "wicked and lying terror with which the Romanists have long intimidated and dulled our conscience." In sharp and pungent German prose, he contrasted the chicanery required to defend the papacy with simple, biblical accounts of faith. Every believer was a priest. The notion of a "spiritual estate" of ordained clergy operating on a different level was a spurious "invention" leading to gross injustices. "If a priest is murdered, the whole country is placed under interdict," Luther noted. "Why not when a peasant is murdered? How does this great difference come about between two men who are both Christians?" Luther set up a ferocious contrast between the freedom suggested by the New Testament and the coercive instincts of the papacy, reaching for what would become one of the proof texts of radical dissent: "A spiritual man judges all things, yet he is judged by no one" [1 Corinthians 2:15]. "We ought to become bold and free on the authority of all these texts," Luther urged. "We ought not to allow the Spirit of freedom (as Paul calls him) [2 Corinthians 3:17] to be frightened off by the fabrications of the popes, but we ought to march boldly forward and test all that they do, or leave undone, by our believing understanding of the Scriptures. We must compel the Romanists to follow not their own interpretation but the better one."[24]

The protest gathered pace in *The Freedom of a Christian* and *The Babylonian Captivity of the Church*, both also of 1520. The latter tore down the penitential machinery of the medieval church, defending personal faith as the sovereign possession of the individual. "Neither pope, nor bishop, nor any one else, has the right to impose so much as a single syllable of obligation upon a Christian man without his own consent," Luther declared. All who violate the sacred ground of conscience were guilty of "tyranny." "It is solely on behalf of this liberty that I cry aloud," Luther continued, "and I do so with good conscience, and in the faith that it is not possible for either men or angels rightfully to impose even a single law upon Christians except with their consent; for we are free from all things." Christians have to accept the rule of law, Luther acknowledged, "Yet, whatever the impositions may be, they are to be borne in such a way that we preserve liberty of conscience; the conscience that knows and affirms unhesitatingly that an injury is being done to it."[25]

Part of what it meant for Luther to articulate a "theology of the cross" was to interpret history as a drama of good and evil, "spirit" and "flesh." One of the grounds of his excommunication in 1520 was the brave contention that "to burn heretics is contrary to the will of the Spirit."[26] Scribbling his heresies in the haunting security of Wartburg castle, where he had been mysteriously installed after the Diet of Worms, Luther had privileged access to that debate. His status as the "wild boar" of Christendom sharpened his critique of papal arrogance and deepened his spiritual interpretation of history. "I am not terrified because many of the great persecute and hate me," he wrote in 1521. "Rather, I am consoled and strengthened, since in all the Scriptures the persecutors and haters have commonly been wrong and the persecuted right. The majority always supports the lie and the minority the truth." "The cross and condemnation [were] infallible signs of the true Church." "All histories show that the true Church has always endured suffering at the hands of the false."[27]

Luther's theology of suffering predated his dispute with the papacy. When he spent four weeks in Rome in 1511, he was drawn above all to sites of Christian suffering, such as the catacombs on the Via Appia, where thousands of martyrs lay buried.[28] Such places were reminders that the true dynamic of history lay beneath the pomp of empires. Suffering was more than a symbol of righteousness: it was proof. As Luther reasoned: “Every Abel has his Cain and every Isaac his Ishmael, every Jacob his Esau and every Israel his Edom, every David his Saul, and every Christ his Judas. ‘All that will live godly in Christ Jesus shall suffer persecution.’ ”[29] “Blessed are they who suffer persecution for my sake,” Jesus proclaimed. “Where you see or hear such,” Luther added, “know that this is the holy Christian Church.”[30] As Luther demystified the papacy as an alliance of power and philosophical “fabrications,” he proposed an almost physical criterion of authenticity: persecution. The persecuted represent Christ; those who “resort to fists” or stoop to “murder,” on the other hand, “*are not Christians.*” “If one judges the tree by its fruits,” he maintained, “it is evident who are the true Christians.” “We do not,” therefore, “kill, banish, and persecute anybody who teaches other than we do.”[31] Luther was so confident that God was on the side of the oppressed, he wondered if there had ever been a heresy that had not expressed some truth. Even where the heresy was flagrant, violence somehow dignified it, inviting sympathy with error. Persecution had the effect of “justifying the heretics.”

This was a radical stance, expounded in his most influential defense of conscience, *On Secular Authority* (1523). Here Luther argued that physical coercion profaned the Christian faith and defeated its own purposes. In the face of error, “God’s Word is the sole recourse, and if this does not avail worldly constraint is vain, though the earth be inundated with blood. Heresy is a spiritual thing which can be cut with no iron, burned with no fire, and drowned with no water.” As the apostles had urged, “The weapons of our warfare are not carnal.” Religious violence was not only a sin, a monstrous distortion of the Church’s spiritual mission, it represented a failure of judgment. For, “faith and heresy are never so entrenched as when they are opposed by sheer violence apart from the Word of God, for everyone can see that such violence lacks a just cause, since it proceeds without the Word of God, and can defend itself only by pure force like a brute beast.” Luther was pleading the same rights for “heresy” as “faith,” and subjecting a thousand-year-old policy of persecution to sarcastic contempt. “See what wise lords these are who wish to drive out heresy, but succeed only in fortifying their enemies and making themselves suspect and in the wrong,” he scoffed. “With force you will merely entrench, not expel.”[32]

It is not just freedom of conscience that is significant here: it is the power of conscience as a collective resource to be invoked against tyranny. Luther was not creating a modern conscience: he was catalyzing it from powerful, dormant resources. His theology of salvation was bracingly paradoxical; it turned an economy of merit upside down. But there was nothing counterintuitive about his aching cleavage between Christ and conscience, on the one hand, and murderous, usurping authority, on the other. "The common man is waking up," he warned the German rulers in 1523, "The scourge of the princes, which God calls 'contempt' is gathering momentum among the common people, and there is grave danger that insurrection cannot be avoided unless the princes begin to show themselves to be truly such by ruling justly in the fear of God with mercy and mildness. People will not put up with your tyranny and arbitrariness any longer."[33]

Luther became the bestselling author of the age. Humanism had prepared an audience, but Luther went where twinkle-toed satirists feared to tread. He created a culture. Having walked the long road of monastic discipline he was able to speak to "a whole generation of nuns and monks who, though drawn by the message of Evangelical freedom, still felt in conscience bound by their vows."[34] In 1525 he sealed the narrative of liberation with the most subversive iconoclasm of all: matrimony. After an unpropitious start, his marriage to the industrious and long-suffering Katherine, a former nun, was very happy. Part of his revolt against scholastic theologies that seemed to confine Christianity to the mind was an affirmation of the body, the material world, and legitimate sensuality. Luther was no Puritan. Letters to his wife from theological summits contain jovial asides on the quality of the local beer. When he was unable to attend the marriage of a close friend, he provided more detail than was strictly necessary in assuring the man that he and Katherine would be "united" with the couple in spirit on the night of the wedding.[35] Luther enjoyed his music, his cards, and his food. He was a one-man rebuttal of the flesh-hating metaphysics of medieval Christendom. It was not only for his stubbornly Catholic theology of the Eucharist that Luther was sometimes described as "the real presence." There may have been no surer index of a conscience released from punitive asceticism than Luther's expanding waistline.

Yet there was substance beneath the bluster. Souls had been crippled by the long winter of denial. Pleasure, exuberance, and occasional overconsumption were weapons to be hurled against the old devil of self-scrutiny. The advice Luther gave to his children's tutor, who was suffering from some sort of depression, suggests the mood of liberation: "Never be alone. Act foolish and play. Drink a good deal. It would even be a good idea to commit a sin—but not a gross one."[36] Luther's "charisma," noted a biographer, "could be a burden to his surroundings."[37] No one denied that he had it. Luther's amnesty on a regime of self-denial came to many like an announcement of spring. His vision of faith as freedom shattered a "contritional" worldview and breathed hope to nervous hearts. But as the gathering promise of spring turned into the riotous exuberance of summer, the merits of discipline began to reassert themselves. Faith assumed a new dignity, a new air of authority. The raging waters of revolt were guided toward the exacting turbines of doctrine, and not all of them agreed to enter.

The Power of Doctrine and the Doctrine of Power: Luther's Counter-Reformation

Luther once reflected that Augustine only came to the triumphant clarity of his theology of grace through his bitter dispute with Pelagius. It was a perceptive but ominous insight. Luther thrived on conflict. He found eloquence in the heat and anger of disputation. But he also tended to overstate his case, to demonize his opponents, to cast criticism as heresy. As Luther's ideas were challenged, stretched, and manipulated by friend and foe alike, the instinct was to sharpen and codify the message—until a message of liberation looked like a doctrine of control. The motive power of conscience, with which his revolution began, was first disciplined by theology: the doctrine of faith. It then succumbed to a political authoritarianism that looked very like the "Babylonian captivity" against which it had formerly protested. Chronology and Luther are never easy partners. Rival impulses run side-by-side. Yet there is no doubt that his theology underwent a process of hardening and defensive exaggeration, inviting reaction and dissent. Luther shattered "faith in authority" only to establish "the authority of faith," Marx once reflected. He replaced one kind of "servitude" with another.[38] The counterattack of radical Protestantism cannot be understood apart from the "counter-Reformation" unleashed by Luther himself.

The Power of Doctrine

Luther's approach to the Bible is perhaps the clearest symbol of this paradox of a subjective authoritarianism: a personal and deeply emotive piety assuming the metallic rigor of dogma. One the one hand, he brought reverence, sedulous precision, and the humble submission that "we are beggars" before the ancient oracles. On the other hand, he could be brusque to the point of cavalier about a set of documents that contained the gospel but were far from synonymous with it. Discovering, in *sola fide*, what he considered the real treasure of the scriptures, Luther was prepared to reorganize if not sell the rest. A concern for the "spirit" over the "letter" of scripture signaled a robust approach to tension and ambiguity. The Bible was the shadow of the true, "alien" Word of God; the "sheath in which the sword of the spirit is contained."[39] The Word and the Bible are, he insisted, "as different as Creator and creature."[40] "If [our] adversaries press the Scriptures against Christ," he once wrote, "we urge Christ against the Scriptures."[41] If theology were a matter of words and grammar, the devil himself could claim expertise.

But convinced, as he was, that the Pauline teachings on justification by faith represented the jewel and pinnacle of the scriptures, Luther sought to codify the principle—taking him back into the forensic jousting of line-by-line exegesis. He at once spiritualized the Bible as an untidy "vessel" containing this precious jewel and objectified it as a timeless and incorruptible authority. In practice, this meant that some books were more important than others; some apostles more worthy of the term. It is well known that Luther would have excluded James's works-conscious "epistle of straw" from the canon, and his commentaries were dominated by the master principle of *sola fide*. Surveying the whole Bible through this polarizing lens, Luther nurtured a theology as hungry for the "letter" as any of his opponents. The tremulous discovery of faith became a dogmatic formulation, hard and precise. And the casualties of certitude were conscience, ethics, and any interpretation of Christianity that would elevate love above faith.

Luther's years of tribulation armed him to interpret doubt as an instrument of the devil. Uncertainty about salvation was, for the recovering ascetic, the very gateway to hell. The emphasis sharpened in a series of conflicts with evangelical radicals and the humanist scholar, Erasmus, both of whom emphasized the ethical demands of Christianity to a degree that unsettled Luther. It was not that Luther was unconcerned about ethics. His fear was that any confusion of faith with ethical performance threw the burden of salvation back onto the cringing believer, nullifying the supremacy of Christ and the principle of grace. To remain pure from the admixtures of "works" and "monkery," faith had to assume a certain independence from ethical rigor. Luther thus moved from a stance in which faith had priority over ethics to a position of frequent hostility, in which scruples of conscience became the very whispers of the devil. Luther was redefining Christianity as something external to the believer, a heavenly transaction. The effect was to disable the rhythms of equity and moral sense from which his theology of protest had first emerged. Conceiving faith as fortitude against fear and doubt, Luther cast moral delicacy as temptation: a draining anxiety over matters that should be turned over to an all-consuming Savior. Clarity of faith and sensitivity of conscience became almost mutually exclusive values.

"This is the reason why our theology is certain," Luther asserted in a characteristic statement, "it snatches us away from ourselves and places us outside ourselves, so that we do not depend on our own strength, conscience, experience, person or works but depend on that which is outside ourselves, that is, on the promise and truth of God which cannot deceive."[42] In the struggle of faith, Christ was the "defender" and conscience the "accuser." A favorite verse was from the first letter of John, where fear turned into hope with the apostolic assurance that "God is greater than our heart." As Luther added with breathless relief: "The defender is greater than the accuser, even to an infinite degree. God is the defender, the heart the accuser. Is this the relation? Yes, indeed it is."[43] "Christ," Luther wrote elsewhere, "is far more than our conscience. . . . When the conscience assails you, He says: 'Believe!' "[44] "Such an evil beast and wicked devil is conscience," he wrote in his *Lectures on Genesis*. "For all authors, sacred and profane, have depicted this monster in horrible fashion."[45] The erosion of affection recalls the words of an English monarch for an irksomely dutiful archbishop: "Who will rid me of this turbulent priest?"

Lutheran spirituality became, in one scholar's phrase, a running "battle against that fatal human disease, the oppressive 'superego' of conscience."[46] Christians were saved while they were still sinners, and the life of faith was one of glorious imperfection. It was worse to try to buy your way into divine favor than to stumble into carnal indulgence. To worry about sins of the flesh was worse than to commit them, as Luther urged in a remarkable letter to his friend and co-reformer, Philipp Melanchthon:

> If you are a preacher of grace, then preach a true and not a fictitious grace; if grace is true, you must bear a true and not a fictitious sin. God does not save people who are only fictitious sinners. Be a sinner and sin boldly, but believe and rejoice in Christ even more boldly, for he is victorious over sin, death, and the world. As long as we are here we have to sin. This life is not the dwelling

> place of righteousness, but, as Peter says, we look for new heavens and a new earth in which righteousness dwells. It is enough that by the riches of God's glory we have come to know the Lamb that takes away the sin of the world. No sin will separate us from the Lamb, even though we commit fornication and murder a thousand times a day. Do you think that the purchase price that was paid for the redemption of our sins by so great a Lamb is too small? Pray boldly—you too are a mighty sinner.[47]

Since this world is not the theater of righteousness, it is foolish to labor for it. To do so is to invite suspicion about the quality of your faith. But in setting faith so defiantly against Christian instinct and scruple, Luther was also sowing the seeds of religious doubt. That he defended his theology so vigorously from the letter of scripture only raised the stakes. As the self-conscious restorer of New Testament Christianity, Luther was subject to unresting scrutiny. The perception of his sternest critics was that he had simply requisitioned the Bible to promote a theology of self-exoneration, license, and sin. Luther's response was to sharpen his case against theologies of merit and morality, defining true religion as belief, not behavior or purity of conscience. But this was a dangerous contrast to assert before an audience that he had all but educated himself on the irrefragable claims of conscience. The restless conscience, so righteous against fallen popery, now had to sit quietly before the majesty of faith. And triumphant faith, once so eager for the confirmatory glow of charity, now had to resist all appearance of a theology of works. Fearing that error still lurked in the heaving edifice of a meritorian Christianity, Luther attempted to burn the house down. When he pushed the argument to the claim that faith is greater than charity in the eyes of a holy God, he galvanized his critics, setting in train a bruising dialectic of love and orthodoxy that would run into the Enlightenment and beyond.

Luther's *Commentary on the Sermon on the Mount* (1532) provides a window into an evolving dogmatism. Luther declared in the preface that his interpretation was "the true, pure Christian meaning," but his hostility to literal readings of the Beatitudes may have set new standards for the personal appropriation of a text. It was as if he had taken the least Lutheran passage of the New Testament as a deliberate exercise in the supremacy of faith over a naïve ethicism. He condemned the "dazzling," "showy" works of "counterfeit saints," who believed that their "big beautiful works of love" endeared them to God.[48] He interpreted the command to do "good works" and let them "shine before men" in terms of preaching rather than acting. Christ, Luther insisted, was more concerned about mind than action: the quality of faith, not the spurious beauty of the deed. When the text seemed to contradict him, Luther appealed to higher sources. The command to perform good deeds, so that people "may see your good works and glorify your Father," prompted the qualification that Matthew, "together with the other two evangelists, Mark and Luke, does not in his gospel treat so fully and profoundly upon the great subject of Christ as St. John and St. Paul." Matthew, Mark, and Luke, he explained, "speak and exhort much about good works; as indeed both should in Christendom be insisted upon, yet each in proportion to its nature and dignity: that one should first and most of all hold forth faith, and Christ, and afterwards inculcate works."[49] Luther was ranking the gospels according to his own criterion of *sola fide*, and he was redefining the meaning and status of "works" in the religious life.

"By good works here [Matthew 5:16]," Luther insisted, "he means the practicing, illustrating and confessing the *teaching* concerning Christ," not dundering philanthropies. The intention was not to prescribe "common works," which anyone could perform, but "the true Christian work, namely correct teaching, insisting upon faith and showing how to strengthen and keep it." Charity encouraged pride and a spirit of emulation, Luther warned, whereas the true work of "teaching or preaching takes from us all the glamour of holiness." The sects were trying to build heaven on earth, and their zeal masked a desire to stand on equal terms with God. "Crazy saints," oblivious of the "difference between an earthly and a heavenly kingdom," had succumbed to the monastic sin of spiritual pride.[50]

Luther's *Commentary on Galatians* (1535) marked the climax of his theological revolution—a supreme statement of the priority of doctrine over works, and a thunderous account of faith as a "training" of the "conscience to believe that God approves of you," whatever the circumstances.[51] Luther wrote with triumphant relish of the need to "send Moses with the Law back to Mount Sinai," and he ridiculed the literalism of the sects. He likened the "fanatic's" emphasis on charity to the Galatian affinity for the Jewish law, condemning it as a "pseudo-Gospel," which exchanges "Christian liberty for the weak and beggarly elements of the world." To change the world was to usurp Christ. To fret over sin was to violate the purity of faith. To rhapsodize about love was to suggest ignorance of the gospel, which stands apart from all terrestrial fumbling:

> I cannot say it often enough, that we must carefully differentiate between doctrine and life. Doctrine is a piece of heaven, life is a piece of earth. Life is sin, error, uncleanness, misery, and charity must forbear, believe, hope, and suffer all things. . . . But with doctrine there must be no error, no need of pardon. There can be no comparison between doctrine and life. The least little point of doctrine is of greater importance than heaven and earth. Therefore we cannot allow the least jot of doctrine to be corrupted. We may overlook the offenses and errors of life, for we daily sin much. Even the saints sin, as they themselves confess in the Lord's Prayer and in the Creed. But our doctrine, God be praised, is pure, because all the articles of our faith are grounded on the Holy Scriptures.[52]

It is difficult to overstate the significance of such statements: with the claim that doctrine suffers "no error" Luther was preparing the ground for a policy of persecution; with the claim that charity pertains only to this fallen earthly life, he was subverting the basic psychology of Christian ethics. Throughout the commentary, Luther portrayed the instinct for good works as a natural competitor to faith, accusing the "fanatics" of "idolatry" for attaching "more importance to charity than to faith in Christ."[53] "Our quarrel," he explained, "is not with those who live in manifest sins. Our quarrel is with those among them who think they live like angels, claiming that they do not only perform the Ten Commandments of God, but also the sayings of Christ, and many good works that God does not expect of them. We quarrel with them because they refuse to have Jesus' merit count alone for righteousness." "Faith trusts in God and is never wrong," Luther urged, but "Charity trusts in men and is often wrong."[54]

A younger Luther had ridiculed scholasticism for defining a Christian by what he or she knew, rather than what they were. He thrilled to mystical commentary that drew its energy from experience not doctrine. But the tables had now turned. Luther spent much of his commentary warning people to resist the smoke and mirrors of feeling, doubt, and nervous moral ardor. He spoke of the accusing conscience like a curse, and he asserted ominous rights of self-defense for his imperious doctrine of faith:

> The pure doctrine takes precedence before charity, apostles, or an angel from heaven. . . . Let others praise charity and concord to the skies; we magnify the authority of the Word and faith. Charity may be neglected at times without peril, but not the Word

> and faith. Charity suffers all things, it gives in. Faith suffers nothing; it never yields. Charity is often deceived but is never put out because it has nothing to lose; it continues to do well even to the ungrateful. When it comes to faith and salvation in the midst of lies and errors that parade as truth and deceive many, charity has no voice or vote. Let us not be influenced by the popular cry for charity and unity.[55]

Finally, Luther declared, "Cursed be any love or harmony which demands for its preservation that we place the Word of God in jeopardy!"

Luther did not deny that Paul enjoined love as a principle of Christian living, but he relegated it to the status of a duty, a sequel, an exercise in good housekeeping:

> It was the custom of the apostles that after they had taught faith and instructed the conscience they followed it up with admonitions unto good works, that the believers might manifest the duties of love toward each other. In order to avoid the appearance as if Christianity militated against good works or opposed civil government, the Apostle also urges us to give ourselves unto good works, to lead an honest life, and to keep faith and love with one another. This will give the lie to the accusations of the world that we Christians are the enemies of decency and of public peace.[56]

"In order that Christians may not abuse their liberty," Luther continued, "the Apostle encumbers them with the rule of mutual love that they should serve each other in love."[57] The pinched and pragmatic tone of such statements was not lost on Luther's critics, nor was the almost proprietorial vigor with which he handled his text. When the passage on the "fruit of the spirit" seemed to elude his emphasis on the supremacy of faith and the separation of doctrine and ethics, Luther offered two rather nervous paraphrases of what he thought the apostle was really trying to say: "I have not forgotten what I told you about faith in the first part of my letter. Because I exhort you to mutual love you are not to think that I have gone back on my teaching of justification by faith alone. I am still of the same opinion." "Do not for a moment think that I am reversing myself on my stand concerning faith. Faith and hope must continue. By faith we are justified, by hope we endure to the end. In addition we serve each other in love because true faith is not idle. Our love, however, is faulty."[58]

In terms of a skeptical backlash, long underway by the 1530s, the significance of such statements is not only the sense of a theological mauling: the foisting of a dogmatic template on a more complex body of teaching. It is the suspicion that the Bible itself had been pummeled and abused in pursuit of a personal agenda. Luther claimed the right "to curse and condemn all men who in the least point corrupt the Word of God," but he was not immune to the same charge.[59] He invoked the authority of an apostle for a war on a heresy defined as little more than the "idolatry" of love. For a small army of dissidents, the link between *sola fide* and moral amnesia was unmistakable. And as the supremacy of doctrine spilled into a policy of persecution, the chemistry of revolt entered a new phase of intensity.

The Doctrine of Power

Luther's boldest liberties had been articulated from the shadows of princely protection. Implicit in the attack on papal corruption was the idea that secular rulers would step into the breach, becoming what Luther would later term "emergency bishops." Luther's disputes with "fanatics" such as his former collaborator, Andreas Carlstadt, demonstrated his early concern for stability and order. Luther showed restraint with Carlstadt, and he remained uneasy about coercion. But if his theology retained correctives against violence it also provided sanctions. Luther's theology of the "two kingdoms"—an extension of his doctrine of salvation—implied a certain tolerance of suffering and imperfection. The world is fallen. Until the day when the lion lies down with the lamb, she must remain a lion. This was a theology that could commission power with a clear conscience and would one day leave a door open to real tyranny.[60] There are continuities.

The first stage in Luther's descent to a previously unthinkable policy of persecution was the ostensibly "secular" policing operation of 1525. Luther's initial reaction to the peasant uprisings of 1525 was sympathetic. The peasants' demands included religious rights, such as the ability to call their own pastors, and economic rights, including the freedom to gather wood in the forests and fish from the rivers. The peasants had hoped to tie their insurgency to Luther's reforms, and Luther must have known that their invocation of his authority was more than tactical. His first response to the revolt was an "Admonition to Peace," which addressed the demands of the peasants and blamed the princes for the escalating conflict. But having witnessed some of the violence committed by peasants at first hand, Luther changed his mind, throwing his full weight behind the princes.

Against the Robbing and Murdering Hordes of Peasants (1525) was a fierce rebuke to the peasants and a counsel of revenge for Christian rulers unsure "how they are to act in the matter with a clear conscience." It made the case for reprisals and, with startling ferocity, outlined the method: "Let everyone who can, smite, slay and stab, secretly or openly, remembering that nothing can be more poisonous, hurtful or devilish than a rebel." Assuming personal responsibility for the carnage, Luther added, "I will not oppose a ruler who, even though he does not tolerate the Gospel, will smite and punish these peasants without offering to submit the case to judgment." In fact, he reasoned, "If he can punish and does not—even though the punishment consist in the taking of life and the shedding of blood—then he is guilty of all the murder and all the evil which these fellows commit." "It is," he advised with crisp and loaded clarity, "the time of the sword, not the day of grace."[61]

The Mayor of Zwickau said that he could not regard the pamphlet as a theological work, calling as it did "for the private and public murder of the peasants." "Is the devil, and those who do this, to be our Lord God?" he wondered, with bitter sarcasm.[62] But the work was all too theological, condemning leaders such as Thomas Müntzer for profaning the gospel as well as disturbing the peace. They had confused the kingdoms. They would now perceive the difference between a secular and a spiritual sword. To hesitant rulers, Luther urged the clarity of the issue. God was on the side of the princes. Having chided the rebels for dragging the gospel into a social conflict, Luther assured the princes that the Bible demanded retribution. The slaughter could be performed with "a good conscience" because the peasants were self-evidently damned:

> It is to their advantage that the peasants have a bad conscience and an unjust cause and that any peasant who is killed is lost in body and soul and is eternally the devil's. But the rulers have a good conscience and a just cause and can, therefore, say to God with all assurance of heart, "Behold, my God, thou hast appointed me prince or lord, of this I can have no doubt; and though hast committed to me the sword over the evildoers (Romans XIII). It is thy Word, and cannot lie. I must fulfill my office or forfeit thy grace.

> Therefore will I punish and smite as long as my heart beats. Thou wilt judge and make things right."[63]

Luther thus went further than the grim articulation of princely duty: he argued that salvation was at stake. The separation of the kingdoms, so clear in the denunciation of the rebels, vanished in the fury of revenge. God would look upon obedience as an act of faith:

> Thus it may be that one who is killed fighting on the ruler's side may be a true martyr in the eyes of God, if he fights with such a conscience as I have just described, for he is in God's Word and is obedient to him. . . . they may die without worry and go to the scaffold with a good conscience, who are found exercising their office of the sword. They may leave to the devil the kingdom of the world, and take in exchange the everlasting kingdom. Strange times, these, when a prince can win heaven with bloodshed, better than other men with prayer![64]

Luther's proof text was the passage in Paul's letter to the Romans where Christians are exhorted to obey rulers, who do not bear the sword in vain. Luther turned a warning to Christian citizens into a mandate for rulers, brandishing it like a sword of his own: "Stab, smite, slay, whoever can," he concluded. "If you die in doing it, well for you! A more blessed death can never be yours, for you die obeying the divine Word and commandment in Romans XIII, and in loving service of your neighbor." "To this let every pious Christian say Amen! For this prayer is right and good, and pleases God; this I know."[65]

It would have been impossible for such statements not to provoke a debate about what it meant to "know" the mind of God. Luther's screed was made to look even worse by appearing at the very moment that the princes of Saxony and Hesse destroyed the rebel armies at the battle of Frankenhausen.[66] In a single day, nearly 6,000 peasants were killed, including Müntzer, while only six of the princes' soldiers were wounded.[67] Luther may not have influenced the outcome, but he had sanctioned the carnage in graphic and potently theological terms. The ease with which Luther declared the world a place of necessary destruction was, for a number of erstwhile devotees, a chilling commentary on a theology of treacherous duality. *Sola fide* seemed to come with a compassion filter—an idea Luther even appeared to embrace. As he boasted many years later: "Preachers are the greatest of slayers. For they urge the authorities to execute their office strictly and punish the wicked. In the revolt I slew all the peasants; all their blood is on my head. But I pass it on to our Lord, who commanded me to speak thus."[68]

It should be no surprise that Luther changed his stance on religious persecution. In the tragic figure of Müntzer, Luther had a lasting image of the spiritual zealot as revolutionary-in-waiting. In the primacy of doctrine over ethics he had a rationale for the heavy shepherding of coercion. Although Luther remained uneasy about the persecution of heretics, preferring to cite blasphemy or sedition as the basis for punishment, his mature theology eroded the rights of conscience to the point of annihilation. Unorthodox consciences were self-evidently corrupt. Hesitation was sin. This was a complete inversion of his earlier stance. When Carlstadt attempted to abolish the Catholic Mass by force in 1522, Luther spoke movingly of the duty of winning converts by persuasion, not force: "Why? Because it is not in my power or hand to fashion the hearts of men as the potter molds the clay and fashion them at my pleasure. I can get no farther than their ears; their hearts I cannot reach. And since I cannot pour faith into their hearts, I cannot, nor should I, force any one to have faith. That is God's work alone, who causes faith to live in the heart." "We have the right to speak," he urged, "but not the power to act." "I will preach it, teach it, write it," he concluded, "but I will constrain no man by force, for faith must come freely without compulsion."[69]

Ten years later, faith seemed to mean something different. The heretic was no longer a misguided brother: he was an enemy. At the very moment that Luther was writing to hostile princes, urging leniency toward persecuted evangelicals, he was instrumental in denying basic freedoms to Anabaptists within what was effectively his own jurisdiction of Prussia, Hesse, and Saxony. In such areas, Lutheran orthodoxy was established in territorial churches, which granted ultimate authority to secular princes and considerable powers to the clergy. In 1527 Luther established a system of "ecclesiastical visitations," which used secular authority to enforce church attendance. Gradually, sanctions against nonconformists increased until rejection of "the ministerial office" was regarded as a blasphemous slander on an ordained servant of God. Finally, and against all earlier instincts, such an offense merited death.

Luther knew as well as anyone that the official grounds of "blasphemy" and "sedition" were mostly spurious. No one seriously claimed that Anabaptists worshiped different gods or that their piety was deliberately sacrilegious. Sedition was rare. But the Peasants' War and the disastrous siege of Münster in 1534–35, cemented the connection between religious and political radicalism. The libertarian pieties of earlier years were quietly laid to rest. "Luther himself took the initiative in treating absence from church as blasphemy, to be met with the threat of banishment and excommunication. In 1536 he had come to regard imprisonment and death as preferable to banishment, which simply spread the infection elsewhere." Finally, the fiction of "blasphemy" was tacitly acknowledged. Heretics would be punished as heretics.[70] The celebrated "protest" made by the Lutheran princes before the Holy Roman Emperor at the Diet of Speyer (1529) juxtaposed quivering demands for liberty of conscience with furious anathemas on the Anabaptists, demanding the death penalty for persistent error.[71] "Protestantism" was born in unblushing contradiction.

Luther's invocation of Moses as a patron of legitimate coercion was a source of particular resentment in radical circles. Having distinguished the "old" and "new" covenants with such exultant finality, having extolled the virtues of Christ over Moses with sonorous eloquence, it was a matter of distress that Luther now claimed Moses as a model of salutary violence. "It is written of Moses that he was the meekest man on earth," Luther reasoned, "but nevertheless when the Jews prayed to the golden calf and angered God, Moses struck many of them dead and thus reconciled God again." Transferring the authority of the law to the new reign of doctrine, Luther claimed that Moses would willingly acquiesce in a judicious policy of coercion. And he applied the uneasy logic in grim anathemas against the Jews. Claiming that Moses would have been the first to acknowledge the obsolescence of the old law under Christianity's new covenant, Luther argued that he would have been "the first to burn their synagogues."[72] Personality played a part in all of Luther's fulminations—but so too did theology and the very arts of inference and deduction that he had long scorned as the carnal currency of scholasticism. Luther had become his own worst nightmare: a philosopher.

Luther had inspired too many people to know the difference between "spiritual" and "carnal" religion to get away with such contortions. He had written too much about the sanctity of conscience to confine it to a confessional cage. A counterattack was underway. In the *Freedom of a Christian*, Luther described the sense of unworthiness before a holy law that leads a person to faith: next to the majesty of the law, even the proudest soul will sense the necessity of grace. Faith bridged the gap between a pure God and an unworthy soul. But as Luther argued in his critique of the papacy, the psychology was reversed in the face of tyranny and injustice. Next to an unholy, arbitrary law, the claims of conscience wax strong. We do not quail before injustice: we challenge it. We might be sinners before God, but we are bold and free before human imposters.

The story of radical dissent was an essay on this principle, turning the fire of the liberated conscience on the fresh captivity of doctrine. Luther first armed his critics, then he provoked them. He was the burning prophet of the free conscience and the high priest of "confessional" control. He was the evangelist who seemed to lose faith in his gospel, succumbing to methods he had once condemned as cast-iron proof of sin. He could not, however, call back the radiant energies he had unleashed any more than he could translate the New Testament back into Greek. Conscience would not blow apart the Lutheran settlement any more than the Genevan experiment or the crumbling might of Rome. But it would generate a culture of dissent at once hotly spiritual and coolly rational, taking the painful steps between medieval and modern worlds that Luther had started and so unceremoniously abandoned.

2

"*To Kill a Man Is Not to Defend a Doctrine. It Is to Kill a Man*"

THE WARS OF RELIGION AND THE VIRTUES OF DOUBT

Coercion is a rather foolish thing in the Kingdom of Christ.
—SEBASTIAN FRANCK, *Paradoxes*, 1534

He who once said, "I believe" now says, "I know."
—SEBASTIAN CASTELLIO, *On the Art of Doubting*, 1563

PIERRE BAYLE, THE French philosopher who became a kind of posthumous tutor to the Enlightenment *philosophes*, was obsessed with the role of the Reformation in the making of modern thought. A Calvinist refugee, driven into Dutch exile by persecution in 1685, Bayle was a penetrating interpreter of the costs of confessional warfare. But his usual sympathy for the underdog deserted him as he weighed the merits of Sebastian Franck, the sixteenth-century spiritualist. Franck, Bayle harshly asserted, used mystical language to dissolve the wall of separation between God and humankind. He was a pantheist and a forerunner of the dreaded Spinoza, Bayle's philosophical *bête noire*.[1] Bayle's analysis suggested a rigor that Franck neither possessed nor claimed, but it was not without diagnostic virtue. Franck was one of the fiercest voices of the radical Reformation: part of a "third force" in the struggle between Catholic and Protestant that slowly moved from theology to an independent and austere doctrine of reason, grounded in the mystical conscience. Franck was no philosopher but Bayle was right to interpret his doctrine of conscience as an early expression of "Spinozist" heresies. Franck, Sebastian Castellio, and a handful of "rational Spiritualists" did not anticipate the Enlightenment: they made it happen.

The Sanctuary of the Spirit

If the sixteenth-century spiritualists reflected any school of philosophy, it was Neo-Platonism, not pantheism, though there were similarities. Both wanted to dissociate God from concrete institutions and to redefine what confessional orthodoxies regarded as "providence." Yet it would be a mistake to force such an amorphous and emotional stream of thought into a single category. Most of the spiritualists were in some sense anti-intellectual, condemning confessional religion for spurious and presumptuous precision, and the rationalism that emerged from their protest centered on the moral conscience. Starting from the idea that conscience was the voice of God in the soul, they aimed to magnify this spark of divinity almost to the degree that Luther diminished it. Indeed the sense of a collision between a young and an older Luther was underlined by the fact that his edition of the *German Theology* became the set text of spiritualist dissent, next to kindred works such as *The Imitation of Christ*. Orthodoxy was attacked from a stance of intensified, not attenuated, spirituality. God was known in the heart, and it was from this conviction that the principle of looking inward, not upward to a transcendent God, developed. Metaphysical innovation emerged from the inner motions of the soul: a great reordering driven by a horror of religious violence. Spiritualists moved from the idea that God is profaned by those who kill in his name to the conviction that such a God could be no more than an idol, the invention of "carnal" minds. Persecution put haunting question marks behind the theology it tried to defend.

Thomas Müntzer was a critical figure, exposing Lutheran affinities for power as a betrayal of evangelical instincts, and then demonstrating the folly of trying to play the theocrats at their own game. Müntzer accused Luther of silencing the Word of God by casting his lot with the princes and showing the poverty of his theology by his acquiescence in persecution.[2] Power-hungry theologians had "stolen" the Bible and muzzled the Holy Spirit. Müntzer condemned *sola fide* as an invention of the flesh, quite foreign to the absorbing, life-changing "advent" of faith described in the New Testament. "Zachariah and Mary," Müntzer challenged, "did not attain their faith in the rosy way believed today by this insane world. . . . With such an easy advent this drunken world concocts a faith more deadly than that of the Turks, heathens, and Jews." Luther preached righteousness but despised holiness and virtue. His theology was a smokescreen for power.[3]

These were powerful and enduring insights, but Müntzer's role in the disaster of 1525 both sharpened and undermined the political critique. The Peasants' War confirmed the worst suspicions about the corruptions of power, and it proved the folly of counterattack. The bitter truth of 1525 was that the eschatological drama could not be hurried. With notable exceptions, such as Münster's theocratic experiment of 1534–35, the growing impulse was either to postpone or to spiritualize the millennial hope, leaving New Jerusalems to the devil. The hardening of ecclesiastical power to create a patchwork of rival orthodoxies, soon to be confirmed under a formula that let princes determine the religion of their people, had a powerful sifting effect. As populations were weighed and measured by fixed "confessions," it was the sterner spirits who refused to cooperate. Places that would accommodate them, like the relatively peaceable Strasbourg, became hotbeds of dissent.

The earliest spiritualists were people of intense piety, incapable of insincere conformity. Moving among Anabaptists whose dissidence typically assumed more concrete forms, spiritualists were more than disillusioned drifters. They dissolved the dogmatic structures of the Reformation with an evangelical militancy. Forced to roam between the swinging blades of rival establishments, they worshipped a God of like sufferings: a "de-historicized or existentialized" Christ, who protected them from the harsh deity "monopolized by a theological aristocracy."[4] In the brooding mysticism of unhappy saints like Franck, a sublime, spiritual Christ would eclipse the fallen God of Christendom. The Word known in the heart would hover in judgment over the tainted "letter" of scripture.

Hans Hut, Müntzer's friend and publisher, shows how such theology was almost invented on the run. Forced into exile for refusing to baptize his child, he started to preach a spiritual Christ, condemning rigid adherence to the scriptures. Hut accused the magisterial reformers of trying to be "masters" of scripture but understanding "less of it than apes."[5] Their unhappy constructions underlined the need for broader sources of wisdom, including what he termed the "gospel of all creatures." Christ did not preach with a nervous dependence on a written text, Hut urged. "He did not go through the Bible chapter and verse as our learned theologians do. . . . Christ needed Scripture only to prove his points with the refined scribes." To the "common man," he spoke in the untwisted vernacular of creation:

> The entire world with all creatures is a book, in the workmanship of which one sees everything that is read in the written book. All the elect from the beginning of the world until Moses have taken their lessons from the book of all creatures and have silently partaken of the understanding which is written in them by nature through the Spirit of God in the heart, for the entire law is written into the works of creation. And all men who work daily with creatures, even (as the law shows) the heathen, who do not have the written law but still do the same as those who have it.[6]

Here was a manifesto of dissent. God speaks "silently." The spirit is known "in the heart." The law is written in "creation." The "heathen" has access to all the riches of the Christian—in fact, advantages. Scripture had become a snare, Hut believed: a tangle of formulae that obscured its purest content. He cited a list of contradictory scriptural statements to suggest the absurdity of putting the written text above the spirit of truth. And only a blundering literalism could have conjured the hydra of *sola fide*: "a thoroughly wicked gospel, which . . . does not better man." Like Luther's ever-enabling doctrine of the two kingdoms, *sola fide* was condemned as a license of destruction, a doctrine of the flesh.[7] Hut died in prison in 1527, a symbol of the spiritual incarceration he had dared to criticize.

Hut's list of scriptural contradictions had been compiled by Hans Denck, a critical figure in the making of spiritualist dissent. Denck was an Anabaptist who eventually abandoned a commitment to physical baptism for a more spiritualized piety. The price of heterodoxy was a series of exiles that took him from Nuremberg to Augsburg, to Strasbourg and, finally, to Basel where he died of the plague in 1527. Denck's contribution was a sweeping critique of the Lutheran "solas" and a passionate defense of the inwardness of true religion. In a public trial before he was banished from Nuremberg in 1524, he explained his alienation from evangelical piety: "For a time I prided myself as possessing faith, but I have finally become convinced that it was a false faith, because this faith did not overcome my spiritual poverty, my inclination to sin, my weaknesses and my sickness."[8] He was "rescued" by responding to the accusing voice of conscience, which he came to identify with Jesus Christ.

Drawing directly on the *synteresis* theology of the *German Theology*, Denck described a journey away from the beguiling deceptions of the written word. Scripture now became a "witness," secondary to the "driving" spirit within, which "*is indeed Christ*." Under this new authority, Denck became dismissive of the physical text of scripture, which was "written with human hands, spoken by human lips, seen with human eyes, and heard with human hearts, [and] cannot by itself completely overcome the darkness." "For," Denck reasoned, holding the ace of spiritual experience, "one who is in his household knows how trustworthy the Lord is without the letter."[9] If salvation depended on knowing the scriptures, he added, whole swathes of humanity would be lost. The inner light of Christ, on the other hand, "speaks clearly in everyone, in the deaf, dumb, and blind, even in unreasoning beasts, even in leaves and grass, stone and wood, heaven and earth, and all that is in them, that they may hear and do his will."[10]

Denck continued to insist upon the necessity of atonement, urging that "Salvation is *in* us although not *of* us." But he rejected Lutheran theology as an exercise in self-flattery. Any system that allowed the "love of the neighbor" to be so "wantonly scorned" had to be rejected.[11] "Let none be deceived," Denck warned, "whoever does not love his brother, certainly does not love God." Denck disputed Luther's view that the law remained a "curse" for the Christian and love an extraneous duty, asserting that "whoever does not wish to hear the curse of the Law, definitely has not yet escaped it." True faith inspired a spontaneous love for the law, a desire to meet and exceed its demands. It was the fulfillment of Jeremiah's prophecy about a "new covenant" written on the heart. It was no fevered exemption. Denck excoriated the Reformation's "unchosen and unappointed" leaders, who dared to call an amnesty on a law they so little understood. *Sola fide*, Denck believed, was a backward step, the "carnal wisdom" of men who professed Christ in word but denied him in deed; a philosophy of entitlement that bore no relation to the struggles described by Paul in chapter 7 of Romans. The truth was that the world was "full of such people whose fruit and life were better before they boasted of faith than thereafter." This was a clear allusion to Luther and *sola fide* but Denck was no kinder to the fawning accomplice of *sola scriptura*: "Let him who honors Scripture but is cold in divine love beware lest he make of Scripture an idol, as do all text-educated scribes who are not educated for the Kingdom of God."[12] The spirit and the letter had to be distinguished—perhaps separated.

Luther's response, as Denck was sentenced for heresy in 1525, was characteristically robust: "Satan has carried it so far that in Nürnberg some persons are denying that Christ is anything, that the Word of God is anything, that the Eucharist is anything, that the magistrates are anything. They say that only God is."[13] Or as he later put it: the spiritualist cries, "Geist, Geist, Geist, and then kicks away the very bridge by which the Holy Spirit can come . . . namely, the outward ordinances of God like the bodily sign of baptism and the preached Word of God."[14] It was not an unperceptive summary. But the spiritualist complaint was that responsibility lay with those who abused the sacraments and the scriptures. They did not "kick away" the "ordinances of God" so much as reject a set of profaned symbols. As persecution and violence was added to theological dogmatism, the protest gathered force. Yet it remained a battle within the Reformation: a struggle between a Lutheran principle of conscience and spiritual freedom and the Lutheran supremacy of doctrine. Franck was the supreme example of homegrown dissent.

Sebastian Franck and the Religion of the Spirit

Franck was a Lutheran minister who had joined the side of reform following Luther's mesmerizing defense of his theology at Heidelberg. But he soon worried about a revolution that sniffed "works" in any call to ethical rigor. His conviction that "words" are not enough was deepened by the sorry spectacle of the Peasants' War, in which both sides invoked the "name" of Christ like a magic spell.[15] Revulsion from violence, and the theology that would justify it, pushed Franck from evangelical orthodoxy toward a simplified gospel of love and conscience that bordered on "a kind of theological nihilism."[16] Inspired by the mysticism of Tauler, the humanism of Erasmus, and the spirit/flesh dualism of the younger Luther, Franck produced the most trenchant critique of creedal Christianity of the Reformation era.

When Sebastian Castellio used excerpts of Franck's writings in his tolerationist anthology, *Concerning Heretics* (1554), he chose a pseudonym that was more homage than disguise: "Augustine Eleutherius." "Eleutherius" was a name that Luther briefly adopted during his humanist phase (literally, "the liberated one"), and "Augustine" was a gentle reminder of a shared parentage. Franck, like Castellio, was a true child of the Reformation. Augustine was a source of Franck's confidence in the divine spark of conscience and the soul's independence from worldly authority, and it was from Luther that he acquired the vital distinction between the "fleshly" and the "spiritual" interpretation of scripture. It was as a good Lutheran that he undertook his first literary endeavor of translating a stiff response to Denck's heresies. Scripture, he insisted, is clear to the spiritually enlightened. But in a personal preface Franck provided a glimpse of a coming dissidence: "the kingdom of God," he wrote, "consists not in words but in the act."[17] The next time we hear from him, apart from a short tract on the evils of drunkenness, Franck had taken sides with Denck, complaining darkly that "the devil sits even among the children of God, and Judas among the Apostles."[18] Solidarity with Luther was no more.

Franck's next publication, a translation of a history of Turkey, attacked divisions within Christendom and employed the shaming tactic used by Müntzer: Christians were no better than Turks. In fact, God may be using Christendom's despised neighbors to bring a bickering household to its senses. Whatever they believed, the Turks knew that a religion without works was no religion at all, whereas "we supposed Christians and evangelicals have much belief without works," leading to "a shameless, rough, wild life, letting the appearance, the works die with the faith."[19] Franck declared war on the Reformation. Having resigned his ministry in 1528, he moved to Nuremburg, then to Strasbourg in 1529, where he lived for two years before being expelled in 1531. In 1534 he settled in Ulm, after a miserable period of wandering, before again receiving his marching orders. He was expelled in 1535 with his friend and fellow spiritualist, Caspar Schwenckfeld. He finally settled in Basel, where he died in 1542, wearied by conflict and the manual labor to which his heresies had reduced him for survival.

Franck was a deeply historical thinker whose antipathy to religious violence was heightened by an ability to contextualize it as the conceit of a fallen orthodoxy. Christianity, he repeatedly observed, did not announce itself to the world with sword and flame. Franck's most important work was his *Universal Chronicle of the World's History from the Earliest Times to the Present* (1530), where he applied Luther's taut antithesis of spirit and flesh to the process of historical change. Names and places changed but the old drama continued. Christ continued to suffer at the hands of Judas, Annas, Caiaphas, and Pilate. Indeed "the whole passion" was played out in the experience of the spiritual church, while the spirit of persecution found its home in the visible or established churches.[20] Franck argued that heretics, dying for their faith, were the true representatives of Christ; their persecutors were inspired by the devil. This was an old problem, exemplified by imperious Catholicism, but exacerbated by the rise of an armed alternative. It was harder to be a Christian in the poisoned atmosphere of the sixteenth century than it was under Nero, Franck suggested. "Today one is yanked into the tribunal for merely having opened his mouth and even slightly doubted something having to do with an article of the church," he lamented. "When someone now does not support and parallel everything of the church . . . he has less peace and freedom of belief and speech than if he were living under the pagans and Turks."[21]

The situation was dire but Franck preferred "to be among those whom the world condemned as heretics rather than among those who have been esteemed as saints." For what God calls evil and "what the world calls heresy" are different things. "Many good Christians have been numbered among the heretics," Franck contended. And the added cruelty of burning their works alongside their bodies—depriving posterity of any true assessment of their merits—was another ground for looking askance at orthodoxy. It was a sobering fact that Jesus was sent to the cross by a proud religious establishment. The New Testament would have looked different had it been written by those who sentenced him to death. Church histories were hollow, self-vindicating affairs, useless in the assessment of moral truth. Persecution had turned Christianity on its head but few were alive to the scandal. The question was not how heresy came to rear its ugly head, but how a peaceable religion assumed the terrible prerogative of violence.

Franck portrayed this "new law of persecution" as a grotesque anomaly, so foreign to Christian sentiment that it must have causes outside the faith. But it was not a simple narrative of power crushing theology from the time of Constantine: it was the darker tale of theology evolving into a science of power. Imperial decrees against heresy, Franck noted, were "constantly enlarged" at the behest of "false doctors," until the church "arrived at chains, crosses, fires, and wheels." Treacherous theologians numbed the Christian mind into insensibility, until even torture smacked of compromise:

> Little by little things have grown worse. The devil was at first ashamed to go to such length of impudence among the faithful as to compel anyone to the faith and to introduce force into the affairs of the Church and the faith. This would have been too absurd, not to say ridiculous, not only in the sight of believers, but also in the eyes of the world, that anyone should attempt to bring the unwilling to faith against their hearts, and should try to employ coercion in the affairs of God, who desires the heart and the consent of His worshippers, a truth which is written in the hearts of all men and

> will be approved by all as just. But one thing was introduced after another and the world grew daily more ignorant and estranged from the truth, until Pope Pelagius in 553, being impelled and sent by the father of all the Pharisees (John 8) shamelessly promulgated a decree that heretics who would not suffer themselves to be persuaded by reasoning to the Roman faith (which he called the Christian faith), should be turned over to the civil arm to be constrained and forced. See what we have come to. More and more we have degenerated, until now there is no dealing or disputing with a heretic save by the gallows, sword, and fire.[22]

Augustine had much to answer for, but Franck suggested that the decrees sanctioned in his time were mild compared to "those which now call for beheadings, burnings, and hanging." And he bitterly regretted that these brutal punishments, "in which the bloodthirsty devil so obviously reveals himself," were no longer the monopoly of Rome. Evangelicals had entered the fray.[23]

Evangelicals did not rival the papacy in the scale of their persecutions, but they eclipsed their enemies in hypocrisy and chilling theological justification. The Reformers had the Bible, the fresh insight of salvation, yet they twisted it to justify what they formerly condemned. They had, Franck argued, fallen back on the crueler tenets of the "old covenant." "On this subject Luther wrote excellently," Franck noted, "on 'How Moses should be read, and how far the Old Testament is valid, and how far it is now abrogated,' against those who bring forth Moses from the darkness, shadows, and figures and set him in truth in the place of Christ." "This," Luther had rightly insisted, "is going backwards from the Promised Land to Egypt, from the desert to Babylon, from sonship to servitude."[24] "In this connection," Franck added, "all the works on Christian liberty and on the difference between the Old Testament and the New are relevant." But Luther had turned, betraying his own principles and the gospel itself:

> Some formerly wrote well on the subject because they were in peril, but now that this liberty has become an embarrassment to them, they put on again the worn shoe and sing again the old song. From Christ they return to Moses, from the sun to the shadow, and would restore the force, sword, and law of Moses, although there is One here who is greater than Moses, Solomon, Jonah, and the prophets, who has established a new covenant in the spirit which supersedes

> the old in the letter, namely, Jesus Christ, whom the Father has commanded us to obey.[25]

Franck was calling Luther on his own, exultant contrast between the old and new covenants. He was condemning evangelical violence on clear evangelical grounds. He wrote more candidly to a friend, complaining that the persecutors "mix the New Testament with the Old." When they cannot defend the sword from the gospels,

> they run at once to the empty quiver, that is, to the Old Testament, and from it prove [the legitimacy of] war, oath, government, power of magistracy, tithes, priesthood; and praise everything and ascribe this all forcibly to Christ without his will. And just as the popes have derived all this from it, so also many of those who would have themselves be called Evangelicals hold that they have nobly escaped the snare of the pope and the devil and have nevertheless achieved, with great effort and sweat, nothing more than that they have exchanged and confounded the priesthood of the pope with the Mosaic kingdom![26]

"Evangelicals at court," Franck continued, "are now fashioning for the princes another [Mosaic kingdom] and nicely press the sword into their hands and, as the proverb has it, pour oil into the fire." Persecution was the work of the devil, and the "famous doctors" who justified it were the very "wolves which Paul spiritually anticipated would fall in upon the flock and which John calls antichrists."[27] But the policy, Franck maintained with a certainty gleaned from Luther, had always backfired on its perpetrators. Persecution was an error of judgment quite as much as a failure of charity and justice. As Franck wrote elsewhere, with almost humored despair: "Coercion is a rather foolish thing in the kingdom of Christ."[28]

From the safe house of moral certainty, Franck launched a more penetrating critique of the visible church. His theory was that the Holy Spirit had anticipated the process of decay, using it as a way of tearing "us away from the school of men" and "pulling us into his school, so that we may sit at his feet and hear his word . . . no longer surrendering ourselves to men and looking to them as our masters."[29] God allowed the external church to be "sullied by Antichrist" as preparation for a purer faith and a holier church. Just as Luther had interpreted the "soul-destroying traditions of our pontiffs and opinions of our theologians" as a kind of pedagogical device, divinely conceived "so that you may recognize the work of antichrist,"[30] Franck rationalized the crisis as a lesson in the corruption of institutions, the hubris of theology and the perils of literalism. "All that we have learned since childhood from the papists," he wrote to his friend, "we must all of a sudden again unlearn. Again, the same for what we have received from Luther and Zwingli—all must be abandoned and altered. For one will sooner make a good Christian out of a Turk than out of a bad Christian or a learned divine! For the veil of Moses hinders them, that is, the death-dealing letter of Scripture."[31]

Franck attacked evangelical biblicism as a symptom of carnality and secular ambition. Scripture remained sacred but its virtues evaporated when men presumed to own it. Reformers had turned it into a "paper pope."[32] "The letter of Scripture," Franck declared in his *Paradoxes* (1534) was "the sword of Antichrist." A sword that now, as in the time of the Pharisees, "kills Christ." Without the illumination of the spirit, the Bible was, Franck argued, "a closed book and a confounding labyrinth."[33] In one sense, it was just "ink, paper and letters," he claimed, the visible testimony of the invisible spirit.[34] In another sense, it was a positive liability: an arsenal of judgments easily misappropriated; a charter for persecutors. The inner Word and the written letter were not only distinct, as Luther had maintained, but often at war. "The Pharisees," Franck noted, "killed Christ with the letter because he taught and lived contrary to the letter." "It still happens to this day."[35]

Modern Pharisees, Franck contended, "kill Christ with the literal Christ, using the sheath against the sword and the lantern against the light." This was the work of "Antichrist," an "outward" victory that confirmed Franck's conviction that Christ had to "remain hidden from the world," his only residence the pure conscience of the believer.[36] The Reformation had started well, but it was now "addicted to the letter of Scripture." Franck warned his friend about a nervous literalism that draws the heart away "from the teaching of the Spirit." He counseled against the methods of the reformers, who fear "the Spirit of God as though it were Satan, crowding him against his will into the script and making Scripture [their] god."[37] The Holy Spirit should not be made the "prisoner" of scripture.[38] Chief among those who "understand Scripture according to the letter," Franck warned, was "Luther." The great unlearning had to start with the greatest of reformers. Contrary to what Luther was now teaching, Franck urged:

> Thou shouldst much rather interpret the scripture as a confirmation of thy conscience, so that it testifies to the heart and not against it. Again, thou shouldst not believe and accept something [merely] reported by scripture—and feel that the God in thy heart must yield to scripture. It were better that scripture should remain Antichrist's! Saint Paul speaks not in vain that the letter killeth. And yet it is [visible letters] which almost all and especially the learned divines consider to be the sole, pre-eminent word of God—supposing God's word really could be written.[39]

Franck applied the same logic to the church. The scandal of a warring Christendom proved the folly of trying to institutionalize spiritual truth. The language was again unmistakably Lutheran. God had lost patience with a church "secure in spiritual arrogance, in the semblance of holiness and in delight of self."[40] To the Augustinian mantra, "Outside the church, no salvation," Franck offered the simplest rejoinder: "where, my friend, is this church?"[41] Franck believed that Jesus had personally instituted the sacrament of the Eucharist. But it had been profaned beyond recognition. It was now a symbol of pride and division. The same was true of the other sacraments. In Franck's melancholy analysis, carnal religion had forced God into retreat. Some would say abstraction. Franck's vision of a spiritual church, rising above a fallen Christendom, was grand, generous and hauntingly nebulous:

> let the church of God remain in the Spirit among all peoples and pagans; let them be herein instructed, governed, and baptized by the Doctor of the New Covenant, namely, the Holy Spirit. . . . Consider as thy brothers all Turks and heathen, wherever they be, who fear God and work righteousness, instructed by God and inwardly drawn by him, even though they have never heard of baptism, indeed, of Christ himself, neither of his story or scripture, but only of his power through the inner Word perceived within and made fruitful. . . . [For] just as there are many Adams who do not know there was one Adam, so also there are many Christians who have never heard Christ's name.[42]

Franck wrote of heathens knowing "the power of Christ" as surely as the prophet Job in his hour of need. What distinguished Franck from Schwenckfeld, a fellow spiritualist who worshipped a "celestial Christ," was a certain depth of resignation. Franck believed that honest pagans possessed the spirit of Christ, but what he understood by that became increasingly austere. Schwenckfeld's solution to Eucharistic controversies was to urge a moratorium, a "*Stillstand*," whereby Christians refrained from the sacrament until they could reach a charitable agreement on what it meant. Do not hold your breath, Franck warned. Sacraments were the "toys" that God expected us to leave in the nursery of faith. We are called to walk free, cleaving to the voice within. Schwenckfeld lived in expectation of fresh infusions of the spirit. Franck pointed to a cooler freedom: a rebirth that held the awakened conscience to be God's final offer.

Franck's mysticism gradually lost its fervor. He appeared to rationalize the salvation narrative as the discovery of a God already known. Writing of the "divine image" in every heart, he urged that "we are [all] capable of God and are, in some measure, of divine quality. The light has been lighted in the lantern of our heart, the treasure lies already in the field, has been laid into the ground of our souls." "Whoever allows the lantern to burn and does not prefer the lantern of the flesh, indeed, whoever moves into himself and looks for this treasure, will not find it above the sea nor must look for it in heaven. But the Word, the image of God, is within us."[43]

In his melancholic *Paradoxes*, Franck described the fall of Adam and the salvation of Christ as a drama confined to the individual soul. There was a reductive simplicity that echoed his disenchantment with the visible church. Drawing on the mystical terminology of the *German Theology*, Franck wrote of sin as a process in which "the sun sets" on the sinner. "In such fashion God, who cannot really die, dies in humankind. This is to say, he cannot be sensed any longer. The spirit departs, i.e. hides and loses his dominion and office, overcome by the flesh."[44] The "wall of partition between us and God," Franck suggested, was nothing more than a division "in our own conscience." It was misleading to say that God is "angry with us." It would be more accurate to say we are angry with ourselves, for "this enmity . . . [lies] solely within us." "God does not condemn anyone," he urged, "but everyone condemns himself."[45] Salvation, meanwhile, was a form of self-awakening: a turning to the "illumination, encouragement . . . and prevenient grace" of an already resident force.[46]

The once-evangelical Franck thus moved toward a kind of rationalism, condemning the demand for miracles as the cry of spiritual infancy. He wished "to see a few people cool their foolish zeal," to stop waiting "for a new, special church, calling, baptism or sending of the Holy Spirit (as many do daily), since I know that Christ does not begin something new every day."[47] His disappointment with a fallen church evolved into a sternly reduced expectation of providence, in some sense a loss of faith. While he continued to employ classic images of a God calling "Turks, Jews, Papists, and Sectaries . . . into the vineyard" to receive "the same wage as we,"[48] Franck broke away from the theological structures of salvation. He likened Socrates, obedient to the inward Christ, to the historical Christ, who may have been no more than an expression of the same spirit. And his model of salvation, creating a spirit "utterly without will and arbitrariness" was starkly rational. Franck's distaste for rashly claimed providences inspired him to a vision of spirituality as stability. True "Christians" would be "like their God": "immovable, invincible, unchangeable and impassible, without any passion whatever, so that no chance has room with them any longer."[49]

The Church of Antichrist had "killed" God but Franck's spiritualism appeared to silence him. Phrases like "the Mind of Christ," "the true Light," and "the Lamp of the soul" were interchangeable. God and conscience had blended into an internal struggle against the flesh. "The inward Light," Franck maintained, "is nothing else than the Word of God, God Himself, by whom all things were made and by whom all men are enlightened."[50] But enlightenment was a process, not a prayer. Franck had moved beyond his evangelical roots to a piety that did not gaze into the eternal abyss so much as steel the spirit within. The mystical conscience glowed with an icy radiance.

Defending his theology before the authorities in Ulm, Franck listed his sources: Tauler, the *German Theology*, Staupitz, Luther. He had been trained to interpret the Bible by "Luther," who said "that Scripture is not Christ, but the swaddling clothes and manger of Christ in which Christ lies wrapped."[51] But Franck had moved on. His confidence that Christ would always be with the pure in heart led him to define religion in terms that were ultimately no broader. From hot evangelical convictions Franck had articulated a form of natural religion. His tired plea for freedom in one of his final works suggests how naturally the protest of a mystic could point to a strikingly modern concept of live and let live: "Nobody is the master of my faith, and I desire to be the master of the faith of no one. I allow nobody to have dominion over the one place which I am pledged to the Lord to keep as pure virgin, namely my heart and my conscience. If you try to bind my conscience, to rule over my faith, or to be master of my heart, then I must leave you."[52]

Franck did not live to see the freedom he demanded but his ideas gained currency via a phenomenon that embodied everything he had come to oppose: Calvinism. Franck's struggle with Lutheran orthodoxy found its parallel in the battle between Calvin and Castellio over the legitimacy of Christian persecution. And it was from the frenzied animosities of this debate that a more durable case for "reason" emerged. Franck's rationalism was implicit, a function of his faith in conscience; Castellio's would rest on the explicit conviction that only an untainted, pre-theological force could stand up to the violence of dogma. Reason pressed its case not as intellectual presumption but as shelter.

A Scandal of Scandals

Calvin was a French humanist lawyer who converted to evangelical faith in 1533. Fleeing France as persecutions broke out the following year, Calvin settled in Geneva, where he had initially planned to spend just one night on his way to Strasbourg. William Farel, a fellow Frenchman, persuaded him to stay and lead the reform of the Genevan church. Apart from a brief period of exile in 1538, Calvin made Geneva his own, molding the life of the city with the lapidary precision that defined his *Institutes of the Christian Religion* (1536). Calvin was a peerless preacher, commentator, and theologian, and his vision of renewal promised more than the darting paradoxes of Lutheranism. He provided system, certainty, and an abiding confidence that trials could not throw providence off its stride. Where Luther proclaimed grace and mercy, Calvin asserted sovereignty. God is in control. The world is no accident. There is work to be done before anyone could think about heavenly retreat.

Calvin's Geneva attracted pilgrims from all over Europe, hopeful that this was the real thing: a Christian commonwealth in the making. This is why Calvin's descent to the forced providence of persecution had such a shattering effect. "Wisdom vanishes when force is introduced," Calvin once wrote, condemning a Catholic religion of "fire and sword."[53] But truth was a stern master, and Calvin's imperious vision somehow demanded force. His confidence that "nothing transpires unless [God] knowingly and deliberately decrees it"[54] inspired Calvin to interpret his rise to power as an act of providence and to perceive criticism as a test of faith and will. Heretics represented an opportunity to vindicate divine honor. Citing Augustine's view that "the cause, not the suffering, makes the martyr," Calvin invariably backed himself to define it.[55] With a cleaner chain of command than Luther ever enjoyed, Calvin was able to do more than whisper into the ears of magistrates. Geneva was where providence and politics met.

Calvin was influenced by the Augustinian School of medieval theology, which set God and humankind in fierce and disturbing tension.[56] God could do whatever he wanted ("voluntarism"); and the world we see around us bears only the faintest relation to the divine nature ("nominalism"). Although Calvin's theology engaged the earth and its fullness more dynamically than either medieval Catholicism or Lutheranism, it retained a stark dualism that sometimes bordered on contempt for the created order. Humans had been formed "from the dust" to keep them "humble," and the "corruption" of their bodies was a reminder of how far they stood from their maker. Although Calvin acquired a reputation as a defender of the Trinity, he was often accused of hesitancy toward the idea of a human Christ. His emphasis on the "incomprehensible" and "incorporeal" nature of God strained at the concept of incarnation and surely contributed to the disdain with which he wrote of human affections. A number of contemporaries accused him of blending the Father and the Son into spiritual abstraction, proclaiming an imperious Christ shorn of "all the features of the forgiving and suffering Son of Man."[57] There is no doubt that Calvin worshipped a God of terrifying grandeur, and his doctrine of predestination was the definitive homage to divine "freedom." God did the asking. It was an idea that could generate mighty assurance in one person and despair in another.

Calvin's style of government echoed his theology of imperious sovereignty. Whatever Calvinists claimed about the "mystery" of predestination, it provided an irresistible framework for interpreting conflict. The notion of an "elect," chosen before time, offered a permanent temptation to classify enemies in the spiritual category of the lost. As a recent biographer notes: "Opponents fell into an entirely different ontological category, and to such Calvin revealed how harsh he could be."[58] The paradox was that a towering theology of transcendence could point to an oddly anthropomorphic God, who picks and chooses between his progeny: a God whose "sovereign" government demands instant execution. Having suppressed what he perceived as an attempted coup d'état in 1555, Calvin did not hesitate to present his triumph as God's victory. Over the severed head of one of his chief opponents was the bracing reflection:

For having fallen into the misfortune
Of loving a man more than God
Claude de Genève has his head
Nailed up in this place.[59]

Calvin's passion for divine honor, his hunger for providence, and the glacial clarity of his intellect, insulated him from the doubts that tempered Luther's slide toward coercion. He did not hide behind euphemisms or fret over the difference between heresy and blasphemy. He simply applied "the appropriate medicine."[60]

An additional factor, germane to the skeptical revolt Calvin triggered, was a highly rational conception of faith, defined as "firm and certain knowledge of God's benevolence towards us, founded upon the truth of the freely given promise in Christ, both revealed to our minds and sealed upon our hearts through the Holy Spirit."[61] There was an affective, or emotional side to faith, but this was the strict corollary to mental certitude, rendered in such words as "cognitio," "notitia," "agnitio," and "scientia"—together translating as "knowledge." Calvin held that "where there is no certain knowledge (*cognitio*) of God, there is no religion (*religio*)." Conscience (*conscientia*) was nothing without *scientia*. Truth had to be known. Failures of understanding suggested spiritual poverty. Calvin's ally, Theodore Beza, argued that full certainty of faith was the difference between "the chosen children of God" and "the castaways,"[62] which meant that doubt was more than the sin it became for Luther: it was a sign of "reprobation." Sowers of theological confusion, while theoretically incapable of disturbing the logic of predestination, were monsters in the Calvinist imagination.

Providence, transcendence, and rational precision all combined to weaken the claims of the heretic. Calvin's comments on the holy wars of the Old Testament demonstrate how the providential vision could attenuate natural sympathies: "We may rest assured," he wrote, "that God would suffer only those infants to be killed whom He had already damned and destined to eternal death."[63] Sometimes Calvin evinced horror at the "barbarous" practices of the Hebrews, but he believed that they were somehow accommodated by God, and that the new Israel of faith was similarly favored—indeed more so. For Calvin, faith was always in tension with human relationships, and divine honor trumped human sympathy, every time. The English Puritan, William Perkins, was reasoning directly from the *Institutes* when he asserted that "the father hath authority to dispose of his child."[64] Calvin's comments on the command to "Honor thy father and thy mother" included the insistence that: "Those who abusively or stubbornly violate parental authority are monsters not men! Hence the Lord commands that all those disobedient to their parents be put to death."[65] Calvin seemed to place violence at the very heart of the divine character.

And far from setting a human Jesus against a law-breathing Jehovah, he allowed one to speak for the other.

Calvin's schematic analysis allowed him to juxtapose a preexistent Christ, who inspired David to say, "Do I not hate them, O Lord, that hate thee?", to a New Testament Christ who said "Love your enemies." It was a recipe for persecution.[66] The apostles had not used force, Calvin admitted, but that was "because miracles were then available."[67] There was so much more to Calvin than the implacable heresy hunter, but it was the rationalizing persecutor who inspired a wave of radical protest. Calvin was a master of inference and synthesis, and it was his ability to place persecution within a towering theological framework that attracted a storm of criticism. "Whoever shall maintain that wrong is done to heretics and blasphemers in punishing them," he reasoned, "makes himself an accomplice in their crime and guilty as they are." "There is no question here of man's authority," he insisted, "it is God who speaks." God "demands" such "extreme severity" to preserve his "honor." His clear command was "that we spare not kin nor blood nor life of any and forget all humanity when the matter is to combat for his glory."[68] Calvin's "ideal," writes one scholar, "was Abraham sacrificing Isaac, save that for Calvin all too often no ram was caught in the thicket."[69]

Calvin's moment of vindication came when Michael Servetus, a Spanish physician and notorious antitrinitarian, made the extraordinary error of passing through Geneva in the summer of 1553, as he fled the Catholic Inquisition. It was August 12 when Servetus entered the city on foot, having escaped prison in Lyons, where he was facing the death penalty for his heresies. He was traveling to Italy, where he hoped to work as a doctor, free from theological controversy. Why he chose to spend a night in Geneva remains a mystery. He must have known of Calvin's hostility because his conviction rested on samples of handwriting supplied by Calvin himself. Servetus had corresponded with him several years earlier, sending both annotations on the *Institutes* and excerpts of his own manuscript, *The Restitution of Christianity*. Calvin ended the dialogue as it descended into insults, filing away the offending documents. Servetus dropped off the radar for a few years, practicing medicine under a false name. But when his cover was blown by two cousins living in Lyons and Geneva, respectively, bickering over whose city was softer on heresy, Calvin was drawn into the affair. By providing what turned out to be the decisive evidence of Servetus's handwriting, he collaborated with the Catholic Inquisition to send the Protestant heretic to the stake. Servetus must have known this as he trudged into Geneva having staged a brilliant escape from his French captors. He knew Calvin despised him. He cannot have known that Calvin had previously vowed to ensnare him should he enter the city: "Servetus has just sent me a long volume of his ravings," Calvin wrote to Farel in February 1546. "If I consent he will come here, but I will not give my word, for should he come, if my authority is of any avail, I will not suffer him to get out alive."[70] Seven years later, he proved it.

On the day he was captured, Servetus had gambled that going to church in disguise represented a lower risk than avoiding worship altogether, a frightening commentary itself on the Genevan regime. He was instantly identified by "certain brothers from Lyons," who informed Calvin. Calvin instructed his secretary to enter custody alongside Servetus as "surety" while he drew up the charges. Encouraged by Farel, Calvin masterminded the prosecution and canvassed the support of neighboring cities as he pressed for the death penalty, the legalities of which were precarious to say the least. Ten weeks later, Servetus was taken to a pile of wood just outside the city, sprinkled with sulfur and burnt at the stake for Anabaptist and antitrinitarian heresies. He screamed as the flame was held in front of his face, recovering composure to utter a final prayer of resignation: "O Jesus, Son of the Eternal God, have pity on me!"[71]

For dismayed critics such as Castellio, the manner of the trial was as telling as the outcome. It reeked of cruelty, revenge, and injustice. Calvin had requested the more humane punishment of beheading, but he treated Servetus with contempt throughout the affair, mocking him for losing composure in the face of death. He saw only blasphemy in the Spaniard's stubborn pieties, and he regarded Servetus's reluctance to debate as an admission of guilt. Servetus, however, had sensed the futility of argument. He recognized that he had been trapped and he refused to dignify the trial as a meeting of minds, goading Calvin to acknowledge his real motives: "Deny that you are a homicide and by your acts I will prove it."[72] Servetus had a serious and fervent theology, and he fiercely defended Christ's divinity. But he saw it as a conferred divinity, a secondary status that applied after the birth of Jesus, not before. Servetus had evangelical reasons for downplaying the Trinity, conscious that Jews and Muslims in his native Spain found the doctrine a decisive barrier to engagement. He had, however, mocked the orthodox view as "a three-headed Cerberus" in a letter to the Genevan pastors. He also ridiculed their theology as a paganism of cruel and arbitrary fate, addressing Calvin as "Simon Magus"—a sorcerer condemned in the New Testament for trying to buy spiritual power. And he accused the new priests of reform of an unbiblical separation of faith from love: "For faith you have a deterministic dream, and good works you say are inane pictures," he raged. "With you the faith of Christ is mere deceit effecting nothing. Man is with you an inert trunk, and God is a chimera of the enslaved will." "You close the Kingdom of Heaven before men."[73] These were serious and enduring charges, but the language condemned Servetus to the status of a ranting blasphemer.

Martyrdom only magnified his cause, however. Servetus's challenge that "faith alone does not suffice, for faith will pass away, whereas love alone abides,"[74] distilled the radical Protestant quarrel with the new reign of doctrine. His death dramatized it. Servetus was far more threatening as a martyr for conscience than he had ever been as a wandering malcontent circulating clandestine heresies. It was Calvin, defending a judicial murder with finely toothed legalities, who raised lasting questions about the reliability of religious knowledge.

Reason as Refuge: The Sixteenth-Century Enlightenment

Reactions to the Servetus affair were instant and sharply polarized. While figures as distinguished as Melanchthon suspended confessional hostilities to congratulate Calvin on his brave stand for truth, others voiced their shock and disgust. The news was taken especially badly among Italian evangelicals who had regarded Calvin as a modern apostle. "Throughout the whole expanse of the Italian diaspora," writes one scholar, "poems, apologies, anthologies, and other materials for some time after 1553 tossed like flotsam on the ever-widening waves of despair at what to these Italians appeared to be the foundering of the Reformed Church under its reckless pilot, Calvin." Critics wrote of a new inquisition, a gospel announced "with flames," a reign of "executioners as wicked as the minions of Antichrist."[75] For one horrified observer, the execution of Servetus was the "scandal of scandals" (*scandalum scandalorum*), a damning scar on this boldest of New Jerusalems.[76]

The most famous response was Castellio's *Concerning Heretics; Whether They Are to Be Persecuted and How They Are to Be Treated; a Collection of the Opinions of Learned Men, Both Ancient and Modern*, published anonymously in 1554. It was an anthology of writings against persecution, including substantial excerpts from Augustine and Luther in their "liberal" phases, and material from a younger Calvin. Franck was widely quoted, and Castellio included several pieces of his own under a series of improbable pseudonyms. The volume appeared before Castellio had time to respond to Calvin's defense of his role in the Servetus affair, so he followed it up with a short *Reply to Calvin's book*, and a handful of additional works, which circulated in manuscript.[77] The controversy has been described as Europe's first international debate on toleration. But it was more than that. A debate on freedom of conscience became a plea for faith in conscience, as the ferocity of the Calvinist counterattack raised the problem of religious knowledge with fresh and painful urgency.

Castellio had started with impeccable Protestant credentials. He was a humanist scholar who joined the evangelical cause under the combined influence of Calvin's *Institutes* and the moving spectacle of French Protestants dying for their faith in Lyon, around 1540.[78] Castellio sought out the new master of evangelical theology and briefly lodged with Calvin during his exile in Strasbourg. Calvin was sufficiently impressed with Castellio to install him as rector of his college for clerical training, though tensions surfaced over biblical interpretation. Calvin's typological approach led him to read the Song of Songs as an allegory of Christ and the Church. Castellio considered it a rather dubious love poem. Calvin's exegesis was unerringly theological; Castellio was more historical and concerned for the flavor and power of the language. He was at once more literal and more moralistic than Calvin, reflecting his humanist training and the influence of Luther, whose distinction between the spirit and the letter remained critical for him. The Bible was like a box of treasures or a shell found on a beach, requiring a healthy spirit rather than a brilliant mind to unlock its riches. Moral sensitivity and literary flair were the hallmarks of Castellio's biblicism.[79]

The tension between a doctrinal and an intuitively ethical outlook soon flared into conflict. Castellio objected to Calvin's evaluation of pastors on the basis of their orthodoxy rather than pastoral competence or moral character, citing the cowardice and ineptitude of the clergy during an outbreak of the plague. As people lay dying in hospital, the majority of ordained ministers refused to visit or provide the sacraments. It was left to members of the laity, such as Castellio himself, to serve their needs. Castellio resented the fact that intellectual orthodoxy counted for more than pastoral integrity in the promotion of clergy, rising after one of Calvin's sermons to denounce the Genevan priority of doctrine over duty. He was infuriated that the name of Paul was invoked to support a system that travestied the apostle's example of humble service. Castellio's grievance was partly motivated by his own exclusion from the ministry, but it reflected a genuine distaste for a theology that elevated intellect over life, and orthodoxy over human decency. The protest caused a sensation, and Castellio's position was instantly untenable. He left Geneva in 1545, finding work correcting proofs and gathering wood in Basel. Calvin even wrote a reference, vouching for his "character" and confirming that he had left his post "of his own free will."[80] It was a remarkable gesture after such a public rebuke. The civilities did not last.

Castellio made friends with a handful of Italian and Dutch exiles, and he managed to produce a Latin translation of the Bible in 1551, before finally escaping penury with an appointment to teach Greek at the university in 1553. But word of Servetus shattered all hope of scholarly retirement. Castellio was horrified by the news of the execution and he immediately prepared a response. Thus began a battle that would consume him until his death in 1563. When he wrote of the power of "vexation" to "sharpen" the mind, enabling diverse thinkers "to write many things well and pointedly concerning persecution," he was almost certainly thinking of himself.[81] Castellio was electrified by the scandal, and his fury that the Bible could be so corrupted by men like Calvin and Beza drove him toward a form of theological skepticism. In rocking Calvin's granite pulpit, Castellio loosened more than he intended.

Persecution as Sin

Concerning Heretics opened with the parable of the White Robe. A king goes away, ordering his subjects to wear white garments, and to be wearing them when he returns. When he reappears, however, no one is dressed accordingly. Rather, his subjects are arguing over where the king had been staying, how he would return, and the nature of his person. In fact, they were killing one another, and claiming to be doing it for the king's honor. This, Castellio sighed, was Christendom. "Christ is the Prince of this world." His requirement is that people love one another. Instead he finds us bickering over "the Trinity, predestination, free will" and forgetting that love is the basis of all spiritual knowledge. Something had to change. "Blessed are the pure in heart: for they shall see God," was a critical verse for Castellio, who always linked intellectual clarity to moral purity. Love was not only the test of creeds: it was the condition of them. We cannot think clearly, about God or other people, without a spirit of generosity, he claimed. Sin warps the mind as well as the heart. Protestants, however, had abandoned this principle, condemning the man who strives "to live justly and innocently" as "a heretic on the ground that he seeks to be justified by works." The Bible had been turned upside down, and from the horrible inversion emerged the "blasphemy" of persecution. As Castellio wrote in sorrow for the evangelical cause, "The very persons who at first reproached their adversaries for resorting to the sword because of inability to debate with the truth, now, grown powerful, adopt the methods of their opponents. Having first burned the persons and the books of their critics at a slow fire, they then tilt against the ashes and vanquish in death those whom they could not overcome in life."[82]

Castellio invited his readers to picture Jesus proudly looking on as pious Anabaptists were coldly put to death in his name. The thought did not bear scrutiny. Persecution was a pagan corruption, Castellio believed, betrayed by the language of sacrificial cleansing with which it was typically justified. Heretics were condemned with a ritual finality that exceeded the treatment of the worst criminals. Persecutors wrote of "amputating" the "putrid member," or "purging" the body of Christ, as though God required constant appeasement and invited men to execute his wrath. In the inverted wisdom of "Geneva," Castellio suggested, "heresy is a graver offense than homicide." But none of this had anything to do with God. "O blasphemies and shameful audacity of men," he lamented, "who dare to attribute to Christ that which they do by the command and at the instigation of Satan!"[83] Persecutors, Castellio contended, were guilty of two kinds of murder: physical and spiritual. "Either the victim resists, and you murder his body, or he yields and speaks against his conscience, and you murder his soul."[84] The heretic was "like a piece of bread roasted on the end of a knife. If it moves forward it is burned and if backward it is pierced."[85]

Castellio wrote with the urgency of someone who knew what it was "to see the executioner sprinkle sulphur" in a face frozen with fear. His evangelical conversion occurred in the context of martyrdom and he was in Basel, several years later, when the body of his friend David Joris was exhumed, mutilated, and burned after the authorities discovered that this notorious Anabaptist had lived and died in the city under a false name. An eyewitness described Castellio looking so pale he might have come up from the grave himself. Castellio's writing reverberated with an irrefragable certainty that persecutors violated the will of God. Joris worked with Castellio on the text of *Concerning Heretics*, which contained a letter he had written to Calvin in 1553, pleading mercy for Servetus. He reminded Calvin that Jesus had prophesied to his disciples that a time would come "when anyone who kills you will think they are offering a service to God. They will do such things because they have not known the Father or me."[86] This was the raw, elemental logic applied throughout *Concerning Heretics* and the accompanying manuscripts. As Castellio wrote in a celebrated introduction: "I do not see how we can retain the name of Christian if we do not imitate His clemency and mercy."[87]

Castellio tried to present the scandal from the point of view of an outsider. "When they see us attacking one another with the fury of beasts, and the weak oppressed by the strong, these heathen feel horror and detestation for the Gospel," he suggested. Persecution justified skepticism. As he continued, in clear allusion to Servetus:

> Who would wish to be a Christian, when he saw that those who confessed the name of Christ were destroyed by Christians themselves with fire, water, and the sword without mercy and more cruelly treated than brigands and murderers? Who would not think Christ a Moloch, or some such god, if he wished that men should be immolated to him and burned alive? Who would wish to serve Christ on condition that a difference of opinion on a controversial point with those in authority would be punished by burning alive at the command of Christ himself more cruelly than in the bull of Phalaris, even though from the midst of the flames he should call with a loud voice upon Christ, and should cry out that he believed in Him? Imagine Christ, the judge of all, present. Imagine Him pronouncing the sentence and applying the torch. Who would not hold Christ for a Satan? What more could Satan do than burn those who call upon the name of Christ?[88]

Calvin defended the execution with the claim that heretics "infect souls with the poison of depraved dogma" that "the doctrine of piety" must be defended at all costs. Castellio responded with his most celebrated aphorism: "To kill a man is not to defend a doctrine. It is to kill a man." Calvin characterized heretics as "wolves" devouring the "body of Christ." Castellio was again vivid in reply: "By their fruits ye shall know them. The fruit of the wolf is to eat raw flesh. Therefore they are not the wolves who are killed, but rather those who kill." Calvin claimed that he had fulfilled a Christian duty in delivering a troublemaker to the secular authorities. Castellio's rage dissolved into sarcasm: "Does your piety consist only in hurrying to the fire strangers passing peacefully through your city?"[89]

The role of the high priest of biblical scholarship in the cruel demise of a fellow Protestant raised grave questions about religious knowledge. A plea for clemency and toleration grew into a debate about theology itself as Castellio developed a sensitivity, reminiscent of the early Luther, to the capacity of intellectual sophistication to mask sin. He started to question the very idea of preserving spiritual truth within dogmatic structures. Castellio was orthodox on the doctrine of the Trinity but he wondered whether the very clarity of the concept betrayed a kind of pride of possession, an urge to claim and perhaps own the deity. The fact that someone had died for violating the doctrine invited suspicion. Beza claimed that the doctrine of the Trinity was the keystone of Christianity. Perhaps so, admitted Castellio. But, he countered: "If you had not known it, you would never have burnt a man alive."[90] This was powerful dissent. It shifted attention from doctrine and metaphysics to flesh and blood.

The connection between orthodoxy and violence was painfully apparent to Castellio, who claimed that "scarcely any shed so much blood as those who profess to have true religion." Passion for theology seemed to weaken sentiments of charity and clemency. Orthodoxy seemed to raise rather than lower men's capacity for violence. In Germany alone, Castellio mourned, "so much human blood has been poured out that if as many beasts had been killed men would lament." In France, massacres had become so frequent that "roads and byways, yes, houses and temples, are stained with the blood of those for whom Christ died . . . and who are baptized in His name." And some of the worst crimes were committed in defense of beliefs that are "so far from being based on Scripture that even the very names are not to be found there." "Is that," he wondered, "a good and just cause for burning men alive?"[91]

Much of *Concerning Heretics* was addressed soberly to rulers, urging them to ignore "those who counsel you to shed blood for religion," to "follow the counsel of Christ, not of Antichrist," assuring them that God would punish "cruelty" not "mercy."[92] There was a sense of bypassing the zealots with a practical appeal to a shared humanity. The approach pointed toward the Enlightenment model of the secular state as referee and judge between the sects. But there was a more corrosive skepticism at work in Castellio's sorrowful rage, centering on the notion of theology as a work of the "flesh." To kill a man was not to defend a doctrine: it was to destroy one.

Theology as Flesh

Castellio prefaced *Concerning Heretics* with a verse from Paul's letter to the Galatians: "He that was born after the flesh persecuted him that was born after the Spirit." He revived Luther's typology of Cain attacking Abel, Esau persecuting Jacob, and Christ ever among the sufferers. The innovation was to argue that dogma itself tended to side with abusive power. Experience told Castellio that the whites of theological eyes did not always speak of a pure love of God. When people talked about defending the honor of God, what they really meant was their own. Castellio started to suspect that there was an inverse relationship between theological precision and Christian goodness. It was the zealots who became persecutors, the intellectuals who egged on the princes. Persecution was a fallacy of intellectual presumption and it was the false certainty of theology that inspired one man to "damn" another "forever." Behind the purest theological formulas lurked the desire to play God.

Castellio did not doubt the sincerity of the zealots, but violence proved the corruption of their motives. The New Testament account of Saul, convinced that he was serving God by persecuting the first Christians, was worth pondering. Saul showed how a jealous orthodoxy could function as a mask for anger and hatred. Likewise, today's persecutors "cover" their sin "with the name of zeal and by this spell bewitch the eyes of the people and perhaps even their own." They "declare that all this is done through zeal for Christ and at His command and in His name." But this was only to "cover the cruelty of the wolf with sheep's clothing." For "Christ, who, rather than shed blood, poured forth His own," had no part in the carnage.[93]

Castellio had a way of dismissing theological rigor as the folly of Alpha males, fighting over personal territory. Whole books of scripture had become the possession of proud intellects. It was with similarly brusque logic that he was prepared to dissolve the concept of heresy altogether: "After a careful investigation into the meaning of the term heretic," he wrote, "I can discover no more than this, that we regard those as heretics with whom we disagree." Could there really be just one truth within the jealous dance of rival orthodoxies? There was, he noted, "scarcely one of our innumerable sects which does not look upon the rest as heretics, so that if you are orthodox in one city or region, you are held for a heretic in the next. If you would live today, you must have as many faiths and religions as there are cities and sects. Just as he who travels from country to country must change his money from day to day."[94] It was a subversive analogy. Cherished formulations were melting under the weary gaze of Christian decency.

Castellio was especially impatient of the use of technical logic to defend highly subjective theories. With Lutheran scorn, he castigated "hairsplitting malicious sophists," who profit from complexity and erudition, drawing "on all the arts of the Aristotles and the Ciceros to throw dust in the eyes of the judges." His critique of the legalities deployed in Calvin's *Defense* reflected a growing skepticism toward intellectual sophistication in general. He rebuked Calvin for employing arguments "more rhetorical than Christian" and for substituting complex inferential logic for plain Christian wisdom. Calvin claimed that, strictly speaking, he had obeyed the biblical command merely "to avoid" the heretic, handing Servetus over to the "godly magistrate" for the appropriate legal remedies. To Castellio, the evasion was a symptom of a mind detached from its spiritual moorings: "The excuse of the Sorbonne! Bring water for Calvin to wash his hands. He is innocent of his blood. . . . O Calvin, Calvin, do you think God is like a man to be beguiled by these sophisms of the Sorbonne?"[95] Calvin was claiming a distinction between spiritual and civic jurisdiction that he had openly violated, Castellio insisted. He was invoking God in pursuit of a vendetta that started and ended with himself. Castellio's claim was that Calvin's erudition had scrambled his conscience and mangled the very source to which he claimed to defer: the Bible.

It troubled Castellio that Calvin could appeal to the example of Elijah's fierce judgment against the priests of Baal when Christ had explicitly condemned it. "The persecutors think that we ought to do what Christ forbade to the apostles," Castellio complained. "We are given to understand that they were not come to save, but to destroy. Our adversaries wish to put to death the priests of Baal, although it is not yet apparent who they are." Like Franck, he lamented the persecutors' affinity for Moses over Christ, though he could not resist the suggestion that even Moses would have recoiled from the new religious measures: "If only the persecutors would select the finer portions of Moses, those which better accord with the mercy of Christ. If only they would imitate Moses," Castellio protested.[96]

Castellio's contention was that theological hubris tempted the persecutors to claim authority they did not possess. It was an appalling presumption to "take life away from those to whom we cannot give it, especially in view of the prohibition of Christ." Persecutors claimed prerogatives that not even Jesus assumed. "Christ himself could not save an unwilling Jerusalem," Castellio noted, "and are we stronger than he?" Calvin's argument that if the law punishes secular crimes it should double its zeal for spiritual justice was another victory for philosophical inference over the clear testimony of scripture. "You might as well argue," Castellio responded, that if the prophets killed the priests of Baal, "how much more might the apostles burn the Samaritans?" Or, "If Moses might kill the Egyptian, how much more might Christ? These are the fallacies devised by the sophists to impel men to shed blood."[97]

Castellio despaired of Calvin's ability to dismiss the clemency of a New Testament figure such as Gamaliel, who had become an icon of the tolerationist cause, while reaching into the "the harsher portions of the law" to justify persecution. Gamaliel was the Jewish leader who advised the Sanhedrin not to persecute the early Christians, pointing out that it would be impossible to stop the new faith "if it is from God." Calvin thought it a poor example, for Gamaliel "suspended judgment like a blind man in the dark." He spoke from ignorance, not knowledge. Castellio was horrified that Calvin would criticize someone who opposed the persecution of Christians, while "appropriating" the example of Nebuchadnezzar, whose decree against blasphemy the prophet Daniel had apparently "celebrated." To find in Nebuchadnezzar's "cruelty" a better model than the "mildness" of Gamaliel distilled the fallacy of system, the arrant corruption of the theological mind. Men who were quick to condemn "reason" were the first to conjure chains of logic by which the Bible was reduced to silence.[98]

Castellio returned to the fact that a man who "believed in the Father, Son, and Holy Spirit" had been condemned to death with arguments hewn from the Bible. If Calvin, who mocked Servetus for his "beastlike stupidity" before his accusers, wanted a biblical analogy for the disgraceful scene, he could look in the New Testament. "I do not say that Servetus was like Christ, but the calumny is similar," he ventured. "Christ in the hands of the executioner refused to dispute." The trial of Servetus was a fiction: a rigged encounter in which "the executioner had the last word." The lesson was not that Protestants revered the Bible and would defend it to the last. They "clamor that they do all in accord with Scripture," he noted, but they could not "produce a syllable which commands that men be put to death." The lesson was that theologians knew better than the "Apostles" and "Evangelists," who evidently lacked the "spine" of their self-appointed successors. For Castellio, persecution did not represent an escalation of zeal so much as a total perversion. By sending Servetus to his death, "Calvin showed the weakness of his word to the glory of the sword, which is his god." "This is," he lamented, "truly the profane money changing of souls, for these men make alive souls which God does not make alive and kill those whom God does not kill. . . . When the Son of God comes He will drive out these money changers . . . with His fiery, unconquerable word, because they have profaned and violated the whole sacred temple of God."[99]

These were hardly the words of an untheological mind. The Bible remained Castellio's primary source. But the awkward fact was that the persecutors were nimble with their texts. Castellio was conscious of the futility of quotation and counter-quotation. The need for a firmer criterion of truth was increasingly apparent. So Castellio moved from a piercing plea for toleration to a cautious appeal for doubt, reason, and undogmatic faith.

"Drop the Arguments and Look at the Fruit": The Art of Doubting and the Virtue of Reason

In the *Reply to Calvin*, Castellio started with the principle that biblical faith presupposes a degree of uncertainty. Most of the heroes of the Bible placed their trust in God without knowing where it would lead them. Castellio contrasted the humility of this attitude with the arrogant verities of theology, which dared to map divine mysteries with mathematical precision. The doctrine of predestination was, for Castellio, the ultimate theological folly: claiming knowledge in matters that are not ours to know, while travestying qualities of love and mercy, which are. Creeds were frequently antithetical to the moral essence of faith, he suggested. The argument was set out in the unpublished *Art of Doubting* but it was a position slowly surfacing in the *Reply*, where Castellio justified his stance with a typically practical analogy. The toleration crisis was like a dispute between doctors in which one side cites Hypocrates and the other Galen. "The only recourse for the people," Castellio urged, "is to drop the arguments and look at the fruits and to award the palm to the one which cures the most and the worse diseases." It was "not a question of names but of truth."[100]

True religion required a willingness to let go of cherished formulas, Castellio urged. Indeed, he argued with a degree of optimism for the future, "Religion will be based on an assured faith concerning things which are hoped for, *not known,* as Abraham, when he was called to go out, obeyed not knowing whither he went." Insofar as the Christian had certainty, it would be ethical not intellectual:

> The true Church will be known by love which proceeds from faith, whose precept is certain. "By this shall all men know that ye are my disciples if ye have love one to another." . . . The doctrine of piety is to love your enemies, bless those that curse you, to hunger and thirst after righteousness, and endure persecution for righteousness' sake. . . . These and similar matters are certain, however dubious may be the obscure questions about the Trinity, predestination, election, and the rest on account of which men are regarded as heretics. Many of the saints knew nothing about them.[101]

The use of the future tense was telling. The only way out of the present crisis would be a disciplined reduction of religion to the essentials of loving God and neighbor, and a studied agnosticism as to disputed matters of theology and metaphysics. There needed to be a great unlearning. In Castellio's circle, the "penitent thief," who came to faith next to Jesus on the cross, was virtually a patron saint: a humble spirit so little saved by theology. As were the Ninevites, described in the book of Jonah: a rough people who changed their ways in response to a simple call to purity. Such examples highlighted divine mercy in ways constantly obscured by orthodox theology. They proved that God's timescale is not ours: that there are twelve hours in the day and "one might learn in the eleventh." Knowledge was all about the present, a foolish zeal to sit "in the tribunal of Christ."[102] Faith involved a suspension of certainty and a hope of mercy beyond the terrestrial state of play. Prophecies like Jonah's confirmed Castellio's belief that there was grace beyond creed, mercy beyond a tribal orthodoxy. Theological skepticism and ethical dogmatism were ideas in tandem. Castellio retained a fervent faith in God and an undying esteem for the Bible, but the axis of his piety broke away from any kind of dogmatic orthodoxy. He moved to a form of rational mysticism that required doubt as a condition of trust.

Castellio's boldest statement was the unfinished manuscript, *On the Art of Doubting.* Here he opened with a military analogy. He compared the religious crisis to a situation in which a general, faced with the problem of transporting his army across a swollen river, had to bypass the usual chain of command, offering a reward to any common soldier who could present a workable plan. Acknowledging that he was no prophet, Castellio humbly stepped forward with a solution. Reason would provide a line of rescue, but only for those willing to lay down the weapons of combat. And this was the meaning of doubt: an expression of humility, a prelude to recovery, a condition of living.

Castellio recognized the radicalism of his proposal but he reiterated the rationale: "Today in the Christian churches some of the most saintly persons are put to death indiscriminately. If the Christians entertained a doubt about what they are doing they would not perpetrate such dreadful homicides for which they will have to repent very soon after." The greedy clutch of theology was no minor partner in these awful crimes, Castellio repeated, summarizing the crisis with another penetrating aphorism: "He who once said, 'I believe' now says, 'I know.'" In the arms race of what scholars now term "confessionalization," the idol of precision had turned into a deadly weapon. "New articles of faith" hung over innocent minds like a "snare," binding "the conscience of posterity," and sowing "the seeds of persecution." It was time to cease production, remembering that Christ had rebuked his disciples for wanting "to know the times [and] the seasons" when the kingdom of Israel would be restored.[103] Doubt was intrinsic to discipleship, Castellio averred. Far from any destruction of the Christian faith, it promised retrieval.

But it was in the definition of faith as virtue and practical energy that Castellio's theology began to sound subversive. In contrast to Calvin's account of faith as knowledge, Castellio used words like "actio," implying a disposition and an appetite for the deed. Faith, Castellio insisted, was a moral virtue, something that could not be said of "knowledge."[104] He dismissed the idea that he was making humans the authors of salvation by arguing that the urge to do good comes from God in the first place. It was an impulse felt in the depths of the soul. The Holy Spirit was present in all people, though not everyone heard his voice. Like Franck, Castellio seemed to be identifying the spirit with the tremors of conscience, characterizing faith as obedience to an already resident light. Drawing on the heart-centered spirituality of the *Imitation of Christ* and the *German Theology*, both of which he translated and edited, Castellio articulated a fluid theology of love and duty. He nurtured what an early biographer termed the "admirable heresy" of situating religion in "conscience" and the "moral act."[105]

Castellio did not dismiss scripture, but he cited the Bible in support of the view that spiritual truth had been "inscribed . . . by the finger of God in the hearts of all." It was also etched into the fabric of nature. "The world, which is the work of God," Castellio reasoned, "is unknown to no man and the precepts of love on which hang all the law and the prophets and which are fulfilled in Christ; these are so plain, so natural, and so known to man that even the wicked know them." Christ addressed sinners as people who strayed from a known law. "If you tell a perfect scoundrel he should love God and his neighbor as himself," Castellio insisted, "he will agree." Moral laws could "no more be erased than the other common notions of men. That is why I assert so confidently that what needs to be known can be known with perfect ease."[106] Castellio seemed to be dispensing with revelation. Having written in his *Four Dialogues* that reason is "infirm," needing to be "aided" by the Spirit, Castellio now seemed to equate the work of the spirit with the activity of reason in the conscience. Reason was a divine faculty, the primal wisdom that gave rise to conscience. Working in harmony with the senses, it ultimately transcended them, organizing the chaos of experience.

In his so-called "hymn to reason," Castellio suggested that the incarnation was no interruption of this ancient fabric of divine rationality. Christ embodied what was already there:

> For reason is, so to speak, the daughter of God. She was before letters and ceremonies, before the world was made; and she is after letters and ceremonies, and after the world is changed and renewed she will endure and can no more be abolished than God Himself. Reason, I say, is a sort of eternal word of God, much older and surer than letters and ceremonies, according to which God taught His people before there were letters and ceremonies, and after these have passed away He will still so teach that men may be truly taught of God. According to reason Abel, Enoch, Noah, and Abraham and many others lived before the letters of Moses, and after these many have lived and will continue to live. According to reason Jesus Christ himself, the Son of the living God, lived and taught. In the Greek he is called *logos,* which means reason or word. They are the same, for reason is a sort of interior and eternal word of truth always

> speaking. By reason Jesus refuted the Jews who placed greater trust in letters and ceremonies. Reason worked upon the Sabbath day and taught the Jews that they might remove a sheep from the ditch on the Sabbath without offense.[107]

Jesus was the logos . . . and he taught "according" to it. The tension was unresolved, but the status of scripture was inevitably in doubt.

Castellio was now quick to note the fragility of the biblical narratives, handed down with the errors of "copyists." Historical disputes, and their attendant theological toxins, needed to make way for reason, which would establish the true "tenor" of the text. Where no such meaning could be found, judgment had to be suspended. As Castellio insisted, the meaning of "baptism, the Lord's supper, justification, predestination and many other questions" is simply "not cleared up in Scripture." More significantly, perhaps, falsely esteemed "oracles" such as his long-admired Luther were to be forever silenced. The pagan associations of the term would not have been lost on Castellio's readers. Castellio concluded with a warning not to allow the spirit of the oracles to outlive the men themselves. With a dark prediction of the rise of new "disciples" and a new age of persecution, Castellio signed off with a prayer:

> O God, the Father of light, avert this sequel. Be appeased by the punishments visited upon our fathers and ourselves and enlighten posterity. And thou, Posterity, beware of this outcome. Be warned by our example and do not so adhere to the interpretations of men as not to put them to the test of reason, sense, and Scripture. And you, scholars, avoid this course. Do not arrogate so much to yourselves that you bring the souls and bodies of many into peril by your authority.[108]

It is rarely disputed that Castellio presaged the natural religion of the Enlightenment, that vague amalgam of faith in self and starry hosts above. Yet this was a profoundly spiritual rationalism, reaching more urgently for the leaven of mysticism than the grain of historical criticism. Castellio's reason was a new version of the *synteresis* of medieval mysticism, "that created organ of the uncreated [God] in the depths of the human heart."[109] Castellio turned to the classic texts of medieval *synteresis* theology—Paul's letter to the Romans and the writings of the apostle John—to argue that the "divine seed" was in the "hearts" of everyone, and God was with all who love. Indeed to love was to be born of God.[110] "The reason of which we speak," he explained, "searches, finds, and interprets truth." "Reason teaches what is good and what is evil, and this instruction gives birth to conscience."[111] This echoed Tauler's two-level account of conscience as a "ground" and a voice, "groaning" in the soul. And it reflected a passage in Romans that spoke of the subjective conscience "bearing witness" to an objective law. Jerome's eagle was alive and well, seeking and exposing new sins, including the tranquilizing darts of Protestant theology.

Castellio died in 1563, the year he wrote the *Art of Doubting*. Calvin and Beza had succeeded in bringing him to trial in Basel on charges of denying the inspiration of the Epistle to the Romans, which he defended. But the waves of defamation and abuse were less easily dismissed, contributing to his decline. Calvin's final curse—"May God consume you, Satan!"—suggests the tone of an unsparing campaign to destroy his most eloquent critic. As a biographer of Calvin writes: "His response to those he regarded as a threat was to seek total victory and their humiliation. He could explain this in terms of divine justice, but, in the case of a man like Sebastian Castellio, it was unvarnished vindictiveness."[112] "Christ is my dignity," Castellio responded, but the feud diminished him. Slanders, such as the rumor that he had supported himself by stealing firewood, cost him friends and allies. In the year of his death he faced renewed charges of heresy, presented by a citizen of Basel but secretly drawn up by Beza. He concluded that his critics shared one essential trait: they lacked the "spirit" and "mercy" of Christ, without which discussion was impossible.[113] One biographer concludes that his opponents were motivated by "visceral hatred" and had "no desire to understand" his thought—a fitting commentary on much of what Castellio had written.[114] Montaigne, the French skeptic and man of letters, described his treatment as a reproach on the very century in which he lived.[115]

"I will fight with all my might against this monster," Castellio wrote of his battle against persecution. "If I cannot kill it I hope at least to wound it severely."[116] It is sobering to reflect that his fulminations against religious violence were inspired by an early and relatively mild phase of the Wars of Religion. He grieved over a France "desolated" by sectarian hatred a full decade before the St. Bartholomew Day massacre. He wrote of a "war of extermination" as the "logical outcome" of confessional strife three generations before the Thirty Years War. Castellio's reduced religion of love and his instinct to back rulers against zealots was the prototype of the Enlightenment settlement. And as his ideas, with those of Franck and a handful of co-travelers, began to stimulate the early Enlightenment in the Dutch Republic, it could be said that his ambition of wounding the "monster" came to fruition. But toleration came at the price of an enduring skepticism. It was the demystification of survival: biblical in origin but increasingly dissolvent in tendency. In rescuing Christ from the persecutors, radical dissenters first spiritualized him as a "celestial" deity, above the religious fray, and then appeared to rationalize him as conscience. This was done with a certainty that the beating heart of conscience was the "true Light" of God in the soul. But the distinction between the "the Self that dwells within" and the ordinary work of the mind was one that would be difficult to sustain.[117] This was the story of the following century. Bayle was right: there were acids in the gentle rhapsodies of the mystics. Yet they were Christian acids, raining on the paradox of violent faith.

3

The Metaphysics of Mercy

CALVIN AND SPINOZA

There is no fear in love; but perfect love casteth out fear: because fear hath torment. He that feareth is not made perfect in love.

—1 JOHN 4:18

ON JULY 27, 1656, the Spanish-Portuguese Synagogue in Amsterdam delivered an extraordinary decree of excommunication on one of its members. Alluding darkly to his "evil opinions and acts," his "abominable heresies," and "monstrous deeds," the board expelled the 23-year-old Baruch de Spinoza from "the people of Israel," cursing him "with all the castigations which are written in the Book of the Law." No one was to communicate with him or even pass within "four cubits of his vicinity." He was to be cut off with a permanence apparently unprecedented in this community: for "the Lord will not spare him," and "the Lord shall blot out his name from under heaven."[1]

This was the harshest writ ever pronounced on a member of the synagogue and, unlike most bans of the period, it was never rescinded. Spinoza offered no appeal. He walked away, with an insouciance that enraged his adversaries, daring to liken his experience to "the exodus of the early Hebrews from Egypt."[2] If there were any proof of his contempt for the religion that had sustained his parents as refugees from the Inquisition, it was the maddening ease with which he accepted his fate. The radical, "Collegiant" Christians with whom he now decided to live became and remained his closest friends. Fourteen years later he published the *Theological-Political Treatise*, a landmark of religious criticism that conferred continent-wide notoriety. Feared at the time as a chillingly assured atheist and identified more recently as "the supreme philosophical bogeyman of Early Enlightenment Europe,"[3] Spinoza was, for Ludwig Feuerbach, "The Moses of modern freethinkers and materialists."[4]

According to one admirer, Spinoza "fundamentally and decisively shaped a tradition of radical thinking which eventually spanned the whole continent, exerted an immense influence over successive generations, and shook western civilization to its foundations." When Rousseau and Voltaire brought "philosophy" to the people in the eighteenth century, urging everyone "to live according to Nature," their project was "little more than footnotes to [an] earlier shift," effected chiefly by Spinoza. His "sweeping rejection of tradition and authority" and his "underlying pantheism" unleashed a stream of radicalism that closed the confessional age. Modernity hunters need to set their watches a century earlier. It was in the seventeenth century that "the real business" was done, before Voltaire had been invented.[5]

Such an emphasis on the Enlightenment as a single, if fractious, movement is welcome. And the notion of critical philosophy as an "awesome dynamic force," assailing "ecclesiastical authority" with unprecedented power, is a helpful corrective to stereotypes of arid rationalism.[6] My only dissent is from the assumption of secularism: the notion that figures like Spinoza and Bayle (whose influence was comparable) attacked religious authority from a stance of outright unbelief. On the contrary, it is in such figures that the passion of spiritual protest is most powerful. The "unbelief" that they represent is heterodoxy, not atheism. Their criticism was driven by positive convictions about God, the Bible, and faith. They were builders as well as destroyers.

The notion of a secular Spinoza owes more to his critics than his work. Theologians condemned Spinoza as "the most impious, the most infamous, and at the same time the most subtle Atheist that Hell has vomited on the earth," and such invectives have entered the bloodstream.[7] A recent work entitled, *A Book Forged in Hell: Spinoza's Scandalous Treatise and the Birth of the Secular Age*, is a case in point: it attaches a claim of secularism to a sectarian insult. Spinoza's "God," we are told, is really an "It," wholly innocent of the "moral characteristics traditionally attributed to God by many Western religions," including "goodness, wisdom and justice." By "God" what Spinoza really means is "Nature."[8] Others have neutralized Spinoza's language with elaborate distinctions between the "esoteric" and "exoteric" meanings of his texts, insisting that he should never be taken at his word, least of all when he is talking about God.[9] Yet Spinoza never apologized for his spiritual convictions, he never referred to his God as "It," and, if he was capable of subtlety and shrewdness of expression, outright deception was hardly his style. As one writer has suggested, the quest "to decipher what Spinoza must have really meant" as he waxed lyrical on "God's internal help" may turn out to be "our problem, not his."[10]

The claim of this chapter is that Spinoza's criticism was not a first draft of scientific naturalism but an extension of the Radical Reformation's spiritual protest against dogma and all its works. Far from a coded expression of atheism, my suggestion is that Spinoza's bracing vision of divine "immanence"—of a God dwelling in the fibers of nature—is a fervently spiritual reaction to theologies of transcendence and arbitrary judgment, chiefly Calvinist. Spinoza was not trying to destroy Christian faith: he was trying to rescue it from historical corruptions. His project was part of a wider revolt against Calvinism in English and Dutch Protestantism—and one that contained striking consistencies. Spinoza lived and worked with the kind of Christians that can embarrass a biographer, and he may have learned as much from them as they from him.

Friends of Religious Liberty: Calvinism, Conscience, and the Making of a Philosophical Culture

Spinoza's lifestyle has led some scholars to romanticize him as "a loner, the individual par excellence, who demands to be understood in terms of his private being and beliefs, not in terms of any social or historical framework supposed to provide him with the essential ingredients of his identity."[11] Some have urged that we do not read "too much" into "Spinoza's friendship" with "pious" Christians such as Jarig Jelles and Pieter Balling, who apparently failed to grasp the "latent hostility" of his philosophy to their religious worldview.[12] Others have portrayed Spinoza's relationship with the Collegiant Christians as a glorified tutoring arrangement for "mediocre pious souls," whose philosophical efforts were inevitably "clumsy and superficial."[13] Spinoza did not see it that way. He clung to his friendships as a spiritual lifeline, insisting on candor and intimacy with new correspondents, such as Henry Oldenburg. "Between friends," Spinoza wrote to the Englishman, "all things, and especially spiritual things, ought to be in common."[14] Spinoza extolled the virtues of friendship in his deepest philosophical works and it is fanciful to suggest that his Christian circle was innocent of his radicalism.[15]

When Spinoza took his battle to the Calvinist authorities with the *Theological-Political Treatise*, his Mennonite friend, Jarig Jelles, wanted to stoke the controversy with a bold Dutch translation. Spinoza feared the consequences of such a move and implored him to drop the plan, adding: "I have every confidence that you will do me and our cause this service."[16] It was another Collegiant, Jan Rieuwertsz, who published Spinoza's works, and another member of the same religious circle, Simon de Vries, who provided him with a pension, Spinoza accepting only half of what was offered. There was intimacy, respect, and common purpose in this mysterious collaboration between an excommunicated Jew and a group of unchurched Christians. Both were survivors of religious persecution and both looked to philosophy to meet needs denied by theology. Yet neither the Collegiants nor Spinoza supply evidence of a clean break, a decisive departure from theological reasoning. The Collegiants, in tandem with English radicals of the same period, provide the model of a rationalism developing from, not against, spiritual religion.

The Collegiants were a group of Christians who emerged from the struggle between Arminian and orthodox Calvinists in the early seventeenth century to pioneer a new mode of fellowship: without creed and without clergy. Calvinism had been instrumental in the formation of the United Provinces of the Netherlands in 1579, mobilizing the revolt against Habsburg oppression as a historic, divine deliverance. But, as a governing philosophy, it proved hard and unforgiving, and the conviction that Calvinism represented a pure and providential dispensation elevated dissent to the status of treason. That it came from such an impeccably pious source as Jacobus Arminius, a once-trusted theologian at the University of Leyden who had trained in Geneva at the feet of Theodore Beza, heightened the sense of betrayal.

Arminius had become suspicious of predestinarian orthodoxy, and the strain that the so-called "eternal decrees" placed on many "passages of Scripture." The idea of Christ dying only "for the elect" offended him, and while he was careful in the disclosure of his suspicions, the mere emphasis of his preaching was enough to precipitate a historic cleavage.[17] Arminius died before the conflict played out at the Synod of Dort between 1618 and 1619. The defeat of his supporters ("Remonstrants") signaled a purge of the Dutch Reformed Church and led to the execution of the aged statesman and Arminian sympathizer, Johan van Oldenbarnevelt. It also triggered a wave of bitter reaction, echoing Castellio's dispute with Calvin. Some considered Castellio the "real founder" of Arminianism.[18]

Others complained of "Castalio's stinking bones" coming "out of the Grave again."[19] It is no accident that his complete works, filled with bitter complaints about his one-time friend Calvin, were published in 1611–12 as the crisis unfolded, creating what one scholar has termed a "Castellio renaissance" in the Dutch Republic.[20] Some feared that they were living through his bleaker predictions for the coming century.

One such was Hugo Grotius, the celebrated philosopher and jurist who was imprisoned for his part in the crisis. Grotius is sometimes portrayed as a secular thinker, soberly sketching a post-theological framework for law and politics. But he could not have been any less the disinterested secularist as he escaped prison in a large trunk to make his case for toleration. And there was nothing generic about his critique of religious authority: "Immense evils must inevitably beset any kingdom," he complained, "where the rulers allow themselves to be led, not by God, but by the spirit of Calvin who is much closer to the spirit of Elias than to that of the Gospel. . . . Far from us be that spirit who has been a murderer from the beginning." Writing bitterly of "what happened to Servetus at Calvin's hands," Grotius was a harried, reluctant skeptic, who diagnosed the malady of religious violence in a gleefully divisive theology of exclusion. His conviction that "all true Calvinists are professed enemies to liberty"[21] was sharpened by access to Castellio's *Art of Doubting*.[22] Like many of his contemporaries, however, Grotius came to such ideas independently. Doubt was a reflex, an involuntary response to the stimulus of persecution.

The Collegiants, whose network spread like an emollient ivy after the trauma of Dort, were anticlerical by accident rather than design. Consisting initially of Remonstrants deprived of their ministers by persecution, the first "colleges" were simply private gatherings for Bible study, sung worship, and "free prophecy." It was only when the exiled ministers returned that the principle of congregational autonomy was firmly established, as the animus against Calvinist authority evolved into a generalized anticlericalism. Here the insights of Sebastian Franck and Caspar Schwenckfeld were significant, alongside Castellio's, disseminated by the important figure of Dirck Coornhert (1522–90).[23] Coornhert was a self-educated polymath and a veteran of the Dutch Revolt who became an influential advocate of religious freedom. As a disaffected Catholic, he was quick to perceive Reformed religion as the rising threat to freedom of conscience, and he found inspiration in the work of sixteenth-century radicals and the mysticism of the *German Theology*.[24] Coornhert's brusque rejection of Calvinism as a gospel of power and a crime against common sense set the tone of Collegiant dissent.[25] His suggestion of a pared-down ministry of Bible readings provided a model for the new colleges, which cemented measures he had considered temporary.

The colleges grew quickly, as the Arminian core attracted a vigorous penumbra of Mennonite Anabaptists, spiritualists, and antitrinitarians, known as Socinians. From the first college, which met in the village of Warmond in 1620 and moved to Rijnsburg the following year, the movement spread across the Netherlands with the most active colleges emerging in Amsterdam, Rotterdam, Haarlem, and Leiden. Spinoza attended the Amsterdam college, as did the Moravian educator and philosopher, John Amos Comenius.[26] Somewhere between a Protestant "conventicle" and a French salon, the Dutch college represents a vital link between Reformation and Enlightenment.[27]

At no point did the Collegiants consciously or explicitly exchange "spirit" for "reason." It was through a developing doctrine of conscience, based on principles first "outlined at Worms"[28] that a deeply spiritual rationalism emerged. Intellectual "reason" did not eclipse conscience in the Dutch colleges: it grew out of it, preserving the alacrity of the mystical lineage. One of the mottoes of the movement was the advice of St. Paul, "Do not treat prophecies with contempt but test them all; hold on to what is good,"[29] and it is impossible to engage the Collegiants without sensing the shared rhythms of intellectual and spiritual liberation: an urgency to "read, understand, examine and judge" springing from hot sensations of religious exile. Interest in the philosophy of Descartes emerged from such unlikely sources as Sebastian Franck, whose urge to abandon all "artificial," acquired knowledge coalesced with the search for "clear and distinct ideas." Philosophy was asked to fulfill religious needs, which is why language of regeneration clung tenaciously to intellectual accounts of "enlightenment."[30]

The Collegiants did not need to construct a skeptical crisis to advance new criteria of religious knowledge. The Arminian crisis, and the ongoing pressures of sectarian disputation, made an eloquent case. The emergence of antitrinitarian theology within the movement was anything but the outcome of rational biblical analysis. It was an instinctive reaction to a symbol of religious tyranny: "all had a vague feeling," notes one scholar, "a suspicion they found it difficult to justify or even articulate, that belief in the Trinity was . . . connected with the system of persecution, intolerance and religious coercion."[31] Confidence in the mind as the arbiter of religious truth grew in proportion to fading respect for religious tradition.

The decisive figure in the transition from spiritualism to rationalism was Galenus Abrahamsz, a Mennonite pastor who became the leader of the Amsterdam college around 1650. Galenus absorbed the ideas of Franck and Schwenckfeld from Adam Boreel, one of the founders of the college, who had imbibed the spiritualist formula from Coornhert. Most of the Collegiants had been originally committed to "visible" churches and concrete "confessions," moving to spiritualist and rationalist alternatives only after conflict and disillusionment. For Galenus, this involved a bitter dispute in his Mennonite community, inspiring him to broaden long-standing indictments of established churches to radical traditions such as his own. God had no part of the cycle of uncharity and recrimination, and those who claimed to hear his voice were probably listening to their own. On one occasion, Galenus confronted a zealot who was defacing a sign outside his house, which displayed his medical credentials. The man explained that God had "told" him to remove this ungodly symbol of worldly pride. When Galenus asked the man if he would have run the knife through him as well, if "God" had so instructed, the reply was affirmative. The incident terrified Galenus and hastened his skepticism.[32]

Conditions in Amsterdam were mild by European standards, but the multiplying "intolerances and fanaticisms" of the Dutch Republic cast their own doubts on providence.[33] As Spinoza later commented, there was truth in the Dutch saying, "every heretic has his text."[34] Personal grievances and a bleak assessment of the Reformation legacy convinced Galenus that churches were "merely human institutions." Confessions were "the uninspired work of fallible humans."[35] It was time to abandon the project of an earthly, incarnated purity. As another Collegiant expressed the same sadness: though some ages have known God's presence, "ours is unblessed."[36] This was the true meaning of disenchantment: disappointed faith.

As one authority on the movement has shown, the Collegiants started to use "Cartesian ideas to express rationalistic convictions that evolved organically" from their theology. And since "reason was identified so closely with the spiritual inner light, reason was spiritualized almost as much as spirit was rationalized."[37] When the Collegiants attempted to distinguish their position from the "spiritual arrogance" of some English Quakers who had joined their circle, they produced a "rationalist" tract that was immediately mistaken for the work of the Quaker they were trying to correct. *The Light upon the Candlestick* (1662), written by Pieter Balling in consultation with Spinoza, circulated for many years as a work of Quaker spirituality, mistakenly attributed to the man named-and-shamed in the title, William Ames. Using the words "Light," "Spirit," and "Christ" interchangeably, yet characterizing enlightenment in Cartesian phraseology as, "a clear and distinct knowledge of truth in the understanding of every man," the pamphlet dissolved the boundaries between spiritualism and rationalism.

Identifying reason with "The Light of Truth, the true Light which enlighteneth every man that cometh into the world [John 1:9]," the author at once pointed to the Johannine proof text of spiritualist Christianity and to a more sober and self-contained rationalism: a quiet empowerment to navigate the "Sea of Confusion" created by "Scholastic Learning, study and disputing"; a holy and confident poise, for weighing and judging the scriptures. External authorities, including the "toyes" of religious ceremony, made way for this sublime inner light. As the writer urged with almost poignant modernism: "We direct thee then to look within thyself." The days of institutionalized truth were over, as was the Reformation's tyranny of words, texts, and cradling language: "Things are not for words, but words for things," urged the writer. "The letters, the words are not the Scriptures, but the mind alone."[38]

The inner light had lost charismatic qualities of direct inspiration, but it retained the zeal of the accusing conscience: "This Light," the writer explained, "is that which makes manifest and reproves sin in man, shewing him how he has strayed from God, accuseth him of the evil which he doth and hath committed; yea this is it which judgeth and condemeth him." It also retained evangelical propensities, bringing whoever obeys its voice "into union with God, wherein all happiness and salvation doth consist." "For this is a living Word, and transmiteth man from death to life, is powerful, & enableth a man to bear witness of it self every where."[39] Salvation was within, but it remained a kind of rescue, with a fierce exposure of sin and a buoyant conversion to living truth. The sense of power and security generated by the inner "Light" is more than redolent of the spirituality of Quakers such as George Fox and Samuel Fisher, who once characterized salvation as being "hid as in a Pavilion from the strife of Tongues."[40] Whatever the differences between Quakers and Collegiants, both were part of a common reaction against Calvinist "scholasticism," seeking truths that transcended words. And it was among the English radicals that Spinoza's ideas found their most powerful analogues and, almost certainly, direct inspiration.

"Teeming Freedom" and the Taming of Calvinism: England's Spiritual Revolution

It is hard to picture the "polite and commercial people" of the eighteenth century, and the benighted "shopkeepers" of the nineteenth, as Milton's "nation of prophets," turning the world "upside down" in a frenzy of spiritual zeal. But this is what England became during twenty dizzying years of civil war, between the disastrous reign of one king, later executed, and the restoration of the monarchy, in 1660, after a brief and fateful republican experiment. Competing reformations, and the relaxing of censorship laws under the "Protectorate" of Oliver Cromwell, between 1653 and 1658, triggered an effusion of radical thought and literature, including bold theories of democratic representation and communist ideas that anticipated Marx. As Gerrard Winstanley said of the great years of overturning: "the old world . . . is running up like parchment in the fire."[41]

Among many parallels with the Dutch ferment was the recognition that to overthrow kingly power was only to scratch the surface of questions of equality and freedom—especially if the republican alternative was sustained by a fierce theology of control. Here too, the diffusive power of Calvinism acted as a goad to theological invention. Although it was the Catholic leanings of Charles I that precipitated the revolution, it was Calvinism that dominated the Church of England from the late sixteenth century through the civil war. Calvinism was a permeating force in British culture: inspiring, energizing, and terrorizing in equal measure.

Calvin had characterized the experience of the "reprobate" as a "foretaste of hell" and it was the perceived link between uncertainty of faith and cosmic rejection that drove many to despair and beyond. As a study on this "persecutory imagination" confirmed: "Many actual suicides resulted from religious despair. Cambridge was notorious for them in the 1580s and 1590s, the period of its greatest domination by puritan preaching." Sixty years later, fear of "reprobation" remained "the pre-eminent aspect of the problem of suicide." A mental doctor in London counted ninety-one individuals "doubtful of salvation" or "tempted to despair of salvation" among his patients. One diary recorded the fate of a man who tried to drown himself, having failed to end his life by other means. The desperate individual, described by the unfriendly commentator as "Mr Monk," ran "forth in his shirt very bloody, flourishing his sword in his hand and leapt into the Thames (at Botolph's Wharf) and hit himself on a boat."

Rescued by some watermen, he was taken home where "he did roar most hideously, crying that he was damned, and he had prayed often, and God would not hear him. . . . He lay crying very strangely and hideously till the next Wednesday, and then he died."[42]

Another writer tried to explain the phenomenon of theology-induced suicide. Typically, he observed, guilt and expectation of punishment

> overcharges the wounded *conscience,* when withall a man apprehends himselfe to bee wholly destitute of true *grace,* and deserted and forsaken of God; given over to a reprobate sense; *whereby* he cannot rest, but is comfortlesse, and at last is swallowed up of utter desperation; living as if he were continually in *hell,* sensibly feeling, as he thinks, the flames and tortures of the damned, in his conscience; *For* ease out of which estate, men many times kill themselves, hoping to mend themselves by change; although it be but, as skipping out of the frying-pan into the fire.[43]

This casual assumption that such torments were only the prelude to greater agonies in hell provides its own commentary on the penetration of Calvinist thought. Hell was on the mind. To say that predestinarian logic had been internalized in seventeenth-century England would be an enormous understatement.

Recent scholarship has sought to balance the stereotype of a joyless and "pathological" Puritanism terrorizing the population.[44] The emphasis of the Westminster Confession on "enjoy[ing]" God is often cited. Yet the volume of despair generated by predestinarian theology remains staggering, and the fact that some people enjoyed a buoyant spirituality may have exacerbated the torments of those who had been taught to interpret their alienation as some sort of cosmic decree. The Westminster Confession spoke of God's "pleasure" in choosing the elect—"but the elect only"—to eternal life, while passing over "the rest of mankind" for eternity. Such was "God's Eternal Decree."[45] Evidence that minds were tortured by this unhappy formula is substantial. Indeed predestinarian fear was the very seedbed of spiritual and rational dissent.

Anna Trapnel, who overcame Calvinist terrors to become an influential millenarian prophet, suffered anxieties so violent that she often considered taking her life: "And I was damn'd, one set apart for destruction, and I was strongly tempted to destroy myself," she recalled. "I have been waked in the night for this very purpose, and directed where to have the knife, and what knife I should take; and these assaults followed me not seldom, but very often."[46] The poet, John Donne, suffered similar afflictions, hovering between fear and flattery of the terrible God:

> *I durst not view heaven yesterday; and to day*
> *In prayers, and flattering speaches I court God:*
> *To morrow I quake with true feare of his rod.*
> *So my devout fitts come and go away*
> *Like a fantastique Ague: save that here*
> *Those are my best dayes, when I shake with feare.*[47]

Donne's fear that his wife's death was ordained to discipline his affections drove him to the brink of unbelief in a God who could command loyalty by taking away "she whome I lovd." "The burden of being human under a God of Calvinist character seems to Donne too heavy," writes one scholar.[48] Others spoke of a strange yearning for hell, in which at least the torture of uncertainty would be taken away. A Cambridge divine found an entire parish in a state of distress because "they could not be persuaded that Christ died for them." Richard Hooker, a notable exception to the Reformed model, softly broached the taboo of doubt with the acknowledgment that his audience may regard a single bad thought as evidence of damnation.[49]

Robert Burton's pioneering study on *The Anatomy of Melancholy* (1621) grieved over the religious sources of this "epidemical disease," which "crucifies the Soule in this life" and threatens "torments in the world to come."[50] Burton is said to have anticipated Freud's work on "guilt, repression, and obsessional neurosis" in his analysis of the problem.[51] His study opened with a discussion of "Original Sin," which transformed "man," "the miracle of nature," into a miserable being subject to illness, fear, unhappiness, and death. Burton was provocatively vague as to whether it was the *fact* of original sin or the *theory* of innate corruption that was ultimately responsible for the misery. Is it, in other words, human nature or a misanthropic theology that drives us to despair? Is Adam or Augustine responsible for the agony? Either way, "Religious melancholics" occupied a large section of the book, their condition characterized by habits of self-mortification and a crushing fear of the deity. *The Anatomy of Melancholy* went through five editions before Burton's death in 1640.[52]

Some did take the nuclear option of atheism, rejecting "not only the Eternal Decrees but even the existence of God."[53] But a more influential response was reformulation, involving a redistribution of grace and a reconception of the divine character. This is where striking parallels with Spinoza's philosophy emerge—what I have termed a metaphysics of mercy. When Thomas Laucock, an English "Ranter," clapped his hands upon his heart and said heaven is "within me, within me!," he was expressing an idea common among evangelical radicals, and he was also making a metaphysical statement, whether he liked it or not. As he proceeded to mock the idea of a transcendent God, high above the creation, he reinforced the point. What or where is Christ, he wondered sarcastically, "three or four story high above sky?" His interviewer claimed to have received similar answers from George Fox. Others abolished Hell in the twinkling of an eye, reducing it to inner torments calmed by the inner light. For one Ranter, there was "no Christ but within; no Scripture to be a rule; no ordinances, no law."[54] A philosophy of "immanence" started with the certainty of a God resident in the heart, and the very concept of democracy sprang from a religious experience of "equality."

Among the most important clusters of dissent was a group called the "Levellers," which united around demands for religious tolerance and popular sovereignty. In 1647 they produced a remarkable document called *An Agreement of the People,* which called for a new and democratic constitution and the abolition of "all arbitrary Power." The request was made on the basis of "the equity" of God, the all-loving creator. This was "the first proposal in history for a written constitution based on inalienable natural rights,"[55] a prototype of Enlightenment egalitarianism. As well as anticipating the American and French Revolutions by more than a century, the Levellers developed radical metaphysical concepts. One of their leaders, Richard Overton, denied the immortality of the soul, characterizing hell as a state of mind, conjured by religious authorities to buttress their power.[56] In *The Araignement of Mr. Persecution* (1645) Overton attacked his "Presbyterian Adversaries" for dwelling on the afterlife simply to "maintaine their repute."[57] The whole architecture of heaven and hell was a political construct that needed to be destroyed for the health of the people.

Like his democratic thought, Overton's metaphysics emerged from a theology of freely available grace. Overton developed a "monistic understanding" of the natural world as a corollary of his belief that Christ had died for all and his resurrection was effective for the whole of creation. This inspired him to reject the traditional doctrine of transcendence. Overton's conviction that "there is no beyond," that "every place must be materiall," was no materialist denial of God's existence. It reflected the belief that Christ, having saved the world, "must be within the compasse of the Creation." Overton applied the language of sin to theologies of judgment that weighed down on the "poore deceived people," leaving them "bestiallized in their understandings," "unman'd" and even "degenerated from being men." Such theology made people ignorant of "how far God by nature hath made them free." A cruel orthodoxy had made people "grosly ignorant of themselves, and of their own natural immunities."[58]

William Walwyn, another Leveller, offered a similarly bracing formula. Walwyn's Calvinist tutelage had been a hard schooling in law and judgment: "yokes of bondage" from which he escaped through a decisive conversion experience. Walwyn recalled his long inability to think beyond established authorities, until the scriptures, "taken in singly, and void of glosse" came to his assistance. Liberated by "that pearle in the field, free justification by Christ alone; I became master of what I heard, or read," he recalled.[59] Intellectual and spiritual awakening were coeval. Walwyn's conversion from predestinarian theology to a belief in "free grace" signaled a passionate commitment to religious and political freedom, and a fierce contempt for the "slaverie" of orthodoxy.[60] His book, *The Power of Love* (1643), suggests the basic cleavage between love and fear that animated so many of the radicals. "In Love's free state all powers so levelled be," wrote one, "That them affection governs more than awe."[61]

Thomas Hobbes took a less democratic approach, but he submitted the same complaint about power finding a home in theology. Part of the work of his "Leviathan" was to defend true religion from the "Kingdom of Darkness," defined as "a confederacy of deceivers that, to obtain dominion over men in this present world, endeavour, by dark and erroneous doctrines, to extinguish in them the light, both of nature and of the gospel; and so to disprepare them for the kingdom of God to come."[62] Hobbes denounced Presbyterian ministers who "brought young men into despair and to think themselves damned because they could not . . . behold a beautiful object without delight."[63] Large sections of *Leviathan* were devoted to the correct interpretation of scripture, and Hobbes's quarrel with the new scholastics, who cast "atoms of Scripture, as dust before men's eyes, make every thing more obscure than it is . . . [for] their own advantage," was classically Protestant. "For if an inward assent of the mind to all the doctrines concerning Christian faith now taught, whereof the greatest part are disputed, were necessary to salvation," Hobbes protested, "there would be nothing in the world so hard as to be a Christian." "The thief upon the cross" and "St. Paul himself" would fall foul of today's denticulate orthodoxy, he sternly contended.[64]

If Hobbes did not share the evangelical inspiration of the radicals, it is notable that many appreciated his assault on the new priests of scripture. An admiring inventory of radical thinkers of the revolution compiled by a Quaker in 1666 included, among familiar members of the awkward brigade, "Brave Mr. Hobbs."[65] It is difficult to separate "secular" and "religious" streams of thought, in England or the Dutch Republic. The conscience that was tearing through the chambers of orthodoxy was not dry or inarticulate: it was passionate, theological, and inflamed with biblical concepts of justice and mercy. No one embodied the phenomenon more vigorously than Gerrard Winstanley.

Winstanley emerged from a conventional English parish to lead one of the most radical sects of the revolutionary era, the "True Levellers" or "Diggers"—so called for their insistence on economic equality and their willingness to "dig" up common ground in order to achieve it. Convinced of the complicity of orthodoxy in the sins of political and economic oppression, Winstanley developed a ferocious evangelical rationalism, which attacked organized religion as "the bondage of the Serpent." Winstanley's radicalism was a drama of salvation in which orthodoxy once again played the part of sin. As he described his own conversion:

> by tradition from the mouths & pen of others: I worshipped a God, but I neither knew who he was, nor where he was, so that I lived in the darke, being blinded by the imagination of my flesh, and by the imagination of such as stand up to teach the people to know the Lord, and yet have no knowledge of the Lord themselves, but as they have received by hearsay, from their books, and other mens words. I spoke of the name of God, and Lord, and Christ, but I knew not this Lord, God, and Christ; I prayed to a God, but I knew not where he was, and so, walking by imagination, I worshipped that devill, and called him God, by reason whereof my comforts were often shaken to pieces, and at last it was shewed to me, That while I builded upon any words or writings of other men, or while I looked after a God without me, I did but build upon the sand, and as yet I knew not the Rock.

Winstanley challenged his followers to reject the idol of orthodoxy and turn to the "teacher within yourselves (which is the Spirit)."[66] But language remained an obstacle: the words "God" and "Christ" were inseparable from the old servitude of fear. Thus, he explained, "I am made to change the name from God to Reason, because I have been held under darknesse by that word as I see many people are."[67]

Winstanley found it hard to keep his promise. His rationalism was too pious and too devotional, exchanging the God of fear for "the Spirit of meeknesse and humility," the spirit of "the Child Jesus." Such a spirit, Winstanley urged, "frees the creature from all distempering fears and passions," notably those generated by the ecclesiastical "Antichrist."[68] Peace of mind and heart were again defined as escape from the terrors of orthodoxy. "Many times," he reflected, "when a wise understanding heart is assaulted with this doctrine of God, a devil, a heaven and a hell, salvation and damnation after a man is dead," minds were brought to the brink of "madness." Such doctrines made a person "heavy and sad, crying out he is damned, God hath forsaken him and he must go to hell when he dies, he cannot make his calling and election sure. And in that distemper many times a man doth hang, kill or drown himself." "So," he challenged the clergy, "this divining doctrine, which you call spiritual and heavenly things, torments people." It was nothing less than torture.[69]

Winstanley's message of a Christ known in the heart, yet immanent and effective in the fabric of nature, was offered with medicinal urgency. "Jesus Christ at a distance from thee," he urged, "will never save thee; but a Christ within is thy Saviour." Winstanley rejected the transcendent God, who lived "beyond the sun," and the historical, "outward" Christ, who "died at Jerusalem." Both seemed to jeopardize his democratic gospel of freely available grace. To historicize Christ was to limit him and to intellectualize the faith was to destroy it: "The Spirit is not confined to your Universities," he berated the orthodox clergy, "but it spreads from East to West, and enlightens sons and daughters in all parts."[70] Mercy pointed to pantheism.

Winstanley was a man of ebullient, irrepressible piety, shaking with biblical visions of "equity" and justice, yet little of the historic structure of the Christian faith survived his burning restoration. He esteemed a Bible, "written by the experimentall hand of Shepherds, Husbandmen, Fishermen, and such inferiour men of the world." But the propensity of theologians to smother its "plaine language" with "their darke interpretation, and glosses" tempered his praise for such a porous and fragile vessel.[71] Like many of the radicals, Winstanley combined reverence for the text with disdain for what it had become. Next to the living Christ known in the heart, the written word was a stolid companion. And given its abuse in the service of ecclesiastical and "kingly" power, in the policing of the land and of the Sabbath, the Bible could no longer be indulged with the usual ceremony. It had been profaned and it was, to some extent, beyond repair. Followers of Winstanley destroyed Bibles in his parish church, in a rare but scarcely exceptional incident.[72]

Spinoza's future correspondent, Henry Oldenburg, noted a rage for biblical criticism in the 1650s, including the view that "the whole story of the creation seems to have been composed in order to introduce the Sabbath . . . from motives of merely political prudence."[73] In December 1654 a radical called Thomas Tany burnt a Bible on a London common, "because the people say it is the Word of God, and it is not." All religion, he said, was "a lie, a cheat, a deceit, for there is but one truth, and that is love." Hell and damnation were states of mind. God and the soul were one. Written documents were a curse.

The line between prophecy and rage may have been thin, but there can be no doubt that the fiercest criticism emerged from the hottest piety. The nemesis of dogma was spiritual experience. The chemistry of revolt was Christian. Winstanley identified his vindicating spirit of "reason and equity" with Jesus Christ, "the true and faithful Leveller." He conjured a philosophy of history from the biblical principle of the new covenant—announcing a "new law of righteousness," "the law of freedom," "the breaking of the day of God." It was with a pulsating inner confidence reminiscent of Luther that figures like Winstanley arraigned the foundations of Christendom. To the accusation that his beliefs "will destroy all government and all our ministry and religion," Winstanley responded with smoldering poise: "It is very true."[74]

Parallels with Spinoza are strong enough to link both to the ferment of evangelical anti-Calvinism. What makes the English connection even more compelling is the possibility that Spinoza was intimately involved with it—learning to navigate the blasted terrain of scripture alongside those ungovernable prophets, the Quakers.

"What Canst Thou Say?" The Inner Light and the Broken Scriptures

George Fox was another melancholy pilgrim who trudged through predestinarian lowlands to discover what Thomas Carlyle termed an "enormous sacred self-confidence."[75] His followers acquired the name "Quakers" from their tendency to tremble in moments of spiritual ecstasy, but like many such terms of reproach, it was designed to mislead. The essence of Quaker spirituality was not shaking before a terrible God. It was peace. A classic expression was Fox's testimony that "the mind may be seasoned and stilled in a right understanding of the Lord."[76] Here again was spirituality conceived as escape from religion. Fox's "renewal" to the "innocency and righteousness" of "the image of God by Christ Jesus" was naturally unmediated by clergy. Christ was within, enlightening anyone who would cleave to his quiet instruction.

It was the clerical monopoly of biblical interpretation that pushed Quakers into a stance of daring criticism: an assault on the "letter" of scripture as the weapon of "dark" clergy and the source of myriad persecutions. Margaret Fell, who later married Fox, recalled the first time she heard him preach on the fragility of the written text. She was "cut . . . to the heart" as the young prophet rode casually over the sacred ground of biblical authority. "You will say," Fox challenged, " 'Christ saith this, and the apostles say this'; but what canst thou say?" Could a written document be compared to the Word inscribed on the heart? Was historical testimony worthy of the name? "Art thou a child of the Light, and hast thou walked in the Light, and what thou speakest, is it inwardly from God?" Fox continued, enjoying the rising tension. As he spoke of a Christ who was "the Light of the world, and lighteth every man that cometh into the world [John 1:9]," Fell suddenly perceived that the scriptures had hidden as often as they had revealed. They were complicit in a life of ordinary, earth-bound piety. Fell rose to her feet in a faint gesture of protest. Then she sat down in her pew "and cried bitterly." "I cried in my spirit to the Lord, 'We are all thieves; we are all thieves; we have taken the scriptures in words, and know nothing of them in ourselves.' "[77] The letter had to be diminished for the spirit to live. It was not intellectual virtuosity that enabled people like Fox to look askance at the historical integrity of the Bible: it was spiritual intensity. It is no wonder that the Quakers produced some of the most virulent biblical criticism of the century.

Samuel Fisher was a "General" (Arminian) Baptist who joined the Quaker movement in 1654 and became its leading controversialist, traveling widely and suffering numerous imprisonments. Fisher was a tireless evangelist, instrumental in the conversion of William Penn, who praised his unique blend of vigor, abrasiveness, and flair.[78] Fisher's boldest sortie was an attempt to convert the Pope and the Sultan on a single grand tour, and his most important work a nine-hundred-page attack on Protestant biblicism and Calvinist orthodoxy, the *Rustick's Alarm to the Rabbies, or the Country correcting the University and Clergy* (1660). The *Rustick's Alarm* was a savage, wickedly humorous assault on the "textmen" of the universities and a bold defense of the individual soul as the true site of revelation. The tone was coarse and aggressive but Fisher knew the ancient languages as well his Puritan adversaries, and he was able to supplement an essentially moral indictment of orthodoxy with a battery of technical objections. Fisher ridiculed the Calvinist affinity for proof texts and the superstition of believing that these cherished landmarks had come down from the apostles without corruption. He mocked his opponents for "Pin[ning] the Everlasting Gospel of God on so Tickelish a Point, as Mens Mistaking, or not Mistaking, in Writing out the Bare letter of if."

John Owen, the leading exponent of textual literalism, claimed that God had performed the same miracle for transcribers of the text as the original writers, arguing that the surviving documents were precise expressions of the divine will. Fisher did not know where to begin. Vowels had been added. Mistakes abounded in the earliest copies. And nowhere in the Bible had God promised to preserve written copies of his words. Translation involved guesswork, and the little that was known about the process of transcription did not inspire confidence. The modern text may have passed through as many as a hundred hands, each as capable of error as any other. The canon was assembled by men of questionable spirituality, long after the contents had been written.[79]

The surviving text was a series of compromises, Fisher concluded, yet schools of orthodoxy converged around single, contested phrases. And then there were internal contradictions, such as the problem of Moses writing of his own death or describing himself as the most humble of men. Fisher went further than Hobbes in questioning the integrity of the text, and he claimed to represent the whole Quaker movement. Quakers did not "own the bare external text of scripture entire in every tittle," he explained, "but say it hath suffered much loss of more than vowels, single letters, and single lines also, yea, even of whole epistles and prophecies of inspired men."[80] Fisher believed that the Bible contained a message of salvation but was by no means synonymous with it. The written word was "fallible and falsified," a shadow of that "pure . . . living, Word and Spirit of God," which was known to Abel, Enoch, and Noah long "before your pretended Rule was written." The "eldest of your Originalls are but upstarts," Fisher challenged the guardians of orthodoxy. They were nothing compared to the Word that "was made flesh, and dwelt in us."[81] The "much altered outward text" was a forest of confusion without this "true touchstone." The Bible was "a Bulk of Heterogenous Writings," "truss[ed]" and "croud[ed]" into a canon with varying degrees of wisdom and expertise. To turn it into an infallible "standard for the trial of all spirits, doctrines, truths" was to play a very dangerous game. The tail was wagging the dog. The irony, Fisher coolly contended, was that biblicism was not biblical: God sent his son, not a book.[82]

When Christians confused the medium with the message they committed idolatry, Fisher claimed. Puritans worshipped arrangements of words the way Catholics worshipped Mary.[83] Theologians were the worst offenders, claiming to honor the text but shamelessly bending it to their custodial instincts, "wip[ing] away" the natural sense of offending passages "with a wet finger."[84] The defenders of the Bible were its destroyers. True reverence would involve an admission of obscurities and difficulties of translation, but Fisher had reached Franck-like conclusions about the motives of "orthodoxy." "Dark minds diving into the Scripture divine lies enough out of it to set whole countries on fire," he lamented. The "letter" was "too weak an engine to set to rights what's out of order."[85] If for no other reason, the capacity of cold-eyed divines to contrive a theology of predestination from the letter of scripture condemned the Protestant method. Fisher's opponent, John Owen, happened to be the architect of a doctrine of "limited atonement"—the notion that Christ died for the elect, and only the elect. To Fisher, the "tender" and fervent evangelist, this was nothing short of blasphemy. It justified his belief that the primitive dentistry of literalism was sin dressed up as scholarship.

Fisher did not mince his words. Predestination turned God into a monster. To talk of grace in the context of a theology that confines the better part of the humanity to hell was an offense to language, not to say conscience. If a king offered a pardon to 1,000 men on terms that 999 could not fulfill, Fisher reasoned, it would not be "mercy" to pardon the thousandth. "Are ye not ashamed," he challenged the Calvinists, "thus to engross the grace of God . . . among yourselves and a few like your sinning selves? . . . For the elect are very few with you." "Are ye not ashamed to make God not only tyrannical but hypocritical and as dissembling as yourselves?" The Calvinist scheme turned God into "a merciless tyrant and arrant hypocrite," like a master holding out meat to a starving man in the full knowledge that he cannot take it. It was to conceive God taunting humankind in the language of the fairground: "Come to me, and here is meat for thee. . . . But if thou wilt not come I will knock thy brains out." Fisher likened the Calvinist offer of salvation to the gift of an inheritance located on "the moon." Metaphors of distance and hostility were again contrasted with a true spirituality of intimacy. Heaven was not so distant or exclusive, Fisher pleaded. Her doors were open to "every humble, broken and contrite spirit."[86]

Fisher was inevitably accused of atheism. But he returned the compliment, accusing the orthodox of making "your own Graves with your own Hands and pluck[ing] up your own Religion by the very Roots." Calvinism was giving the Bible a bad name and weakening the claims of Christianity itself.[87] Fisher's biblical criticism was an exercise in rescuing God from the apparatus of oppression. His theological universalism, proclaiming a "light" effective in all lands, was fired by evangelical zeal. Yet this was rugged and potentially destructive criticism, placing high expectations on the purity of the inner light. Fisher's arguments flowed seamlessly into the deism of John Toland and Charles Blount.[88] They also appeared to surface in the work of Spinoza, with whom Fisher almost certainly became acquainted during his European adventures.

Spinoza and the Quakers

When the Quakers established a mission in Amsterdam in 1655–66, they made immediate contact with the Collegiants, identifying them as kindred spirits and potential collaborators. They remained close until disputes of the kind that prompted *The Light upon the Candlestick* caused a rift. Spinoza was known to the Collegiants when the first Quakers arrived, and he seems to have been the person entrusted with the task of translating two tracts written by Margaret Fell for the conversion of the Jews. The translator was mentioned several times in correspondence, but never named. He was "expert in several languadges" including Portuguese, Dutch, and Hebrew, but not English, and he remained "very friendly in his way."

Mention of Portuguese instantly ties the translator to the Spanish-Portuguese synagogue, and reference to his heresies places him among only four Jews to have been excommunicated for ideological reasons in this period. The date of the clearest reference to the translator, William Ames's letter of April 17, 1657, points tantalizingly to Spinoza as the mysterious collaborator. At this time: one of the four was dead; one was still being paid by the Jewish community and was yet to be excommunicated; and one was in continuing negotiations for readmission that lasted until May of that year, and, having issued a penitent apology, was the least likely of the four to have assisted in a subversive missionary project. Only Spinoza fits the description of one "cast out" from the Jewish community at that time. It is unlikely that there was another disaffected Jew in the city who could read Dutch, Portuguese, and Hebrew as well as Latin, let alone one who moved in radical Christian circles.[89]

A number of Dutch scholars and historians of the Quakers assumed that the translator was Spinoza, and it is a measure of the freight attached to his name that exhaustive reconstruction of the connection still meets with skepticism. Ames and Spinoza had mutual friends in Balling and Pieter Serrarius, among others. Serrarius was a member of the Amsterdam college, well connected and active in Christian–Jewish relations in preparation for what he believed to be Christ's imminent return. He once traveled to London to join discussions on the readmission of the Jews under Cromwell, and it was he who put Spinoza in touch with Henry Oldenburg and the scientist, Robert Boyle. It is likely that Serrarius was also the link between Spinoza and the Quakers. Fell's *Loving Salutation to the Seed of Abraham*, urging the Jews to "turn to the light within you," was a project close to his heart, and in the kindly Jew now living in his circle he had a valuable, if controversial, window into that world.[90] It may be that a studious reluctance to mention the name of the translator reflected a desire to protect him from further indignities. Whatever his views on the tracts themselves, we can be confident that the person described by Ames in the letter to Margaret Fell in 1657 was Spinoza:

> There is a Jew at amsterdam that by the Jews is Cast out (as he himself and others sayeth) because he owneth no other teacher but the light and he sent for me and I spoke toe him and he was pretty tender and doth owne all that is spoken; and he sayde tow read of moses and the prophets without was nothing tow him except he came tow know it within; and soe the name of Christ it is like he doth owne: I gave order that one of the duch Copyes of thy book should be given tow him and he sent me word he would Come toe oure meeting but in the mean time I was imprisoned.[91]

Assuming this was Spinoza, the letter indicates that he was excommunicated for a spiritualist interpretation of the scriptures: that to "read of moses and the prophets *without* was nothing tow him except he came tow know it *within*." He recognized "no other teacher but the light," indeed "the name of Christ it is like he doth owne." He was even prepared to attend a Quaker meeting, until the plan fell through when Ames was arrested.

The possibility that Christianity was at the root of Spinoza's unusually bitter expulsion gains credence from the heightened sensitivity of the Jewish community to Christian proselytism in this decade. A number of virulently anti-Christian works emerged in the 1650s, including a ferocious attack on Christian theology by Rabbi Saul Levi Morteira, the chief rabbi of Amsterdam in Spinoza's time.[92] No other writ of expulsion plumbed the depths of dismay like Spinoza's, and no other alienated Jew insisted on referring to Jesus as "Christ" and interpreting the "Old Testament" in the light of the "New." Whatever the facts of the *herem*, Spinoza was now moving among spiritualist Christians and his criticism suggests direct influences, especially from Fisher.

It was Fisher who took Fell's tract to Amsterdam in search of a translator, which means that he and Spinoza were probably working alongside one another for several months. This would account for what a leading authority terms "the striking similarities in Spinoza's biblical criticism to that of Samuel Fisher and for the recurrent use of Quaker terms and concepts in Spinoza's writings."[93] Fisher and Spinoza offered similar arguments about the weakness of the text and "offered the same examples to prove them," indicating that their biblical criticism was "probably a joint creation, born out of their meeting over a period of six months or more in Amsterdam."[94] Yet this was more than the bizarre convergence of theology and philosophy that some have seen it to be—a serendipitous collusion in which philosophy borrows ideas from an eccentric and obsolete partner. Spinoza's philosophy was an expression of spiritualist theology, no less potent than Fisher's or Winstanley's, and sharing many of the same features: a priority of inward over outward revelation, a blurring of the boundaries between God and nature, and a certain experiential fervor proud to identify with the "new covenant" announced in the Bible. Spinoza was a "born again" believer.

Born Again: An Evangelical Philosophy

Scholars have often distinguished Spinoza's Collegiant friends from his more philosophical circle, which included figures like Franciscus Van den Enden, Lodewijk Meyer, and Adrian Koerbagh. Van den Enden was an ex-Jesuit who taught Spinoza Latin and probably introduced him to Descartes. Meyer was a trenchant Cartesian, who published an important work urging the submission of theology to philosophy, and Koerbagh was a vociferous critic of Reformed orthodoxy who was jailed for blasphemous views in 1668 and whose subsequent death in miserable prison conditions was one of the inspirations for the *Theological-Political Treatise*. Yet the notion of two incompatible worlds is misleading. Meyer had friends among the Collegiants and, like Spinoza, used Jan Rieuwertsz as his publisher. Spinoza developed his early interest in Descartes in the same circle and, if anything, drew greater sustenance from spiritualist influences as he moved away from the static dualism of the Cartesian system.

Having attended lectures at Leiden in 1655–57 and published a short summary of Cartesian thought, Spinoza started to develop a personal philosophy that bridged the great mind–body divide asserted by "the illustrious Descartes." He offered an account of human nature that broke down the wall of separation between God and the human person and dissolved the ghostly interplay of mind and matter that Descartes—following centuries of "dualist" anthropology—had taken to be the core of the rational experience. Spinoza's radicalism lay in his "monist" response to this awkward relationship: a theory that God, humanity, and matter do not interact in moments of weakness and condescension; they are part of a single "substance." Like some of the English radicals, proclaiming a God who is truly among us, Spinoza felt that traditional theories of transcendence collapsed on experience. Spinoza frequently appealed to psychological testimony to illustrate and even demonstrate his ideas, asserting in the *Ethics*, for example, that "we feel and know that we are eternal."[95] While he aspired to build a system of geometric solidity and purity, any encounter with his works reveals the emotional force behind the logic. The criticism that flowed from his pen in the *Treatise* was no bystander's lament. It was the expression of a profound and intense spirituality.[96]

Spinoza set out the bones of his philosophy in a *Short Treatise on God, Man and His Well-being* (c. 1660) and a semi-autobiographical *Treatise on the Emendation of the Intellect* (c. 1661). Both developed an almost mystical account of understanding as "intuition"—a "third kind of knowledge" which transcends both the cobbled wisdom of daily living and the more strenuous "reasoning" of the philosophers. Reasoning had its place, but it labored before the deeper questions of existence and the tyranny of uncontrolled passions, including such ancient enigmas as how to tame the tongue. Developing ideas that would mature in the *Ethics,* Spinoza offered an account of spiritual understanding as emancipation from injurious emotion. Far from a creed of intellectual aloofness or Stoic resistance, Spinoza articulated an experience of spiritual ecstasy. "This knowledge," he urged in the *Short Treatise,* "brings us to the point where we attribute everything to God, love him alone, because he is most magnificent and supremely perfect, and offer ourselves entirely to him. For that is what true religion and our eternal salvation and happiness really consist in."[97]

Spinoza denied that "reason" alone could release the mind from its bondage to "evil" passions, defending as an evangelist the right "to speak of our Love of God." He spoke of the wearying dominion of "sadness, despair, envy, fright, and other evil passions, which . . . are the real hell itself," commending especially the power of love to overcome fear. True knowledge of God "brings us to the point where we do not fear God, as others fear the devil," Spinoza claimed. "For how could we fear God, who is himself the greatest good, and through whom all things that have any essence—and we who live in him—are what they are?"

If this sounded like George Fox, urging the power of spirit to "still" the mind, Spinoza's climax rivaled the more exuberant "enthusiasts." "I do not say that we must know him as he is," Spinoza cautioned, "it is enough for us to know him to some extent in order to be united with him. For even in the knowledge we have of the body we do not know it as it is, or perfectly. And yet," he countered, "what a union! what a love!" Knowledge was salvation, and salvation was no courtly metaphor. In a passage that invites comparison with Jonathan Edwards's theology of the "affections," Spinoza rose to a rhapsodic climax:

> When we become aware of these effects, we can truly say that we have been born again. For our first birth was when we were united with the body. From this union have arisen the effects and motions of the [animal] spirits. But our other, or second, birth will occur when we become aware in ourselves of the completely different effects of love produced by knowledge of this incorporeal object. This [love of God] is as different from [love of the body] as the incorporeal is from the corporeal, the spirit from the flesh. This, therefore, may the more rightly and truly be called Rebirth, because, as we shall show, an eternal and immutable constancy comes only from this Love and Union.[98]

Part V of the *Ethics* offered an extended discussion of this electrifying, "third kind" of knowledge, and there can be no doubt that it reflected a genuine personal stance. Scholars have questioned the sincerity with which Spinoza linked this experience to Christianity, but the similarity of his theology to a whole genre of spirituality conceived as relief from "fear" should temper suspicion. Spinoza had not labored under predestinarian anxieties, but he knew what it was to be "cursed" in the name of an angry God, and it is hard to dispute the experiential passion of an escape that he characterized as a personal "exodus." The relief of breaking out of a "hell" of uncertainty to a state of "eternal and immutable constancy" was classically evangelical, the irony being that this was the kind of fervid spirituality from which many of the Collegiants were rowing back. Spinoza's mystical rendering of philosophical freedom seemed to put grace back on the table. Reason was greatly esteemed but the highest form of knowledge was an intuitive, experiential love of God. This was his brave alternative to pervasive, destructive theologies of fear. Such was the substance of a radical Enlightenment.

Spinoza saved the strongest expressions of his philosophy for the *Ethics*, where he cannot be suspected of playing games to please a Christian audience. Here salvation is characterized as "the constant and eternal love towards God" and explicitly linked to the Bible: "This love or blessedness is, in the Bible, called Glory, and not undeservedly," he adds.[99] Here too he characterized sin as a slide into fear and bondage to the passions: a psychological condition rather than an event. This was resonant with the radical Protestant world and the urge to reconceive doctrines in ways that could simultaneously account for the harshness of orthodoxy and the consolations of personal experience. The curses of orthodoxy reflect an unbroken condition of sin; salvation is from, not within, the tangled wreckage of imperious Christendom. Spinoza's contrasting sentiments about superstition, religion, and philosophy reflect such a framework. He condemned superstition as sin; he praised religion as law, promoting obedience but rarely touching the heights of blessedness; and he extolled philosophy as the true and holy road to salvation: a new covenant. The force of the contrast between philosophy and religion has been construed as a clean break from theological reasoning. Yet Spinoza presented this higher state of blessedness as the fulfillment of the Judeo-Christian narrative. Philosophy was the great moving on from leaden duty to spontaneous virtue of which Paul had written. And the model was not Spinoza or even an apostle: it was Jesus Christ.

The Stable God and Sin of Superstition

Spinoza broke off work on the *Ethics* to write the *Theological-Political Treatise,* a more urgent, aggressive, and practical offering, though the two should be read in tandem. The context was the renewed political activity of the Dutch Calvinists and the ending of a period of relative calm known as the "True Freedom." The death of Adrian Koerbagh saddened and angered Spinoza, who considered his treatment a betrayal of the principles of the Republic and listed freedom of speech among his motives for writing.[100] This freedom, he wrote to Oldenburg, "I want to vindicate completely, for here it is in every way suppressed by the excessive authority and egotism of preachers." The other reasons for writing were to counter the "prejudices of theologians," the intellectual barrier to freedom, and to refute the personal calumny of "atheism" persistently made against him by "the common people." All three aims point to a struggle with the "Voetian Calvinists," who favored the use of state authority to suppress theological novelty and whose theology most resembles what the *Treatise* identifies as "superstition."[101] "Though Spinoza does not mention them explicitly," writes one scholar, "it is safe to assume that his repeated complaints against 'the theologians' in his correspondence were directed most of all against orthodox Calvinist theologians."[102]

The Voetians were followers of Gisbertus Voetius, firebrand rector of the University of Utrecht, who had been responsible for driving Descartes out of the Dutch Republic and whose Aristotelian proclivities made him the symbol of a Protestant "neo-scholasticism." Inspiring a small army of Reformed ministers, known as the *predikanten,* the Voetians campaigned for what one scholar has termed the "Calvinization" of everyday life—from policing the universities to banning ice-skating parties on Sundays.[103] Fired by millenarian fervor, the Voetians were behind the latest wave of theocratic zeal and they emerge as the primary target for Spinoza's criticism, including many of his comments on Judaism. When the *Treatise* was published in 1670, Spinoza had been out of the Jewish world for nearly fifteen years and faced more urgent challenges than the revival of a Jewish theocracy. "The clear and present danger of the time," writes one scholar, "was not the attempt by Jews to reestablish their ancient kingdom, but the attempt by Christian Millenarians to use the ancient scenario as a political programme for the day."[104] Spinoza identified the activities of contemporary persecutors, who revile and attack "men of outstanding probity and known virtue," with the hypocrisy of "Pharisees."[105] While his comments on Judaism are consistently harsh, they often feel like a vehicle for a more immediate problem: militant Calvinism.

First, Spinoza offered an ethical critique: the eternal contrast between a religion of love and a religious culture of hate. The title page of the *Treatise* quoted a verse from the first epistle of John: "By this we know that we remain in God, and God remains in us, because he has given us of his spirit." For Spinoza, the spirit was known above all by ethical fruit, and the failure of an angry orthodoxy to produce it was the starting point of criticism. This was emphasized in the preface, which condemned a reign of superstition that threw everyone "back into servitude" and turned "rational men into brutes"—the very language used in the *Ethics* to describe the Fall. Spinoza spoke of a decay that left "nothing" of the "religion of the early church."[106] "I have often been amazed," he reflected, "to find that people who are proud to confess the Christian religion, that is [a religion of] love, joy, peace, moderation and good will to all men, opposing each other with extraordinary animosity and giving daily expression to the bitterest mutual hatred. So much so that it has become easier to recognize an individual's faith by the latter features than the former."[107]

These were familiar indictments and Spinoza echoed the Anabaptist theory that the rot set in soon after the age of the apostles, when established churches offered a "worldly career" to people motivated by "sordid greed and ambition," so that the "worst kind of people came forward to fill the sacred offices." He affirmed the view that, under the peculiar incentives of Christendom, "New and controversial doctrines" emerged as the tools of clerical ambition, so that churches became places of permanent disputation. Scripture made way for "the speculations of the Aristotelians and Platonists" and "what is really divine in Scripture" assumed a secondary relationship to "human fabrications."[108]

But there were contemporary provocations that made older debates feel academic. Spinoza refined his wording to leave little doubt as to his target. With sarcastic allusion to the "profoundest mysteries" that modern Aristotelians discover in their Bibles, Spinoza appeared to broach the taboo of predestination. Such "mysteries" were the conceit of men who claimed to regard scripture as "true and divine throughout" but whose appetite for destruction proved that they "do not really believe Scripture but merely assent to it." To such, Spinoza claimed, the Bible was a tool not a guide. As he lamented in a passage clearly intended for Calvinist consumption:

> Dear God! Piety and religion are reduced to ridiculous mysteries and those who totally condemn reason and reject and revile the understanding as corrupt by nature, are believed without question to possess the divine light, which is the most iniquitous aspect of all. Clearly, if these men had even a spark of divine light, they would not rave so arrogantly. They would learn to revere God with more good sense, and surpass other men in love as they now surpass them in hatred. Nor would they persecute so fiercely those who disagree with them, but would have compassion for them.[109]

Spinoza accused the orthodox of hating men more than they loved God, quoting the apostle John before launching another assault:

> "And by this we are sure that we know him, if we keep his commandments. He who says, I know him and does not keep his commandments, is a liar, and the truth is not in him." From this it likewise follows, that the true antichrists are those who persecute honest men and lovers of justice because they differ from them in doctrine and do not adhere to the same tenets of belief as themselves. For we know that those who love justice and charity are faithful by this measure alone, and he who persecutes the faithful is an antichrist.[110]

This was not the jaded cynicism of an outsider. "Antichrist" was a central category of spiritual radicalism in the seventeenth century, a concept first popularized by Luther in his battle with the papacy.[111] Spinoza's use of the term has occasionally embarrassed his admirers, who have sometimes translated it as "enemies of Christ" to soften the note of sectarianism.[112] Others have attributed such language to Spinoza's "circuitous tactic" of packaging his philosophy in Christian terminology: a sustained and guileful subterfuge.[113] But Spinoza's biblical affinities were too profound to be reducible to tactics, and his privileged treatment of the Johannine writings—with their emphasis on the light of Christ in the soul and the litmus test of love—was consistent with his radical Protestant milieu. Spinoza was securing his intellectual critique on the moral ground of biblical ethics, accusing the orthodox of hiding sinful designs behind complex theological structures. He was developing a version of Castellio's challenge to Calvin: if the Bible is your standard, why don't you treat it with more respect? But he was also going beyond ethical critique, toward a new conception of God himself. Like the English radicals, summoning a pantheist theology from the raw material of spiritual experience, Spinoza developed a theology of "immanence" as an expression of what he considered the truth of the divine character.

This has been the most controversial, and misunderstood, aspect of Spinoza's philosophy. Scholars continue to identify the sixth chapter of the *Treatise* as a "sweeping denial of miracles," with further claims that "between the rise of Christianity and the mid-eighteenth century . . . only Spinoza categorically denies the possibility of miracles and supernatural occurrences." It was, writes one authority, this brazen denial that inspired respectable philosophers to label him "Spinoza Atheorum pessimus" ("Spinoza the worst of atheists").[114] But Spinoza cannot be defined by critics who may or may not have bothered to read him. Spinoza did not "deny" either miracles or the supernatural. He voiced skepticism about events perceived to have been miracles, urging that signs and wonders are typically natural events whose causes are as yet unknown, but he clearly affirmed a belief that God is capable of "extraordinary" manifestations of his power and that the Bible endorses such events. "Unless we are willing to do violence to Scripture," he wrote in the *Treatise*, "we must concede without reservation that the Israelites heard a real voice" when God spoke directly to Moses.[115] Spinoza's account of miracles is deflationary, rather than categorically hostile, and it springs from a theological conviction of divine equity and consistency. Far from a denial of providence, Spinoza's metaphysics emerged from a positive and fervent understanding of divine activity in the world.

Spinoza's central vision of an "indwelling" God, who does not hover in judgment above creation, was rooted in one, abiding principle: that God "cares for all" people.[116] His suspicion of miracles was part of a wider critique of theologies of grace and favor, where the problem is not so much prodigies of nature but the moral disaster of a partial God. It was sheer superstition, he suggested, to picture God as some tribal deity "holding royal power and seated on a throne which [people] suppose is in the dome of the sky above the stars."[117] The Old Testament often spoke of God in human language, but Spinoza deferred to the first letter to the Corinthians to defend his own understanding of a fair and just deity. Here, Spinoza noted, "Paul concludes that God is the God of all nations, that is, God is equally well-disposed to all, and all men are equally under law and sin, and that is why God sent his Christ to all nations, to free all men equally from the servitude of the law." Indeed, he added: "Paul teaches exactly what we want to affirm."[118] A stylist might demur at the use of the word "all" five times, and "equally" three times, in the same sentence. But Spinoza had more pressing worries in his urgent, restless treatise. The conviction that God "cares for all" disciplines everything he had to say.

Such statements were the constant background to Spinoza's suspicions of arbitrary providence. When he set out the seven "fundamentals" of true religion in chapter 14 of the *Treatise*, Spinoza's first assertion was that God "is supremely just and merciful." The third was that, "He is everywhere present and all things are manifest to Him; for if things were believed to be hidden from him, or if it were not known that he sees all things, there would be doubts about the equity of his justice by which he directs all things."[119] In other words: to doubt that God is "everywhere present" is to doubt his goodness. Metaphysical order and moral consistency were non-negotiable values. Miracles had to represent causes that were hidden rather than a God mischievously pulling strings for a privileged elect.

Spinoza repeatedly contrasted this New Testament vision of equity and universality with what he considered the selfish particularity of Judaism and contemporary "superstition." In the section "On the vocation of the Hebrews," Spinoza acknowledged that Moses sought "special external help from God" and seemed to have performed "great miracles," but, he suggested, it was only because the people were "obstinate" that such signs were necessary. The thrust of the chapter was a rebuke to the idea that God loved the Jews more than other people. God does not parcel out favors to a chosen few. The piety that consists of thanking God for such imagined favors is little more than pride. The miracles performed by Moses and other prophets, Spinoza suggested, "could not yield any true idea and knowledge of God." "Miracles could not demonstrate to them [the Jews] that God cares equally for all men: only philosophy can teach this."[120] "True joy and happiness," Spinoza urged, with predestinarian theologians no doubt in mind, "lie in the simple enjoyment of what is good and not in the kind of false pride that enjoys happiness because others are excluded from it."[121]

The Christian contours of the argument were especially evident in the assertion that the Jewish law was never intended to be permanent. The prophets knew that the law would not last forever. They balanced the necessary particularity of the Jewish law with the promise of a different mode of access to God in the future: "a new and eternal covenant of God, a covenant of knowledge, love and grace." "That this eternal covenant of God, the covenant of knowledge and of love [would be] universal, is entirely evident," Spinoza suggested, "from Zephaniah 3:10–11," and many other texts. It was "unthinkable that it has been promised only to pious Jews."[122]

That Spinoza was setting Christian principles against the theocratic hunger of the Calvinists, rather than unfurling some anachronistic banner of naturalism, is also evident from the *Ethics*. Here he defined God as "a being absolutely infinite or perfect," the "indwelling and not the transient cause of all things."[123] He protested against "my opponents," who attribute to God an "absolute free will," distinct from his "understanding." "The multitude," Spinoza complained, "understand by the power of God the free will of God," likening this freedom "to the power of kings." Under such a theology, God is invested with human "passions" and understood to be permanently at our service. This was superstition, the conceit of those who convince themselves "that everything which is created is created for their sake." It was a theology born of "blind cupidity and insatiable avarice." Men dared to attribute "storms, earthquakes, diseases" to divine caprice, in willful ignorance of the Bible's assurance that "good and evil fortunes fall to the lot of pious and impious alike."[124]

Spinoza's language confirmed the primary target of Calvinism. Spinoza expressed his agreement with "our opponents" that everything happens by "the decree and will of God," but he refused to picture a God glorying in the freedom to tear up his own creation. God's "will" and his "intellect" could not be in a state of nervous contradiction. This would convict God of "imperfection or change," opening a door to atheism: for who could trust such a God? Spinoza was wrestling with a "voluntarist" theology of untamed divine "freedom" and his reaction is redolent of a theologian like Thomas Aquinas, for whom "divine decisions" were always "in line with eternal truth," and for whom God's actions always reflected a solid stratum of "divine rationality." The material fabric of creation, was, for Aquinas, consistently "in line with the very truth of God's character."[125] The controversial phrase used in the *Ethics*, "*Deus sive Natura*" ("God or Nature"), can also be translated, "God *as* Nature." This was not a doctrine of nature's "autonomy" or independence. It was a theology of consistency. Spinoza's central complaint against theologies of arbitrary providence is that they impugn the character of a God who cares for all. His resistance to "final causes" or directional readings of natural history—brusquely rejected as "human figments"—is theological from first to last.[126] Spinoza was trying to protect God from the theologians.

Closely following this concern for divine equity is a sensitivity to the moral effects of superstition. To picture a God towering over you in moods of variable warmth is to nurture a nervous, ungenerous spirituality. Where a true understanding of God enables one to "partake of the divine nature" (a New Testament phrase used several times in the *Ethics*),[127] "superstition" promotes fear, anxiety, and resentment of those who appear to be enjoying riper bounties, Spinoza contended. Superstition is essentially selfish, he suggests, promoting both aggression and a kind of competitive asceticism: a cult of self-denial. A neglected theme of the *Ethics* is Spinoza's insistence on "joy" and "mirth" as marks of spiritual health, and his disdain for a torturing rigor that seems to "account as good all that brings pain, and as bad all that brings pleasure." Spinoza offered a holistic critique of his puritanical opponents, "who know better how to rail at vice than how to teach virtue, and who strive not to guide men by reason, but so to restrain them that they would rather escape evil than love virtue." Such "superstitious persons," he complained, "have no other aim but to make others as wretched as themselves," making them "generally troublesome and odious to their fellow men." As Spinoza protested in a passage that might qualify his reputation for furrowed intellectual austerity:

> Assuredly nothing forbids man to enjoy himself, save grim and gloomy superstition. For why is it more lawful to satiate one's hunger and thirst than to drive away one's melancholy? I reason, and have convinced myself as follows: No deity, nor anyone else, save the envious, takes pleasure in my infirmity and discomfort, nor sets down to my virtue the tears, sobs, fear, and the like, which are signs of infirmity of spirit; on the contrary, the greater the pleasure wherewith we are affected, the greater the perfection whereto we pass. . . . To make use of what comes in our way, and to enjoy it as much as possible (not to the point of satiety, for that would not be enjoyment) is the part of a wise man. I say it is the part of a wise man to refresh and recreate himself with moderate and pleasant food and drink, and also with perfumes, with the soft beauty of growing plants, with dress, with music, with many sports, with theatres, and the like, such as every man may make use of without injury to his neighbor.[128]

Spinoza was at war with the Protestant ethic as well as Calvinist theology. Ethical and metaphysical critique went hand in hand.

The chapter on miracles in the *Treatise* was thus a fragment of a wider theology of equity and spiritual harmony. The innocent-sounding assertion that "God's understanding is not distinct from his will" took up an old quarrel with the voluntarist deity of the theologians.[129] Spinoza maintained that it was the dangerous God of superstition, not the generous God of nature, who leads "to atheism." And he emphasized that by "nature" he meant not merely "matter and its properties, but other infinite things besides matter."[130] Nature was suffused with divine energy, and its "eternal, fixed and immutable order" was a source of wonder and reverence.[131] This was neither naturalism nor pantheism but a theology of the "indwelling" God. Such a deity, Spinoza maintained, can act with "natural or supernatural" power, but the "greater miracle" lay in the former.[132] Spinoza balanced grudging acknowledgment of Old Testament miracles with stern reflections on their moral consequences. Rather than mythologize the miracles of the Exodus, for example, he suggested that God had allowed Moses to perform them on account of "the obstinate temper and spirit of his people."[133] Such events, however, could only represent the intensification of natural causes. "Miracles require causes and circumstances," Spinoza insisted. "They do not follow from the kind of autocratic government the common people ascribe to God."[134]

Instead of inspiring true reverence, however, the signs performed in the Old Testament generated pride and division, Spinoza suggested. Memory of the Exodus caused the Jews to imagine "that the Israelites were dearer to God than other men."[135] "The Israelites," he continued, "were unable to form a sound conception of God despite all those miracles." Indeed they were more inclined to bend the knee to "false gods" having witnessed them. After Moses performed wonders to release the Israelites from Egypt, they worshipped "a calf." "This was shameful!" Spinoza protested. If the Bible recorded miraculous events, it was "also evident from Scripture itself that miracles do not yield true knowledge of God."[136] Spinoza was more generous toward the New Testament narratives, acknowledging that the apostles established their authority with signs and wonders, but he emphasized the temporary quality of the phenomenon. The greater concern of the apostles was to teach.[137] Finally: both testaments confirmed that "miracles may also be performed by imposters."[138] This alone ought to invite suspicion of rashly claimed providences.

Spinoza's discussion ended on a rather agnostic note: the Bible affirms miracles but it does not promote "them as doctrines necessary for salvation." It was "up to every man to hold the opinion about them that he feels best enables him to subscribe with all his mind to the worship of God."[139] Ancient writers as distinguished as Josephus believed in the occurrence of miracles, though not confining them exclusively to the Jewish people. We have to tread carefully. Spinoza was willing to suspend hostilities over miracles if people would agree that they are neither exclusive to one religious group nor foundational to piety.[140] He maintained that it was orthodox theologians, who "evidently hold that God is inactive whilst nature follows its normal course," who opened the real path to unbelief.[141]

The Divine Law and the Tainted Scriptures: Restoring Religion

If Spinoza's discussion of superstition was tirelessly negative, characterizing it as sin and deceit, indeed a "cloak" for "aggressive license,"[142] his account of religion was profoundly ambiguous. The religion of the Jews, spelled out in wearying detail by Moses, came close to the "servitude" Spinoza identified as superstition. Even the purest religion fell short of the ideal of philosophical freedom. Yet Spinoza acknowledged that not all were capable of philosophy. Salvation could also be known by "obedience." The Bible contained a single "divine law," Spinoza argued, which could be perceived inwardly as spiritual truth (philosophy) or obeyed as duty and law (religion). Whichever path was taken, however, this divine law was not to be confused with the written text of the Bible. Spinoza's biblical criticism emerged from a reverent but reductive account of a law that could be known as moral duty or philosophical enlightenment but not historical truth. He did not subordinate the Bible to philosophy: he reduced it to ethics.

The scandalized reception of the *Treatise* conferred on Spinoza the reputation as the father of biblical criticism, but he wrote in the wake of Hobbes, Fisher, and Isaac La Peyrère, and often with more caution. La Peyrère was a French Huguenot, whose *Prae-Adamitae* (1655) was the first to raise questions of chronology and historicity that would dominate biblical criticism for years to come. Whom, for example, had Cain to fear if no one else was alive when he killed his brother? Like Fisher, La Peyrère had written under evangelical impulses, sacrificing historical infelicities for what he considered the spiritual integrity of the gospel. Although he recanted his heresies under duress, La Peyrère had considered his work a contribution to the spread of the faith, "which is in Christ."[143] Spinoza's determination to sift and weigh the Bible's contents according to a single principle places him within a Protestant tradition that reaches all the way to Luther and the interpretive élan of *sola fide*. Like Luther, Spinoza was not immune to the proof text. But he spoke for the radical Reformation's primacy of love against the booted splendor of doctrine.

It was Spinoza's confidence in the simplicity of the divine law that enabled him to treat questions of historicity with often-brisk indifference. With Fisher, he argued that however "distorted," "truncated," "badly written," or "frequently altered" the outward text, the moral "dignity of Scripture" was undisturbed:

> for Scripture would be no less divine even if written in other words or in a different language. Thus, no one can question that in this sense we have received the divine law, uncorrupted. For we see from Scripture itself, and without any difficulty or ambiguity, that the essence of the Law is to love God above all things and one's neighbour as oneself. And this cannot be adulterated nor penned in a slap-dash, error-prone manner.[144]

Spinoza's attack on the "superstitious veneration of the letter"—a worship of "paper and ink" no better than "adoring images and pictures"—reflected a bold certainty as to essence of the divine law.[145] Anchored in love, we can relax about historical details. Literalism is idolatry.

Scholars have noted the similarity of these comments to Fisher's critique of Protestant "bibliolatry." If anything, Spinoza was more hesitant to criticize the New Testament than Fisher. He worked harder to link the divine law to the gospel narratives: to resolve the tension between a universal law and a very specific exemplar. "After Christ's coming," Spinoza wrote, "the Apostles preached religion to all people everywhere, as the universal law, based solely upon Christ's passion." The particularity of this narrative was compatible with the universal and eternal quality of the message, he argued. For the Bible tells us that the gospel message was really nothing "new, except to those people who did not know it: 'he was in the world,' says John the Evangelist 1.10, 'and the world did not know him.'"[146] This was a foundation text of spiritualist Christianity. Spinoza used it to link the historical Christ to the pan-historical light within.

The New Testament narrative mattered, therefore, but as the renewal and exemplification of an ancient law of love. Paul summed up the whole of scripture when he urged in the letter to the Romans that whoever "loves his neighbor, with the intention of obeying God, has fulfilled the law."[147] The ultimate goal was to be able to serve God without the sentiment of following a "law," but Spinoza explained the necessity of a written code as part of a historical process of education. God provides what is necessary in the given circumstances, which is why he was sometimes described in the Bible as "El Shaddai"—the "God who suffices." He "gives each person what suffices for him."[148] When the Israelites emerged from Egypt, where they suffered as slaves and were "accustomed to Egyptian superstition," they needed a written law, and they needed to picture God "as a legislator obliging them to live well by the command of the law." "For this reason the right way of living or the true life and worship of God was more servitude to them than true liberty and the grace and gift of God." Moses "taught them in the same way as parents teach their children prior to the age of reason."[149] Only Solomon, before he started behaving "unworthily of a philosopher," showed a true affinity for unmediated knowledge. The prophets were simply men of "extraordinary virtue" and fertile imagination, which enabled them to command the fleeting respect of the people.[150]

For Spinoza, spiritual gifts were invariably shorthand for moral excellence. He constantly equated "the spirit of God" with "his kindness and mercy."[151] Amassing vast support for this sober conception of a fair God requiring justice from his people, Spinoza condemned the urge to build dogma from the raw timber of the text. He established "from the Bible alone" that love is the mark of true religion, before assessing other interpretations from this sole "ground" of judgment. Scripture demands love, and love judges scripture. Love was "the end and substance of revelation."[152] It was this simple, if circular, logic that gave Spinoza's biblical criticism an almost anti-intellectual quality. Even his more technical discussions of the fragility of the surviving texts and the precariousness of the "canon" were guided by the priority of ethics. His horror at "the audacity of those rabbis who wanted to exclude this book [of Proverbs], together with Ecclesiastes, from the canon of sacred writings" expressed the balance of sympathy.[153] These were the treasures of a mixed inheritance.

The shared crime of the two schools of interpretation he wished to challenge was the confusion of a Bible written in "everyday language" with spurious philosophical systems. The Cartesian error of using philosophy to establish what the prophets really meant to say, and the Calvinist folly of divining "profoundest mysteries" from earthy apostolic effusions, were condemned alike. Spinoza adopted an almost Lutheran tone as he lambasted those who tried "to demonstrate the authority of Scripture" with "stronger arguments" than those used by "the prophets in their time."[154] He ridiculed those who employed "mathematical proofs" to upgrade what was "solely a moral certainty" for the authors.[155] The prophets conjured images to move "hearts to obedience and devotion." They "spoke in human terms."[156] It was an extraordinary arrogance for philosophers and theologians to translate a pure moral vernacular into a private intellectual code, so that "the Church now resembles a university and religion a field of learning or, rather, ceaseless learned controversy." The very people who claimed to despise philosophy (Calvinists) reached for the "fabrications of Aristotle or Plato" to unlock its secrets, while the self-conscious admirers of philosophy (Cartesians) relentlessly sacrificed "the literal sense" of the Bible for their "preconceived opinions."[157] To "suppose that philosophers cannot err in interpreting Scripture" was to produce a "new ecclesiastical authority and a novel species of priest or pontiff, which would more likely be mocked than venerated by the common people."[158]

These were Protestant fulminations, crashing down on the new scholastics. Spinoza's demand that philosophy and religion are respected as distinct categories of knowledge was intended to protect both. Scripture existed to encourage faith and obedience in those who typically fell short of the demands of philosophy. It was rarely concerned with philosophical truth. Spinoza was as appalled by the muzzling of ancient prophets by pretentious intellectuals as he was disturbed by Calvinist zealots policing the universities. Scholars have sometimes interpreted Spinoza's separation of philosophical "truth" from biblical "ethics" to mean that people could believe what they wanted, provided they lived decent lives. Yet Spinoza's list of the "fundamentals" of scripture, the "ignorance of which makes obedience towards [God] impossible," was anything but an agnostic's charter. Understood within its own limits, scripture spoke firmly and clearly.

Spinoza again made his point through John: "Whoever loves [i.e., his neighbor] is born of God and knows God; he who does not love, does not know God; for God is love."[159] Worship consisted "solely in justice and charity," and all who "obey God in this rationale of living, and only they, are saved." "Finally," to conclude his summary of "the intent of the whole of Scripture," Spinoza listed his seventh "dogma":

> God forgives the repentant their sins; for there is no one who does not sin, and therefore if this were not clearly established, all would despair of their salvation and would have no reason to believe that God is merciful. But anyone who firmly believes that God forgives men's sins with the mercy and grace with which he directs all things and is more fully inspired with the love of God for this reason, truly knows Christ according to the spirit, and Christ is within him.[160]

People "do not agree about everything," Spinoza added with almost droll understatement. Most opinions are better left to private judgment. Yet this was the last of seven dogmas "that are absolutely required for obedience to God." "God is merciful," he "forgives," to deny this is to promote "despair."[161] Having resolved much of the Old Testament into ethics, Spinoza offered a more theological reading of the New: to believe that God forgives sins is to know "Christ according to the spirit."

If the Bible can thus promote salvation, the question arises: why do we need philosophy? If there is such purity in the text, why is the contrast between philosophy and religion so sharp? The answer was partly to be found in Spinoza's positive interpretation of philosophy-as-new-covenant, and partly in a bleak appraisal of the costs of sectarian strife. Although he was confident that his reductions were more faithful than the self-furnishing theories of his adversaries, Spinoza's analysis contained a dark current of realism and resignation. The Bible had been compromised by conflict, perhaps permanently. A purer course was necessary. Even if the Bible could be summarized as a counsel of love, the historical reality was that it had been stained by controversy and ruined as a symbol of unity. "Something intended to promote the practice of piety and religion is called sacred and divine and is sacred only so long as people use it religiously," Spinoza urged. "If they cease to be pious, the thing in question likewise, at the same time, ceases to be sacred. If they devote that thing to impious purposes, the very object that before was sacred will be rendered unclean and profane."[162] This was the story of the Bible.

Scripture contained its own warnings, Spinoza insisted. A certain place was called "the house of God" by Jacob, because he worshipped God there, but "the very same place was called 'the house of iniquity' " by Amos and Hosea because the Israelites were "accustomed to sacrifice idols there." "Words acquire a particular meaning simply from their usage," Spinoza ventured, and if the acquired meaning contradicts the original sense all sanctity is lost. If, he reasoned, "it becomes accepted usage to construe the words in the contrary sense, then both words and book which were formerly sacred will become profane and impure." This was "entirely evident from many passages of Scripture." For Jeremiah, a temple "frequented by murderers, thieves, idolaters and other wrong-doers" was no longer "the temple of God." The long-profaned "ark of the covenant" perished along with the Temple, "although there was nothing more sacred or venerated among the Hebrews." The tablets on which the Ten Commandments were written proved to be similarly dispensable. And now the Bible itself. Spinoza stared his opponents in the eye and said it is you, not us, who have corrupted the word of God. Quoting Jeremiah against those who "pervert" and profane the text, he challenged: " 'How can you say, we are trained in the Law of God and are its guardians. Assuredly, it has been written in vain, vain is the scribe's pen!' That is, even though the Scripture is in your hands, you are wrong to say you are guardians of God's Law, now that you have rendered it ineffective."[163]

Spinoza accused "theologians" of ransacking the scriptures to "extract their own thoughts and opinions," acting in a spirit that belied the claim of reverence for the "divine authority." "There is nothing they interpret with less hesitation and greater boldness than the Scriptures, that is the mind of the Holy Spirit." "If people truly believed in their hearts what they say with their lips about Scripture," he challenged, "they would follow a completely different way of life." There would be "fewer bitter controversies" and "less blind and reckless ambition to distort our interpretation of the Bible and devise novelties in religion." With bitter allusion to the "profound mysteries" that theologians believed to be "hidden in the Holy scripture," he accused his contemporaries of reducing religion to the defense of "purely human delusions." "Far from consisting of love, it has been turned, under the false labels of holy devotion and ardent zeal, into the promotion of conflict and the dissemination of senseless hatred."[164]

This was superstition, not religion, but the contagion reached back into the sources. There came a point when sacred texts became tainted oracles, when the Bible was inseparable from the "fictions" ascribed to it. The bloom was off the rose. Whole books of the New Testament were synonymous with controversy. It was impossible to enter them without breathing the odor of disputation. Spinoza was expressing what many of his Collegiant friends had already concluded. His contention was that the apostles had anticipated the problem, never intending their writings to acquire the status of dogma. The truth of the apostolic literature was that there was a higher road to salvation than law, duty, and labored virtue: inward knowledge. Paul taught it, and Christ demonstrated it. Radical, dangerous Spinoza was nothing less than a preacher.

The Power of Reason and the Mind of Christ

Those who would exclude Spinoza from the sweep of Christian history face a roadblock in his reverence for Christ and his esteem for Paul as a pioneer of philosophical reasoning. More than Solomon, Paul exemplified the philosophical method, the purity of reason. But Christ was on a different level: effortlessly embodying the wisdom to which others could only aspire. Religion was a legitimate but labored path to blessedness. Philosophy would not scorn it so much as transcend it. "Anyone," Spinoza maintained, "who abounds in the fruits of love, joy, peace, long-suffering, kindness, goodness, faithfulness, gentleness and self-control, against whom (as Paul says in his Epistle to the Galatians 5.22) there is no law, he, whether he has been taught by reason alone or by Scripture alone, has truly been taught by God, and is altogether happy."[165] Yet Spinoza left no doubt which of the approaches he preferred. The Bible was like the training wheels on the bicycle or the hand resting on the shoulder of the child. When the rhythms of philosophy were in motion, both could fall away.

Spinoza was clearly advocating no break with New Testament ethics, and he continued to cite John on the primacy of love. The novelty was to suggest that the vigorous reasoning employed by an apostle such as Paul (representing Spinoza's "second" kind of knowledge) and the intuitive spiritual knowledge embodied by Christ (the "third" and highest type) were the models of a new, post-religious wisdom. In one sense, Spinoza's critics were right: he was urging a separation of the religious and philosophic paths to holiness. He was reducing, even diminishing, the status of scripture, theology, and clerical authority. But Spinoza understood this as the fulfillment, not the desecration, of the Christian faith. He hits a note of intensity as he enters the New Testament material. Sarcasms evaporate. The engagement could hardly be tactical for it constitutes the climax of his argument. The three-part structure of superstition, religion, and philosophy leans indulgently toward the New Testament sources and the Christian concept of the new covenant.

As we have seen, the difference between religion and philosophy was the mode of appropriation: religion issues orders; philosophy quietly instructs. Spinoza situated philosophy within a biblical architecture of law and grace. It was the fulfillment of the promise of a law "divinely inscribed upon the hearts of men." Or as he quoted Paul: a "letter from God . . . written not in ink but by the spirit of God, not on tablets of stone but on tablets of flesh, on the heart."[166] This was a new mode of understanding, superseding the mechanical ordinances of the prophets. Spinoza's account of reason was a version of the spiritualist principle that a law ceased to be law when it was grasped internally. Reason, "the true light of the mind," was the power that turned law into freedom. Spinoza's model ultimately transcended rational certainty, reaching a kind of spiritual ecstasy, but it built on the foundation of a rational inner light. This was the logic of *The Light upon the Candlestick*, written by his close friend Balling. Spinoza pressed the argument further to suggest that submission to the inner light of reason was precisely what Paul meant by "faith."

Spinoza appealed to the apostle in support of his conviction that "the Bible fully endorses the natural light of reason and the natural divine law." The divine law was the imperative of love; reason was the ability to grasp it—clearly defined in Romans 1:20, where the apostle wrote of the "hidden things of God" being seen "through the understanding in his creatures, as well as his power and divinity . . . so that they are without a way of escape."[167] Like Castellio, Spinoza inferred "reason" from texts traditionally used to affirm the universality of conscience. Romans 1:20 was a cherished source of the medieval *synteresis* theology with which Luther's revolution began. Spinoza modified it by translating "heart" as "mind" and construing "faith" as a form of intellectual perseverance: "[Paul] says that no one is justified by the works of the law but by faith alone (see Romans 3.28), by which he certainly means nothing other than full mental assent."[168] Spinoza thus intellectualized the evangelical conversion narrative.

Assent to reason presaged the ascent to divine communion: the intellectual love of God. "That man," Spinoza urged, "is necessarily most perfect and most participates in the highest happiness who most loves and most enjoys, above all other things, the intellectual knowledge of God, who is the most perfect being. This then is what our highest good and happiness is, the knowledge and love of God."[169] Although rooted in the mind, this "blessedness" transcended words and energized the whole person, bringing "peace," "stability," and banishing deleterious thoughts of death.[170] Philosophy was not intellectual retreat. It was life in its fullness. As Spinoza urged in the *Ethics*: "A free man thinks of death least of all things, and his wisdom is a meditation not of death but of life."[171]

Although, Spinoza argued, the apostles remained prophets urging obedience and performing "signs" in keeping with the Jewish tradition, their primary work was to announce this new mode of access to God. If John was the advocate of love, Paul was the great differentiator between toiling obedience and unencumbered freedom. While the apostle urged that it is good to obey the law, he also contended that "no one is blessed unless he has the mind of Christ in him (see Romans 8.9) whereby, undoubtedly, one may understand God's laws as eternal laws," rather than thudding precepts.[172] Or as Spinoza paraphrased Paul's argument in the first letter to the Corinthians: "God sent his Christ to all nations, to free all men equally from the servitude of the law, so that they would no longer live good lives because the law so commanded, but from a fixed conviction of the mind."[173] This was true salvation: when the moral truth of the divine law is perceived inwardly as a natural effect of knowing God. It was Spinoza's doctrine of grace. As he insisted, "true knowledge of God is not a command but a divine gift."[174]

Spinoza's God was not honored by the extravagant gesture, but this was not to deny the experiential force of a true "idea of God," which conveys meaning "not in words, but in a much more excellent manner." It was a sensation of release and discovery that "every man who has experienced intellectual certainty has undoubtedly felt within himself."[175] It was at once intellectual and joyous; rational and super-rational. As Spinoza explained in an important annotation:

> For the love of God is not obedience but a virtue necessarily present in someone who rightly knows God. Obedience on the other hand, concerns the will of someone who commands, not the necessity and truth of a thing. . . . [For] divine commandments seem to us like decrees or enactments only so long as we are ignorant of their cause. Once we know this, they immediately cease to be edicts and we accept them as eternal truths, not as decrees, that is, obedience immediately turns into love which arises from true knowledge as inevitably as light emanates from the sun. By the guidance of reason therefore we can love God but not obey him, since we cannot accept

> divine laws as divine as long as we do not know their cause, nor by reason can we conceive of God as issuing decrees like a prince.[176]

Spinoza insisted that this two-speed model of law and reason was entirely biblical. Paul spoke the language of duty when he needed to. But the thrust of his ministry was to reach beyond law to this buoyant, intuitive mode of perception. Reason opened a door to a purer knowledge of God. The law lost the odor of obligation when finally perceived as "eternal truth." At such a time, "obedience immediately turns into love," flowing from knowledge as naturally "as light emanates from the sun." This "third kind" of knowledge rendered coercion obsolete. It was the death of superstition and perhaps the end of religion too. Spinoza is quietly firm in his conviction that inward knowledge of God rendered "pastors," "ceremonies," and "histories" obsolete for those who could attain it.[177]

Application preceded intuition, however, and Spinoza delighted in showing how the apostles modeled philosophical exchange as the prelude to intuitive knowledge of God. The apostles switched between "prophesying" before crowds and more sophisticated "teaching." Where the Old Testament prophets, in religious mode, had prefaced their statements with "Thus says God," the New Testament epistles were lively dialogues—collaborative, respectful, and teeming with phrases like, "we therefore think" or "for I think." Such expressions suggested a healthy appetite for debate and a holy reluctance to dogmatize. To forge dogmas from the agile and deeply personal reasoning of the epistles was to travesty the genre. Paul, Spinoza suggested, was the master of winning respect by eschewing "prophetic authoritativeness," attempting to convince the Corinthians " 'as a weak man and not by command' (see 1 Corinthians 7.6), or writing that, 'I speak to you as to intelligent men; judge for yourselves what I say.' " Whereas prophetic authority did "not permit participation in argument," apostolic teachings were carefully and sensitively reasoned. The apostles' "letters contain nothing," Spinoza suggested, "but brotherly advice mixed with courtesies (which of course are totally alien to prophetic authority), like Paul's excusing himself at Romans 15.15 by saying 'Brethren, I have written to you rather too boldly.' "[178]

Spinoza's tone was breathless as he contrasted Old Testament authority with New Testament persuasion, littering his discussion with phrases like: "But in the New Testament . . ." and "But the Apostles. . . ." The apostles straddled religious and philosophical modes, but they pointed clearly to a future of rational enlightenment. For, "although religion, as the Apostles preached it by simply telling the story of Christ, does not come within the scope of reason, nevertheless everyone can acquire the essence of it by means of the natural light of reason, for, like the whole of Christ's teaching, it consists primarily of moral doctrine." The natural light precluded the necessity of miracle or supernatural inspiration. As Spinoza explained, "the Apostles did not need supernatural light to adapt to the common understanding the religion which they had already confirmed by miracles so that everyone could easily accept it from his heart." Although miracles bought a hearing, they actually hindered the reception of Christianity in the authentic chamber of the "heart." Miracles were a fading currency, as were dramatic claims to apostolic status. Paul grasped this with liberating candor. His renunciation of apostolic rights in the letter to Philemon was, for Spinoza, a signal example of philosophical wisdom. It showed that even where there was authority to "command," persuasion was the higher road. A negotiating apostle was something to marvel at.[179] As Spinoza wrote in the *Ethics*, "minds are not conquered by force, but by love and generosity."[180]

If Paul was the model of ingenuous reasoning, richer in a page than all the "Aristotelian trifles" of the theologians,[181] Christ was on a different level. Whereas Paul's writings, such as the letter to the Romans, were characterized by "long deductions and arguments," of which Spinoza warmly approved,[182] Christ possessed an ease and immediacy of grasp that suggested direct access to God, even divinity. Paul reasoned but Christ embodied the "Eternal Wisdom" of God. As Spinoza urged in an astonishing passage:

> For a person to know things which are not contained in the first foundations of our knowledge and cannot be deduced from them, his mind would necessarily have to be vastly superior, far surpassing the human mind. I do not believe anyone has reached such a degree of perfection above others except Christ, to whom the decrees of God which guide men to salvation were revealed not by words or visions but directly; and that is why God revealed himself to the Apostles through the mind of Christ, as he did, formerly, to Moses by means of a heavenly voice. Therefore the voice of Christ may be called the voice of God, like the voice which Moses heard. In this sense we may also say that the wisdom of God, that is, the wisdom which is above human wisdom, took on human nature in Christ, and that Christ was the way of salvation. . . . Therefore if

> Moses spoke with God face to face . . . Christ communicated with God from mind to mind.[183]

Spinoza thus located the difference between the labor of obedience (religion) and the freedom of inward revelation (philosophy) in the contrast between Moses and Christ. This was no isolated example. Later in the *Treatise*, Spinoza wrote: "We assert therefore that, apart from Christ, no one has received revelations from God except by means of the imagination," which, he added, was inferior to the knowledge perceived by a "perfect mind." "God revealed himself to Christ or his soul directly," without "words or visions." Christ surpassed and nullified the law by internalizing it. For "although," Spinoza noted, "he too appeared to issue laws in the name of God, one must see, that he understood things truly and adequately. Christ was not so much a prophet as the mouth-piece of God."[184]

Christ was unique, untouchable, but the model could be emulated. It was, Spinoza believed, Christ's hope that his disciples would exchange mechanical obedience for inward perception. Christ came to teach "eternal truths," and "if he sometimes prescribed them as laws, he did so because of the ignorance and obstinacy of the people." "To those who *were* capable of learning about the heavenly mysteries, he undoubtedly did teach things as eternal truths and not as commandments. Hence he freed them from servitude to the law and yet in this way also confirmed and stabilized the law, inscribing it deeply in their hearts." "Paul too seems to indicate as much in certain passages," Spinoza added.[185]

Spinoza took the Sermon on the Mount as the supreme example of Christ's ability to internalize cumbrous, external precepts. It was an essay on the higher status of philosophy. Religion says adultery is wrong. Philosophy goes further, exposing the insidious mastery of lust, the motive that precedes the transgression. This was Christ's genius: transcending the written law to teach "universal truths," commending "spiritual" rather than "physical" rewards, offering liberation from the treadmill of religion. Christ cared more about "the consent of the mind" than the ability to refrain from the deed. He embodied a virtue that was its own reward. Language of punishment was just a "human" way of characterizing bondage to the passions.[186] Christ "openly commends" the Mosaic Law, Spinoza admitted, but by refusing to impose it "as a legislator" he demonstrated his emancipation from the religious mode: the priority of the renewed mind over the merely disciplined body. It was "less external actions that he sought to correct than people's minds."[187] Christ was,

Spinoza declared to a distinguished visitor, who reported the statement to Gottfried Leibniz: "the supreme philosopher."[188]

Like many of the Christian spiritualists, Spinoza acknowledged a mystical Christ whose supreme gifts were not to be confused with the orthodox doctrine of incarnation. For Spinoza, God did not assume human flesh in Christ any more than he took on "the nature of a cloud" in the desert. Yet Christ's status was undiminished. He was a man "endowed with eternity."[189] As Spinoza explained to Oldenburg: "I do not think it necessary for salvation to know Christ according to the flesh: but with regard to the Eternal Son of God, that is the Eternal Wisdom of God, which has manifested itself in all things and especially in the human mind, and above all in Christ Jesus, the case is far otherwise. For without this no one can come to a state of blessedness, inasmuch as it alone teaches, what is true or false, good or evil."[190] "Only by the Spirit of Christ," he warned a former student who had converted to Catholicism and now berated him for his heresies, "can we be led to the love of justice and charity."[191]

Christ gave "by His life and death a matchless example of holiness," Spinoza believed, but he did not physically rise from the dead. The resurrection was a triumph over "spiritual" death—of the kind suggested by Christ's own phrase, "let the dead bury their dead." As Spinoza attempted to justify his stance to Oldenburg: "Christians interpret spiritually all those doctrines which the Jews accepted literally," and the same was true of the resurrection. "The utmost that Christ says of Himself is, that He is the Temple of God, because, as I said before, God had specially manifested Himself in Christ. John, wishing to express the same truth more forcibly, said that 'the Word was made flesh.'"[192] Thus, Spinoza affirmed: "I accept Christ's passion, death, and burial literally, as you do, but His resurrection I understand allegorically." "He appeared to His disciples; but in these matters they might, without injury to Gospel teaching, have been deceived," Spinoza suggested. Oldenburg was not impressed by Spinoza's selective allegorization. But Spinoza was unmoved, asserting the redundancy of a doctrine of physical resurrection with what he considered his trump card: Paul, chief among the apostles who just happened to be the only one who never knew Christ as a man. "Paul," Spinoza observed, "to whom Christ afterwards appeared, rejoices, that he knew Christ not after the flesh, but after the spirit. Farewell, honourable Sir, and believe me yours in all affection and zeal."[193]

Oldenburg struggled with several aspects of the *Treatise*, but he warmly affirmed Spinoza's attempt to "to exalt and establish the true object of the Christian religion and the divine loftiness of fruitful philosophy."[194] Their correspondence ceased not because Oldenburg suddenly grasped Spinoza's subversive intent but because Leibniz failed to deliver one of his letters, a matter that distressed the Englishman. Spinoza's emphasis on the "spirit" of Christ was not unusual among the Christians with whom he associated. It was this concept that enabled him to affirm that "the Turks and other non-Christian nations; if they worship God by the practice of justice and charity towards their neighbour . . . have the spirit of Christ, and are in a state of salvation, whatever they may ignorantly hold with regard to Mahomet and oracles."[195] And it was this pan-historical, "Logos" Christology that enabled him to read an eternal Christ into the earliest history of Judaism. This emerged powerfully in Spinoza's comments in the *Ethics* on the Genesis account of the Fall, characterized as a descent from freedom to fear. "This freedom," he argued, "was afterwards recovered by the patriarchs, led by the spirit of Christ; that is, by the idea of God, wheron alone it depends, that man may be free, and desire for others the good which he desires for himself."[196] Spinoza prepared the *Ethics* for posthumous publication. He had no reason to court a Christian public with feigned pieties, even if he were capable of such a thing.

Spinoza did not "empty" Christian terms of their contents, or use the word God "in a sense unknown to all Christians."[197] As one scholar has recently argued, Spinoza's *Ethics* contains a clear and powerful doctrine of "eternal life." She identifies the central theme of the work as the capacity of love to cast out fear, arguing that "it might be possible to read the *Ethics* as a philosophical exposition of the theology of 1 John—an exposition that firmly situates the latter text in the 17th-century context by its emphasis on the harmful effects of fear, and its insistence that the hatred fuelling sectarian conflict needs to be overcome by love."[198] As she continues: "While Spinoza's reinterpretations of the theological doctrines taught by the Dutch Reformed Church involve revisions so radical and subversive that they drew the charge not just of heresy but of atheism, his interpretation of eternal life echoes the First Letter of John quite simply and straightforwardly. This biblical text does not need to be twisted or revised in order to be strikingly relevant to the theological-political situation that Spinoza faced."[199]

Privately, Spinoza remained a man of undimmed spirituality whose philosophical virtuosity did not preclude the value of prayer. One of his letters shows him protesting, yet again, against the idea that he had confounded "the divine nature with human nature." While he maintained that pure "understanding offers our mind and body to God freed from all superstition," he did not rule out devotional, supra-rational, modes of access. "Nor do I deny," he explained, "that prayer is extremely useful to us. For my understanding is too small to determine all the means, whereby God leads men to the love of Himself, that is, to salvation. So far is my opinion from being hurtful [to religion], that it offers to those, who are not taken up with prejudices and childish superstitions, the only means for arriving at the highest stage of blessedness." He added a comment that could have been aimed at his modern interpreters: "When you say that, by making men so dependent on God, I reduce them to the likeness of the elements, plants or stones, you sufficiently show that you have thoroughly misunderstood my meaning."[200] "The supposition of some," he wrote in another letter, "that I endeavor to prove in the *Tractatus Theologico-Politicus* the unity of God and Nature (meaning by the latter a certain mass or corporeal matter)" was, he insisted, "wholly erroneous."[201] Immanence did not mean naturalism. A doctrine of divine necessity was not a creed of blind determinism. The whole thrust of the *Ethics* is the power of the enlightened mind to break out of the tyranny of the passions. And while philosophy is clearly preferred to religion in the *Treatise*, Spinoza made an "earnest request" that readers examine his chapters on their relationship "again and again" to accept that his quarrel was not with faith as such, but with that misnamed religion which promotes "hatred, conflict and anger." He implored readers "to understand that we have not written them simply to make some novel remarks, but to correct abuses, and indeed we hope one day to see them corrected."[202]

With the possible exception of Bayle, there was no more influential critic of organized religion in the seventeenth century. No one did more than Spinoza to establish philosophy as a culture, a way of life. Spinoza was also a great advocate of science, busily swapping notes with Oldenburg and Boyle on a range of contemporary discoveries. But his religious criticism did not emerge from his scientific interests. For all its promise and prestige, science was, to borrow Fisher's phrase, "too weak an engine" to mobilize the sentiments evinced by Spinoza or any of the radicals quoted above. Almost all of the criticism we have encountered sprang from a stance of positive spirituality: the molten progeny of an unsilenced Reformation. The Christian conscience, conceived as "inner light," "reason," or raging indignation, was the enduring solvent of orthodoxy. The impulses that inspired Franck to oppose Luther, and Castellio to challenge Calvin, were alive and undiminished. When the English heresy hunter, Thomas Edwards, cited "a golden saying of Luther," "Cursed be that Charity which is kept with the losse of the doctrine of faith,"[203] he confirmed the basic cleavage between dogma and ethics that summoned a culture of dissent. Spinoza always suspected that dogma was an alibi for power and in arguing so he was dependent on both the Bible and the Christian subculture in which he found a home. Spinoza has a place in a history of unbelief through what he started, not what he was. The analogy with Moses may have been more profound than Feuerbach intended.

Spinoza remained a dark and distrusted figure in the Christian world until a handful of German admirers started to rehabilitate him in the following century. The English radicals who had so briefly turned the world upside down were put back in their boxes in a "restoration" as stern as anything that had come before. But as the classic study of English radicalism wondered: "How absolutely certain can we be that this world was the right way up"—an age of peace and order "in which poets went mad" and philosophers were "afraid" of the emotional disturbance of music?[204] The same question can be asked of religious history and the coercive logic of "secularization." We think of a religious culture assailed by a secular philosophy, we acquiesce in the sifting language of faith and "infidelity," piety and secularism. But can we be sure that we are viewing the matter the right way up?

4

In Search of a Father

VOLTAIRE'S CHRISTIAN ENLIGHTENMENT

I see the mercy of God where you would see only his power.
—VOLTAIRE, "On the Interpretation
OF THE NEW TESTAMENT," 1767

WHEN E. P. THOMPSON defined history as the "rescue" of ordinary people from "the enormous condescension of posterity," it was not Enlightenment philosophers that he had in mind.[1] Powdered prophets, preaching revolution under the instruction of the finest Burgundy, represented the wrong kind of history, a confusion of status with influence. History is from "below." Greatness has been greatly exaggerated. Scholars who place more emphasis on ideas, meanwhile, have often been no kinder to the Enlightenment. From the terror of the French Revolution to the horrors of industrialism, no malaise of modernity has escaped association with the self-admiring *philosophes.* Since the early 1800s, exposing the follies of Enlightenment reason has been the chosen blood sport of the Western intellectual—a tradition that goes back to Edmund Burke, Romanticism, and the in-house criticism of Jean-Jacques Rousseau. The situation reaches absurdity when men who campaigned for religious tolerance, penal reform, and a profusion of humanitarian concerns are routinely implicated in the dissolution of Western morality—even the barbarism of Auschwitz; when a gritty human rights agenda, pursued over decades by scholar-activists like Voltaire, can be dismissed as a philosophical "fiction"; when an era of hopeful and historic reform can be damned as a game of innocents—"the Enlightenment project," in the reductive appellation of an influential critic.[2]

If the first fallacy of historical analysis is to look at the evidence from the wrong end of the telescope—to judge the past by the present—the second is downright distortion. The revolutionary violence of the 1790s was no more the fruit of a naked and instrumental reason than the Enlightenment itself was. The "reason" for which the eighteenth century contended was not the all-seeing eye of René Descartes. It was a cautious, chastened, and deeply moral phenomenon, rooted in a Christian tradition that the philosophers at once challenged and refined. Finding classic expression in Rousseau's "Profession of Faith of a Savoyard Vicar" (1762) or Kant's *Religion within the limits of Reason alone* (1793), Enlightenment reason did not symbolize the imperialism of the intellect so much as the battered protest of the soul. And in Voltaire, the supreme embodiment of Enlightenment vigor, the ratio of moral to intellectual certainty was arguably greatest. Voltaire fought religious authority with the righteous sword of conscience. Where Rousseau and Kant allowed the flashing blade to eclipse theology altogether,[3] Voltaire remained open and attentive to the supernatural. The leading critic of Christianity in the modern era was a stubbornly religious thinker, whose fury against a persecuting orthodoxy was again rooted in positive theological convictions.

Although Kant's perorations on a law "inscribed in the heart of all human beings," "free from every dogma," place him within the tradition of Christian moral dissent, he cannot be allowed to speak exclusively for it. He represents the conclusion of a drama that is very much alive in figures like Pierre Bayle and Voltaire. However resounding the echoes of a Pietist tutelage, the triumph of the independent conscience over the "infancy" of faith is, in Kant, vigorous and decisive. He is clear that "morality in no way needs religion . . . but is rather self-sufficient by virtue of pure practical reason," the law written on the heart.[4] Kant's aversion to prayer, to the "foreign influence" of grace, or any of the principles of "ecclesiastical faith," is unwavering.[5] He mocks the "crafty hope" and "lazy confidence" of those who expect moral goodness to fall "in their lap, as if it were a heavenly gift from above." "Universal human reason must be recognized and honored as supreme commanding principle in a natural religion," he writes. Any "revealed faith" which "is to come ahead of" such a religion "is a *counterfeit service* through which the moral order is totally reversed," a "slavish" piety, a "groveling delusion," a "fetish-making," a "courtly service"; a "surrogate" for the honest work of "conscience." "Enthusiastic religious delusion is," Kant suggests, "the moral death of the reason without which there can be no religion."[6]

The kinship of such sentiments to the sterner currents of the radical Reformation and the early, "spiritualist" Enlightenment, is unmistakable.

Yet Kant was not one to fret over access to the means of grace. The door was now closed. When Kant spoke of "deny[ing] knowledge in order to make room for faith," the faith he had in mind was a strangely circular affair. Ripping through what remained of the great medieval "proofs" for God's existence, Kant built a fortress of conscience. But it was a haunting security that swore a rescued God to silence. The moral law reverberates in the soul, but prayer is for weaklings. "Once the doctrine of the purity of conscience . . . has been sufficiently propagated," Kant wrote to a friend, "when this true religious structure has been built up so that it can maintain itself in the world—then the scaffolding must be taken down."[7] By "scaffolding," Kant meant the dogmatic structures of Christian faith. In Kierkegaard's arresting summary: "If in this connection I then say that it is my duty to love God, I am actually pronouncing only a tautology." "God" and "duty" are one. Morality has swallowed religion.[8]

Although I would continue to quibble with language of secularization, Kantian "autonomy" does represent a line in the sand. It proves that a religious impulse—the Protestant conscience—can create an outlook that is no longer expectantly religious. But the unbounded confidence in human resources that flows from Kant's pen cannot be taken for the essence of the Enlightenment. To read the movement as a steady ascent toward Kant's triumphant formula is to modernize it prematurely: turning a living drama between conscience, faith, and religious authority into a sterile procession. It is to mistake a defiant and sharp-edged conclusion for a deeply contested process. It is again to read the cause from the outcome—or the perceived outcome. How many people, of the modern West, came to think like Kant is a matter for debate. Even among the philosophers, his chiseled clarity was rare. Voltaire was not a man who could peel away from a church with total contempt for the "delusionary" endeavor within. While his animosities were often riper than Kant's so too were his pieties. His appeals to conscience were powerfully informed by what he considered right understandings of God. Natural religion was never very natural for Voltaire. This, I will argue, was a formula closer to the essence of Enlightenment than either Kantian "autonomy" or the reign of unbridled intellectual reason that is persistently mistaken for it.

The awkward fact is that Voltaire was at his most religious or theological during the years of his most aggressive attacks on orthodoxy. Condemned in his own time as a "diabolical" infidel, comparable with "Judas Iscariot" among the "supreme representatives of impenitence and unbelief,"[9] and scorned by modern philosophy as a phrasemaking dilettante, Voltaire was in fact a defiantly Christian thinker who embraced the status of philosophical "ignorance" with pride.[10] He hated intellectual pretension and despised any philosophy that privileged ideas over human decency or practical experience. Voltaire's moral judgments were more than "linguistic survivals from the practices of classical theism," in the classic indictment of Enlightenment ethics.[11] Within an army of destroyers, Voltaire was notable for the virulence of his anticlericalism and the tenacity of his religious belief. The claim of this chapter is that the two were connected. The nineteenth-century historian W. E. H. Lecky classed Voltaire with Luther among a handful of thinkers who had profoundly modified the opinions of humankind.[12] My contention is that the comparison is merited in terms of substance as well as scale. The "natural law" that Voltaire set against the arrogance of orthodoxy was Christian in all but name. And while he initially proposed it as an antidote to theology, he was always conscious of limitations. A parallel, and eventually dominant, stream of his thought is a quest for a theology of mercy to complete a lively but ultimately barren doctrine of conscience. Finding "revelation" in his own cast of spiritual heroes, Voltaire emerges as a powerful critic of natural religion, turning finally from scorn to hushed appreciation of Jesus Christ. Voltaire was not chasing the gods out of human affairs. He was searching for one.

Science and Conscience

The primacy of moral reason, or conscience, in Enlightenment criticism should not be conceived in terms of competition with intellectual reason, or science. The claims of science against inherited systems of thought remained ethical and deeply resonant with the revolt of conscience against creed. Science and conscience can be distinguished, not divided. The "dare" to "think for yourself," issued by Voltaire long before Kant made it synonymous with "the age of Enlightenment," remained a demand for courage as well as clarity.[13] The status of Newton and Locke as giants of natural philosophy implied a sense of heroism and the triumph of light over darkness. One of Newton's editors characterized his work as the historic illumination of questions merely "named" by others,[14] and it was with his usual blend of mischief and profundity that Voltaire cast his lot with the English master against a beleaguered Descartes, "born to uncover the errors of antiquity [only] to substitute his own."[15] Knowledge was emancipation. Locke's researches into the mechanics of intellectual formation exuded a Lutheran contempt for the presumption of tradition and the folly of "taking things upon trust." The vast majority, Locke regretted, "misimploy their power of Assent, by lazily enslaving their Minds to the Dictates and Dominion of others in Doctrines which it is their duty carefully to examine." "The floating of other Mens Opinions in our brains," he famously urged,

> makes us not a jot more knowing, though they happen to be true. What in them was Science, is in us but Opinatrety, whilst we give up our assent to reverend Names, and do not, as they did, employ our own Reason to understand those Truths, which gave them reputation. . . . In the Sciences, every one has so much, as he really knows and comprehends: What he believes only, and takes upon trust, are but shreads.

Truth was no respecter of persons. Enlightenment was an attitude, a determination of the soul. "I have not made it my business," Locke piously declared, "either to quit or follow any Authority in the ensuing Discourse: Truth has been my only Aim."[16]

Locke's *Essay Concerning Human Understanding* (1690) became the gospel of the new "empiricism": the principle that ideas have to be discovered, grasped, and known before they can aspire to the status of truth. This has been described as a "sensationalist" theory of knowledge for its reliance on "sense" and "experience," and it is no accident that the Lockean model was appropriated by the evangelists John Wesley and Jonathan Edwards in an analogous quest for religious certainty.[17] Reformation and Enlightenment cannot be separated. The empirical mood was restless and irreverent, backing personal conviction over second-hand authority, every time. When one of Voltaire's characters responded to an enquiry about his religion by placing his hand on his chest and saying, "My law is here," the homage was to both conscience and empiricism.[18] Science was moral, and morality was practical and experimental—though the kinship should not be overstated. It would be hard to exaggerate the status of Newton and Locke as icons of Enlightenment and the bearers of a new kind of intellectual authority but they remained priests rather than prophets. They brought light, not heat, leaving the moral universe much as they found it.

While the Newtonian revolution raised doubts about a certain kind of providence, it strongly supported a theology of creation and divine order.

Science remained "natural philosophy" and, for many, a branch of theology. Newton's demonstration that the planets do not move on invisible structures but by an awesome poise of gravity and velocity acquired the status of a revelation. It suggested wisdom, power, and unimaginable precision in the making of the cosmos. And, for the time being, it enabled theologians to laugh at the folly of atheism. The weaknesses of "physical theology" would be revealed in the nineteenth century, when conflict and development replaced design in the scientific imagination, but in the meantime, science was on the side of the angels, and Voltaire joined the choir. But as the trauma of the Lisbon earthquake revealed to him, if not others, in 1755: a theology of perfect order rings hollow in the midst of a perfect disaster. And more than silence or inarticulacy, Lisbon demonstrated the dangers of a scientific mentality that could equate physical events with the mind of God. Voltaire was scandalized by efforts to explain away the suffering as a minor and necessary kink in the chain of providence. Providential "optimism" was a bystander's charter, an anesthetic for the soul. The fatalism of natural philosophy matched the cruelty of scapegoating Inquisitors. Voltaire condemned both.

Voltaire's reaction marked a turning point in his career, and he would never again write of "natural law" with such confidence, but it also revealed long-brewing tensions between moral and scientific consciousness. The potential for scientific concepts of order and physical necessity to nourish a theology of resignation was a sore point of the early Enlightenment. Voltaire's rage against Newtonian "optimists" such as Alexander Pope, whose glib assurance that "Whatever is, is right" so infuriated him, placed him within a distinguished tradition of moral dissent. Voltaire's insistence that science can neither explain nor justify the suffering consequent upon a natural disaster said something about his own, restless conscience and it offered the same comment about the conservatism of natural philosophy that English radicals had made in the seventeenth century. Many had feared the "mechanical philosophy" of Locke and Newton as a new doctrine of control, sanctifying inequality and tethering political privilege to property and education. Indeed some scholars have suggested that the scientific revolution helped to end the political revolution, offering "consoling truths" for a "hierarchical society."[19] In 1691 Robert Boyle endowed a series of lectures to promote understanding of the interrelationship between Christianity and science. The tenor of the project is suggested by the comment of the Boyle lecturer of 1697 that, if "there is no God nor religion," then "all men are equal."[20] Voltaire remained an admirer of Locke and a disciple of Newton but it was from neither that he gleaned the minerals of revolt or his war cry of anticlericalism: "*Écrasez l'Infâme!*" ("Crush the Infamous!"). Voltaire's criticism was too visceral to be reducible to any secondary authority, but if there was a model and an icon it was the forgotten man of the early Enlightenment: Pierre Bayle.

Bayle and the "Empire of Conscience"

Insofar as the Enlightenment represented an attitude or a "climate of opinion," rather than a body of teaching or a worldview, Bayle provided the template. As the twentieth-century philosopher Ernst Cassirer argued, "the real philosophy of the Enlightenment is not simply the sum total of what its leading thinkers . . . thought and taught" but a "pulsation of the inner intellectual life," registering less in the content of "individual doctrines than in the form and manner of intellectual activity in general."[21] The mood was aggressive and skeptical, rather than speculative or theoretical, and the taste was for history and fact over logic and detachment. The medicinal chaos of Bayle's *Historical and Critical Dictionary,* which began appearing in 1696, rather than the austere precision of Spinoza's *Ethics,* was the order of the day. Bayle cared little for science and even less for philosophical systems, finding his calling in destruction, not construction. His was a ministry of holy confusion unleashed in the name of health and humanity. Bayle personified philosophy as criticism, not certainty, and his animus against the hubris of intellectual reason set the tone of a movement that would be as hostile to rationalism as theology. "Reason," he declared in a vintage effusion of 1703, "is like a runner who doesn't know that the race is over."[22] It is blind to its futility. In Bayle, the Enlightenment moved from the purity of speculation to the anarchy of history and a pragmatic, essentially moral quest for tolerance. Perfection was off the agenda.

Bayle's *Dictionary* has been described as the "arsenal" of the Enlightenment, the prototype of the great Encyclopedias of the 1750s, and his *Philosophical Commentary* (1686) was the boldest appeal for religious toleration of the early modern period, surpassing the radicalism of Locke and Spinoza in its sympathy for the demon of atheism. No other author commanded such an imposing presence in private libraries of the eighteenth century.[23] For Voltaire, he was nothing less than the "immortal Bayle," the "great and wise," "the attorney general of philosophers."[24] The evocative image of David Hume, slipping away to France to write his skeptical masterpiece, *A Treatise on Human Nature*, with eight volumes of Bayle in his luggage, tells its own story.[25] "The acute and penetrating Bayle" was a philosopher's philosopher. He was also a Christian, who defended the burden of criticism as the birthright of "a good Protestant."[26]

Bayle was a Calvinist Protestant (Huguenot) driven out of France by the persecutions unleashed by Louis XIV in the 1680s, a wave of belligerence that culminated in the Revocation of the Edict of Nantes in 1685. The Edict of Nantes, issued by Henry IV in 1598, had granted rights to French Protestants and symbolized the end of the Wars of Religion. The Revocation signaled their return. Bayle's vast and unstinting output was a direct response to the reopened wound. French Protestants had not enjoyed liberty in the seventeenth century, but lives were now in danger, and as someone who had briefly converted to Catholicism, Bayle's was in acute jeopardy. In 1681 he joined the estimated 200,000 Huguenots who fled to the Netherlands, where he conducted a literary campaign against intolerance that consumed him for the rest of his life.

His first contribution was a *General Criticism* of a grossly partisan history of Calvinism, which had been written to justify the persecutions.[27] This set the tone for a series of piercing counterattacks. In the same year, Bayle published his *Miscellaneous Reflections on the Comet* (1682), which condemned the superstition and spiritual one-upmanship prompted by the passing of a comet in 1680. To believe that God used natural events to reward one people and punish another was idolatry, he asserted. And this, he claimed, was worse than atheism, for it travestied the character of God, who was the Father of the whole of humankind.[28] It was here that Bayle aired the subversive thought, couched as innocent historical observation, that theological orthodoxy and moral integrity are not two sides of the same coin. Christians, Bayle reflected with cool understatement, are not always motivated by charity and a pure love of God. Religion is no safeguard of morality. Indeed a society of virtuous atheists is not beyond the realm of imagination. This was not to announce a divorce between theology and morality, but it was a rebuke to a religious tyranny justified as the preservation of moral order. Not only did orthodoxy fail to generate virtue, the extent of the failure pointed an accusing finger at its theology. "Our life," Bayle lamented, "destroys our doctrine."[29]

In 1684 Bayle started to edit a monthly journal, the *News of the Republic of Letters*, which diffused the gently millennial hope that colonies of tolerance and generous piety were finally lifting the fog of superstition and persecution. It was here that the motif of enlightenment gained fresh currency: an expression of spiritual and mental liberation, the promise of a new era. “We are now in an age,” Bayle wrote in April 1684, “which bids fair to become daily more and more enlightened, so much so that all preceding ages when compared with this will seem to be plunged in darkness.” Bayle was part of a vigorous culture of dissent: pious, irreverent, sometimes salacious, but united against the criminality of persecution. “Eyes that are enlightened by the light,” proclaimed a pamphlet of 1687 “[can see] that France . . . is in the grip of a Catholic fury.”[30] It was a time of stirring hope but, for Bayle, the darkness returned in November 1685, when news came of his brother’s death at the hands of the French authorities, following an arrest of which he was indirectly the cause. Unable to lay their hands on the author of the *General Criticism*, they had arrested his brother, Jacob, a young Huguenot pastor. Kept alive for five months in a squalid cell and visited daily by a Jesuit who offered to release him if he would abjure, Jacob finally died. Bayle never forgave himself for his role in his brother’s demise, and he never forgave the theological machine that brought about his death.

Bayle did not lose his faith in God. He clung to an austere belief in a God whose goodness could not be doubted, even if his ways were truly obscure. “I die a Christian philosopher,” he wrote to his friend, Pastor Terson, hours before his death in 1706, “convinced of and filled with God’s goodness and mercy.”[31] What he never recovered was any confidence in a link between the ways of God and the ways of Christendom. The death of other family members, and the taste of persecution within the exiled Calvinist community, took a heavy toll. The penchant for deflating and debunking religious authority became a career. And Bayle did not go after soft targets. His attack on Augustine, as the fateful originator of the doctrine of persecution, is a stunning example of sustained polemicism and that “pulsation” of the inner life to which Cassirer referred. Bayle’s *Philosophical Commentary on These Words of the Gospel, Luke 14.23: “Compel Them to Come in, That My House May Be Full,”* written in the wake of his brother’s death, is a breathtaking assault on a figure revered throughout the Christian world, and a seminal document of European Enlightenment.

Bayle managed to produce nearly 800 pages expounding a single verse from the New Testament, a passage from the fourteenth chapter of Luke’s gospel, in which a master instructs a servant to invite strangers to a banquet with the words: “Compel them to come in, that my house may be full.” The verse had been used by Augustine, in his controversy with a fifth-century sect, to build a case for coercion, or what Bayle termed, in the Church's extenuating parlance, "the charitable and salutary Violence exercis'd on Hereticks."[32] A verse suggestive of God's generosity, Bayle protested, had been turned by Augustine, in his rage against the Donatists, into the proof text of persecution. Every persecutor cited Augustine, Bayle noted, and only recently had the Archbishop of Paris attempted to justify the "calamities of our Brethren of France" with a treatise on *The Conformity of the Conduct of the Church of France for reuniting the Protestants, with that of the Church of Africk for reuniting the Donatists to the Catholick Church.*[33] *For Bayle, the tawdry repetition of Augustine's jaundiced sentiments was a picture of what theological reasoning had come to be: an exercise in making God and the Bible serve us, not the other way round. To extract a rationale for "smiting, imprisoning, kidnapping, and putting to death"*[34] *from an invitation to a party was a savage indictment of the theological mind.*

It infuriated Bayle that Augustine could use the sacred image of a "Shepherd" to justify measures that could result in the death of one of the sheep. It baffled him that Augustine could cite the "Violence [with which] Saul was forc'd by Jesus Christ to acknowledge and embrace the Truth," as some sort of template for persecution when Saul's conversion was, first, not an act of violence in the ordinary sense and, second, not something that could be tried at home. God looked on the heart, not conformity to an institution, Bayle insisted. To force hearts into unwilling cooperation was a violation of conscience and the voluntary principle of the gospel. Bayle showed how each of Augustine's examples fell apart on these grounds, travestying the freedom announced in the New Testament. He differentiated the theocratic prerogatives of the Old Testament from the spiritual demands placed upon the Christian. To defend coercion was to plead ignorance of God's character, the nature of faith, and the plain word of the Bible. The dissonance between the savagery of persecution and the "Character of Jesus Christ," whose "reigning Qualitys" were "Humility, Meekness, and Patience" was of the kind that a small child could appreciate. Christ demanded no more than a "voluntary Obedience," he disdained force, he praised *"the Meek, and the Peace-makers, and the Merciful,"* and he blessed his persecutors, going to his death like a "Lamb led to the slaughter."[35] But the grown-ups knew better, and the consequences were disastrous.

The "Cruelty" and "tyrannical Insolence" perpetrated in Christ's name cast fresh doubt upon the "Christian Religion," Bayle observed, bringing shame on its "adorable Founder." The link between persecution and unbelief was undeniable and, Bayle suggested, perhaps necessary. It is no wonder, he noted, that "the Age we live in is full of Free-Thinkers and Deists." It is no surprise that persecutions, "drenching" the world in "cruelties" have fomented horror, distrust, and contempt for religion, sowing "perhaps some Seeds of Atheism." "We can't stop the mouths of Infidels, or hinder their charging Christianity with these things," Bayle warned, "since they may find 'em in our Historys." And though "the Church of Rome" held the "whip-hand for so many Ages past," Protestants were now deep in the mire. Bayle drew a comparison between the rights of "the Sects which have separated" from Rome and the "Reproaches" of "Infidels" against Christianity. We have brought it on ourselves, he concluded, and the future was bleak. To acquit "our Religion at the expence of its Professors," was an almost impossible task. For Christians and Christianity were inseparable. Bayle speculated that the natives of China or Japan would do better, under God, to resist a Christian religion "stain'd with Blood" than subscribe to a blackened orthodoxy. But it was a point of burning conviction to Bayle that Christ should be spared association with the carnage: "if we can't save Christianity from this Infamy, at least let us save the Honor of its Founder, and of his Laws; and not say, that all this was the consequence of his express Command to compel the World."[36]

Scholars have been quick to infer from Bayle's sympathy for atheism a veiled expression of his own. It is more likely that his ability to distinguish Christ from the "Professors" of Christianity kept his faith alive. There is no evidence that he abandoned his religion. He continued to attend a Protestant church and his philosophical skepticism crackled with religious ardor. Bayle's leading biographer affirms the sincerity of his religious convictions, noting his affinities with the "Spiritualist 'left wing' of the Reformation," with its emphasis on moral rigor, intellectual humility, and "the altruism of the Gospel."[37] Bayle was no mystic but his sense of historical corruption led him to an almost mystical reverence for the purity of conscience. He was certain that the case for persecution was a tissue of sophistry but, like Spinoza, he sensed the degree to which the Bible had been disabled as an arbiter of truth. From a vigorous defense of his passage, Bayle moved to a stance of virtual resignation. Argument is futile. Truth may be known but proof is elusive. Bayle could go the distance with Augustine, responding to every sleight of hand with aquiline ferocity, but he tired of the labor. He seemed to rebuke his own erudition with a shift from disputation to moral sense, intellect to conscience. "If limits are to be assigned to speculative truths," he suggested, "I think there ought to be none in respect of the ordinary practical principles which have to do with morals." Religious ideas must be referred "to that natural conception of equity *which illumines every man that comes into the world*."[38]

This was a direct quotation from the first chapter of the fourth gospel [John 1:9]—the *locus classicus* of the spiritualist doctrine of the inner light. This "distinct and spritely Light," Bayle explained, "enlightens all Men the moment they open the Eyes of their Attention." It was the "irresistible" witness of "God himself." As Bayle continued in language redolent of the German mystics, "we can never be assur'd of the truth of any thing farther than as agreeable to that primitive and universal Light, which God diffuses in the Souls of Men, and which infallibly and irresistibly draws on their Assent the moment they lend their Attention. By this primitive and metaphysical Light we have discover'd the rightful Sense of infinite Passages of Scripture, which taken in the literal and popular Meaning of the Words had led us into the lowest Conceptions imaginable of the Deity." Conscience protected God against theology and the Bible against deathly commentary and invention:

> Shou'd a Casuist therefore come and inform us, he finds from the Scriptures, that 'tis a good and a holy Practice to curse our Enemys, and those who persecute the faithful; let's forthwith turn our Eyes on natural Religion, strengthen'd and perfected by the Gospel, and we shall see by the bright shining of this interior Truth, which speaks to our Spirits without the Sound of Words . . . that the pretended Scripture of this Casuist is only a bilious Vapor from his own Temperament and Constitution.[39]

Interior truth outshone the fading testimony of words. The heart was more reliable than the mind. As Bayle argued elsewhere: "In religious matters, the rule of judgment does not lie in the intellect but in the conscience, which means that we should accept things . . . on the grounds that our conscience tells us that in so doing we shall be doing what is agreeable to God."[40] Intellectual skepticism was thus married to moral and spiritual conviction, indeed driven by it. Bayle was no relativist.

The tone of the *Historical and Critical Dictionary* was darker than the *Philosophical Commentary*, and the iconoclasm more abrasive, as Bayle conducted a guerrilla campaign against system and all its works. The *Dictionary* has been described as the "graveyard" of intellectual systems, a dismantling of "the mental universe" of the early modern period.[41] Yet

Bayle justified his criticism as an attempt to break the rhythms of reflexive hatred and ritual hostility. The task required persistence and aggression. He aimed to show the "weak side" of every dogmatism with a view to taking it out of service. The article that landed him in the deepest trouble was what many considered his character assassination of the biblical king David. But this was no frivolous exposé. Bayle was scattering his shot under one of the hallowed vehicles of theocratic ambition: a figure claimed on both sides of the confessional divide as a model of godly violence. In puncturing David's aura of sainthood, Bayle was opposing both Catholics and fellow Huguenots, who appealed to Old Testament wars to justify violence.[42] He raked over David's adventures with the solemn insistence that if David was a man after God's own heart, it must have been for his penitence, not his sins. Yet the charges of heresy rolled in. As Voltaire later commented: Bayle was "reproached with not praising actions which were in themselves unjust, sanguinary, atrocious, contrary to good faith, or grossly offensive to decency." He was reduced "to poverty" for failing "to eulogize [David's] cruelties and crimes." "Did not Bayle perform a service to the human race when he said that God . . . has not consecrated all the crimes recorded in that history?" he wondered. The "mortal war" declared on Bayle for his article was a dismal commentary on its theme, Voltaire reflected, "while the philosopher, oppressed by them all, content[ed] himself with pitying them."[43] Bayle had more than pity for his critics, but Voltaire was right about the motives of his attack on a figure who, "by the testimony of God himself . . . was a man of blood."[44]

Voltaire sensed a suicidal dignity in the embattled skeptic, reminiscent of Samson destroying the temple of the Philistines before "sink[ing] beneath the ruin he has wrought."[45] Yet Bayle spared the New Testament his fury, he cited Paul against the vanity of philosophy and he never wrote of Christ with anything less than profound reverence. Although Hume would delight in his intellectual agility, and the atheists, Diderot and Holbach, would gorge on his anticlericalism, Bayle also provided inspiration for the heart-centered spirituality of German Pietism, becoming a favorite author for one of the movement's leaders, Count Zinzendorf. Bayle helped to fuel Zinzendorf's "rejection of rationalism, and supported his effort to base spiritual truth on religious experience rather than philosophy."[46] These were not among the ironies of history. As Voltaire will demonstrate, such a dichotomy between a "secular" and a "Christian" appropriation of Bayle is unsustainable. Bayle clung to his twin anchors of the goodness and mercy of God and the clarity of conscience. This was the essence of natural religion and the foundation of the Enlightenment critique of religious authority. Bayle's repatriation of spiritual authority from creed to conscience was another manifestation of the heart religion of the Reformation. And men of less certain spirituality shared the momentum of the transfer, fueled by the memory and experience of persecution.

In *The Heavenly City of the Eighteenth-Century Philosophers* (1932), Carl Becker gently mocked the *philosophes* as theologians in denial, "skeptics who eagerly assent to so much." Of the strange dogmatism of natural religion, Becker queried, "How comes it, we ask, that you are so well acquainted with God and his purposes?" The *philosophes* were drawing on the moral capital of a religion they were attempting to destroy. Searching for "intellectual collateral to guarantee their bright promises," they translated faith in God into faith in Nature, ever capitalized in bending reverence.[47] Becker received short shrift from later authorities, one of whom dismissed his thesis as a work of charming eccentricity, possessing "every virtue save one, the virtue of being right."[48] But Becker was right about unacknowledged moral sources, and he could have pressed his argument further.

The Heavenly City mostly sidestepped the materialism of Baron d'Holbach, whose *La Systeme de la Nature* (1770) became the manifesto of aggressive atheism, yet here was a remarkable case in point. Holbach condemned superstition for smothering "the great law of nature—which says, '*love thy neighbor as thyself.*' " He criticized sacraments for either exonerating or "fettering" the natural rhythms of "conscience." And he evinced a Spinozan contempt for theologies that torture minds with warnings of "the eternity and dreadful nature of their punishments."[49] Holbach shared the radical Protestant horror of hellfire preaching, publishing a French translation of a work by the English Baptist, Samuel Richardson, *Of the Torments of Hell* (1657). This was an "annihilationist" tract, arguing that lost souls will vanish after death rather than face an eternity of punishment.[50] In spite of his reductive metaphysics of body and matter, Holbach remained a fierce advocate of conscience.

In another work, Holbach quoted the English moralist, John Trenchard, who excoriated "religious ceremonies" as "disastrous inventions by means of which man substitutes the physical movements of his body for the honest and regulated movements of his heart."[51] Religion was an artificial constraint, violating the goodness of the heart. Salvation was found in nature and nature's law: "Come back, runaway child, come back to Nature," Holbach urged, "She will console you, she will drive from your heart the fears that confound you, the anxiety that torments you, the passions that unsettle you, the hatred that keeps you from the men you should love."[52] Holbach cited "the mild maxims of the Evangelists" against the cruelty of superstition, commending "virtue," "reason," and "truth" as nature's "assisting deities," capable of banishing "error from our mind," "wickedness from our hearts," and causing "goodness to occupy our souls."[53]

Unlike Spinoza and Bayle, Holbach really was an atheist, yet the genealogy of dissent is clearly shared. Having coined the term "anthropomorphic" to belittle the instinct to create gods in the human image, Holbach offered a "theomorphic" vision of nature. If a figure like Holbach was still trading in enemy currency, it should be no surprise that Voltaire, a fierce critic of atheist materialism, was drawing on the same resources. Becker was right to identify Voltaire as chief among the reclaimers of "the Christian story": the "apostle who fought the good fight, tireless to the end, writing seventy volumes to convey the truth that was to make us free."[54] But the recovery was more profound than the transferred zeal and prophetic tonality Becker saw in him. Voltaire was more than a fiery advocate of law, conscience, and duty: he was a preacher of grace.

The Prodigal Son: The Making of a Philosopher

François-Marie Arouet was born in 1694 and educated by Jesuits at the prestigious Collège Louis-le-Grand, between 1704 and 1711. Impressing and exasperating his teachers in equal measure, and resisting his father's disciplines, Voltaire's early life offered a glimpse of what was to come: an earnest irreverence, an unending dance between freedom and authority, a training in evasion. Voltaire always believed that he was an illegitimate child and the decision to identify himself by his bullish *nom de plume* was symbolic of an irrepressible individuality. The prospect of following his father into the law struck fear into the aspiring poet, and Voltaire duly botched the clerical assignments that stood between him and his inheritance. But it was not long before his knowledge of France's legal system was more intimate that he would have hoped, as his penchant for provocation earned a series of arrests, exiles, and the lasting suspicion of the royal court. In 1717 he spent eleven months in the Bastille for mocking the regent in verse, returning in 1726 following a humiliating dispute with an aristocrat. Agreeing to leave the country on his release, Voltaire spent a formative exile in England from 1726 to 1729, assembling his first missile against the French establishment, the *Philosophical Letters* or *Letters on the English* (1733).

If praise for a neighbor was ever going to be interpreted as an insult to the fatherland, it was here. The faux-innocence of the *Philosophical Letters* fooled no one, and Voltaire was once again packing his bags, heading to the Lorraine for a fifteen-year house arrest in the chateau de Cirey with his mistress, Émilie du Châtelet. This was a time of extraordinary productivity for Voltaire. He had been writing plays and poems for years, but he now turned to history, science, and a new genre that he essentially pioneered, the "philosophical tale." Praise for the new science had flowed in the *Philosophical Letters,* but Émilie deepened Voltaire's interest and the couple devoted themselves to the study and propagation of Newton's work. For a brief period, Voltaire looked like he had matured into a more sober intellectual, and his appointment as Royal Historiographer of France (1745) and election to the French Academy (1746) signaled his arrival in an establishment that had rejected him so harshly in 1726.

But Voltaire had lost none of his fight, even if he no longer took fencing lessons to see off his enemies. A time of crisis, following Émilie's death (1749), a disastrous period serving as philosopher-in-residence to Frederick the Great in Berlin (1750–53), and then the calamity of the Lisbon earthquake (1755), reignited Voltaire's radicalism. Admission to an establishment did nothing to arrest the rhythms of arbitrary rule, Voltaire discovered, his disappointment with Frederick heightened by the fact that here was a true man of learning, a philosopher King. And the Lisbon disaster raised questions that no grasp of physics could answer. The world was not as it ought to be, and humans had a habit of making it worse. It was here, in contemplation of the cruelty of nature and the corruption of power, that Voltaire turned "hopefully to learned Bayle," finding in Bayle's rugged skepticism a working philosophy of action and salutary doubt. "In criticism he was," wrote a modern admirer, "the direct descendant of Bayle."[55]

Bayle helped Voltaire to navigate between the old world of tradition and arbitrary authority and the new empire of reason, whose fragility was so brutally exposed by the earthquake. Voltaire's most famous work, *Candide,* radiated an abhorrence for religious violence and intolerance that had energized him since his schooldays. To this it added a pungent critique of philosophical optimism and intellectual complacency. Voltaire emerged as both the icon of Enlightenment and its leading critic, making good on his challenge that philosophy must be practical or hold its tongue. It is striking that Voltaire's most dynamic interventions against religious persecution came in the 1760s, in the wake of *Candide*'s celebrated conclusion that it is all very well to talk, but real life consists in action. Although Candide's sober ambition to "cultivate our garden" has been interpreted in terms of Stoic resignation, or an Epicurean aspiration to enjoy what is near to you and forget the rest,[56] Voltaire's startling activism, when he finally had a garden of his own at Ferney, near the safety of Geneva, casts doubt on such theories. The final two decades of his life, which produced the *Treatise on Tolerance* (1763), the *Philosophical Dictionary* (1764), and a stream of radioactive pamphlets and short stories, were definitive in terms of Voltaire's influence and status. It was as the "defender of Calas"—the persecuted Protestant family whose rehabilitation Voltaire had undertaken—that Voltaire was feted on the streets of Paris shortly before his death in 1778.[57] Diderot once said that he envied Voltaire his role in the Calas affair more than any of his literary triumphs. Voltaire was not unique in conceiving philosophy as action but he exemplified the principle, drawing on volatile reserves of moral energy and a passionate, if heterodox, theology of his own.

The standard approach has been to say that Voltaire was a deist, and deists were rationalists, drawing lessons from nature not revelation, and aiming for the most part at destruction. This is to draw a line between "Christianity" and a philosophical rival which was not always visible at the time. Most of the English deists who influenced Voltaire cited Spinoza and Bayle among their sources, and recent work on the seminal figure of John Toland has emphasized his Protestant pedigree, identifying his *Christianity not Mysterious* (1695) as a "reforming Dissenter work."[58] Toland's attack on "priestcraft" was a Protestant critique of Catholic "idolatry" extended to all ministers. He condemned the clergy not for their Christianity but their lack of it. He maintained that the clergy's pride, ambition, and spirit of "emulation," and not Christianity as such, were the "real source[s] of all those heresies, which make so bulky and black a catalogue in ecclesiastical history."[59] He defined "priestcraft" as the "design'd abuse and reverse of religion," not the logical outcome of Christian faith.[60] In *Christianity not Mysterious*, Toland aligned his theology with what he considered real Christianity, criticizing the modern urge to wrap dogma in philosophical jargon, and complaining of "those Gentlemen who love to call Names in Religion," in an attempt to isolate their enemies. He wished to "assure them, that I am neither of Paul, nor of Cephas, nor of Apollos, but of the Lord Jesus Christ alone, who is the Author and Finisher of my

Faith." "The only religious Title therefore that I shall everown," he fiercely maintained, "is that most glorious one of being a Christian."[61] If deism was heresy, it was Christian heresy.

Another deist, Thomas Chubb, produced works such as, *The Glory of Christ, The True Gospel of Jesus Christ asserted*, and *A Vindication of God's Moral Character.* Matthew Tindal quoted Jesus against an "Old Testament" psychology of persecution, noting that Christ had "rebuked" his disciples for wanting to call down fire on the ungodly.[62] Deism extended the fault line of moral criticism that runs from Castellio to Arminianism and the spiritual dissent of the seventeenth century, drawing on the biblical criticism of the Quaker, Samuel Fisher, and the "immanentist" metaphysics of the bolder English "enthusiasts."[63] The God of vengeance was judged by the God who was known in the heart and could be gleaned from Nature's revolving feast. There was grandeur in criticism: a sense of possession. There were anti-Christian writers among the deists, such as Peter Annet, but even in hostility, debts to Christian sources were constantly apparent. Voltaire drew on the anticlericalism, biblical criticism, and rhetorical aggression of the English deists, which often amounted to Bayle at one remove. And he shared the deist impulse to situate revelation in creation rather than a disputed text—an instinct that again places him within, not outside, the Christian culture.

Voltaire did not coin the "watchmaker" analogy later associated with the Anglican theologian, William Paley, but he made it his own in the struggle against the new "imposter" of atheism. "I shall always be convinced that a watch proves the existence of a watchmaker and that the universe proves the existence of a God," he wrote in his *Elements of Newton's Philosophy* (1745).[64] In 1768 he was as confident as ever that "you can be a very good philosopher and believe in God. The atheists have never answered the argument that a clock proves the existence of a clockmaker."[65] Voltaire maintained deep admiration for liberal Anglicans, such as Archbishop Tillotson, Christian philosophers such as Samuel Clarke, and above all, the Quakers. He shared the zeal of orthodox theologians for natural theology, and he had equally respectable French sources for his two guiding principles of conscience and mercy.

Long before Voltaire encountered Bayle or the deists, he completed his own apprenticeship in the dialectics of sectarianism at school and in the family home. As René Pomeau, a leading French authority on Voltaire, demonstrated, his deism was above all an "anti-Jansenism."[66] It was a protest against a hyper-Augustinian branch of Catholicism that mirrored the Arminian struggle against Calvinism in the Netherlands. Voltaire's brother, Armand, was a fierce Jansenist, and at the Collège Louis-le-Grand he was in a nursery of reaction to the vigorous sect. Some of Voltaire's teachers, such as René-Joseph Tournemine, were major theologians in their own right, forging influential responses to the austerity of Jansenism, and flouting the cultural shibboleths of the movement. The Jesuits encouraged the young Arouet in drama and poetry, and arranged for some of his work to be published.

Voltaire was in touch with some of his teachers twenty years after he left the school, approaching Tournemine when he was in need of philosophical allies on his return from England. Relations soured over divergent considerations of Newton but Pomeau insists that Voltaire, "brilliant student of the Jesuits," drew vital nutrients from his liberal Catholic education. The religious culture of the school, including the official catechism in use, manifested certain "deistic tendencies," including an impulse to reduce the gap between human and divine wisdom, felt to have been overplayed by Augustinian rivals. Pomeau writes of a certain heterodoxy germinating "within the breast of orthodoxy," even a tendency "to transform Christianity into a natural religion."[67] Heterodox or not, the Jesuit catechism emphasized mercy over judgment, free will against predestination, and the positive credentials of conscience—all central Voltairean concerns.[68]

The bravest offering on the anti-Jansenist menu was the banned work of Archbishop Fénelon—a pastoral theologian of the late seventeenth century whose mystical affinities had incurred the official censure of Rome. Fénelon's *Maximes des saints* (1697) had popularized the spirituality of Madame Guyon, who exalted inner experience over clerical authority, inviting comparisons with the Quakers. Condemned, as Voltaire later remarked, for preaching the "fatal heresy" of "pure and perfect love," Madame Guyon was imprisoned as "a person dangerous to the state"—fulfilling her own prophecy, as Voltaire dryly added, that, "All hell shall rise up to stop the progress of the inward spirit and the formation of Christ Jesus in souls."[69] Voltaire considered her an egotist and a fanatic, but his sympathy for her "Quietist" heresy over her orthodox persecutors was clear, and in Fénelon's urbane and sanitized translations, he was imbibing at least some of the Quietist spirit.

Fénelon's *Maximes* preached the priority of love over dogma, and a quality of disinterestedness imperiled by a proud and possessive orthodoxy. Love, as Voltaire later summarized Fénelon's stance, must be "neither debased by fear, nor exalted by the hope of reward." Fénelon extolled the conscience as "the voice of God" in the soul and he placed a daring emphasis on Jesus as an ordinary human distinguished by extraordinary love.[70] And perhaps most significantly for Voltaire, Fénelon insisted that God is not a "powerful judge" so much as a "tender" and compassionate "Father."[71] Voltaire struck a note of discovery when he returned to Fénelon's works in the 1760s, writing to a friend that Fénelon's doctrine of "pure love" "could render even Paris happy."[72] The "virtuous and tender Fénelon" became a much-cited "sage" in his later works. But echoes of the heretic prelate and the mystical conscience are visible throughout his career. Voltaire was the kind of student who was always learning more than he let on.

A "*Spark of Heavenly Fire*": *Voltaire's Accusing Conscience*

One thing that scholars have agreed upon is that Voltaire was a destroyer: in philosophy a skeptic; in theology an enemy of every dogma. Even Pomeau, who has done more than anyone to expose his theological debts, portrayed Voltaire's religion as an icy affair, "a de-christianized Christianity," which pleads the divine principle of tolerance but expects little in return from a cool and distant deity.[73] Voltaire can be read this way, especially in his more somber reflections following the Lisbon earthquake. But my suggestion is that there is more vigor, definition, and purpose in Voltaire's criticism than such interpretations allow. Voltaire often appears torn between a clean, de-theologized natural religion—which would end scholastic "squabbles" once and for all—and a more generous, affirmative theology, which would supply the weaknesses of conscience with gentle dogmas of its own. The two concerns run side by side, and Voltaire may be as elusive of chronological classification as Luther, but my claim is that a more positive theology of forgiveness ultimately dominates Voltaire's leaner assertions of natural law. And even when Voltaire is at his most anti-theological, or seems to be, the vigor of his religious convictions is palpable. Scholars have been too quick to equate philosophical and theological skepticism with outright unbelief. Like Bayle and Spinoza before him, Voltaire launched his volleys with the elemental poise of someone who knew that some truths are eternal.

One way to interpret this tension between natural law and positive religion is to see the first as Voltaire's doctrine of creation and the second as his doctrine of redemption—with superstition serving for him, as for Spinoza, as sin. This would account for some of the ambivalence of Voltaire's writing about conscience, combining enthusiasm and disappointment. Clearly, Lisbon was a turning point, and it is notable that Voltaire's most fulsome expression came in the *Poem on Natural Law* (1756), written shortly before the disaster. Here, Voltaire defended the divine origins of the heavenly chaperone against those who would reduce it to a social skill. As he challenged: "Did men create the sense of guilt or shame? Their soul and faculties did mortals frame?" Voltaire placed himself within a spiritualist cast of thought as he defended the divinity of conscience as a "seed of virtue" sown in "every heart" by the God to whom every person "owes" their life. The mystical pedigree was clear as Voltaire commended this "bright ethereal spark of heavenly fire," this "generous flame," as an active principle, which "makes the obstinate repent." Voltaire defined superstition as the occlusion of this sacred instinct. Why, he wondered, had this mighty principle failed to arrest "so many years" of "religious wars" and "pious rage"? The answer was theology—of a kind that invites souls to "withdraw" from "nature's law," tempting them to believe that their passions reflected God's will, and empowering them to reject ordinary morality under the princely fiction that "the Pagan virtues were but crimes at best."[74] This was a clear allusion to Augustine and signaled a central target of Voltaire's criticism.

Such theology, daring to "to damn mankind" on the authority of a capricious deity, was capable of corrupting the soul. It could turn out the lights. This was the essence of "fanaticism," the soured fruit of superstition, defined in the *Philosophical Dictionary* as "the effect of a false conscience, which makes religion subservient to the caprices of the imagination, and the excesses of the passions."[75] Voltaire's portrait of "Mahomet" as a cold-blooded killer was prefaced with the explanation that this was a man in whom "superstition had totally extinguished . . . the light of nature,"[76] a diagnosis extended to Calvin, who had "brilliant mind" and an "atrocious soul"—the two somehow linked.[77] Even when Voltaire spoke through the voice of "Nature," as in the *Treatise on Tolerance*, he retained a spiritual sense of a created good requiring protection from the perversions of theology, the passions, or any combination of the two. "I have placed in each of your hearts a seed of compassion with which to help one another through life," spoke Voltaire's Nature. "Do not smother this seed; nor must you corrupt it; for it is divine. And do not substitute the pathetic squabbles of academic dispute for the voice of nature."[78] It was in a similar spirit that Voltaire could condemn the doctrine of "Original Sin" as Christianity's "original sin."[79] The goodness of conscience reflected the goodness of creation.

The trademarks of Voltaire's heroes were openness, candor, and guileless good nature. Candide combined "true judgment with simplicity of spirit," a humble soul endowed "with the most gentle of manners." "His countenance was a true picture of his soul."[80] *Le Huron ou L'Ingenu* ("The Huron or the Ingenuous") was another adventure built around the clarifying innocence of an honest hero, a Native American whose rough candor cut through the embroidered deceptions of the old world. Superstition and theology were the corsets of virtue and the prisons of conscience. Voltaire often contrasted the purity of untutored peoples with the cynicism of what passed for Christian morality. The "savage beauty" of Alzire's heart, in Voltaire's South American drama, could be read from her countenance. Her face never "belie[d] her heart." "Dissimulation and disguise" were "European arts." "Shame," a "European phantom, Which fools mistake for virtue."[81]

When non-Christian religions exchanged conscience for social honor, however, Voltaire could be equally harsh. In *Zadig*, he set another of his "ingenuous" heroes in conversation with a widow preparing to throw herself on her husband's "funeral pile." Discovering, to his horror, that the woman actually wanted to die on her husband's ashes, Zadig slowly brought her to the admission that her real concern was for "reputation." "Zadig having forced her ingenuously to confess, that she parted with her Life more out of Regard to what the World would say of her, and out of Pride and Ostentation, than any real Love for the deceased," she changed her mind.[82] A life was preserved and the adventure continued. This was purest Voltaire.

Even in his darkest broodings on the cruelty of the universe and the inscrutability of the creator, Voltaire clung to the sacredness of human life. When the weary and disillusioned Martin described the shadows of hanged men as "horrible blots" on the world, Candide cautioned against resignation: "'They are men who make the blots,' said Candide, 'and they cannot be dispensed with.'"[83] When Martin "concluded that man was born to live either in a state of distracting inquietude or of lethargic disgust," the rebuke was again gentle but firm: "Candide did not quite agree."[84] Life went on. The philosophical skepticism that Voltaire aired in the Lisbon poem, in *Candide*, and in such idiosyncratic gems as *The Ignorant Philosopher* (1766), was sustained by an enduring humanism of sympathy and moral purpose. "I always reduce, so far as I can, my metaphysics to morality," Voltaire told Frederick, dismissing metaphysics in another letter as: "Fine names that nobody can explain, for what nobody can understand."[85] Contrary to the stereotype of an Enlightenment drunk on reason and intellectual presumption, the mood of the period was enduringly skeptical, taking down the "enchanted castles" of the seventeenth-century "romanciers," and dragging philosophy before the bar of conscience quite as often as theology. Conscience and skepticism were forces in concert.

Voltaire's wicked portrait of Pangloss, that unfeeling professor of "metaphysico-theologico-cosmolo-nigology," who could talk but never act, was a monument to what one scholar has termed the Enlightenment's "anti-intellectualism"—a beefy impatience with theory and intellectual pretension that could provoke Samuel Johnson to "refute" the idealist metaphysics of Bishop Berkley by kicking the nearest "stone,"[86] or enable the Bayle-like Martin to explain his "hard[ness] of belief" in three simple words: "I have lived."[87] Reality was in. Speculation was out—leading the same scholar to conclude that "the Enlightenment was not an Age of Reason but a Revolt against Rationalism."[88] Hume's contention that reason does not get out of bed until nudged by one of the passions was an example of a wider revolt against a bookish, unblooded intellectualism. Passions could be moral as well as physical. Voltaire's were both.

When Candide and Martin managed to discuss philosophy for "fifteen successive days," they found that "on the last of those fifteen days, they were as far advanced as on the first." And "they consoled each other."[89] Not so Pangloss ("All Tongue"), whose intellectual rigidity stiffened in the breeze of events: "I am still of my first opinion . . . for I am a philosopher and I cannot retract." Voltaire satirized his facile intellectualism with the same vigor with which he cursed the crashing bromides of optimism in the Lisbon poem—where the "Dreams of the bloodless thinker" were implicated in the loss of human life; where silence was preferred to "grim speculat[ion] on the woes of men"; where the urge to explain was condemned as another species of cruelty.

As the exhausted travelers in *Candide* arrived at their destination in Turkey, Pangloss picked out a friendly local, hoping to engage him "a little about causes and effects, about the best of all possible worlds, the origin of evil, the nature of the soul, and the pre-established harmony." "At these words, the Dervish shut the door in their faces." The reanimating decision of Martin and Candide to "work . . . without disputing" was also Voltaire's: a bruised humanism crawling out of a tunnel of hollow reasoning.[90] It was a recovery of nerve that symbolized a transfer of responsibility from mind to heart, discourse to action. This is why much of the period's criticism exudes an earthy, almost unscholarly quality.

This was especially true of Voltaire's attitude to the Bible. Like Bayle, Voltaire was more troubled by the thought of why God would choose to harden Pharaoh's heart than whether he was capable of doing so.[91] Bayle had made conscience preeminent over scripture, and morality the measure of metaphysics. "Should a thousand times as many Miracles as those of Moses and the Apostles be wrought in confirmation of a Doctrine repugnant to these universal Principles of common Sense," Bayle urged, "Man, as his Facultys are made, could not believe a tittle on it."[92] Voltaire applied the same principle, reducing questions of historicity to ethics and dismissing the divine deliverances of holy warfare as the conceit of a tribal imagination. As one scholar writes, "Voltaire's most indignant criticisms of Old Testament miracles concern their alleged immorality, as for example with Joshua 10:12–14, where God lengthens the day to give the Israelites more time to kill the Amorites."[93] There was venom in Voltaire's writing, there can be no doubt. But the ethical criterion was constantly evident, enabling him to hold fire when the Bible enjoined justice and mercy, or when love extended beyond the clan, as in the book of Ruth.

Voltaire often praised the naivety of the biblical style, and he frequently quoted from the book of Ecclesiastes (also a favorite of Spinoza's).[94] It would be hard to deny similarities between the Genesis account of Joseph and the adventures of Zadig—an open-hearted man, enslaved, accused of plotting an affair with his master's wife, and redeemed by an ability to interpret dreams, administer debt, and forgive his enemies. Voltaire's commentary on "Joseph" in the *Philosophical Dictionary* reveals a tension between an urge to historicize the Old Testament as a collection of folk tales and a desire to extract a lost message of forgiveness. Voltaire wanted to argue that the story was not unique to the Jews at the same time as distinguishing it from a sea of Arabic and classical folklore. "It is more affecting than the 'Odyssey,'" he insisted, "for a hero who pardons is more touching than one who avenges." "Almost all in it is wonderful," he continued, "and the termination exacts tears of tenderness." Joseph's capacity to "receive," "pardon," and "enrich" the brothers who sold him into slavery was a jewel within the dust of ancient fables. The Arabs had their "ingenious fictions," Voltaire granted, "but I see among them no adventures comparable to those of Joseph."[95]

Voltaire's wrath was as agile as his wit, his fury consistently uneven. His ability to praise a Joseph while excoriating a "monster" such as Joshua reflected clear priorities, and his constant search for heroes and exemplars suggested a desire to rewrite, rather than destroy, the Christian narrative. By seeking to stimulate and challenge the conscience of his readers, Voltaire was admitting the need for sources beyond the self. His affinity for a more explicit theology of redemption was not, therefore, the awkward U-turn some have held it to be. It was the acceleration of impulses always surging behind the cool visage of natural religion. The more closely Voltaire's polemicism is examined, the clearer it becomes that he was not attacking religion in the abstract but a very particular kind of superstition. Indeed to know Voltaire's enemy is in a sense to know his God. The clarity and articulacy with which he assailed Augustine, and Augustinian strains of theology, suggests that the real battle of the Enlightenment was not between natural religion and Christianity: it was between two Christianities. One reason Voltaire's de-theologized model of natural religion did not travel far without seeking theological sustenance was because there was little "natural" about it in the first place. It was another Christian protest against a flesh-cutting theology of exclusion.

Against the Tyrant God: Unmasking Superstition

Critics of Voltaire's early works quickly identified assaults on arbitrary divinity in plays such as *Oedipe* and *Mahomet* as veiled attacks on Jansenism. Voltaire's Oedipus committed crimes through no fault of his own, crying out in the final act of the drama: "Merciless gods, my crimes are your crimes." It was, as one scholar suggests, a theological statement, in which, "The Jesuit vision of a just God [was] implicitly championed in contrast to the Jansenist God of wrath and obligatory sinfulness." Voltaire set a "Jesuit morality of conscience and intention" against the fatalism of "Jansenist morality."[96] By the time he wrote the *Philosophical Dictionary*, some four decades later, subtlety was no longer the condition of dissent. Voltaire's contribution to a debate on which Christian heresy Islam most clearly resembles consisted of the blunt aspersion that "Mahomet" was neither Arian, Manichean, nor Donatist: "he was rather a Jansenist, for the foundation of his doctrine is the absolute degree of gratuitous predestination."[97]

Voltaire was gleefully enraged by the cruel and unvalorous psychology of predestination—and psychology was what he came to consider it. In a historical discussion of the sectarian hostilities that had divided France since the mid-seventeenth century, he placed full responsibility with the Jansenists, adding that their dispute with the Jesuits was based on "exactly the ground of the quarrel between the [Calvinist] Gomarists and Arminians" in the Netherlands. The malaise was all the more depressing given that Dutch "eyes" had now opened to the "atrocious" consequences of such fanaticism. And Voltaire, rarely pedantic of citation, was surgical in locating the seed of destruction: "We . . . read on page 165 [of Jansen's book *Augustinus*], 'That according to St. Augustine, Jesus Christ did not die for all men.' "[98] Jansenism was the joy of damning your brother on God's irrevocable authority. Pascal was the past master, squandering his talents on a mean and vindictive campaign against the Jesuits. It was thanks to Pascal, Voltaire claimed, that Jansenists struggled to think of Jesuits as human beings, let alone Christians.

For someone who gained a reputation for crude and indiscriminate mockery, Voltaire was remarkably precise of aim. He rarely missed an opportunity to identify the toxin of superstition with either Jansenism or Augustine himself: "A little Jansenist stands by," ran one of his poems, "St. Austin's works and saintly pride, Both equally his heart divide."[99] When the generous Huron came face-to-face with religious bigotry in a prison cell, it was inevitably the contortions of Jansenism that he had to unravel. When he finally taught Gordon, the repentant Jansenist, how to forgive a woman who had sinned, the narrator added that "the aged Gordon would have condemned her at the time he was only a Jansenist; but having attained wisdom, he esteemed her, and wept."[100]

As a young man Voltaire reflected that it would be better not to be born at all than to be predestined to hell, and the injustice of such theology never ceased to agitate him.[101] What kind of God creates in order to destroy? Such was the concern of his most virulent criticism. The *Épître* à *Uranie* ("Letter to Urania") (1722) was a poem written to a lover who had been unnerved by Voltaire's angry impieties. Casting himself as a "new Lucretius" tearing away the "blindfold" of superstition, Voltaire sought to convince her of the seriousness of his intent and the goodness of his God. The letter circulated in manuscript after

Voltaire carelessly showed it to the poet Jean-Baptiste Rousseau, who released it in retribution for a typically Voltairean insult. (Rousseau had written an "Ode to Posterity"; Voltaire said he did not think it would reach its destination.)

Voltaire had every reason to worry about where his own poem would end up. In the presumed safety of clandestine verse, he declared war on a punitive Christian orthodoxy. The God of superstition, found in the "sanctuary" of religion was, he declared, a "tyrant, whom we must hate." Voltaire sought a "father," whom he could "love," but the God of superstition was simply unlovable: a cruel master who made humans in his image, only to watch them decay; a God who invented guilt, only to invite punishment; a God who made us love pleasure, only to torment us with pain. Voltaire likened him to a craftsman despising the labor of his hands: a heartless operator, prepared to "lose us all."[102]

But, whispered the voice of tradition, what about the cross? Hadn't God relented of his fury, offering a way out of despair? No, thundered Voltaire. The cross changed nothing. The poem reaches its sharpest intensity as Voltaire condemns Christ's death as "useless!"—"*inutile*!"—for, even now, not all would be saved. The callous God of orthodoxy proposed to "plunge us back into the eternal abyss." Voltaire's fury coils around the crime of applying words like "clemency" to a theology of terror. But the tone softens as he introduces the reader to the true God, who is nothing like the God of Christianity. This reasonable deity, Voltaire urged, takes more pleasure in a "modest" Buddhist or a "charitable dervish" than a "ruthless Jansenist" or an "ambitious Pontiff." Indeed, he could be addressed directly. From talking of the tyrant God, Voltaire now prayed to the God of justice and peace, "imploring" him to "hear" his "meek and sincere voice." "My unbelief should not displease you; My heart is open to your eyes." "The unfeeling blaspheme you," Voltaire continued, but, "I, I revere you." "I am not a Christian, but it is to love you more."[103]

The final verses were addressed to the reader, assuring her that the true God is one who "consoles" and "enlightens"; a God who has "engraved" a true law of righteousness in every heart; a God to whom the heart of the just is "precious"; a God who will not visit his "undying hatred" on a soul as "naïve" and "candid" as hers. Such a God could be trusted to value justice and charity above "honors" and "homage":

> *If we can offend him, it is by our injustices,*
> *He judges us by our virtues, And not by our sacrifices.*[104]

This was Voltaire under the defiant banner of "natural law," boldly declaring that he is not a Christian and casting the choice between the God of orthodoxy and the God of Nature as a terrible either/or. Yet this was a knowing doubt and a deeply certain defiance. The true God desires justice, not sacrifice, and will one day reward it. Voltaire did a better impression of an Old Testament prophet, announcing God's will and promising relief from his "anger," than a modern-day Lucretius, denying his existence. His fury against a "pitiless" Jansenism and a power-corrupted papacy was palpably biblical, his final verses redolent of the words attributed to Jesus in the New Testament: "Go and learn what this means, 'I desire mercy, and not sacrifice.' "[105] The Christianity skewered on Voltaire's sword of justice was a theology of wrath and limited salvation. The maneuver was dashing and defiant; the weapon, another form of Christianity.

Voltaire's Christian pedigree was rarely more palpable than in the *Philosophical Letters* (1733), where he appended a blistering attack on Pascal to his gentle praise of English tolerance. Life, Voltaire protested against a figure he regarded as the supreme misanthrope, is more than a death sentence, and religion more than a set of crushing paradoxes. Humans are neither as "evil" nor as "unhappy" as Pascal contended. Voltaire accused him of turning his sectarian quarrels into a scurrilous indictment of humanity: "He writes against human nature more or less as he wrote against the Jesuits. He attributes to the essence of our nature what applies only to certain men." In setting human and divine nature so far apart, Voltaire accused Pascal of claiming "to know more about [religion] than Jesus Christ and the Apostles." Voltaire offered a double critique of Pascal's asceticism and his doctrine of salvation. The first was a protest on behalf of creation, redeeming nature from the status of a cosmic blunder; the second was a protest on behalf of God's character, relieving him from charge of tyranny. To present God as a dice-rolling tyrant, tormenting his progeny with deliberately opaque prophecies, was to praise in him what could never be praised in a person. He who had poured such righteous scorn on the God of the philosophers was guilty of a grosser travesty: he had turned God into a theologian, delighting in "obscurities of erudition"; a Lord of paradox, not love.[106]

"How can you," Voltaire barked at Pascal through the mist of mortal separation, "without blushing, admit in God, those very things for which mankind are adjudged infamous and are punished?" "If, in your system, God only came for so few people, if the small number of the elect is so terrifying, if I can do nothing at all by my own efforts, tell me, please, what interest I have in believing you?" Indeed:

> Have I not an obvious interest in being persuaded to the contrary? How can you have the effrontery to show me an infinite happiness to which hardly one in a million has the right to aspire? If you want to convince me, set about it in some other way, and don't sometimes talk to me about games of chance, wagers and heads or tails, and sometimes frighten me by the thorns you scatter on the path I want to follow and must follow. Your reasoning would only serve to make atheists were it not that the voice of the whole of nature cries out that there is a God with a strength as great as the weakness of those subtleties.[107]

The rocks were crying out. So was the Bible. Voltaire's article on "Original Sin" in the *Philosophical Dictionary* simmered with the same molten eloquence. If the "strange notion" of original sin were a true account of the human condition, Voltaire contended, marriage would be a crime and the New Testament a lie. Christ said nothing about the eternal agonies of unbaptized infants. The doctrine was the invention of Augustine, a man at once "debauched and penitent, Manichean and Christian, tolerant and persecuting—who passed his life in perpetual self-contradiction." Augustine had burdened the race with his own perversities, slandering God as a remorseful creator, and creating a religion of fear—rarely more offensive than in pitiless speculation on the eternal destiny of children. Of such, Voltaire complained, "men have now attained such a degree of superstition that I can scarcely relate it without trembling." Voltaire allowed the Jansenist theologian, Pierre Nicole, to explain in ponderous technicalities how children revealed tendencies "to concupiscence" even before the "act" of sin, and how evil resided in the "will" rather than the deed, thus provoking divine wrath. He then cut in on behalf of the putatively depraved infant: "Well said, Nicole; bravo! But, in the meantime, why am I to be damned?"[108]

For Voltaire, these were no academic disputes. This was the theology that was dividing a nation, arresting the cause of toleration, and sharpening barbarous statutes against heresy and impiety. The link between theological "misanthropy" and religious violence was clear. "The superstition that we must drive from the earth," he wrote in 1767, "is that which, making a tyrant of God, invites men to become tyrants."[109] The *Treatise on Tolerance* was similarly revealing of his basic animus: "But, in truth," he addressed the advocates of coercion, "do we know all the ways of God and the full extent of His mercy? Is it not permitted we should hope in Him as much as fear Him? Is it not sufficient to be faithful servants of the Church? Must each one of us presume to take upon himself the authority of God and decide, in His place, upon the eternal fate of our fellow men?"[110] Or as he urged more simply in a "sermon" of 1767: "I see the mercy of God where you would see only his power."[111]

One scholar has interpreted the preoccupation with mercy in Voltaire's later works as a decisive transition from firebrand to peacemaker. "Can we," she wonders, with a play on his adopted theme, "forgive Voltaire for having ceased to be Voltaire?"[112] Noting a similar transition, Pomeau emphasized the pressure of atheism from the 1760s and an almost scrambled theology of counterattack. Yet the concern for forgiveness was long-standing. What changed was Voltaire's willingness to cite figures like Fénelon and Jesus Christ as his exemplars. Like the spiritualist Christians of the seventeenth century, Voltaire developed a model of "enlightenment" that centered on religious qualities of illumination and conferred mercy. This central beam of Voltaire's project has been nervously excised from his literary estate. For a man who did not like theology, Voltaire did rather a lot of it.

The Frail Conscience and the Father God: Voltaire's Religion

I do not confound superstition and religion, my dear philosopher. . . . Superstition has always produced trouble and discord: religion maintains brotherhood, learning, and peace.

—VOLTAIRE TO M. BERTRAND, January 1764

Superstition is to religion what astrology is to astronomy, that is the very foolish daughter of a wise and intelligent mother.

—VOLTAIRE, *Treatise on Tolerance*, 1763

A stupid priest excites contempt; a bad priest inspires horror; a good priest, mild, pious, without superstition, charitable, tolerant, is one who ought to be cherished and revered.

—VOLTAIRE, *Philosophical Dictionary*, 1764

Voltaire's search for a "father" rather than a "tyrant" was more than the rhetorical flourish of the *Letter to Urania*. The idea dominated his theological writing. Voltaire's burden was not to demystify so much as to correct. His guiding authorities were the Christian "heresies" of Pelagianism, Socinianism, and Quakerism, as well as Fénelon's mysticism. "Pelagius," Voltaire contended against Augustine, denied that children could "possibly be guilty before they can even think" and he "considered God, not merely as an absolute master, *but as a parent,* who left His children at perfect liberty, and rewarded them beyond their merits, and punished them less than their faults deserved."[113]

There was esteem for conscience among Voltaire's Christian allies, but there was also a recognition of limits. And it was from such recognition that Voltaire gradually increased the theological quotient of his philosophy. Voltaire's critique of conscience preceded his falling out with Jean-Jacques Rousseau, but there can be no doubt that an insufferable rival bragging about being "intoxicated with virtue" hastened his suspicions. Voltaire admired Rousseau's *Émile* (1762), where a "profession of faith" by a "Savoyard Vicar" asserted the primacy of conscience over dogma with unsurpassed eloquence. But Rousseau the man was another matter. Voltaire sensed delusion in a sublime appeal to conscience that left a man free to behave as he wished. It was with more than personal spite that Voltaire let it be known that the author of a soaring, saintly treatise on education had surrendered all five of his own children to a Paris orphanage, never to see them again.[114] The eight-page pamphlet of 1762, entitled *Sentiment des citoyens* ("How Citizens Feel") reflected Voltaire's growing awareness of the infirmity of conscience—even, or especially, when the scaffolding of doctrine had been removed. The point was made with elegant economy in the *Philosophical Dictionary*: "There is a natural law; but it is still more natural to many people to forget it."[115]

In *Candide*, James, the gentle Anabaptist, rebuked Pangloss for denying the reality of sin. After one of Pangloss's sermons on the perfection of the natural order, James politely responded: " 'It is more likely,' said he, 'mankind have a little corrupted nature, for they were not born wolves, and they have become wolves; God has given them neither cannon of four-and-twenty pounders, nor bayonets; and yet they have made cannon and bayonets to destroy one another.' "[116] This was to resist the twin extremes of philosophic optimism and Augustinian pessimism—a balance that increasingly characterized Voltaire's own stance. Depravity was not natural or total, but it was real enough. The *Dictionary* entry for "Conscience" suggested Voltaire's ability to balance the proto-Kantian verities of the *Poem on Natural Law* with the Lockean wisdom that consciences are made, not given. Voltaire took the provocative example of David in the Old Testament, "who sometimes possessed a conscience tender and enlightened, at others hardened and dark," to suggest the fallibility of this rock of virtue. He admitted that history was littered with persecutors, assassins, and arrant debauchees who lived and died "without the slightest feeling of remorse." The problem could be demonstrated at both ends of the social scale, and Voltaire defined the task of regeneration in unapologetically religious terms: "it is judicious," he announced with homiletic grandeur, "to endeavor to awaken conscience both in mantua-makers and in monarchs." Indeed, "it is necessary to preach better than modern preachers usually do, who seldom talk effectively to either."[117]

It is true that Voltaire's pieties deepened with age and the rising threat of atheism, but even in the supposedly deistic phase, the message was strangely evangelical. Even before Voltaire developed this explicit critique of conscience, his tolerationist writings offered an implicit one. Voltaire's epic poem about Henry IV, the clement king who ended France's Wars of Religion, was one of his proudest achievements. He spent much of his time in England trying to find a publisher for it, and he even wrote an "Essay upon the civil wars in France" to highlight the cause and the work. Poring with lurid fascination over the St. Bartholomew Day Massacre, and raising its peacemaking hero to god-like status, *La Henriade*, first published in 1723 as *La Ligue, ou Henri le Grand* ("The League, or Henry the Great"), distilled Voltaire's religious concerns. The poem pleads for the Christian virtue of mercy over nature's highest offer of justice. Voltaire interrupts a fast-paced narrative to reveal the spiritual education of his hero.

Henry is described as seeking a "greater boon" than a "crown," namely, "enlightening grace." His animating conviction that "God created us, he wills all sav'd," follows a lengthy dialogue with an angel, who assures him that God's mercy is greater than his anger, and a similar conversation with a "sage" on the island of Jersey. "God," the angel informs him, can "subject" his people "without tyrannizing" them. He "is a sire who schools his sons," not the "tyrant" described "on earth." He "is always stable." Although there is a place called "hell" where the truly vicious are punished, "mankind's creator" takes no pleasure in the suffering of "the creatures of his hands." "If infinite he, it is in his rewards," the angel affirms. "Free in his gifts, to vengeance he sets bounds."[118]

When the conquering king puts the divine vision into practice, pardoning and even feeding his enemies, Voltaire describes it as the offer of "grace" to "these rebels." The defeated soldiers are "rendered to life" by Henry's "kind commands," honoring their conqueror as "the brilliant image of our God." If this was to employ New Testament language of incarnation, the description of Henry delivering food on the tips of "those lances, which had ever carried death," recalls prophetic images of "swords" turning into "plowshares" and "spears" to "pruning hooks." Voltaire turns Henry into a savior, melting the hearts of his enemies. Natural law would have justified Henry in delivering judgment, not mercy; it would not have brought peace. Throughout the poem, the concept of "enlightenment" implied spiritual illumination and gathering wisdom, sometimes incorporated into a prayer: "Enlighten, Lord, his heart, thee born to know: A master give to France, the church a son."[119] Voltaire's epic was an essay on the character of God and the preeminence of mercy over justice. With hardly a word about Jesus himself, Voltaire presented Henry as a Christ-like deliverer, the "image" of God, marshaling his people with a radiant scepter of mercy.

Alzire offered a comparable drama of terror, justice, and mercy. *Alzire ou les Americains* ("Alzire or the Americans") was written during Voltaire's house arrest at Cirey and first performed at the Comédie-Française in Paris in 1736. It was well received and it remained one of Voltaire's favorite works. It was staged many times at Ferney, and it was performed in Paris during his triumphal, and ultimately fatal, return to the city in 1778. *Alzire* has been classed alongside *Zaire, Mahomet,* and *Merope* as "one of his four dramatic masterpieces."[120] Set in Lima at the time of the Spanish conquest, the play sustains a three-way tension between a religion of fear and vengeance, an ancestral piety of natural law and just deserts, and a true religion of mercy and forgiveness. Voltaire's fiercest censures are clearly aimed at the first, the religion of vengeance represented by the implacable figure of Guzman, but his critique of a natural religion that would swing the sword of justice on its conquerors is powerful. Voltaire praises the candor and integrity of the Native Americans Alzire and her lover, Zamor. He acknowledges the superiority of their religion of reciprocity to the mendacity of a conquering Catholicism—a lust for gold disguised as faith in God. But he ultimately exposes the poverty of a religion that would either kill or die to defend its honor. Prefaced with Alexander Pope's phrase, "To err is human, to forgive divine," *Alzire* concludes with a laying down of arms and a moving scene of reconciliation.

The action starts with the aging governor of the colony, Alvarez, offering advice to his son, Guzman, as he hands over power. As if to repent of his part in the conquest, Alvarez admits that he had for "too long" "neglected" the God in whose name the American land had been taken. He now understood the superiority of clemency to arbitrary power, and he wished his son to continue accordingly. Having been spared death by a magnanimous native, Alvarez had learnt the wisdom of restraint and the necessity of generosity. Guzman was to do likewise. Guzman, however, rejects his father's advice. He warns his father that "power" is "lost by mildness." Only "severity" ensures "obedience." The natives must be made to "tremble" at their conquerors, forced to "embrace our faith" and to submit to the "one God." Alvarez is dismayed by his son's arrogance and his dullness to the consequences of these "tyrant maxims." A religion that brings nothing of "heaven but its thunder," which serves "a God of peace with war and slaughter," can only foment hatred and rebellion. Alvarez reminds Guzman that he owes his life to these "wild barbarians," whose virtues exceeded their own:

> *In short, I blush to own it, we alone*
> *Are the barbarians here: the simple savage,*
> *Though fierce by nature, is in courage equal,*
> *In goodness our superior. O my Guzman,*
> *Had he, like us, been prodigal of blood,*
> *Had he not felt the throbs of tender pity,*
> *Alvarez had not lived to speak his virtues*

Hearts that are "oppressed," Alvarez reasons, are "never conquered." And God is not honored by force. The "true God, my son, The God of Christians is a God of mercy."[121]

Alvarez's reign of mercy had mollified some of the natives, whose leader, Montezuma, gave his daughter, Alzire, to marry Guzman. Alzire, however, was in love with the leader of the resistance to the Spanish conquerors, the wild-hearted Zamor. Presuming Zamor to be dead after a long absence, however, Alzire reluctantly consented to the marriage, before suffering the shock of Zamor's return. Zamor was a noble character, and it was he who had spared Alvarez's life many years before. But he now had renewed cause to avenge the blood of his people with that of the "proud Guzman." Following a series of threats, Zamor mortally wounded Guzman, before handing himself over to Alvarez to be killed, having completed his work of revenge.

In the face of death, however, Guzman experienced a change of heart. Before the attack, he had refused his father's request to pardon Zamor for his insults. With similar pride, Zamor had disdained a tactical conversion to Christianity that would have saved his life at that point. But with Guzman dying, and Zamor facing death for the attack, the folly of vengeance and the wisdom of mercy slowly dawned. In the hour of death, the "mask" of Guzman's bloodstained piety came off. With fading power of body, he finally summoned the courage to "imitate Alvarez," whose love had been unswerving throughout. The Christian conqueror finally converted to the faith he had hitherto sullied:

O my father,
The mask is off, death has at last unveiled
The hideous scene, and showed me to myself;
New light breaks in on my astonished soul:
O I have been a proud, ungrateful being,
And trampled on my fellow-creatures: heaven
Avenges earth: my life can never atone
For half the blood I've shed: prosperity
Had blinded Guzman, death's benignant hand
Restores my sight; I thank the instrument
Employed by heaven to make me what I am.

Guzman's speech did not end with his conversion, however. As "light" broke in on his "astonished soul," he found the power to forgive his adversary and to pardon his crime:

A penitent: I yet am master here;
And yet can pardon: Zamor, I forgive thee,
Live and be free; but O remember how
A Christian acted, how a Christian died.[122]

Zamor, whose refusal to "worship deities . . . bathed in our own blood" had hitherto sealed his loathing of the Christian God, was overwhelmed by his enemy's change of heart. As Guzman not only pardoned him, but entrusted Alzire to his care, with the words, "live and hate me not," Zamor—"Amazed, confounded"—fell at his feet and announced his own conversion to Christianity.

By heaven; the Christian's law must be divine:
Friendship, and faith, and constancy I knew
Already; but this soars above them all:
I must indeed admire and love thee, Guzman.[123]

Earlier, when a pragmatic conversion would have saved him, Alzire had directed Zamor to "hear the voice of conscience; act as she alone directs thee." Under such a dispensation, Zamor had proudly refused to convert—conscience and honor uniting against the humiliation of bowing to a foreign god. You "scorn our proferred mercy," Alvarez lamented, as Zamor elected to "die with honor." When it finally occurred, Zamor's conversion was presented as liberation from pride and honor, triggered by Guzman's act of mercy. Guzman also pardoned his estranged wife, Alzire, who had never loved him: "I cannot see thee weep and not forgive thee." Hearts are not conquered by force, Alvarez had said all along, though it took the sacrificial death of Guzman to prove it. The play concludes with Alvarez turning to Alzire's father, Montezuma, with a somber reflection on the costs of mercy:

I see the hand of God in all our woes,
And humbly bend myself before that power
Who wounds to heal, and strikes but to forgive.[124]

"We may smile," writes one biographer, at Voltaire's "guileful, politic attempt to present himself as the truest of Christians." But as the same scholar acknowledges, Voltaire attached unusual importance to the play, endorsing its message in a "heartfelt, sincere, and uncharacteristically personal" preface.[125] Voltaire claimed that *Alzire* was written "with a view of showing how far superior the spirit of true religion is to the light of nature."[126] And audiences took it seriously. Rousseau was reduced to tears when he saw the play in Grenoble in 1737. If it was written for the censors, it assumed a strange method of appeasement, accusing the Catholic Church of tyranny, cruelty, and avarice under the pretense of civilizing the New World. Voltaire did not pull his punches. He may not have realized how closely he was reconstructing the central event of Christianity with his drama of a dying son forgiving his enemies, or how theological the characterization of Alvarez felt—described by Montezuma as "a god, Sent down from heaven to soften this rude world, And bless mankind."[127] But the

Christian vigor of the play was unmistakable. It was again the condition of "enlightenment." Having made peace with Alvarez, Montezuma praised him as the revealer of the "will of heaven," whose "gentle manners" had

> *Enlightened our dark minds; what mighty Spain*
> *Unconquered left, thy virtue has subdued:*
> *Thy cruel countrymen's remorseless rage*
> *Had rendered even thy God detestable,*
> *But that in thee His great perfections shine,*
> *His goodness, and His mercy; in thy heart*
> *We trace his image . . .*

This was the essence of Voltaire's religion: the God of mercy defeating the idolatry of power and conquest. Alzire's grievance against a European God who stood as "the partial parent of one world, And tyrant o'er another," was assuaged, and by action not words. Alvarez prayed that God would "enlighten and preserve" "this new world" and he exposed the fragility of natural religion—a Eurocentric formula, no doubt, yet a potently Christian one.[128] The deist was behaving like an evangelist.

Voltaire's preference for the more affirmative term of "theism" was partly a response to the "poison" of atheism, which was apparently spreading in the 1740s and 1750s. It also enabled Voltaire to situate his philosophy within what he considered the warmer strains of Christian faith. Contact with English Quakers and a number of Socinian ministers in Geneva supplied more than rhetoric. Ideas flowed in both directions. Scholars often dismiss Voltaire's theism with the assurance that "we are no longer really speaking of the Christian God,"[129] but Voltaire refused the distinction, castigating fanaticism as corruption and sacrilege rather than the worship of another deity. When Zamor protested that the God of Alvarez could not also be the God of the "cruel tyrants," Alvarez responded in terms that crystallize Voltaire's stance: "It is the same, my son, But they offend him, they disgrace his name."[130] Voltaire refused to put clear water between fanaticism and true religion by identifying them with different Gods. His war cry of "*Écrasez l'Infâme!*" ("Crush the Infamous!"), was aimed at a persecuting orthodoxy not Christianity per se. He continued to portray enlightenment in terms of conversion, a change of heart. Criticism was repair and recovery—almost a religious act in itself.

This was even true of his critique of miracles. Against elaborate theories of multiple providences, proposed by figures such as Nicolas

Malebranche, Voltaire offered the Spinozan retort that God can be nothing but fair. If a wolf happens to find a lamb for his supper, "while another is dying with hunger," this was not because "God has given the first wolf a particular grace." In the *Dictionary* article on "Grace," Voltaire accused orthodox theologians of succumbing to a paganism of insecurity and cringing fear. He likened them to "the combatants in Homer, who believed that the gods were sometimes armed for and sometimes against them." "Reverend fathers," he playfully admonished, "you are terrible genii; we foolishly thought that the Eternal Being never conducted Himself by particular laws like vile human beings, but by general laws, eternal like Himself. No one among us ever imagined that God was like a senseless master, who gives an estate to one slave and refuses food to another; who orders one with a broken arm to knead a loaf, and a cripple to be his courier." "The universal theologian, that is to say, the true philosopher," he continued, "sees that it is contradictory for nature to act on particular or single views."[131] This was not naturalism. It was theology.

It was in such a spirit that Voltaire could claim "the great philosophers, Penn and Locke" as stout and worthy allies, despite some obvious and substantial differences.[132] And perhaps most strikingly, he was prepared to change his mind about some of the seventeenth-century "romanciers," roundly mocked in his earlier work, including the long-maligned Spinoza. Voltaire concluded that Bayle had been wrong to infer atheism from Spinoza's brave philosophy of immanence. Spinoza, he now suggested, was a saintly antidote to the hollow cult of atheism. In the *Dictionary* entry for "God," Voltaire repented of his prejudices and condemned the "multitude of those who cry out against Spinoza, without ever having read him." He quoted Spinoza's "profession of faith" with excited approval. A true love of God, "received, not by the relation or intervention of other men, but immediately from Him," was no menace to the state, Spinoza had insisted, though it put an end to superstitious ceremonies designed to buttress clerical power. This "love of God," Spinoza had written, "banishes fear, uneasiness, distrust, and all the effects of a vulgar or interested love. It informs me that this is a good which I cannot lose, and which I possess the more fully, as I know and love it." "Are these the words of the virtuous and tender Fénelon," Voltaire finally interjected, "or those of Spinoza?"[133] The Christian mystic and the Moses of freethinkers were kindred spirits. And it is notable that both had affinities with those admirable "Primitives called Quakers."[134]

Voltaire devoted the first four of the *Philosophical Letters* to the Quakers, more than all of the other sects put together. He was charmed by the rugged candor of the "Friends," cringing, by comparison, at his own habits of bowing and spluttering "feeble compliments" to new acquaintances. The Quakers will look you in the eye, tell you the truth, and never raise their hats in courtly deference. They were eccentric of creed and spirituality, but they possessed the priceless gift of liberation from the worship of human grandeur. They practiced what they preached, refusing to bear grudges even in sustained persecution. The Quakers "say *thou* to kings and cobblers alike, never bow to anybody, [and have] nothing but charity towards men and respect for the laws." Finding their faith in deed not word, they stood apart from the vanity of religion, especially those ritual desecrations of a gospel of peace that marked the nation's military victories. As one of the Quakers explained, "we groan in silence over the murders that cause this public rejoicing."[135]

Voltaire's commentary on the "miracles" that followed George Fox's arrest was suitably skeptical, as was his account of the "trembling" from which the sect acquired its name, but it was indicative of his priorities that Quaker virtues eclipsed the oddities of their piety. Among the Christian settlers in America, the Quakers were distinguished by the charity and tolerance extended to native peoples, gaining respect to the degree that "the other Christian conquerors and destroyers of America" inspired "hatred." The "illustrious William Penn" was, for Voltaire, an unambiguously great man, whose government of Pennsylvania presented "a really novel spectacle: a ruler whom everyone addressed as *thou*, to whom they spoke wearing their hats, a government without priests, a people without weapons, citizens all equal . . . and neighbors without jealousy." These "peaceful Quakers" were, Voltaire claimed, "loved" by the natives of the country.[136]

These were Voltaire's reflections of the 1720s and 1730s. In the *Dictionary* article on "Church," written nearly forty years later, Voltaire juxtaposed hoary indictments of a power-corrupted priesthood with stirring praise for the Quakers as a remnant of Christianity's original virtue: "Jesus Christ had baptized none. The associates of Penn declined baptism." "Charity was in high esteem with the disciples of the Saviour; those of Penn formed a common purse for assisting the poor." Whatever their errors, these "imitators" of the "first Christians" represented "an astonishing model of order and morals to every other society of Christians," Voltaire urged. He also wrote of an American sect that had broken off from the Quakers, a society that "rejects the doctrine of original sin as impious, and that of the eternity of punishment as barbarous"; a society not without foibles of biblical interpretation but, in spite of such errors, "the most just and most inimitable of men."[137]

"I will tell you," he once wrote to a friend, "that I love the Quakers." He claimed in the same letter that, if he could have endured the seasickness, he would have settled in Pennsylvania for "the rest of my career."[138] The Quakers were more than a foil for Voltaire's anticlericalism, and when the new "imposter" of atheism was at its most threatening, it was to the enlightened spirituality of the Friends that Voltaire turned for the definitive expression of his theology of peace and mercy.

The hero of *La Histoire de Jenni, ou Le Sage et l'Athée* (1775) ("The History of Johnny, or the Sage and the Atheist") was a man of boundless energy, patience, and charity, introduced with inspired subtlety as "Freind." Confusingly cast as an Anglican clergyman and a member of the British Parliament, Freind was also described as a Quaker and the grandson of William Penn in Voltaire's improbable, didactic romp. Voltaire again presented a philosophy of tolerance and a theology of forgiveness as two sides of the same coin, with a polemical alignment of Augustinian misanthropy and Holbachian atheism as mutually sustaining follies. A savage orthodoxy, Voltaire had long argued, is an invitation to atheism. But atheism is no refuge. Voltaire's tract is an attempt to reclaim the Enlightenment for the right kind of religion. An early scene sees "our worthy philosopher Freind . . . enlightening the priests of Barcelona," having rushed over to Spain to rescue his son, Johnny, from a perilous encounter with the Inquisition.[139] Enlightenment is once again spiritual—only this time a double rescue from the errant relations of superstition and atheism. Voltaire may have written one of the finest pieces of religious apologetics of the eighteenth century.

If Zadig invited comparisons with Joseph, the adventures of the dissolute young Johnny bring a New Testament parallel to mind. A son travels to Spain, racks up enormous debts, assaults his creditor, fumbles through a series of unsuitable liaisons and finally flees to America in the company of an adulterous woman ("Mrs. Clive-Hart") and an atheist friend ("Birton"). Freind, Johnny's long-suffering father, goes in pursuit of his son, releasing him from the Spanish Inquisition, paying off his debts, and finally boarding a boat to America with the aim to "Restore my only son . . . or bury myself with him." When Johnny is finally brought to a tearful repentance and a moving reconciliation with his father, he chooses to marry the demure love of his youth, and the story ends with a joyous wedding. Even Birton, now a humbled believer, joined the festivities: "The worthy Freind was as a father to all."[140]

Although interviews with Spanish bachelors of theology and journeys under vaulted skies afford ample scope for Voltairean homiletics, Johnny's restoration is effected primarily by his father's example. Freind constantly resists the temptation to lecture, cajole, or threaten his son, believing this would drive him further into his transgressions. If the policy of tireless affirmation has an air of unreality, Freind's sacrifices give the narrative substance. His kindness is unceasing, yet shown to be anything but cheap. Johnny's repentance springs from an awareness of the depth of his father's love. The poverty of conscience without the stimulus of forgiveness and exemplary action is suggested throughout the narrative, especially during the American leg of the adventure.

Freind's entrée to the New World was eased by his status as Penn's grandson, enabling him to engage in spirited conversation with a Native Indian, whose daughter Johnny had led astray. This gave Voltaire an opportunity to preach a familiar sermon on the wickedness of the European invaders (minus the Quakers), and to praise the natural religion of the natives, as far as it went. Quizzed by Freind about his piety, the Native American gave perhaps the neatest summary of natural religion ever expressed: "'My God is there,' and he pointed to heaven. 'My law is here,' and he put his hand on his breast."[141] Freind admired the statement but a discussion of the justice of killing Mrs. Clive-Hart, who died in the scramble to recover the chief's daughter, revealed important tensions. Clive-Hart had shot at one of the natives while his back was turned, so they killed her. Why, asked Freind's companion? "Because we are just," replied the chief. "Every one should be treated according to his desert." Freind was moved to disagree, urging that such licensed retribution, and the custom of "burning captives," was "execrable" and "inspired a ferocity destructive to the human race." It served Freind's cause that the atheist Birton chipped in with some extenuating thoughts on cannibalism, defending the custom of "boiling and roasting a neighbor" on impeccable materialist grounds. No one listened. Freind finally convinced the Native Americans to desist from capital punishment: "They all swore by their great Manitou, that they would not burn men and women again." The narrator described it as a victory greater than all the "miracles" performed by the Jesuits in the New World.[142]

The degree to which Voltaire made Christianity speak to the book's assembled errors of persecutory Catholicism, bacchanalian hedonism, Holbachian atheism, and deistic natural religion, was constantly evident—in the plundering of the biblical account of the "Prodigal Son" and in Freind's explicit affirmations. In the hilarious "dialogue of the 'Buts,'" in which every statement by Freind was met with a belligerent "but" from the Spanish Bachelor of Theology, Voltaire took up a series of Lutheran objections to a philosophy-intoxicated and flesh-denying Catholicism. When the Bachelor sniffs heresy in Freind's aversion to eternal punishment, Freind responds: "It does not become me to limit the compassion or the justice of God." "I believe with Jesus Christ that we ought to love God and our neighbor, forgive our enemies, and do good for evil. These are the maxims of Jesus." Freind's ability to "keep his temper" throughout the goading dispute was central to the apologetic, winning the praise of observers. When his companion explained that he was from a tolerant and undogmatic sect known as the Quakers, it seemed to the astonished Spaniard "like another universe." "And," Voltaire added, "he was right."[143]

Voltaire saved his loftiest thoughts for Freind's donnish exchange with Birton on the journey back to England. Birton, reproved by the narrator for "having the turn of mind that mistakes probabilities for demonstrations," was treated with more patience by Freind, who winsomely commended the argument for design as the party sailed under "spangled" skies. The meat of Birton's dissent revolved around the problem of evil, however, and Freind did not shrink from the challenge. The tone intensified as Freind staged a bold defense of a providential universe. The world does contain suffering, but not without limit, and most of humanity's ills are "brought on ourselves." For "men are perverse, and make a detestable use of the liberty that God has given and ought to have given,—that is, the power of exercising their wills, without which they would be simple machines." Epidemics that depopulated North America were unleashed by European settlers. When Birton quoted Augustine on the ubiquity of earthquakes and other torments, Voltaire used Freind to settle some familiar scores with the "African rhetorician" who was so "prodigal of exaggerations." Natural disasters are not the natural order of the world. There are blessings as well as curses within the short span of life. Augustine "wrote of earthquakes as he did of the efficacy of grace, and the damnation of children dying without baptism," Freind warned: with gross error and excess.[144]

Suffering could not be ignored, but it could not be treated as the normal human condition, Freind maintained. Taken as a whole, nature's bounties pointed to a generous God: "a compassionate father," not a heartless "tyrant." And human history, checkered apprenticeship though it might be, offered glimmers of light. "If there be crime in the world," Freind pleaded, "there is virtue as well." If there have been episodes of shame, from the "the abominations of Christians in Mexico and Peru" to the St. Bartholomew Massacre in France, had there not been "people who have always held in abhorrence the shedding of blood?" If history has been a sequence of wars, have there not been people such as those "whom they attempt in vain to ridicule by the name of Quakers . . . who have always hated war?" Are there not places, such as "the Carolinas, where the great Locke dictated laws," where "all citizens are equal; all consciences are free; all religions good; provided they worship God"? God should not be on trial for human crimes. For, "He lets the sun shine on the evil and the good." Voltaire was quoting from the Sermon on the Mount.

Although the scales of terrestrial justice were ever fallible, Freind continued, there was a higher court of appeal. All "just spirits," he insisted, "will be happy one day; if they are not so now." "Happy! How? When? Who told you so?" spluttered the young materialist. Freind's reply was cool and brief: "His justice." The principle of equity that stirs in every human heart was planted by God. The "voice of conscience" was a signal of God's existence. Belief was as natural as breathing. Freshly apprised of his own transgressions, Birton finally agreed. When he apologized to Freind for "speaking lightly of virtue," the homage was gently parried: "Rather apologize to the Supreme Being, who can reward and punish eternally," urged the humble sage.[145] Yet all was forgiven.

Freind's willingness to quote figures like Epictetus, Marcus Aurelius, and Cicero alongside Jesus raises the question of competing influences. Some have interpreted Voltaire's moralism as Stoicism with a sprinkling of Christian terminology, or even a mixture of Stoicism and Epicureanism: a cool resignation to the world as it is.[146] A famous study of the Enlightenment summarized the movement as "a volatile mixture of classicism, impiety, and science; the *philosophes*, in a phrase, were modern pagans." Chief among them was Voltaire. "While there might have been some doubt about the purity of Montesquieu's paganism," assured the author, "there could be none about Voltaire's."[147] A leading biographer and influential editor of Voltaire's works offered the summary "conclusion that Voltaire was at most an agnostic." And, he added, "were any tough-minded philosopher to maintain that this type of agnosticism is indistinguishable from atheism, I would not be prepared to contradict him."[148] Yet there must be doubts about Voltaire's "paganism," and suspicion toward any attempt to reinvent him as an atheist. Such verdicts reveal little more than the power of modern thought to remake the past in its own image. "History," Voltaire once quipped, "is after all only a pack of tricks we play on the dead."[149] His "atheism" is a case in point. Voltaire's moralism was too dynamic to be reducible to science, classicism, or impiety. Johnny, Birton, Guzman, Zamor, the Jansenist Gordon in *The Huron*—to take a handful of examples—were all souls in need of transformation. This was achieved through a fresh apprehension of God, revealed in the goodness of true believers. Conscience was not enough.

Voltaire's heroes, including Henry, Alvarez, and Freind, were active spirits some way from the Stoic virtue of "apatheia" (the freedom from all passions) or the Epicurean quality of "ataraxia" (tranquility). In the *Letter to Urania*, Voltaire cast himself as a "new Lucretius," tearing off the blindfold of superstition, but this was as far as the parallel went. In *De Rerum Natura*, Lucretius characterized happiness as a person's ability to observe a storm-tossed ship or a fierce battle from a distant "fortress of indifference."[150] Voltaire's problem was that he was incapable of indifference. John Morley, a nineteenth-century agnostic and an admirer of Voltaire, suggested that he bowdlerized his classical sources, turning figures like Cicero into exemplary monotheists when they were anything but uncomplicated forerunners.[151]

Voltaire's humanism was too mindful of the single life to be at one with a Stoicism that could commend the spectacle of gladiatorial violence as a lesson in how to treat death with "contempt," to take an example from Cicero.[152] Ludwig Feuerbach identified a profound cleavage in Western thought between a Christian culture that valued the individual as bearing the image of God and a "heathen philosophy" that "subordinated the part to the whole." He quoted a letter from the Roman orator Sulpicius to Cicero, chiding him for grieving over the loss of his daughter: "Great, renowned cities and empires have passed away, and thou behavest thus at the death of an *homunculus*, a little human being! Where is thy philosophy?"[153] The letter shows that Cicero was not immune to grief or compassion, at least for a family member, but it also suggests the gulf that separated classical antiquity from a Christian world that Voltaire invariably attacked for failing to honor its principles, not for the principles themselves. If Feuerbach was right about a fundamental difference between classical and Christian "anthropologies" (theories of the human person), Voltaire was on the Christian side of the fence. Voltaire was an eclectic thinker who drew on many sources, but in works like *Le Henriade, Alzire,* and *Jenni,* it is a liberalized Christianity of compassion and mercy that wins out. Hannah Arendt suggested that Christianity all but invented the concept of forgiveness in western thought. "The Discoverer of the role of forgiveness in the realm of human affairs," she wrote in the shadow of twentieth-century totalitarianism, "was Jesus of Nazareth."[154] Even before Voltaire rediscovered Fénelon, his writing suggested the same insight. Voltaire dramatized the sterile reciprocities of natural law: the incapacity of even enlightened philosophies of justice to break cycles of violence and recrimination. Voltaire did not believe that the forces of good and evil could be left to reach their own "equilibrium." He was an unconvincing Stoic.

What is even clearer is that Voltaire was no Epicurean, reducing life to soulless matter and committing himself to a path of studied insensibility. In the *Poem on the Lisbon Disaster,* he raged against the Epicurean conception of human nature as a "temporary blend of blood and dust," "put together only to dissolve." When Voltaire turned "hopefully to learned Bayle" as an example of faith without certainty, hope without optimism, it was because the Epicurean alternative to a glib and heartless providentialism horrified him. He felt the tug of a brutal and honest demystification, calling the world as it is, but he could not give up on providence, or the sanctity of human life:

Tormented atoms in a bed of mud,
Devoured by death, a mockery of fate.
But thinking atoms, whose far-seeing eyes,
Guided by thought, have measured the faint stars,
Our being mingles with the infinite . . .[155]

The squinting mystic rose up from the dungeon of despair. The temptation of atheism was held at bay. In *Jenni,* superstition, atheism, and hedonism were exposed as kindred contagions. Theologies of cruelty, persecution, and blind fate will foment unbelief, and unbelief will decimate virtue. Augustine and Holbach are cousins. But William Penn, the hope of the new world, sailed between the errors of both. As Voltaire wrote to a friend, having completed his crowning apologetic: "I have always regarded atheists as impudent sophists; I have said it, I have printed it. The author of *Jenni* cannot be suspected of thinking as Epicurus."[156] It can be no surprise that he came to a new evaluation of a man kept in the shadows of his earlier works: Jesus Christ.

The Man of Peace: Voltaire's Christ

Voltaire's attitude toward Jesus is one of the enigmas of his life and work. In the *Letter to Urania,* he wrote of the "insult" of the incarnation and the futility of the cross. In the *Philosophical Letters,* he made unflattering analogies between George Fox's ability to conjure a new religion from the spurious vapor of miracle and Christ's. And in the "Sermon of the Fifty" (1752), another clandestine document, he ridiculed the idea of a God dying "on a gibbet," adding that "Josephus [was] too serious an historian to mention such a man" as Jesus.[157] On other occasions, he wrote with warmth, blaming the paradoxes of orthodox Christology on a Platonic ambush of early Christendom. Gradually, however, affirmation and praise eclipsed criticism and ridicule. By the late 1760s, Voltaire was extolling Christ as the purest theist: he worshipped God, forgave his enemies, served the poor and unmasked the sins of priesthood with unrivalled penetration. Voltaire had always needed models, and like Spinoza, he started to argue that the special status of Christ was consistent with a belief in divine equity. As he wrote in a sermon "On Superstition" in 1767: "It does not offend our good sense that he has chosen to link one man more closely to himself than others; that he has made him a model of reason or virtue. No one can deny that it is possible for God to shower his finest gifts on one of his works." God had given Jesus "more light, and more talents than any other." Jesus was no deity, Voltaire maintained, but he possessed rare and perhaps unique "light."[158]

Such statements started to flow from Voltaire's pen. The first time he wrote of Jesus with real enthusiasm seems to have been the *Dialogue du douteur et de l'adorateur,* (1763) ("Dialogue of a Doubter and an Adorer"), where he praised the "beautiful maxims" of the Sermon on the Mount, especially the phrase, "Blessed are the poor in spirit." He lamented the "corruption" of the "simple and natural religion of Jesus," which was a law of love: "This is," he insisted, "the eternal law of all men, and it is mine: this is how I am a friend of Jesus; this is how I am a Christian. If someone has been an adorer of God, an enemy of false priests, persecuted by scoundrels, I unite myself to him, I am his brother."[159] Voltaire expressed irritation with the sort of trivializing critiques in which he had formerly indulged. An English deist had ridiculed the story of Jesus healing the ear of the soldier in the garden of Gethsemane. At least, Voltaire responded, the story showed Jesus to be a man of peace.[160]

In *Dieu et les hommes* (1769) ("God and Man"), a sweeping critique of revealed religion, Voltaire went out of his way to defend the character of Christ: "The greatest enemies of Jesus must admit that he possessed very rare qualities to attract disciples," he volunteered. Jesus had an "energy," a "force," and a "tenderness" that defied classification.[161] Voltaire often combined criticism of the gospel narratives with stirring defense of Christ's moral teaching and personal bearing.[162] He always admired the story of the Good Samaritan, where the orthodox "priests" are shown to be perfect barbarians, while the charitable "heretic" and layman emerges as the true "man of God." "Voilà la doctrine, voilà la morale de Jesus, voilà sa religion," Voltaire concluded.[163]

While he was campaigning on behalf of two Protestant families, both of whom had suffered cruel miscarriages of justice, someone criticized Voltaire for stirring up controversy, urging him to "let the dead bury their dead." Voltaire's response was swift and indignant: "I found an Israelite in the desert—an Israelite covered in blood; suffer me to pour a little wine and oil into his wounds. You are the Levite, leave me to play the Samaritan."[164] Such allusions abounded, as Voltaire appeared to repent of insults past. In the *Profession de foi des théistes* (1768), ("The Theists' Profession of Faith") he extolled Christ as a moral icon: "We never talk about Jesus, whom we call the Christ, with derision, with contempt," he insisted. "On the contrary, we regard him as a man distinguished among men for his zeal, his virtue, for his love of brotherly equality." His exhortations were occasionally "rash," but he was a true "reformer" who fell "victim to fanatical persecutors."[165]

Voltaire followed Bayle in structuring his case for toleration around the words and example of Jesus, offering a mercifully briefer commentary on those much abused words of Luke's gospel: "compel them to enter." Voltaire offered a damning contrast between an Augustine who, "having once preached charity and benevolence, then turned to advocate persecution," and a sublimely consistent Christ.[166] Christ was one who "forgives the sinners," who offers no fiercer censure to the woman taken in adultery than the command that "she be faithful in future." He was a kind and genial spirit who "even indulges harmless enjoyment." Voltaire cited his favorite New Testament passages to affirm that Christ was a man of "patience, gentleness and forgiveness." When Jesus spoke about God it was in terms that no healthy mind could disdain: "Witness the father who welcomes back the prodigal son; the laborer who arrives at the last moment but is paid the same as the others; the good Samaritan." Jesus, Voltaire continued, commanded Peter to put away his sword in the garden, and he reprimanded the sons of Zebedee for wishing to call down fire on men who had done nothing more than insult them.[167] He was a defuser of mistaken zeal and a revealer of self-serving fanaticism, though it cost him dearly. For exposing the Pharisees as "blind guides, which strain at a gnat and swallow a camel" and "clean the outside of the cup," Jesus paid with his life.[168] But even in death, he "asked his Father to forgive his enemies."[169]

As Jacques Derrida noted in a late essay, Voltaire did not commend tolerance as common sense or ordinary knowledge but as a distinctly Christian prerogative. Voltaire's "lesson of tolerance" was "an exemplary lesson that the Christian deemed himself alone capable of giving to the world, even if he often had to learn it himself." "When Voltaire accuses the Christian religion and the Church," Derrida observed, "he invokes the lesson of originary Christianity, 'the times of the first Christians,' Jesus and the Apostles, betrayed by 'the Catholic, Apostolic and Roman religion.' The latter is 'in all its ceremonies and in all its dogmas, the opposite of the religion of Jesus.' " Early Christianity was more than an ornamental feature of Voltaire's philosophy. "In short, a little in the manner of Kant, believe it or not, Voltaire seems to think that Christianity is the sole 'moral' religion," averred Derrida, without obvious approbation. "In this respect," he concluded, "the French Enlightenment, *les Lumières*, was no less essentially Christian than the [German] *Aufklärung*."[170]

The jewel among the eulogies was the "meditation" that Voltaire added to the section on "Religion" in the *Philosophical Dictionary*. It is an astonishing symbol of Voltaire's transition from critic to admirer, assuming pride of place in his flagship of dissent. The account began with a description of the philosopher meditating on the immensity of nature and the harmony of the "infinite globes," wondering whether a child born under Sirius's rays would "love and care as we." An angel interrupted the reverie and took him up into the heavens. It was a chilling vision. The "aerial creature" guided the philosopher to a desert, a place of "desolation," where the bones of slaughtered men and women lay in mournful silence. This was not hell. It was not a place of judgment. It was a sphere of pity, where the sages of antiquity grieved over the sufferings of humanity. In one grove lay the scattered bodies of the "Jews who danced before a calf," in another, the remains of "Christians slaughtered by each other for metaphysical disputes"—so numerous that they could "have mounted right to the sky." Finally, he surveyed bones of "twelve million Americans killed in their fatherland" by religious conquerors.[171]

The philosopher's tears were the signal that he could enter the groves of the sages, the curators of this museum of suffering, whose reward for a life of virtue was to live, though never forget. Passing from virtuous Roman kings and lofty Pythagoreans to Socrates, who spoke generously of his accusers, the philosopher was taken to a higher place, "situated above the thickets where all the sages of antiquity seemed to be tasting sweet repose." The angel had promised that understanding would follow a display of compassion. The final stage of the journey was an interview with one who lived apart from the other sages and grieved more than any:

> I saw a man of gentle, simple countenance, who seemed to me to be about thirty-five years old. From afar he cast compassionate glances on these piles of whitened bones, across which I had had to pass to reach the sages' abode. I was astonished to find his feet swollen and bleeding, his hands likewise, his side pierced, and his ribs flayed with whip cuts. "Good Heavens!" I said to him, "is it possible for a just man, a sage, to be in this state? I have just seen one who was treated in a very hateful way, but there is no comparison between his torture and yours. Wicked priests and wicked judges poisoned him; is it by priests and judges that you have been so cruelly assassinated?"

"Yes," answered the man, before submitting "with much courtesy" to a series of breathless queries. Had he come to found a new religion? Did he sanction violence when he spoke of bringing not "peace, but a sword"? Were his followers supposed to covet power? Was the sacrament of confession necessary for a life of virtue? Answering "no" to each of these questions, and declaring his abhorrence of the "murders" performed in his name, Voltaire's celestial Christ explained twice that his only command was to "Love God with all your heart and your fellow-creature as yourself." Why, then, had the priests put him to death? "They saw that I knew them." A sobering awe descended on the importunate philosopher as Jesus affirmed his equal concern for "the Jew and the Samaritan." A meditation that started with misty reflections on the immensity of nature concluded with a clarifying focus and a pledge of allegiance: " 'Well, if that is so,

I take you for my only master.' Then he made me a sign with his head which filled me with consolation. The vision disappeared, and a clear conscience stayed with me."[172]

Orthodox or otherwise, there is no question that Voltaire could write of Jesus with emotional force. Privately, he bristled at aspersions cast on Christ's character in Holbach's *Christianity Unmasked* (1767), protesting in the margins of his own copy that "the morality of Jesus was not perverse," and reproaching Holbach for "exaggerating the evils of Christianity."[173] Scholars have scratched their heads over this change of direction but Voltaire may have been moved to identify the Christian provenance of his philosophy for the simple reason that it was true.

The Burdens of Philosophy

When you get down to it, I am a decent fellow, and my priests, my vassals and my neighbors all approve of me.

—VOLTAIRE TO MME DU DEFFAND, APRIL 1760

It is good that there should be people like me in this world.

—VOLTAIRE TO MME FONTAINE, OCTOBER 1760

. . . j'écris pour agir.

—VOLTAIRE TO A.M. VERNES, APRIL 1767

Dissenters from the notion of a religious Voltaire may cite a personality and a lifestyle more in keeping with the fast-living Johnny than the saintly Freind. Ever the anti-Manichean, Voltaire would respond, first, that there was method in his madness, and second, that he grew up. Voltaire was never a libertine, and his ridicule was always more than mockery. His ability to command an international audience was testimony to a mind engaging profound and pressing realities. Although he held grudges and pursued his detractors with fretful alacrity, he was also a man of considerable generosity who took his responsibilities at Ferney seriously. Reaping a windfall from some rather dubious investments, Voltaire dispensed his wealth with proud benevolence, bailing friends out of debts, and pouring his money into commercial ventures to provide employment for his tenants. The chancer who had left England under a cloud of financial suspicion became a genial grandee, moving to solve an economic crisis by setting up a watch-making enterprise in his chateau. Voltaire converted his beloved theater into a workshop, touting his wares among princes and tsars—including Catherine the Great, who gamely placed a large order, having initially thought she was being offered a gift. Nothing in half measures.

"Oh how I love this philosophy of action and goodwill," he wrote to a friend, outlining, to another, an almost pastoral vision of the philosophical life:

> The real philosopher clears uncultivated ground, adds to the number of ploughs and, so, to the number of inhabitants: employs and enriches the poor: encourages marriages and finds a home for the orphan: does not grumble at necessary taxes, and puts the agriculturist in a condition to pay them promptly. He expects nothing from others, and does them all the good he can. He has a horror of hypocrisy, but he pities the superstitious: and, finally, he knows how to be a friend.[174]

While the Keynesian bounties were falling on Ferney, Voltaire was fighting a series of darker battles against persecution and injustice, from the celebrated cases of Calas, Sirven, and La Barre, to miscarriages of justice in the military. He also spearheaded a campaign against slavery in French territories, an issue raised in *Candide* and other works. He was one of the first European intellectuals to condemn a trade that "enriches" nations by "destroying" human beings, and he did something about it. Voltaire found energy in his philanthropies and relief from the depression to which he was often reduced. The anniversary of the St. Bartholomew Day Massacre was an annual trauma for Voltaire, the day on which "the pen trembles in my hand,"[175] and it was the revived specter of persecution in the 1760s that prompted his most dramatic interventions in public life.

When news reached him of the torture and execution of Jean Calas, a Protestant falsely accused of killing his son for converting to Catholicism, Voltaire wrote in horror to one of his clerical admirers, Cardinal Bernis: "This adventure grips my heart; it casts sadness over my pleasures and corrupts them."[176] He looked into the case, met the family, and fought a three-year battle for Calas's exoneration. He also commissioned an engraving of the Calases hearing news of the acquittal, copies of which were sold to support the family. A portrait of Voltaire in his bedchamber by Jean Huber shows the Calas engraving hanging proudly by his bed, and there is no doubt that Voltaire counted his involvement in the case among his greatest achievements. "This is no longer a time for jesting," he wrote to a friend as he threw himself into the case, "witty things do not go well with massacres."[177] It was in direct response to the Calas affair that he launched his tolerationist missile of 1763, which opened with a tremulous introduction: "The murder of Calas, sanctioned by the sword of justice on 9 March 1762, in the city of Toulouse, is one of the most extraordinary events to claim the attention both of our own age and of posterity."[178]

Voltaire took up a number of similar cases, including the scandal of a 19-year-old aristocrat, The Chevalier de la Barre, who was sentenced to a brutal and humiliating death in 1766 for some high-spirited impieties committed with a group of friends. The poignancy of the case was heightened by the discovery of a copy of the *Philosophical Dictionary* among the boy's possessions, a fact that may have increased the severity of the sentence. This horrified Voltaire, who wrote a piercing account of the episode and fought for several years to have the guilty verdict lifted from the one remaining member of the group, who had escaped to Prussia. He was 80 when he wrote *Le Cri du sang innocent* ("The Cry of Innocent Blood"), which led at last to the boy's exoneration. Voltaire was famously solicitous for his own safety, rarely putting pen to paper without at least two escape-routes in place. But his sympathy for those who did fall between the blades of a cruel regime was unfeigned, and part of his contempt for Rousseau centered on the younger philosopher's refusal to involve himself in similar cases of persecution, even when directly canvassed. The French system, Voltaire wrote to the lawyer representing the Calas family, "sets too little store by the life of men."[179] Like Spinoza, Voltaire was maddened that his writing continued to invite the charge of atheism. "I've been persecuted ever since I wrote *La Henriade*," he complained to Frederick. "Would you believe how often people have reproached me for depicting the Saint Bartholomew Massacre in such an odious light? I have been called an atheist because I said that men weren't born to destroy each other."[180]

Voltaire's religion certainly contained a streak of pragmatism and patriarchal decorum, tangible in the infamous adage that "if God did not exist, we would have to invent him." His appearances at the parish church at Ferney did not always exude spiritual intensity. When he rose to preach a sermon in 1766, he dazzled the faithful with his thoughts on the subject of "theft." Taking communion on Easter Sunday in 1766 served the dual purpose of impressing the workers and infuriating the bishop, who was duly incensed and demanded a personal confession of faith. This signaled a game of cat and mouse that continued, with a revolving cast of clergy, until Voltaire's death. The most Voltaire was willing to do was to say that he was a loyal member of the established Church. On one occasion, he feigned life-threatening illness so that he could receive absolution—before emerging to take a walk with one of his servants in the garden.

Beneath the fun and games, however, was a serious desire to avoid the disgrace of excommunication. Voltaire remained a man of real, if idiosyncratic, piety. While he was winding up his bishop with meretricious devotions, he was also quietly attending Mass in the chateau. Mass was celebrated by Father Adam, a dissident Jesuit priest and a long-time resident at Ferney, who became one of Voltaire's closest confidants. When a Jesuit condemned Voltaire as a turncoat and traitor, Voltaire had to restrain himself from announcing that he had a Jesuit living under his roof. As well as saying Mass, Father Adam's duties involved playing chess with the patriarch, both of which occurred frequently enough to incur the displeasure of Voltaire's mistress, who complained in 1769 that he had no "relaxation other than going to Mass and no recreation apart from Father Adam."[181] When the bishop placed a ban on Father Adam's services, Voltaire sought an immediate replacement, engaging a community of Franciscan monks. It is hard to find a biographer who regards this as anything more than provocation, but there was, as ever, substance beneath the theater. Voltaire wanted to attend Mass and go to Confession, and he took a genuine interest in the monks who performed the deed. When he discovered the extent of the Franciscans' poverty, he negotiated with a government minister to arrange an official pension. He received a letter of thanks from the head of the order in Rome, conferring on him the title of "Spiritual Child, Benefactor and Temporal Father of the order of Saint Francis."[182] Voltaire was delighted, immediately taking to signing his letters, "Friar François, unworthy Capuchin."

Among the more remarkable aspects of Ferney's monastic makeover was Voltaire's decision to improve mealtimes with edifying readings from august texts—a practical response to the graying philosopher's verdict that "very few people have in themselves a fund of useful conversation." Voltaire proudly enforced the practice when a delegation from the Dijon *Parlement* was entertained to dinner. Rather than enjoying the company of Europe's most celebrated wit, the bemused officials ate their meals in silence while a sermon was read from a lectern. This was clearly a prank, but it is significant that the regimen was in place at all. The menu of learning included the sermons of the "Racine of the pulpit," Jean-Baptiste

Massillon. Voltaire referred to the arrangement in a letter complaining of his clerical persecutors: "I am a better Christian than they are," he wrote to a friend. "By taking communion I edify all the inhabitants of my estates and all my neighbours. Not only do I do my own duty, but I also send my Catholic servants regularly to church, and my Protestant servants regularly to the temple, and I employ a schoolmaster to teach the children their catechism. I even have public readings at mealtimes from the history of the Church and the sermons of Massillon."[183] Voltaire wrote more anxiously to another friend of his dependence on Father Adam and his fears of being deprived of a legitimate confessor: "I have with me, as I think you know, a Jesuit who was deprived of his right to perform religious services, as soon as they found out he was living in my profane hovel. His bishop has been badly advised, for he risks making me die without confession, a misfortune for which I shall never be consoled."[184]

Interrogated by the probing and bumptious Boswell, Voltaire refused to be pinned down as any sort of orthodox Christian. He did not believe in the incarnation, or the resurrection. It is unlikely that he uttered blasphemous insults on his deathbed, and Pomeau is surely right to discount the scabrous mythologies that arose on both sides of the clerical fence. Voltaire faced death with neither the terrors of dawning judgment nor the defiance of an unbeliever. He was neither the returning prodigal nor the untroubled pagan. Although his death in Paris rendered the plan obsolete, Voltaire's arrangement for his tomb at Ferney offers a tantalizing commentary on a career of ambivalent fury. The tomb was to be constructed in a very particular fashion, half inside the church and half outside. It was a strange, though not unrevealing, arrangement. He would be neither in nor out. In the elegant summary of an English historian: "He often did things in jest, but seldom in jest only."[185]

Voltaire now rests in the Panthéon in Paris, where he and Rousseau continue their quarrel in stoniest silence—two giants of philosophy and fathers of the revolution united only in death. Jean-Jacques was the darling of the Jacobins but Voltaire, achieving a kind of apotheosis in his frail final years, was the icon of Enlightenment. Adorned with images of "Philosophy" overwhelming the monsters of "Superstition," and the "Spirit of Genius" leading Voltaire and Rousseau to the temple of "Glory and Immortality," the Pantheon was conceived as a symbol of reason's triumph over Christianity: an imperious church converted into a towering sanctuary of secular sainthood. But three times, in the coming century, the Pantheon was converted back into a church; and three times it was stripped of its altars and religious imagery, and restored to secular honor. All that remains is a giant stone cross, "a great monument of French classical art, killed icy and naked by the troubles of French history."[186]

Like Voltaire, Rousseau, and the revolution itself, the embattled edifice raises eloquent doubts about simplistic, one-way visions of secularization. Yet it would be a mistake to understate the scale of Christianity's crisis in a culture where a single beleaguered Church represented a whole religious tradition. The fate of Christianity and the status of its ministers may not be synonymous. But they are linked. Anticlericalism took its toll. The *philosophes* did not create the malaise of a persecuting orthodoxy and they cannot be blamed for the Church's crisis, but in exposing the problem they also deepened it. There was a school of nineteenth-century thought that saw Voltaire as a prophetic witness to a slumbering Church, and Voltaire was not above personal comparisons with Luther and Calvin. Lytton Strachey considered him one of the most misunderstood thinkers of the modern age, known "by his name . . . and not by his works."[187] Yet there are reasons for his status as the icon of French secularism.

The attempt to extract conscience from the fires of confessional warfare and to build a religion of love around the dimming jewel was a brave and difficult endeavor. Voltaire perceived the fragility of natural religion very early, thrusting his fictional heroes into the role of an improvised revelation. He plundered the Bible and finally claimed Jesus for the cause, molding a philosophy of criticism and mercy around the original subverter of religious authority. If the motives were still Christian, however, the outcome was not, as poetic liberties flowed into the rage of revolution. Voltaire believed in a God of justice and mercy. He truly believed that Fénelon's doctrine of "pure love" could have made Paris happy. But the ratio of fury to forgiveness remained an unhappy one, and that is how Paris remained.

5

"A Damnable Doctrine"

DARWIN AND THE SOUL OF VICTORIAN DOUBT

For we must not mistake ourselves, we have as much that is automatic in us as intellectual, and hence it comes that the instrument by which persuasion is brought about is not demonstration alone. How few things are demonstrated!

—PASCAL, *Pensées,* quoted in George Romanes, *Thoughts on Religion,* 1895

THE HOLLYWOOD MOVIE *Inherit the Wind* (1960) dramatizes the fears of a small American community that Darwin and his theory of evolution stood as an atheist conspiracy against Christian civilization. Based on the Scopes Trial of 1925, in which a high school teacher was prosecuted for violating a state ban on the theory, the film captures the anxiety buried in the very name of Darwin. The central character, "Matthew Harrison Brady," who prosecuted the young teacher, was based on William Jennings Bryan, who spoke for more than an isolated fringe when he claimed that "the evolutionary hypothesis is the only thing that has seriously menaced religion since the birth of Christ."[1] With comparable drama, Sigmund Freud placed Darwin alongside Copernicus as the source of one of the "two great outrages" upon humanity in the history of the West: the first removed the earth from the center of the universe; the second "robbed man of his peculiar privilege of having been specially created, and relegated him to a descent from the animal world."[2] The wreck was bound to be total.

Influential as such analysis has been, it has always felt like a search for a scapegoat, on one side, and wishful thinking, on the other. Darwin did not destroy religious faith in the nineteenth century nor did he put the seal on a long and definitive struggle between science and religion. Whatever the historical liberties of the screenplay, it was the genius of *Inherit the*

Wind to expose the degree to which attitudes to Darwin obscured more visceral tensions. Evolution functioned as a symbol for many people, including those who understood and embraced it. Cross-examination of the teacher's fiancée revealed that his animus against the fundamentalists was rooted in issues more personal than biology. He had ceased to attend church following the death of one of his pupils and, more precisely, the pastor's callous verdict that the child was now burning in hell. When the fiancée put a milder gloss on the matter, the otherwise silent teacher rose and shouted across the courtroom: "Tell him what your father really said, that Tommy's soul was damned, writhing in hellfire. Religion's supposed to comfort people, not frighten them to death." As groans of dismay erupted around the room, the fiancée pleaded that "it wasn't God he abandoned, only the church."[3]

This was a conceit of the screenplay, though not an outrageous one. In the historical version of events, it was not Scopes who initiated the battle against the anti-evolutionists but a group of activists led by a man called George Rappleyea. Rappleyea was a Methodist whose liberal minister had put his mind to rest on the question of evolution. He was not fanatical on the subject, however, and it was indeed a child's funeral that prompted his battle with the fundamentalists. A 6-year-old boy, the son of one of Rappleyea's workers, had died in a railroad accident. Rappleyea attended the funeral, where he witnessed an appalling exchange between the officiating minister and the child's mother. As the preacher arrived, the mother was "moaning: 'Oh, if I only knew he was with Jesus! If I only knew that!' " The preacher responded with words of savage disdain: "The ways of the Lord are His. You know and everybody here knows that this boy had never been baptized. He had never confessed Christ. There can be no doubt but that at this moment, he is in the flames of Hell." Rappleyea pulled the preacher aside and rebuked him for "torturing" the grieving mother. The preacher replied that it was his "duty to preach the word of God." Rappleyea told him that "if your conscience won't let you think of anything to say that will bring a little comfort to that poor creature, shut up." He left the church shaking with anger, his role in setting the Scopes trial in motion an act of measured revenge: "Well, a few days later," he recalled, "I heard that this same bunch, the Fundamentalists, had passed that anti-evolution law, and I made up my mind I'd show the world."[4]

The Victorian crisis of faith, like the Scopes trial, was a fact as well as a myth. It was a time of painful and intense disenchantment, in which the Bible and orthodoxy came under sustained attack, but it was driven by conscience, not science. The strongest assaults emerged from a set of ethical concerns that reprised the moral critiques of Spinoza, Bayle, and Voltaire, and largely preceded the bombshell of natural selection. Science became a symbol and a weapon of unbelief, but it was rarely a cause, even among scientists themselves.

Christians were prominent in this "second scientific revolution" and the outlook that it nurtured did not overwhelm the life of faith. It challenged and, for many, destroyed the "natural theology" of perfect design associated with William Paley, but it also opened doors. The new vision of nature as a vast network of hidden causes, supple connections, and infinitely transferable energy soon acquired a "numinous" quality for Victorian minds, acting as either a substitute for God or a new way of interpreting the divine. Whatever Victorians *should* have believed about nature or evolution, many continued to link science to "creation." There were sharper instruments available for the honest doubter of the nineteenth century, penetrating beyond texts and chronologies to the dogmatic core of the Christian faith, and first among them was conscience.

Such has been the verdict of a small but vigorous literature since the 1950s,[5] inclining some to the view that the warfare of science and religion was little more than a "storm in a Victorian teacup."[6] In the second half of this chapter, I will offer a new interpretation of this "ethical revolt," arguing that the Victorian conscience, like Voltaire's, was more theological than scholars have acknowledged. In the first, I will show how science and religion came to live in relative harmony in the nineteenth century, arguing that the warfare of science and religion was actually part of the wider revolt of conscience against religious authority. As in the Enlightenment: conscience and science can be distinguished but not separated. When "science" assumed a stance of aggression toward religion, it did so with resources that were less than purely scientific. My claim is that the hostility of activists like John Tyndall and T. H. Huxley, "Darwin's bulldog," was less the product of "untrammeled" scientific consciousness than a form of righteous anticlericalism—hard on theological arrogance but soft on ultimate questions of religious knowledge. The revolt of science against theology was part of a broader ferment, a storm within a storm, and if there was a shared resistance to orthodoxy it was a matter of morality rather than clean, intellectual clarity. Calvin played a larger part in the Victorian crisis of faith than Darwin.

The Flow of Energy and the Fate of the Soul: Science and the Myth of Materialism

The strength of the Darwin-slays-God thesis has always depended on what is meant by "God." There is no doubt that scientific naturalism, culminating in natural selection, shattered the apologetic structures of eighteenth-century theology. It was hard to think of God as a heavenly Mechanic when nature was no longer understood as a machine. But even in the eighteenth century, when the apologetics of design coasted regally in the jeweled carriage of Newtonian physics, faith had roots in the more supple realities of sentiment and "moral sense." Voltaire's transition from "spangled" skies to the testimony of the heart in the lachrymose adventure of *Jenni* was typical of a period in which "probability" was preferred to "proof" in the defense of religious faith. And Voltaire's determination to turn suffering to the good, by linking evil to human choice and error, rather than arbitrary divine action, was consistent with the most sophisticated apologetics of the eighteenth century. The emphasis echoed the evangelical theology that dominated British and American religion in the early to mid-nineteenth century. Conscience and sin became the vital grounds of Christian apologetics.

In the turbulent years of the early nineteenth century, questions of guilt and judgment weighed more heavily than the symmetry of creation. In a time of war and breakneck industrialization, a theology of disorder was more compelling than the point-scoring mantras of order and "perfect contrivance." There was a degree to which the flow and chaos of naturalism spoke more eloquently to the drama of living than the static precision of the older, Paleyan apologetics. Voltaire's rage against those who would explain a natural disaster in terms of providential harmony found its analogues. There were theologians who actually welcomed Thomas Malthus's vision of scarcity, struggle, and conflict as the natural course of civilization, when it appeared in 1798, for the simple reason that it described the world in which they lived. By the time Darwin appeared with a model announcing conflict and adaptation as nature's *modus operandi*, much of his work had been done. Not only had Malthus alerted him to the role of struggle in the refinement of organic structures, giving him "a theory by which to work,"[7] he had prepared an audience. The God of perfect design came and went in the era that invented him. The God of the evangelical revival had deeper roots in the psyche than Paley's dazzling metaphors.

As "development" eclipsed "design" as the default perception of the natural world, there were at least precedents for accommodation.

This is not to say that arguments over the age of the earth, or the creation and transfer of energy, lacked drama. Eighteenth-century philosophy was, in metaphysical terms, "dualistic." It conceived matter as "inert" until acted upon by an outside force—a principle that seemed to preserve the necessity of the deity. But as conflict and struggle were theologized, in the wake of Malthus and the rage of competitive "Christian economics," it became just as acceptable to think of God acting within as above nature. The shift from a mechanical, dualistic view of matter to a more fluid model of causation took place within the religious culture. Chemists, such as Joseph Priestley, echoed Spinoza in perceiving an interconnected world as evidence of a loving God. And while evangelicals placed more emphasis on judgment, many were equally receptive to the idea of a natural world breathing the thoughts of the creator. Such was the attitude of the "uniformitarian" school of geology, which emerged triumphant in the 1830s and 1840s with an awesome vision of an ancient earth turning under constant, "uninterrupted" forces. Charles Lyell's *Principles of Geology* (1830–33) made a literal reading of the "days" of Genesis all but impossible. The earth was much older than hitherto imagined. But the idea signaled excitement as well as trauma. God did not slumber. The new law of "continuity," in George Eliot's phrase, "the great conception of a universal regular sequence, without partiality and without caprice,"[8] was ripe for theological appropriation. Even among Christians who emphasized divine wrath and judgment, consistency was a vital principle. Discoveries that seemed to tie God's hands could be interpreted otherwise.

When Friedrich Wöhler discovered that he could synthesize "urea," a fluid found in the body, from inorganic matter, he wrote urgently to a friend: "I have just witnessed the great tragedy of science: the slaying of a beautiful theory by an ugly fact."[9] But to a Romantic generation, reclaiming nature from a bleak and instrumentalized industrial firmament, the thought of life inhering in matter was highly attractive. The correlating discovery in physics that energy is not created so much as constantly "transferred" (The First Law of Thermodynamics) was equally rich in potential. At a time when the "immanentist" metaphysics of German Romanticism were popularizing a view of nature as radiant with spiritual life, the notion that energy worked in a similar way was a source of some excitement. It is no coincidence that many of the leading scientists of the period were drawn to this German stream of thought, mediated by the important figures of Samuel Taylor Coleridge and Thomas Carlyle.[10]

While scientific naturalism was, in practical terms, a continuation of Enlightenment empiricism, philosophically it was more inclined to what earlier scientists considered Spinozan heresies. Romanticism blurred the boundaries between body and soul, God and nature, work and play. It rebelled against a tyranny of reason and a desiccated picture of the human person as a rational mind attached to a fallen body. To minds frustrated by what Coleridge termed the "mechanico-corpuscular philosophy" of Descartes and Locke, naturalism contained the potential for correction and enrichment. By the time Darwin published the *Origin of Species* in 1859, the urge to ennoble nature as a living feast was widespread. Joy was found less in the perfect melon, exquisitely contrived to satisfy a family of six,[11] than in the fluid mystery of creation. As biology threatened to drag the human frame into the primeval ooze, kinder analogies were at hand.

None of this is to deny that evolutionary thought was controversial, especially as it touched on human origins. The provocatively titled *Vestiges of the Natural History of Creation* (1844), which virtually deduced evolution from the first law of thermodynamics, was stamped out like an attempted arson. Critics took comfort in the amateurish bravado of the project, goading the author with pious assertions of the irreducible sanctity of human nature. Such reactions deepened Darwin's anxiety, as he inched his way toward a credible explanation for the transmutation of species. But when fellow naturalist, Alfred Russel Wallace, wrote to him with a very similar account of natural selection, he was emboldened to publish. Their co-authored paper of 1858 fell quietly upon the Victorian public, but the vivid, elegant and perfectly paced *Origin of Species* sailed into national consciousness, leaving Russel Wallace the forgotten partner of a jointly conceived thesis.

Why Darwin's bombshell failed to signal a crisis of faith is partly evident from his writing. The habits that offended scientists, such as the tendency to humanize nature as a force "seeking," "selecting," and "scrutinizing" with "unerring skill" and "visual powers," endeared the work to a Christian readership.[12] Darwin later regretted the confusion entailed by the terms "Creator" and "creation" in the *Origin of Species*, but he must have known what he was doing in the final paragraph of the book, which commended evolution as a window on the mind of God: "There is grandeur in this view of life," he quietly ventured, "with its several powers, having been originally breathed by the Creator into a few forms or into one." It was awesome to reflect "that, whilst this planet has gone cycling on according to the fixed law of gravity, from so simple a beginning endless forms most beautiful and most wonderful have been, and are being, evolved."[13] What Darwin took away from Paley, in a bold section on "Organs of Extreme Perfection and Complication," he gave back in a generous language of providence. All but ridiculing the idea of the first animals flashing "into living tissues" from the nearest elements, he managed to present evolution as a true and dignified doctrine of creation. With time, anything was possible.

Privately, Darwin wrote more darkly of "the clumsy, wasteful, blundering, low, and horribly cruel works of nature,"[14] but he always denied that natural selection proclaimed a world lost in chaos, and it was with pride that he identified a clergyman such as Charles Kingsley among his supporters. When Kingsley urged that "all natural theology must be rewritten," it was not in a spirit of panic.[15] He sensed the grandeur of natural selection, writing to Darwin to express excited approval of the *Origin*. "All I have seen of it *awes* me," he wrote, forcing him to "give up much that I have believed and written." "In that, I care little," he added. "Let God be true, and every man a liar!" Kingsley explained that his observations on animal breeding had long inclined him "to disbelieve the dogma of the permanence of species." Now he had what appeared to be proof. The idea that it pointed to a godless universe was absurd. Darwin confirmed a train of thought with which he had been battling for some time, and the outcome was anything but bleak: "I have gradually learnt to see that it is just as noble a conception of Deity, to believe that he created primal forms capable of self-development into all forms needful *pro tempore* and *pro loco*, as to believe that he required a fresh act of intervention to supply the *lacunas* which He himself had made. I question whether the former be not the loftier thought."[16] Darwin quoted the letter in later editions of the *Origin*. Kingsley wrote his best-loved novel, the *Water Babies* (1862), as a rhapsody on the spirituality of nature, mocking the soulless logic of the older, "mechanico-corpuscular" philosophy. Darwin provided rich material for his "theistic naturalism" as it rose against the miserly calculus of a dualistic worldview: Kingsley's lifelong enemy of "Manichee-ism."

Kingsley was part of a romantic generation of clergy, which sought to balance an earlier emphasis on "atonement" with a broader concern for the meaning of "incarnation." Salvation was not from but within culture. Progress in science, sanitation and social reform were among the purest instruments of providence. Although the embrace of a deeply ambivalent

Darwin sometimes had the feel of an overenthusiastic mother-in-law, the honesty of intent cannot be questioned. By the time of Darwin's death in 1882, Kingsleian awe had become a theological commonplace. Darwin was buried in Westminster Abbey and feted as the latter-day Newton that he certainly was not. He remained vexed by the theological implications of his thesis—happy for others to draw theistic conclusions but brusquely rejecting overtures from the Archbishop of Canterbury to contribute to some sort of concordat between science and theology.[17]

But what mattered was the reception. And between the twin poles of gushing endorsement and angry rejection, it is hard to discern a crisis of faith. Even where hostility was intense, it should not be mistaken for theological crisis. Few of those exposed to the new science seem to have perceived it as a solvent of faith. As the son of the marine biologist, Philip Gosse, who squandered his professional credentials with a hasty rebuttal of evolution, Edmund Gosse would seem a natural candidate for a scientific "disenchantment." He had a front row seat on the evolution debate, and he was saddened by his father's demise. But his alienation from Christianity sprang from a different cause: the stunting of his emotional and aesthetic proclivities by a ferocious Calvinist upbringing. In his searing memoir, *Father and Son* (1907), Gosse insisted that the "extension of [his] intellectual powers" did not trigger "any spirit of doubt or hostility to the faith." "Whether the facts and doctrines contained in the Bible were true or false was not the question that appealed to me," he maintained. His "growing distaste for the Holy Scriptures" had less to do with their veracity than their role as symbols of a domestic incarceration. They were mentally inseparable from a "spirit of condemnation" that had darkened his youth and stifled his talents.[18] To read Gosse is to grasp why the warfare between science and religion, real as it was for a handful of professional combatants, was peripheral to the more emotive dramas of personal faith. Next to bitter alienation from an overbearing parent, the integrity of the Bible's creation account was a matter of small importance.

Scientific reasoning, like the historical analysis of the Bible, could evoke wonder, excitement, and indignation but rarely the fear and loathing characteristic of the more seminal disenchantments. And while the status of natural selection was rising, it was a gradual and uncertain process, leaving room for maneuver. The notion of a Promethean "Science" holding a gun to the theological head obscures the diversity, indecision, and ambivalence of scientific knowledge in this period. The historical reality was almost the inversion of the popular myth. While theologians were eagerly beatifying Darwin in pulpit and print, scientists themselves were often in deep disagreement. Close allies such as Lyell took ten years before accepting Darwin's thesis, and in the face of substantial criticism, Darwin all but rewrote the *Origin*.

Yet to be vindicated by modern genetics, Darwin placed more and more emphasis on the role of physical environment in triggering changes for which he had no obvious cause. He even introduced the notion of organisms passing on "acquired characteristics" to their offspring—the very idea he had once mocked as the dilettantism of the French evolutionist, Lamarck. Later editions of the *Origin* made increasingly vague appeal to the unity of nature in corroboration of its claims, and while Darwin might have been better advised to stick to his guns, leaving the levers of transmutation unexplained, the scale of his editions suggests the fragility of the thesis. As one scholar has suggested, the sixth and final edition was so extensively modified, it should have read, "*On the Origin of Species by Means of Natural Selection and All Sorts of Other Things*."[19]

Against the more bullish accounts of Darwin's "revolution," it is worth noting that the president of the British Association for the Advancement of Science, the leading professional body of scientists, declared in 1894 that natural selection was "not proven."[20] It is also striking that when the "Mendelian" theory of "inheritance" surfaced in the early twentieth century, it was initially perceived as undermining natural selection. Indeed "it took until the 1930s and 1940s for Mendelianism and Darwinian selection to be reconciled."[21] Evolution did not land in the Victorian lap like a burning asteroid. It rolled in on broad currents of naturalistic thought, finding critics and admirers across the mythical boundaries of "religion" and "science." In the real world of Victorian culture, "paradigms" overlapped and relationships survived the tectonic "shifts" that have been read back into the era.

Edmund Gosse's priceless image of Charles Kingsley, esteemed novelist and national celebrity, pacing up and down the garden while his father punctiliously persevered with a Bible study for "certain of the Lord's children," may say more about the period than some of the more famous set pieces. Piety did not jump to attention for science or intellectual prestige. People who should not have been friends often were. Kingsley was the symbol of progressive Anglicanism and a virtual propagandist for Darwin; Philip Gosse was a fierce Nonconformist and an arch-critic of evolution. Yet their friendship survived a very public disagreement over the mechanisms of creation. They continued to spend happy afternoons "trawling" for marine life in

Torbay—even after Kingsley had rebuked Gosse for his belligerence over natural selection.[22]

Others held competing visions in tension. A delightful exchange between two aristocrats in 1836 shows how comfortably new ways of thinking about nature could coalesce with older modes, suggesting the degree to which scientific ideas operate for the nonspecialist on an almost aesthetic plane. "My view," wrote Lord Althorp to Henry Brougham, "raises I think rather higher than yours the wisdom and design which directed the divine mind in Creation, but yours is much more impressive as to the continued government of the universe and the constant dependence in which we exist on the divine will."[23] Here, twenty years before the *Origin*, was the shift from "design" to "development," taking place within a believing framework. The "warfare" of science against religion had more to do with the politics of intellectual freedom than the philosophical legalities of belief. Indeed, it was a religious phenomenon itself.

"This New School of the Prophets": Science as Religion

T. H. Huxley was a leading zoologist, a ferocious advocate of scientific naturalism, and one of the great characters of the Victorian era. Precocious, self-educated, and incurably combative, Huxley's only memory of two years of formal education was of fighting the school bully. By the age of 12, he was reading works of the new "uniformitarian" geology, which, combined with Carlyle, served to weaken his childhood faith. Carlyle taught him that religion could be distinguished from theology, and it was Huxley's ability to pour spiritual energies into the new vessel of science that defined his career. His breakthrough came with the publication of his zoological observations made during a grueling, four-year stint as a naval surgeon on *H.M.S. Rattlesnake*, between 1846 and 1850. The journey took him to the Far East and Australasia, where he identified and recorded a spectacular array of species. Fame, however, did not bring employment, and three years of job-hunting between 1851 and 1854 sharpened his critique of a state shamefully reluctant to support science or reward talent. Huxley delayed his marriage for eight years as he struggled to establish himself. When he finally married Nettie in 1855, a frugal Welsh honeymoon "doubled as [a] coastal survey, with Huxley dredging or dissecting goose barnacles for ovaria." Inspired by Carlyle's vision of a new aristocracy of courage, merit, and toil, Huxley was every inch the warrior of science.[24]

Huxley became synonymous with a confident, declericalized science, assuming the role of intellectual bodyguard to the beleaguered and uncombative Darwin. A tireless promoter of the natural sciences in schools, universities, and myriad public bodies, Huxley was, by the 1870s, the "senior statesman of science" and the symbol of a revolution that was having its way.[25] A teacher of teachers, and a smiter of philistines, Huxley was as dexterous with the pen as the pencil: a virtuoso of polemical prose. It is to Huxley that we owe much of the terminology of the science-versus-religion debate, including "Darwinism," "creationist," and "agnostic." No one has done more to propagate a picture of science and theology as historic forces locked in mortal combat. "Extinguished theologians," he wrote with lurid menace in 1860, "lie about the cradle of every infant science as the strangled snakes beside that of Hercules."[26] Whether he believed it entirely is another matter.

Huxley's skepticism of miracles and the Bible's "cosmogonical and diluvial narratives" was fierce and unwavering.[27] His mocking reflections on the first elephants "flashing" into being from dust were incorporated into the *Origin of Species*, and a lecture explaining life in terms of "molecular forces" shocked the audience when he delivered it in 1868, creating a furor on publication. "No article that has appeared in any periodical for a generation back," reflected the editor, "excited so profound a sensation as Huxley's memorable paper *On the Physical Basis of Life* (1869)."[28] The issue was reprinted seven times and the term "protoplasm" entered the language. Huxley was the uncompromising voice of naturalism, endlessly willing to expound Darwin's "doctrine" and to stare down his "episcopal Goliaths."[29] He wrote with needling persistence of the "sin of faith" and when he turned, with a tenacity that ultimately eclipsed his scientific endeavors, to biblical studies, he established himself as the period's leading religious critic. Mixing historical rigor with facetious reflections on the legality of sending pigs to die in lakes, Huxley was the closest Victorian England came to producing a Voltaire.

Like the French giant, however, Huxley breathed an uneven fire. When a Catholic writer penned an elegant synthesis between evolution and the doctrines of "derivative creation" espoused by Augustine and Suarez, Huxley read up on the offending authors, before penning one of the harshest essays he had ever written. Among a torrent of insults was the claim that no one should imagine that "he is, or can be, both a true son of the

Church and a loyal soldier of science."[30] This came as a shock to the author, who suddenly perceived that the debate was not about ideas, or a common pursuit of intellectual consistency. It was about territory. Huxley's fiercest volleys were aimed at Catholics and "Anglo-Catholics" in the Church of England, whom he regarded as the real enemies of scientific freedom. And while he was unforgiving of the evangelical sin of "bibliolatry," he retained important Protestant sympathies. His wife was a devout Christian who continued to attend church along with their children. The parish priest was a frequent guest in the family home. Huxley and Darwin were godparents to each other's children, and Huxley counted the theologian, F. D. Maurice, as well as Kingsley, among his friends. He taught for many years at their London Working Men's College, acting as principal between 1868 and 1880, and earning the incongruous nickname of "Pope Huxley" for his intensely moralistic approach to science. Toward the "right" kind of Christianity Huxley could be positively friendly, advising a Young Men's Christian Association audience, on one occasion, that the sciences are "neither Christian, nor Unchristian, but are Extra-Christian."[31]

Thirty years after the evolution controversy, Huxley maintained that the real "conflict" of the era was between "Agnosticism and Ecclesiasticism," not science and "theology" per se. The essential target was religious authority, and its often-disdainful treatment of intellectual enquiry. In some instances, theology had been a friend and ally. "But, as between Agnosticism and Ecclesiasticism, or, as our neighbours across the Channel call it, Clericalism, there can be neither peace nor truce," he maintained. "The Cleric asserts that it is morally wrong not to believe certain propositions, whatever the results of a strict scientific investigation of the evidence of these propositions. He tells us 'that religious error is, in itself, of an immoral nature.' " "Now I, and many other Agnostics," Huxley countered, "believe that faith, in this sense, is an abomination." Indeed, "we do feel that the disagreement between ourselves and those who hold this doctrine is even more moral than intellectual."[32]

Huxley's anticlericalism was nurtured in the company of religious "Dissenters" who resented their continuing exclusion from the ancient universities and a range of public offices. Oxford and Cambridge remained Anglican monopolies until the 1870s. An attempt to open Oxford to Dissenters in 1835 was crushed by the "Tractarian" or "Oxford" movement, marshaled by John Henry Newman, who raised the cry against the colleges being "profaned" by "those who have been baptised by strangers."[33] The corresponding complaint that Oxford represented an "antique, gothicized, politico-religious Establishment" was shared by many scientists.[34] It is no accident that Oxford—smoldering epicenter of righteous clericalism—hosted Huxley's most memorable assault on his "episcopal Goliaths." When Samuel Wilberforce delivered his infamous put-down at the meeting of the British Association in 1860, Huxley muttered something about "the Lord" delivering his enemy into his "hands."[35] It allowed him, the honest "David" of science, to rise in defense of truth and serious enquiry. Wilberforce wondered whether the apes were on his grandfather's or grandmother's side. Huxley replied that he would "rather have a miserable ape for a grandfather" than a man "possessed of great means of influence and yet who employs . . . that influence for the mere purpose of introducing ridicule into a grave scientific discussion."[36] The opportunity to cast bishops as purple-vested dilettantes, meddling in the weightier matters of natural law, was a glorious boon. But anticlericalism should not be mistaken for atheism or the emergence of a secular "worldview."

As well as the exclusion of non-Anglicans from Oxford and Cambridge, Huxley faced the problem of theological control within newer institutions such as the British Association, whose early presidents emphasized the interdependence of science and theology. This sounded innocent to some. To Huxley, and the co-founders of the vaguely conspiratorial "X Club," devoted to "science, pure and free, untrammelled by religious dogmas," these were tainted sentiments. They put limits on the scope of scientific research, they encouraged public disdain for non-theological approaches, and they subordinated talent to arbitrary standards of ideological conformity. Huxley felt that to pursue science within the canon of natural theology was to destroy it. Even the mildest language of "providence" represented a hand on the shoulder. Huxley came to regret the ambiguity of Newton's legacy: the stifling assumption that to speak of nature is always to speak of God. The aggression of scientific naturalism was a legacy of natural theology and ecclesiastical politics. It was another protest of conscience against Christendom.[37]

If Huxley's performance in Oxford had the feel of a slightly downbeat Diet of Worms, it was not for want of trying. For a furious skeptic, Huxley was remarkably keen to align his cause with both the Reformation and a duly historicized Bible. In a letter to Kingsley he boasted of representing a "new school of the prophets."[38] He preached "sermons," established Sunday schools, and described the whole movement of scientific naturalism as a "new Reformation," a religion without theology. Dismayed by an

Oxford movement "anxious to repudiate all complicity with the principles of the Protestant Reformation and to call itself 'Anglo-Catholic,'" Huxley paraded his Protestant loyalties. He justified his agnosticism in terms of

> that conviction of the supremacy of private judgment (indeed, of the impossibility of escaping it) which is the foundation of the Protestant Reformation, and which was the doctrine accepted by the vast majority of the Anglicans of my youth, before that backsliding towards the "beggarly rudiments" of an effete and idolatrous sacerdotalism which has, even now, provided us with the saddest spectacle which has been offered to the eyes of Englishmen in this generation.

"Men who can be absorbed in bickerings over miserable disputes," he continued, "can have but little sympathy with the old evangelical doctrine of the 'open Bible,' or anything but a grave misgiving of the results of diligent reading of the Bible, without the help of ecclesiastical spectacles."[39] Huxley presented science as a vehicle for what was good and eternal in the Bible, which amounted to rather a lot. Like William Gladstone's "politics of atonement," or John Ruskin's gospel of art, Huxley's "scientism" was another rumbling vehicle of redemption, fired by evangelical coals. If his anticlericalism raised the cry of "No popery" with distasteful fidelity to the evangelical original, his respect for the moral stamina of the Bible was enduring. When it was proposed that the Bible should be excluded from the curriculum of the new state schools, established in 1870, Huxley came forward as its least expected defender:

> I have always been strongly in favour of secular education, in the sense of education without theology; but I must confess I have been no less seriously perplexed to know by what practical measures the religious feeling, which is the essential basis of conduct, was to be kept up, in the present utterly chaotic state of opinion on these matters, without the use of the Bible. . . . Take the Bible as a whole; make the severest deductions which fair criticism can dictate for shortcomings and positive errors; eliminate, as a sensible lay-teacher would do, if left to himself, all that it is not desirable for children to occupy themselves with; and there still remains in this old literature a vast residuum of moral beauty and grandeur. And then consider the great historical fact that, for three centuries, this

> book has been woven into the life of all that is best and noblest in English history; that it has become the national epic of Britain, and is as familiar to noble and simple, from John-o'-Groat's House to Land's End.[40]

Elsewhere, Huxley described the Bible as the foundation of modern freedom, including the scientist's liberty of enquiry. "Throughout the history of the western world," he wrote in a late essay, "the Scriptures, Jewish and Christian, have been the great instigators of revolt against the worst forms of clerical and political despotism. The Bible has been the Magna Charta of the poor and of the oppressed; down to modern times, no State has had a constitution in which the interests of the people are so largely taken into account." It was "the most democratic book in the world." The Bible, he continued, "insists on the equality of duties, on the liberty to bring about that righteousness . . . [and] on the fraternity of taking thought for one's neighbour as for oneself." "That one should rejoice in the good man, forgive the bad man, and pity and help all men to the best of one's ability, is surely indisputable," asserted the agnostic. "It is the glory of Judaism and of Christianity to have proclaimed this truth, through all their aberrations." The Bible contained its own "refutation" of the "sophistical metaphysics" in which it was later embalmed. Jesus would have regarded the early fathers of the Church as "blasphemous if he could have been made to understand them." Huxley praised "the heretical sects" that had turned the Bible's libertarian impulses against "clerico-political despotism," for this was his cause. "Whoso calls to mind what I may venture to term the bright side of Christianity," he concluded, "is not likely to underrate the importance of the Christian faith as a factor in human history."[41]

Huxley frequently urged respect between science and biblical ethics, quoting a celebrated statement of the prophet Micah on what "the Lord require[s]" of his people: "to do justly, and to love mercy, and to walk humbly with thy God." Where theology adds or "takes away from this great saying of Micah," Huxley warned, it violates "the perfect ideal of religion." But he also counseled against any scientific consciousness that would presume to despise such sentiments. "What extent of knowledge, what acuteness of scientific criticism, can touch this . . .?" he challenged. "Will the progress of research prove that justice is worthless and mercy hateful . . .?"[42] Huxley's Romanes Lecture on "Evolution and Ethics" (1893) issued a warning to those who would draw a social ethic or a political philosophy from nature's struggle. The lecture, he suggested with only partial humor, was a sermon on the principle that Satan is "the Prince of this world."[43] Science could not brush aside the problem of evil.

Huxley coined the term "agnostic" out of genuine reluctance to be associated with the dogmatisms of atheism, materialism, and positivism. He decried the metaphysical arrogance of the "positivist" disciples of Auguste Comte, dismissing the movement as a naïve, ersatz theology—something "like John Bunyan's Pope and Pagan rolled into one." "Physical science," he declared in an essay on "Science and Morals," "is as little Atheistic as it is Materialistic." Huxley refused to reduce human consciousness to physiology. "Consciousness," he wrote in the same essay, "in the hardness of my heart or head, I cannot see to be matter or force, or any conceivable modification of either." He proceeded to defend conscience against the profanity of scientific reductionism: "If there is no spark of worship-worthy divinity in the individual twigs of humanity," he addressed the French materialists, "whence comes that godlike splendour which the Moses of Positivism fondly imagines to pervade the whole bush?" This was both to protect conscience against science and to call science on the sin of idolatry—or the "new Anthropolatry" as he termed Comte's movement.[44] "Idolatry," writes one authority, remained Huxley's "main category" for the criticism of both religion and science.[45]

The background to the solemn, faintly curial disclosure of "agnosticism" in 1869 was an essay by Sir William Hamilton "On the Philosophy of the Unconditioned," which declared that the "last and highest consecration of all true religion" is the *Agnosto Theo* (the "Unknown God"). This worship of an unknown deity, argued Hamilton, was the only aspect of Greek religion of which the apostle Paul approved. Huxley cited the essay, reportedly adding some reflections of his own on "the altar on which he has more than once professed to lay his offerings—that inscribed 'to the Unknown God.' " Thus it seems that the quintessential symbol of Victorian doubt was an expression of a surviving, sorrowful piety. It was with another biblical allusion that Huxley voiced his dissent from glib extremes on both sides of the fence: the false comforts of those who offer "mental peace where there is no peace." "Most of us are idolators," he wrote of the rasher claims of science, "[we] ascribe divine powers to the abstractions 'Force,' 'Gravity,' 'Vitality,' which our own brains have created."[46] "The antagonism between science and religion, about which we hear so much," he wrote in 1885, "appears to me to be purely factitious—fabricated, on the one hand, by short-sighted religious people who confound a certain branch of science, theology, with religion; and, on the other, by equally short-sighted scientific people who forget that science takes for its province only that which is susceptible of clear intellectual comprehension; and that, outside the boundaries of that province, they must be content with imagination, with hope, and with ignorance."[47]

Huxley described some of his earlier effusions as "my heathen letters" and he expressed regret that "99 out of 100 of my fellows would call me atheist, infidel, and all the other usual hard names."[48] It was inevitably to Kingsley that he opened his heart after the death of his son, with the brave conviction that "I am no optimist, but I have the firmest belief that the Divine Government (if we may use such a phrase to express the sum of the 'customs of matter') is wholly just."[49] More publicly, he was prepared to endorse the opaque splendor of Spinoza's God. Quoting a phrase from the *Ethics* defining God as "a being absolutely infinite, that is, a substance consisting of an infinity of attributes, of which each one expresses an eternal and infinite essence,"[50] Huxley proposed that a "God so conceived is one that only a very great fool would deny, even in his heart."[51] The vanquisher of natural theology had not given up on God.

Huxley's agonized blend of hostility and affirmation was far from exceptional. Indeed it was shared by some of his co-belligerents of the "X Club." John Tyndall's presidential address at the meeting of the British Association in Belfast in 1874 was perhaps the fiercest single event in the warfare between science and theology, generating almost a year of comment and reaction. Tyndall berated theologians for trying to police what they could not understand, he ridiculed literalist accounts of creation, and he sketched a dark account of the "dangerous," "destructive" history of clerical interference in scientific enquiry. But every paragraph reveals that his primary target was clerical control, not religious belief as such—the background to his furious polemic being the recent decision of the Catholic University to exclude science from its curriculum.

Tyndall was a leading physicist who had been reared in stern Ulster Protestantism, and his critique bristled with a sense of theological honor: a compulsion to protect a sacred calling from high-handed amateurs. He accused the self-appointed guardians of creation of profaning nature with clumsy and rashly conclusive reasoning. He presented science not as an all-knowing patron, but as a steward of nature's mystery.

"The 'materialism' here professed may be vastly different from what you suppose," he urged. "The whole process of evolution," he insisted,

> is the manifestation of a Power absolutely inscrutable to the intellect of man. As little in our day as in the days of Job can man by searching find this Power out. Considered fundamentally, then, it is by the operation of an insoluble mystery that life on earth is evolved, species differentiated, and mind unfolded from their prepotent elements in the immeasurable past. There is, you will observe, no very rank materialism here.[52]

Tyndall resented natural theology for its rationalism, as much as its technical follies: it knew the answers in advance; it turned the poetry of nature into proofs and propositions; it reduced divine activity to the work of a tinkering "Artificer," "acting by broken efforts, as man is seen to act." Naturalism offered a purer window on the divine:

> Believing as I do in the continuity of Nature, I cannot stop abruptly where our microscopes cease to be of use. Here the vision of the mind authoritatively supplements the vision of the eye. By an intellectual necessity I cross the boundary of the experimental evidence, and discern in that Matter which we, in our ignorance of its latent powers, and notwithstanding our professed reverence for its Creator, have hitherto covered with opprobrium, the promise and potency of all terrestrial Life.[53]

This was a Protestant telling a Catholic intellectual culture not to despise the sacred grammar of a material cosmos. Tyndall proceeded to condemn a Platonizing theology that "caused men to look with shame upon their own bodies," the perpetuation of a medieval outlook that "scorned the earth, in view of that 'building of God . . . in the heavens.' " Tyndall's mandate for science was a hymn to the goodness of creation. When he quoted the eighteenth-century apologist, Bishop Butler, against the life-sapping materialism of Lucretius, the circle was almost complete. He chose the poignant authority of Giordano Bruno—martyred by the Inquisition in 1600—to contend that "matter is not 'that mere empty capacity which philosophers have pictured her to be, but the universal mother who brings forth all things as the fruit of her own womb.' " Theology had exchanged the wonder of nature for a set of tired, Aristotelian formulas. It was the kind of foolish solicitude that would protect a plant by confining it to an airless room. Agitated by the scandal, Tyndall simply found himself preaching: "All we see around us, and all we feel within us—the phenomena of physical nature as well as those of the human mind—have their unsearchable roots in a cosmical life, if I dare apply the term."[54]

Science, Tyndall maintained, held no powers of veto over "those unquenchable claims of [humanity's] moral and emotional nature which the understanding can never satisfy," including those feelings "of Awe, Reverence, Wonder" from which "the Religions of the world" have drawn their strength. Theology had to know its limits, but so too must science. He rebuked those "high-and-dry" intellects that would banish "imagination," "enthusiasm," and "moral force" from intellectual life. He gladly acknowledged that "science itself not unfrequently derives motive power from an ultra-scientific source." Inspired by the idealism of the German philosopher, Fichte, and Carlyle's concept of the heroic intellectual, Tyndall portrayed science as a humble, almost mystical calling; "the yearning of a pilgrim." Science and religion could be reconciled in awe before the "Mystery" of nature. For these branches of knowledge "are not opposed, but supplementary—not mutually exclusive, but reconcilable." Tyndall looked forward to the day when "Heart" and "Understanding" might "dwell together in unity of spirit and in the bond of peace."[55]

In the proposed reconciliation, science held the aces. Theology had to surrender all rights of intellectual leadership. Yet Tyndall's thunderous rhapsody revealed a wealth of biblical assumptions about the sacredness of the natural order and the spiritual "potency" of the forces behind it. Tyndall may not have realized how far his own address exemplified his point about science deriving "motive power" from nonscientific sources. But, of course, this was not science, strictly speaking. It was criticism, clearing a way for science. And criticism was a matter of conscience as much as intellect or technical acumen. This helps to explain the apparent paradox of science being most aggressive toward religion when it was most religious itself. Huxley and Tyndall were no less the heirs of a Protestant Reformation than the "pulpit princes" of evangelical Dissent. It also helps to explain why militant science made such modest inroads into national piety. Heterodox as they may have been, men like Huxley and Tyndall were not trying to convert a nation to atheism or even agnosticism. Their fire was aimed at a particular set of problems, beyond which they recognized limits. Tyndall confirmed in a letter of 1874 that "I am not an Atheist."[56] His rejection of the "main doctrines of Victorian Christianity" was a textbook example of ethical revolt. As he wrote in a journal entry of 1847: "I cannot for an instant imagine that a good and merciful God would ever make our eternal salvation depend upon such slender links, as conformity with what some are pleased to call the essentials of religion. I was long fettered by these things, but now thank God they are placed upon the same shelf with the swaddling clothes which bound up my infancy."[57] It was the old collision between the merciful God and the God of orthodoxy: the nucleus of the crisis of faith.

The pieties of agnosticism attracted the ridicule of the bolder positivists, who belittled it as "a stage in the evolution of religion." But positivism, with its rituals, priesthood, and a rising account of history as progress from "Theology" to "Metaphysics" to "Science" revealed its own debts. Jules Ferry, an important French advocate, summarized Comte's vision as one in which humanity was "no longer a fallen race, doomed by original sin, dragging itself painfully in a valley of tears, but a ceaseless cavalcade marching towards the light."[58] "In the struggle of life with the facts of existence," wrote George Lewes, a leading popularizer of the movement, "Science is the bringer of aid; in the struggle of the soul with the mystery of existence, Science is a bringer of light."[59] The escape from theology was again theological.[60] Positivism was the chief example of what the socialist, Beatrice Webb, termed the "cult of science," an "almost fanatical faith" in rational and technological progress.[61] Webb was not exceptional in surveying "this idolisation of science" with suspicion. The title of Lewes's article of 1878 "On the Dread and Dislike of Science" told its own story, and there was a distinct tendency for people raised on uncompromising formulas to rebel. Science acquired enormous prestige in the nineteenth century, but it was not universal, unqualified or immune to reaction.

John Stuart Mill was brought up on an austere diet of "utilitarian" philosophy: Jeremy Bentham's rigorous prescription of pleasure and pain as the sovereign arbiters of moral reasoning. Instead of converting the age to Bentham's icy formula, however, the Young Turk of philosophic radicalism was himself converted to a more holistic outlook. Following a breakdown in which the limitations of naked "utility" became painfully real for Mill, he discovered a "new fabric of thought" in dialogue with Romantic poets, Carlyle, and liberal Anglicans such as F. D. Maurice. Mill thought Maurice's talents were wasted on theology but he developed a growing sympathy for "Theism," defining his task as not to subvert Christian belief but to create an alliance of "good ethics and good metaphysics."[62] Mill's pursuit of a "Philosophy of Life," "cleared of superstition," was a self-consciously spiritual task. He quoted Goethe's view that "Ages of belief . . . have been the only ages in which great things have been done," adding that "religion has hitherto supplied the only Philosophy of Life, or the only one which differed from a mere theory of self-indulgence."[63] Mill's transition from rationalist liberalism to a more rounded and intellectually reticent activism was characteristic of the era. And his sympathy for "theism" was typical of period in which reactions to orthodoxy often issued in new spiritualities, such as Spiritualism or "Theosophy," rather than atheism or a truly confident unbelief.

Fragmentation, writes one scholar, may have been the real story of Victorian culture: the loss of a "common context" of intellectual exchange; the beginning of the age of the specialist, the unread journal, the lonely babel of academia.[64] It was not the rise of a worldview. Pluralism should not be mistaken for secularism. The situation could not have been further from the vision of irresistible "disenchantment" outlined in Max Weber's famous lecture on "Science as vocation," where he described "rationalization and intellectualization" as the awesome reality of the modern age, mocking "the person who cannot bear the fate of the times like a man." "The arms of the old churches are opened widely and compassionately for him," Weber sneered, provided such a person will "bring his 'intellectual sacrifice.'"[65] Such statements have always contained more aspiration than historical judgment. The notion of the nineteenth century as the last age in which a person could believe in God without committing intellectual suicide belongs to the category of propaganda. There was an erosion of religious belief in this period and it did reveal a sense of "honor" not unlike the kind Weber expected every true thinker to hold. But its motor was not intellectual virtuosity, which could lead anywhere. It was an abiding conviction that certain principles of orthodoxy cannot be true because a moral universe could not allow it.

"Finding Liberty": Doubt as Freedom

The first signal of the true ecology of doubt is timing. Some of the most influential "deconversions" occurred in the 1830s and 1840s, triggered by the political and sectarian tensions of those traumatic decades, rather than scientific discoveries. A number of intellectuals abandoned clerical careers in this period, and freethinking became a small but vigorous presence in public life. Nor was this a purely elite affair. By 1862, the

Westminster Review, a symbol of the new culture, was reporting that "secularism is the religion, or the no-religion, of a large minority of thinking artisans."[66] Science and biblical criticism became weapons of secularism, but they rarely precipitated the loss of faith. Personal experience nearly always preceded theoretical reflection—a not unscientific principle itself. As one historian has written, "just as Christian belief can be, and often is, founded on an emotional response in a given situation, to be confirmed later by intellectually satisfying 'evidences,' so infidelity seems to have frequently been inspired by disgust with the Church and moral revulsion against Christian doctrines, and then sustained by a growing intellectual conviction of the rightness of such a rejection."[67]

A pioneering analysis of Victorian freethinkers found that out of 150 individuals who documented their loss of faith, ideas relating to geology or evolution were influential in only three cases. "The revolution in scientific and theological thinking," concluded the author, "seems largely irrelevant. The loss of faith for Freethinkers was not an intellectual but a moral matter." "It was," she added, "mainly those who had been actively and sincerely religious who were converted to secularism." A child at a Catholic school was asked after a lecture on the priesthood what he would do if a priest hit him: "He was punished for answering that he would hit him back, and having lost faith in priests, at a later age lost it in Catholicism." Another ceased to believe "because his mother had left his crooked foot untreated on the grounds that it was God's will." Charles Bradlaugh, long-time president of the National Secular Society and the first avowed atheist to sit in parliament, lost his faith following a bitter dispute with his church minister. Engaging the minister over discrepancies between the gospels, Bradlaugh was dismissed from his post as a Sunday school teacher. Bradlaugh consequently refused to attend church, he was forced to leave home, and finally he lost his job. "Whilst still a Christian, he became violently opposed to the church and priesthood," imbibing skeptical literature only after falling in with the "Infidels" whom he met at open-air debates. Such were the "petty persecutions" that created a secularist subculture.[68]

Circumstances were often decisive. The English radical, Richard Carlile, was a deist when he was imprisoned for publishing Thomas Paine's theological works in 1819. He was an atheist when he emerged in 1825. George Jacob Holyoake was similarly radicalized when he was imprisoned for "blasphemy" in 1842 following some flippant comments about religion at a public meeting. The dearth of scientific comment in

Holyoake's history of "secularism"—a term he invented as a more dignified alternative to "infidelity"—disappointed an American publisher. But Holyoake, who subtitled the work "a confession of belief," was unrepentant on the matter. Secularism had no care for metaphysics—scientific or religious. Such questions distracted from the essential business of the movement, which was to separate "morality" from "theology."[69] If the process of Holyoake's disenchantment demonstrated the power of experience, his justification pointed to the other, underlying factor in the emergence of unbelief: conscience. Secularists like Holyoake spoke so fervently of "conscience," "character," "duty," and "service," they were often accused of founding a new religion, complete with their own vision of a coming "kingdom" of peace and justice.[70] That is because secularism was in many ways an extension of the evangelical moralism that set the tone of British culture in this period.

The evangelical movement had always valued inward conviction over external "evidences" or written testimony. From John Wesley to William Wilberforce, the evangelical challenge was that "Real Christianity" is more than the "Prevailing Religious System of Professed Christians." Faith was more than dogma; the witness of the heart more than the brittle mandates of creed. George Eliot was still thinking like an evangelical when she wrote that "the tides of the divine life in man move under the thickest ice of theory."[71] The implication was that intellectual change could not eat into evangelical piety like a loss of spiritual nerve. Theologians such as Thomas Chalmers had formalized the priority of conscience over "evidences" in the early nineteenth century, declaring the moral sense a firmer ground for Christian apologetics than the glass house of a perfect cosmos. Ex-evangelicals like John Henry Newman shared the emphasis, scorning "Physical Theology" as tongue-tied on questions of "duty and conscience," and silent on those "hateful cypresses" of "death," "judgment," and "hell"—indeed all the essential "elements of Christianity." As one scholar writes, "there is a sense in which he was more critical of Paley than he was of Darwin."[72] So in taking away Paley and his perfect world, Darwin was taking away nothing that the more dynamic Christianity of the period could not live without.

Conscience was another matter. As Chalmers eloquently acknowledged, a dynamic ally became a dangerous partner when she no longer found a refuge in Christian life and doctrine. To argue that there was a perfect fit between the troubled conscience and the saving power of Christianity required at least integrity of the latter. As early as 1817,

Chalmers identified patterns of aggression that threatened to upset a delicate economy of salvation. It is better, he argued, to risk the accusation of "antinomianism" than to create a religion of unrelenting judgment. To "impair the freeness" of the gospel was "to chase away" the "love" of it, and to leave people "like the children of Israel in the land of Egypt, when required to make bricks without straw." Resentment, if not rebellion, would follow.[73]

This was an extraordinary insight. The evangelical revival had flourished, since the time of Wesley, as a joyous antidote to a religion of law and terror. The evangelical experience was, for one admirer, "a blending in one indivisible act of the sense of sin with the sense of deliverance from it."[74] The novelty of the movement was the emphasis on immediate and buoyant salvation: emancipation from the "psychic strain" of the sterner traditions of holiness. Wesley counseled his preachers to avoid overemphasis on divine wrath and to stress the joy of faith. They were to embody the principle that "a believer walking in the light is inexpressibly great and happy."[75] Freedom was a word constantly used in conversion narratives. Evangelists like George Whitefield invited conversion in terms that bordered on anticlericalism: the priests have deceived you! Salvation is within! It was a potent formula until the tables were turned.

When evangelicalism functioned as law rather than freedom, it began to collide with its own expectations. This was the story of the Victorian crisis of faith. A hardening of the evangelical ethos in the middle decades of the century, combined with the escalating sectarianism of the Oxford movement, made unbelief look like a salutary option to a small but significant minority. Eliot described the process with her customary elegance: "Religious ideas have the fate of melodies, which, once set afloat in the world, are taken up by all sorts of instruments, some of them woefully coarse, feeble, or out of tune, until people are in danger of crying out that the melody itself is detestable."[76]

This was partly the effect of time and routine. It also reflected a sharpening of the evangelical message in response to a number of challenges. Reactions to Catholic resurgence and political radicalism included a more rigid biblicism, a rising emphasis on hell and judgment, and a zeal for prophecy and a coming day of wrath. It was in the third and fourth decades of the century that the fragments of modern fundamentalism were assembled, as frustrated evangelicals such as J. N. Darby abandoned hope of reforming church or world and turned their eyes to Christ's avenging return. Those who did clamor for a Christian society often did so angrily, trampling on traditional freedoms and turning Sunday into a cultural battleground. As F. D. Maurice contended with mounting exasperation: to defend the Lord's Day was not always to defend the Lord. Sabbatarianism was more than a footnote on the process of alienation.[77] John Stuart Mill wrote his treatise *On Liberty* (1859) as a direct response to evangelical "despotism" in the public sphere, and it was in a similar spirit that a number of internal critiques emerged. Evangelicalism created the "eternal microscope" of the Victorian conscience before succumbing to its exacting scrutiny. The unsleeping righteousness that vanquished slavery, blood sports, and a welter of time-honored cruelties, finally turned on the dogmatic structures of Christianity itself.

The sense of a struggle within the world of faith was powerfully conveyed in Francis Newman's *Phases of Faith* (1850), a seminal statement of Victorian doubt and one of a handful of religious works that attracted Darwin's explicit praise. He described it as "excellent."[78] Newman was an outstanding scholar whose double first in classics and mathematics was said to have been one of the highest degrees ever awarded at Oxford.[79] He became a Fellow of Balliol College in his twenties but he left the university when required to subscribe to the Thirty-Nine Articles of the Church of England on the renewal of his Fellowship. After a period as a missionary in Baghdad, he took up various teaching posts, publishing widely on the languages and culture of the Middle East, mathematics, logic, political economy, diet, and classical literature—to name only a few of his interests.[80] But it was his spiritual autobiography, *Phases of Faith,* which placed him at the center of a controversy subsequently known as the crisis of faith. Newman traced his steps from the cool Anglicanism of the family home, to fervent evangelicalism, to a diffuse theism, hostile to dogmatic Christianity. Newman's brother, the future cardinal, predicted that an evangelical piety rooted in the quicksand of private judgment would lead to skepticism. And so it did—but not without the stimulus of ostracism by friends and family. John Henry may have regarded his brother's doubt as a symptom of secular pride and presumption, a bitter fruit of "liberalism." Yet he was no small factor in his brother's regress. Newman versus Newman was the crisis of faith writ large.

Francis Newman's fading respect for the Church of England, for "Christendom," and finally the Bible, was the classic collision between aspiration and experience: between an exalted conception of the Christian life and dispiriting facts. Clashing with his brother over the status of bishops, Francis said that he expected "reality" not "pomp" from a Christian institution, and it was with similarly untamed ambition that he ran into disappointment as a missionary to Baghdad and as a follower of J. N. Darby. It was the intensity of Newman's piety that made it so sensitive to error, failure, and sham. Newman described his faith as a force that had "subjugated" his whole being. It was, "no mere fancy resting in my intellect: it was really operative on my temper, tastes, pursuits and conduct."[81] "I cannot keep half measures in religion," he told his brother, "I must be a truly devoted Christian; I must not let a single five minutes in the day lie waste."[82] Newman wrote of his delight in the Christian scriptures, a "sense of the unapproachable greatness of the New Testament," finding in the letters of Paul, "a moral reality and a depth of wisdom perpetually growing upon me." Yet there was a clue to his later dissent in the "moral chasm" that he identified between the New Testament and the very best early Christian writers, a gulf "so vast" that the status of Councils and Church Fathers was "unintelligible" to him.[83]

This was before he took up his Balliol fellowship, and before the trip to Baghdad, but it was the spark of dissonance that would flare into furious conflict with his spiritual mentor, J. N. Darby. Like many evangelicals, Newman was unmoved by the glitter of "Christian Evidence," looking to "direct moral evidence alone" in his spiritual formation. Darby taught him to scoff at the surface knowledge of traditional apologetics. But as Newman started to query some of the ideas Darby claimed to have drawn directly from the Bible, the relationship strained. The fear dawned on him that the "primitive Christianity" of the Irish zealot was a human construction, a dogmatic interpretation that rested on the moral life like a suit of armor. The Church, Newman came to believe, "had systematized too much," and the effort always came at a cost. Disputes with the ultra-Calvinist Darby on the Trinity convinced him that evangelicals were as complicit as Catholics in turning the new wine of the gospel into the sterile water of system. Thus "began a time of deep and critical trial to me and to my Creed."[84]

Just as Newman was coming to blows with his evangelical mentor, tensions with his brother flared into public humiliation:

> The Tractarian movement was just commencing in 1833. My brother was taking a position, in which he was bound to show that he could sacrifice private love to ecclesiastical dogma; and upon learning that I had spoken at some small meetings of religious people,

> (which he interpreted, I believe, to be an assuming of the Priest's office,) he separated himself entirely from my private friendship and acquaintance.

His "distress was naturally great," not least because John Henry's coldness "cut me off from other members of my family, who were living in his house." Francis was separated from the family at the same time that "one after another" of his evangelical circle "turned against me." Darby wrote a letter of severe reproach, to which Newman replied with a plea for dialogue, but his questions were dismissed as wicked rebellion. The reaction confirmed Newman's conviction "that so vehement a champion of the sufficiency of the Scripture, so staunch an opposer of Creeds and Churches, was wedded to an extra-Scriptural creed of his own, by which he tested the spiritual state of his brethren." Rejected by his brother and a man he had idolized as a living saint, Newman recalled that his "heart was ready to break." "Oh, Dogma! Dogma! how dost thou trample under foot love, truth, conscience, justice! Was ever a Moloch worse than thou?"[85]

It was in the nature of true religion, Newman reasoned, to expect "like qualities in others," to seek in other Christians those "fruits of the Spirit" of which the apostle spoke. Or as "John did not hesitate to say: 'We know that we have passed from death unto life, because we love the brethren.'" To be disowned and excommunicated for asking questions was no small indictment; to lose a brother for daring to speak at a religious meeting was a savage commentary on theological zeal. This almost simultaneous alienation from two warring theologies provided a moment of clarity for Newman, confirming that dogma's follies exceeded intellectual presumption. Theology may be a form of sin, creating a spirituality of cruel insensibility:

> This idea enlarged itself into another,—*that spirituality is no adequate security for sound moral discernment*. These alienated friends did not know they were acting unjustly, cruelly, crookedly, or they would have hated themselves for it: they thought they were doing God service. The fervour of their love towards him was probably greater than mine; yet this did not make them superior to prejudice, or sharpen their logical faculties to see that they were idolizing words to which they attached no ideas.[86]

Newman sensed that a neo-Calvinist phrase like "Jesus is Jehovah" represented a kind of lust for control, an urge to recalibrate the gospels as judgment rather than mercy. Dogma represented an inclination to sharpen the edges, and stiffen the logic, of faith. Newman inevitably cited Calvin, "who burned Servetus," as the personification of the fallacy. "Why have I been so slow to learn," he wondered, "that religion is an impulse which animates us to execute our moral judgments, but an impulse which may be half blind?" It was "clear" to Newman "that A. B. and X. Y. would have behaved towards me more kindly, more justly, and more wisely, if they had consulted their excellent strong sense and amiable natures, instead of following (what they suppose to be) the commands of the word of God." Persecution bears the stamp of orthodoxy but it is "founded on *Hatred*." Creed was the great enabler of uncharity, and Newman lamented his own habits of exclusion: "I began to mourn over the unlovely conduct into which I had been betrayed by this creed, long before I could thoroughly get rid of the creed that justified it."[87]

Newman's alienation was defined by the Calvinism that had dominated his evangelical "phase." He concluded "that the man who worships a fiend for a God may be in some sense spiritual, but his spirituality will be a devilish fanaticism, having nothing in it to admire or approve." Like Voltaire's fury against the "useless" redemption announced by a selective Jansenism, Newman's rage was against a theological machine that seemed to leave the world as it is:

> I saw that the current orthodoxy made Satan eternal conqueror over Christ. In vain does the Son of God come from heaven and take human flesh and die on the cross. In spite of him, the devil carries off to hell the vast majority of mankind, in whom, not misery only, but Sin is triumphant for ever and ever. Thus Christ not only does not succeed in destroying the works of the devil, but even aggravates them. Again: what sort of gospel or glad tidings had I been holding?

"How much better no futurity for any," he wondered, "than that a few should be eternally in bliss, and the great majority kept alive for eternal sin as well as eternal misery! My gospel then was bad tidings, nay, the worst of tidings!"[88]

Newman's commentary also recalls Spinoza's critique of superstition as "bondage" to fear. The doctrine of eternal punishment, he came to believe, was a deadly burden to the soul. "No *use* in the punishment was imaginable," Newman protested, "without setting up Fear, instead of Love, as the ruling principle in the blessed. And what was the moral tendency of the doctrine? I had never borne to dwell upon it: but I before long suspected that it promoted malignity and selfishness, and was the real clue to the cruelties perpetrated under the name of religion. For he who does dwell on it, must comfort himself under the prospect of his brethren's eternal misery, by the selfish expectation of personal blessedness." The pieces started to tumble. Newman rejected original sin as another doctrine that enthrones Satan and leaves humankind in a state of misery: "I saw that the Calvinistic doctrine of human degeneracy teaches that God disowns my nature (the only nature I ever had) as not his work, but the devil's work. He hereby tells me that he is not my Creator, and he disclaims his right over me, as a father who disowns a child. To teach this is to teach that I owe him no obedience, no worship, no trust: to sever the cords that bind the creature to the Creator, and to make all religion gratuitous and vain."[89]

Newman felt that "in dropping Calvinism I had lost nothing Evangelical," but his growing "preference for John's mysterious Jesus," and his contempt for the literalism that had serviced the Calvinist scheme, pushed him beyond even moderate evangelicalism. In classic Protestant fashion, the journey was characterized as a renunciation of a "religion of the letter" for the purity of the spirit. Yet the damage was substantial. The process was stimulated by discussions about the age of the "human race" and the "geological difficulties of the Mosaic cosmogony," which were "at that time exciting attention," but these were peripheral concerns. Conversations with the liberal Anglican, Thomas Arnold, set his mind to rest on the Bible's historical integrity, proving that "a vigorous mind, deeply imbued with Christian devoutness," had nothing to fear from "free inquiry." But he had no such control over his moral anxieties, which bullied his fading orthodoxy and triggered a piercing disdain for "bibliolatry," dogma's partner in the "paralysis" of the "moral sense." "Bibliolatry" was a zeal for the letter of scripture which, "by setting men to the duty of extracting absolute harmony out of discordant materials," constantly tempted them to twist the evidence. The effect was to "benumb conscience" and "corrupt the intellect." Newman's sense of release was thus moral and intellectual, but no reader could mistake the Christian passion of the severance: "I shuddered at the notions which I had once imbibed as a part of religion; and then got comfort from the inference, how much better the men of this century are than their creed."[90]

Newman expressed his theism more positively in *The Soul, Her Sorrows and Her Aspirations: An Essay Towards the Natural History of the Soul, as the True Basis of Theology* (1849). Admirers included Eliot, Holyoake, and Frederic Harrison, a Comtean Positivist. John Henry greeted it with dismay—without deigning to read it.[91] Had he done so, he would have realized that his brother had not descended to paganism. Newman's attempt to retrieve an authentic spirituality from the embers of "cursing theologies" was a strangely Wesleyan affair. The Arminianism that was praised in *Phases of Faith* against the severities of Calvinism surfaced here as a balm of universalism, complete with generous quotation from Charles Wesley on the "Pure, Universal Love" of God. "Though we know," Newman reflected, "that the physical Universe has fixed unfaltering laws, *we cannot help* seeing God's hands in events. Whatever happens, we think of as his Mercies, his Kindnesses; or his Visitations and his Chastisements; everything comes to us from his Love." Sin cannot reign. Suffering melts in a sea of benevolence. The soul finds health in truth. "This," Newman concluded, "seems to be the state which the Wesleyans (to the scandal of other Christians) have denominated Perfection or Full Redemption, after which they breathe in many beautiful and touching hymns." Newman had ceased to identify himself as a Christian, yet his antidote to a terrorizing orthodoxy was a Wesleyan doctrine of love. And in his now "secular" career of social and intellectual activism, Newman continued to behave like a Christian—fighting a lifelong campaign against the "four barbarisms" of war, the penal system, alcohol, and cruelty to animals.[92] The escape from theology was once again theological.

James Anthony Froude was another scholar who abandoned a clerical career over what he perceived as the immorality of orthodoxy—an alienation hastened by the "unkindness" of family members, including a brother (Richard Hurrell) at the center of the Oxford Movement. Froude told the story in a semi-autobiographical novel, *The Nemesis of Faith* (1849), which earned the rare distinction of being burned in an Oxford lecture hall. Froude condemned the morality of the atonement, the slaughter of innocent peoples in the Old Testament, and the febrile extremism so often promoted by dogma. Froude's protest, expressed in a dialogue between his fictional ordinand, Markham Sutherland, and a clerical mentor, was another theological revolt against the apparent fatalism of orthodoxy. "If I am to be a minister of religion," he wrote, "I must teach the poor people that they have a Father in heaven, not a tyrant; one who loves them all beyond power of heart to conceive; who is sorry when they do wrong, not angry; whom they are to love and dread, not with caitiff coward fear, but with deepest awe and reverence, as the all-pure, all-good, all-holy. I could never fear a God who kept a hell prison-house. No, not though he flung me there because I refused." Dissent was again self-consciously Christian:

> I believe that we may find in the Bible the highest and purest religion most of all in the history of Him in whose name we all are called. His religion—not *the Christian religion*, but *the religion of Christ*—the poor man's gospel; the message of forgiveness, of reconciliation, of love; and, oh, how gladly would I spend my life, in season and out of season, in preaching this! But I must have no hell terrors, none of these fear doctrines; they were not in the early creeds, God knows whether they were ever in the early gospels, or ever passed His lips. He went down to hell, but it was to break the chains, not to bind them.[93]

Froude, like his character, abandoned his vocation and was forced to resign his Oxford fellowship. But it was an inconclusive alienation. Froude described himself as hanging, "like Mahomet's coffin between earth and heaven," and it was with Charles Kingsley, that tireless mediator, that he took refuge from the storm created by his "manual of infidelity."[94] Froude's partners in crime, including Carlyle and the German theologian, Friedrich Schleiermacher, do not suggest a mind purged of spiritual affinities. The "nemesis" of faith was a moral sensorium, an impatience of sectarian rancor, an exasperation with the inversions of theology. It was either a product of Christianity or a continuing expression. It was the inner pulse of the holy fury of "secularism."

George Jacob Holyoake was a Unitarian when he was arrested for flippant remarks made at a lecture on Owenite socialism in 1842. The offending comment came in reply to a question about the place of religion in some proposed socialist communities. Holyoake's plea to be spared "vindictive reprehension" did not move a jury of laymen, who committed him to six months in prison. He responded by putting "theism" on trial, writing and editing a range of freethinking publications, including the *Circular of the Anti-Persecution Union* (1845) and *The Reasoner*, which ran weekly from 1846 until 1861.[95] Holyoake described his persecution as "the cradle of my doubts, and the grave of my religion." He did not become an atheist but he ceased to be "a believer in the humanising tendency of Christianity." He retained respect for "pure Theists" such as Francis

Newman, with his "fine conception of God as the Deity of duty" and his brave articulation of "a reverence untinged by terror." Such an ideal, he admitted, "soars into the radiant light of a possible God."[96] But a hell-fire orthodoxy had to be abandoned. Ten years after his imprisonment, Holyoake was still justifying his secularism in terms of Christian virtue. A handbill, advertising one of his lectures promised to demonstrate that, "Eternal Punishments, as taught by Jesus Christ, [are] contradictory to the great precepts on which his own Moral Character reposes."[97]

Holyoake had been "an assiduous chapel-goer" as a boy, earning a reputation as an "angel-child" among visiting ministers. He took his part in family discussions, including one in which he was gravely assured "that there were children in hell not a span long." Not yet 12 at the time, Holyoake "shuddered at such doctrines," prompting his mother to take him to a moderate Baptist chapel, "where the Rev. Mr. Cheadle expressed comforting doubts whether there was any hell at all." The pleasant discrepancy between the Baptist's preaching and his customary diet sustained him for some time. But the tension ultimately served to highlight the cruelty of what he considered Christian orthodoxy.[98] In *The Trial of Theism* (1858), Holyoake placed his finger on the trigger of Victorian doubt, with the solemn assertion that the theology under attack is the boiled truth of the Bible: "the New Testament bids us call God father, yet tells us, or seems to tell us, that if His children disobey Him, He will everlastingly burn them; will take them as a father might take his children in a room with a fire in it, and hold them in the fire for ever." "The relation of man to the God of Christianism," he concluded, "is an essentially penal relation, one which can neither nurture the affections nor morals." It was against this punitive theology of his upbringing that Holyoake asserted the almost Kantian dignity of his doubt:

> God was to me a Fear. Of his being a God of Love, in the human sense of that term, the idea never occurred to me, and was never suggested by my teachers. To trust God, in that sense which casteth out anxiety, was a feeling utterly unknown to me. The only trust in God which I knew was a mingled feeling of awe, terror, and hope. He was to me a judge who had ever on his lips a dread sentence, and whose leniency could only be obtained by abject faith, by an undefined submission of the spirit, and a confessed consciousness of natural guilt—perpetual, oppressive, painful, and humiliating. In the Lord's Prayer I was, indeed, taught to say "Our Father who

> art in heaven;" but I was never able to conceive of him other than as the Father spoken of by Solomon, who held a rod in his hand, and under the conviction that it was best not to spare it. Such was the God of Orthodox Dissenting Theology, in which I had the misfortune to be reared, in which I originally believed, but in which I have, since 1841, ceased to believe, and in which I have no wish to believe again.

Holyoake characterized the process as the exchange of "Creed" for "Life."[99] Evangelical conversion was being reinvented as righteous doubt.

Perhaps the most remarkable of such disenchantments was that of Alfred Russel Wallace, the co-discoverer of natural selection and a symbol of the period's intellectual vitality and eclecticism. Darwin praised Wallace's "heroic" labors, but he was disappointed by Wallace's hesitations over the explanatory scope of their theory. Wallace did not think that natural selection could not account for the aesthetic, spiritual, or mathematical powers of the human mind,[100] prompting an extraordinary letter from Darwin, expressing his fear that Wallace had "murdered too completely your own and my child."[101] Wallace also infuriated Huxley with his misty and rather unmanly proclivity for spiritualism—the Victorian cult of trying to contact the dead. His essays on the subject, including, "Modern spiritualism—are its phenomena in harmony with science?" (1885) and, "If a man die, shall he live again?" (1887), were among his most reprinted works. Wallace was no one's acolyte; an eccentric but not an anomaly.

Wallace's determination to combine evolution with a spiritual outlook was typical of the era, and his willingness to interpret nature's struggle as a stimulus to "sentiments of justice, mercy, charity, and love, which we all feel to be our best and noblest characteristics" recalled the evangelical appropriation of Malthus in the 1820s.[102] Nature is at war, but humans have the capacity to rise above it. Yet Wallace was no evangelical, and the spiritualism to which he committed himself was another reaction to the punitive theology that alienated Newman, Froude, and Holyoake. His spiritualism represented an attempt to establish a level playing field on the ruins of a discarded Calvinism. It was a cobbled answer to "a problem that had haunted Wallace ever since adolescence—predestination."[103] Wallace lost faith in "orthodox" Christianity before he embarked upon his historic labors in the Amazon and the Malay Archipelago, and he clung to his spiritual convictions long after he had established himself in the front rank of scientific discoverers.[104]

The turning point came in his late teens when Wallace read Paine on the problem of evil and a tract by Robert Dale Owen on "the horrible doctrine of eternal punishment as then commonly taught from thousands of pulpits by both the Church of England and Dissenters." Paine could be navigated. His observations on evil, Wallace reflected, "did not really touch the question of the existence of God." Not so eternal punishment. Wallace never doubted the reality of the supernatural but he recoiled from a theology of exultant retribution. He came to the solemn conviction that "orthodox ideas as to [God's] nature and powers cannot be accepted." Hell was again the point of departure:

> I remember one illustration quoted from a sermon, to enable persons to realize to some extent what eternal punishment meant. After the most terrible description had been given of the unimaginable torments of hell-fire, we were told to suppose that the whole earth was a mass of fine sand, and that at the end of a thousand years one single grain of this sand flew away into space. Then—we were told—let us try to imagine the slow procession of the ages, while grain by grain the earth diminished, but still remained apparently as large as ever,—and still the torments went on.

"And then," asked the preacher, "is the sinner any nearer the end of his punishment? No! for his punishment is to be infinite, and after thousands of such globes had been in the same way dissipated, his torments are still to go on and on for ever!" Such sermons, Wallace claimed, were the regular currency of the churches of his youth. He recalled that "a lady we knew well had been so affected by them that she had tried to commit suicide." He therefore agreed with Owen that "the orthodox religion of the day was degrading and hideous, and that the only true and wholly beneficial religion was that which inculcated the service of humanity, and whose only dogma was the brotherhood of man. Thus was laid the foundation of my religious scepticism." Owen's lecture was dated 1840, and Wallace seems to have read it soon after it was published.[105]

Wallace never portrayed his skepticism as the fruit of scientific enquiry, and he was infuriated by the caricature of unbelief as a sinful refusal to submit to the purity of orthodoxy. As he wrote to his brother-in-law in 1861: "I remain an *utter disbeliever* in almost all that you consider the most sacred truths. I will pass over as utterly contemptible the oft-repeated accusation that sceptics shut out evidence because they will not be governed by the morality of Christianity. You I know will not believe that in my case, and *I* know its falsehood as a general rule."[106] The vexed scientist was hinting at a basic law of unbelief: a pattern governed by conscience, not intellect or immorality. He and Darwin may have disagreed over their jointly nurtured "child" of natural selection, but they were on the same page when it came to the morality of orthodoxy.

By his own admission, Darwin was more of a spectator than a participant in the Victorian religious revival. The family tradition was of Unitarian dissent, and Darwin did not suffer overbearing pieties in either church or home. He was, however, briefly set for a career as an Anglican clergyman, and he fully subscribed to the Paleyan apologetics of design as a young man. He considered himself "quite orthodox" during his time on the *Beagle*. His loss of faith was a serious matter, described with gravity in his autobiography. At first sight, the account suggests a mind soberly submitting to the evidence of the natural world. He cited "inaccuracies" in the gospel accounts and the difficulties of believing in miracles in the light of what "we know of the fixed laws of nature." Yet the account blended historical and moral objections, with increasing emphasis on the latter. Darwin recalled that he "gradually" came "to see that the Old Testament from its manifestly false history of the world, with the Tower of Babel, the rainbow as a sign, etc., etc., and from its attributing to God the feelings of a revengeful tyrant, was no more to be trusted than the sacred books of the Hindoos, or the beliefs of any barbarian." Professing reluctance to abandon his faith, and speculating that life would be poorer without the "morality of the New Testament," he moved to a dramatic conclusion:

> But I was very unwilling to give up my belief;—I feel sure of this for I can well remember often and often inventing day-dreams of old letters between distinguished Romans and manuscripts being discovered at Pompeii or elsewhere which confirmed in the most striking manner all that was written in the Gospels. But I found it more and more difficult, with free scope given to my imagination, to invent evidence which would suffice to convince me. Thus disbelief crept over me at a very slow rate, but was at last complete. The rate was so slow that I felt no distress, and have never since doubted even for a single second that my conclusion was correct. I can indeed hardly see how anyone ought to wish Christianity to be true; for if so the plain language of

> the text seems to show that the men who do not believe, and this would include my Father, Brother and almost all my best friends, will be everlastingly punished.
>
> And this is a damnable doctrine.[107]

The final sentence, left hanging in an icy paragraph of its own, was considered too "raw" by Darwin's wife, who had it removed from the second edition. The weary naturalist who had avoided religious controversy for forty years had summarized the crisis of faith in a sentence. Though Darwin claimed that this was an intellectual process to which he was "unwilling" to submit, the moral force of his stance is overwhelming. For the greatest scientist of his time to offer such watery speculations on the sudden appearance of ancient manuscripts is a measure of how peripheral historical arguments had become. Darwin gives no impression of having explored the evidence, or any desire to do so. He reflects that, since he could no longer "invent" the requisite corroboration of the gospels, he reluctantly laid his faith to rest—a less than convincing analysis. Contrary to the claims of reluctance and regret, Darwin is grateful that he no longer has to believe. Why? Because the "plain language" of the Bible indicates that the people "who do not believe," including his closest friends and family, "will be everlastingly punished." One commentator suggests that the phrase "damnable doctrine" was an accidental pun, making him sound angrier than he was. But Darwin was a fine writer in perfect control of his prose. He takes the reader from the outskirts of evidences and proofs to the burning center of the problem: to believe in the Bible is to believe in everlasting punishment. The case may be dismissed.

Some scholars have cited the "bitter and cruel loss" of Darwin's eldest daughter, Annie, in 1851, as the true cause of his unbelief. This would also confirm a moral, rather than a strictly evidential, trajectory, but the sources are inconclusive. The trauma produced no comparable expression of defiance. In a letter to the evangelical Harvard botanist, Asa Gray, in 1860, Darwin admitted that theological questions were "always painful to me." He "had no intention to write atheistically" but he admitted that he did not see "design and beneficence on all sides of us. There seems to me too much misery in the world." "On the other hand," he countered, "I cannot anyhow be contented to view this wonderful universe, and especially the nature of man, and to conclude that everything is the result of brute force." He was willing, therefore, to suspend judgment, with the philosophical disclaimer that "the whole subject is too profound for the human intellect. A dog might as well speculate on the mind of Newton. Let each man hope and believe what he can."[108] This was agnosticism: a true admission of not knowing. It was to illustrate Wallace's point about the problem of suffering: it may raise doubts without proving that God does not exist. But the doctrine of eternal punishment brooked no such ambiguity: it was obnoxious to Darwin and it inspired his only definitive statement of unbelief. Evolution inclined Darwin to agnosticism; eternal punishment pushed him into righteous defiance.

The reactions of Darwin, Wallace, and many other scientists reveal that the vaunted gulf between scientific and religious "worldviews" did not exist. The same problems exercised minds across the intellectual spectrum. F. D. Maurice lost his job at King's College London in 1852 for some equivocating remarks on the reality of hell, and it was for similar heresies that two of the contributors to the liberal Anglican manifesto, *Essays and Reviews* (1860), were convicted for heresy. They were later exonerated by the Privy Council, where "hell" was famously "dismissed with costs."[109] But eternal punishment remained the fuel of a crisis of faith that permeated church and world, rather than divided them. A theologian such as Benjamin Jowett exuded the same distaste for the concept as a philosopher such as Mill. "God," Jowett wrote of the orthodox scheme, "is represented as angry with us for what we never did; He is ready to inflict a disproportionate punishment on us for what we are; He is satisfied by the sufferings of His Son in our stead. The imperfection of human law is transferred to the Divine."[110] Mill differed only in tone: "I will call no being good," he declared with ill-controlled equanimity, "who is not what I mean when I apply that epithet to my fellow creatures, and if such a being can sentence me to hell for not so calling him, to hell I will go."[111]

Herbert Spencer, one of the great advocates of scientific naturalism, justified his unbelief in similar terms, writing of "how absolutely and immeasurably unjust it would be that for Adam's disobedience (which might have caused a harsh man to discharge his servant), all Adam's guiltless descendants should be damned, with the exception of a relatively few who accepted the 'plan of salvation.' "[112] Meanwhile, Alfred Tennyson, who agonized over the cruelties of nature in his poem *In Memoriam* (1849), also revealed the expulsive power of hellfire theology. He nursed a vivid memory of an aunt saying to him as a child, "Alfred, Alfred, whenever I look at you I think of the words, 'Depart from me, ye cursed, into everlasting fire.' "[113] It can be no surprise that such ideas, entering the mind at an early age, operated more powerfully in the making of unbelief than science. Human destiny was a more pressing concern than human origins. Even those who lost their faith often continued to be haunted by the fear of hell.

Most churches were softening their language in the second half of the century. Calvinism was in decline. But liberalization in some quarters prompted intensification in others. A *Westminster Review* article of 1875 found continuing evidence of a "terroristic system" of spiritual training, claiming that children were "habitually" exposed to threats of "unutterable tortures" in hell. Children were urged to conceive their "normal condition" as a "state of hopeless degradation" and God as an "Unseen Power full of anger, harshness and vindictiveness."[114] The writer quoted a volume of *Sermons for the Very Young* (1864), which invited readers to imagine the "shriek of horror" that would be heard in the hour of judgment, when slumbering sinners discover that it is "too late" to repent. "Think, little child, of the fearful story," warned the author. Two doctors placed "religious anxiety and excitement" second on a list of seven "moral causes of insanity."[115] It was in such a context that the Scottish writer, George MacDonald, commenced a project of rescuing childhood from theologies of terror, urging that God himself is "childlike" and quite innocent of Calvinist severity.[116] But such reactions may have come too late. The ethical revolt was an almost tangible phenomenon of the age.

Beatrice Webb reflected that "with most people it is the sense of what is *morally* untrue which first shakes your faith in Christianity; it is moral disapprobation of some of its dogmas which forces you to question rationally the rest."[117] Some blamed the emphasis of preaching, rather than the Bible itself. "God, and immortality, and the Bible have been so taught as to make scepticism the only refuge for morality to flee to," complained a Unitarian in the *Westminster Review.* "Secularism," he claimed, "would only have existed in a few exceptional cases . . . if religion had not been irreligiously preached."[118] Meanwhile, George Dawson, an Independent minister, blamed a regrettable note of aggression in contemporary religion. He concluded a sermon on "The Folly of Abuse" (1871) with a stirring call for humanity and decency: "We must do what we can," he insisted, "to prevent any man being driven to atheism by our theism. In the presence of justice, rebellion grows unholy; in the presence of tyranny, it is a virtue. . . . Let it be ours not to get angry with such as are so unhappy as to have lost their faith. . . . Let us strive when we use the name of God to keep it righteous, and to force no man into doubt by the unloveliness of our faith."[119]

Twenty years later, the Catholic, A. L. Moore, offered a similar verdict on an age of sorrowful disenchantment. He argued that there were two kinds of "difficulties in religion," intellectual and moral, and the latter contained all the active ingredients. Intellectual doubt played its part but it lacked the force and urgency of moral dissent. Whereas, he suggested, "Intellectual difficulties may conceivably wait, moral difficulties cannot."

> What I mean is, we are prepared for much in religion which we cannot fully rationalize. A religion which had no mysteries would not be a religion. And then, if the intellectual difficulties lie mainly, as they so often do, in the speculative region, we may still believe that religion is true. But it is otherwise with moral difficulties. If religion is seen to be immoral, its reign is over. We cannot have one kind of morality for God and another for man. Conscience, which is the formative principle of religion, is also the great destroyer of a religion seen to be immoral.

"The most striking fact in the present day," he continued, "is that unbelief not only claims to be, but so often is, the result of a true protest of the conscience and the moral nature of man." Indeed, if he "were asked what was the main cause of unbelief in the present day, I should say, not science, not new truths in history and criticism, but a higher tone of morality acting upon an immoral travesty of the gospel of Christ."[120]

Moore proceeded to blame Calvinism for the crisis—a partisan, though not wholly unfair, analysis. There were dynamic and genial Calvinists, such as Charles Spurgeon, who proclaimed the "Approachableness of Jesus" and flouted the taboos of Victorian puritanism. Spurgeon preached in music halls, smoked cigars, and peppered his sermons with inviting humor. Yet this was so clearly a ministry of recovery and repair, it arguably highlighted the wider problem. "No one," gushed an article in *Vanity Fair*, "has succeeded like him in sketching the comic side of repentance and regeneration."[121] Spurgeon's determination to challenge fear and terror as default attitudes to God, urging, in an influential sermon, that "the glory of his person lies not in the splendour which repels, but in the majesty which divinely attracts," was a tacit admission of a pastoral crisis.[122] Although there may have been exaggeration or embellishment in the loss of faith literature, it seems that many people were simply scared into doubt.

George Eliot: The Art of Virtue and the Virtues of Art

The final word on the Victorian hybrid of spiritual doubt goes to George Eliot, who lost her faith in her twenties but continued to bring evangelical values to her writing and criticism. She was, for Nietzsche, the bleached icon of a distinctly English "penance": an infuriating insistence on preserving Christian morality after the loss of Christian faith. Yet Eliot was more than the moral "fanatic" that Nietzsche considered her to be.[123] Her dissent from the evangelical culture contained an important thread of aesthetic or sensual protest—a very English search for what continental philosophers termed a "Life Philosophy." She is at once the model of the early Victorian "ethical revolt" and a pioneer of the aesthetic reaction that characterized the generation of Edmund Gosse and Samuel Butler: a crisis of earnestness. Eliot reveals the inseparability of moral and emotional reactions to orthodoxy, and as the translator of Strauss, Feuerbach, and Spinoza, she suggests the kinship of intellectual, ethical, and emotional protest.

Eliot's loss of faith was the classic revolt of conscience against creed. The context was again the sectarian strife signaled by the Oxford Movement. Disturbed by clerical debates over the purity of the Church at the time of the great Councils, she started to wonder whether Christianity had ever fulfilled its moral ideals. A novel depicting the life of an "amiable atheist" provided a further nudge toward doubt. Eliot recalled that she "was considerably shaken by the impression that religion was not a requisite to moral excellence."[124] A critical study on the origins of Christianity confirmed the train of thought. Finally, her own evangelical Calvinism fell under withering scrutiny. The Calvinist doctrine of total depravity lost all reality for Eliot, and the psychology of gratuitous election began to offend her sense of justice. In December 1841 she declared that she was no longer a Christian, facing the consequences of a scandalous apostasy with simmering defiance. As she wrote to a friend:

> Although I cannot rank among my principles of action a fear of vengeance eternal, gratitude for predestined salvation, or a revelation of future glories as a reward, I fully participate in the belief that the only heaven here, or hereafter, is to be found in conformity with the will of the Supreme; a continual aiming at the attainment of the perfect ideal, the true logos that dwells in the bosom of the one

Father. . . . Good bye, and blessings on you, as they will infallibly be on the children of peace and virtue.[125]

Eliot had been notable for her depth of her piety and she brought the same intensity to her dissent, bravely acknowledging the implications for her marriage prospects in a letter to her father: "I could not, without vile hypocrisy and a miserable truckling to the smile of the world for the sake of my supposed interests, profess to join in worship which I wholly disapprove."[126] Religion was now worldliness; unbelief, the hard road of duty. Eliot moved to London and lived for many years with George Lewes, whose estranged wife refused to grant a divorce. She became active in the freethinking cause, writing widely in the *Westminster Review* before establishing herself as one of the greatest novelists of the era. Finding in literature the most powerful vehicle of criticism, Eliot was never far from autobiography. Words crafted for Dorothea in *Middlemarch* might have been chosen for herself: "If [she] ever attained perfect meekness, it would not be for lack of inward fire."[127]

Eliot's pen was at its sharpest in a review she wrote in 1855 on the works of a prolific evangelical preacher and author, Dr. John Cumming. The article distilled her dissent and it dismantled what she considered the evangelical mythology of a holy remnant surrounded by wicked "infidelity." She turned this narrative on its head, exposing the morality of orthodoxy as the true source of spiritual alienation. Rarely has the righteousness of doubt been on more electrifying display. Cumming was a Presbyterian minister who had built up a large congregation at Covent Garden in London. A trenchant Calvinist and a tireless advocate of Christ's imminent return, Cumming personified the dogmatism and world-betrayal that Eliot most despised in contemporary Christianity. She used his material to launch a wider critique of the capacity of dogma to smother charity and basic intellectual honesty.

Throughout the article, Eliot was less concerned by Cumming's ignorance of biblical criticism and continental philosophy than his determination to inoculate his congregation from such diseases with a policy of sustained caricature. Cumming routinely misrepresented critics under the license of a crusade against infidelity, and, she suggested, he doctored evidence in the knowledge that few of his readers would bother to check the facts. She cited a handful of inaccuracies as proof "of the astounding ignorance which was possible in a metropolitan preacher, A.D. 1854."[128]

But it was the arrogance of Cumming's mode of delivery that so infuriated Eliot, suggesting the poverty of his theology. Eliot registered her disgust with the preacher's habits of exaggeration and slander. She lamented his "reckless assertions," "apocryphal anecdotes," and "vituperative imputations"; his "prodigality of misstatement" and "exuberance of mendacity"; his constant "invention" of "illustrative experience"; his addiction to "vulgar fables" and "borrowed narratives." The preacher's very style, Eliot suggested, revealed a chronic contempt for the "moral quality of veracity." Cumming was symbolic of a theological culture that did not consider "delicate veracity" in intellectual debate "a Christian virtue." Eliot wrote of a "total absence from Dr. Cumming's theological mind of any demarcation between fact and rhetoric," accusing him of deliberate dishonesty in his comments on the "atheist" Voltaire. It was easier to slander such a figure than to dignify an infidel with the truth. Eliot censured Cumming for pouring the old venom of anti-Catholicism onto the new demon of unbelief, trading in stereotypes rather than truth. Cumming was an apologist and an intellectual but it did not prevent him treating "infidels" as spiritual "vermin"—"the rats which are to be nailed up as trophies."[129]

This, however, was only the preamble to a critique of the theology that could so arrest the instincts of decency. Eliot's contention was that the Calvinism of a man like Cumming was capable of generating affection for "the clan" but not "the rest of mankind." Cumming's exultantly divisive theology, complete with its own apocalyptic schedule, was no more than "the transportation of political passions on to a so-called religious platform." His theology of the last days was "the anticipation of the triumph of 'our party,' accomplished by our principal men being 'sent for' into the clouds." It was a theology of "egoistic complacency" nourishing a "hard and condemnatory spirit towards one's fellow-men." Cumming's Calvinism was a "dogmatic system" that "stifled," "misled," and "perver[ted]" the "natural good sense and healthy feeling" of its followers, Eliot claimed. "Dr. Cumming's God," she continued, "is a God who instead of sharing and aiding our human sympathies, is directly in collision with them." His "religion may demand a tribute of love, but it gives a charter to hatred; it may enjoin charity, but it fosters all uncharitableness." Love was the only test.

As she reasoned, with a writer's attention to form: "Precepts of charity uttered with faint breath at the end of a sermon are perfectly futile, when all the force of the lungs has been spent in keeping the hearer's mind fixed on the conception of his fellow-men, not as fellow-sinners and fellow-suffers, but as agents of hell, as automata through whom Satan plays his game on earth." It did not matter whether Cumming's "prognostications" about the future contained grains of truth, Eliot warned. His prophecy "must be *a priori* condemned in the judgment of right-minded persons, by its results as testified in the net moral effect of his sermons." Having started with the symptoms of ignorance and intellectual dishonesty, Eliot finished with a devastating analysis of the cause: a dogmatic structure that stifles virtue and provides a greenhouse for "egoistic passions."[130] The sermon ended.

Eliot pursued the same quarrel in the sumptuously wicked character of Nicholas Bulstrode, the evangelical banker in *Middlemarch* (1872). Eliot was again harsh but revealing—of both the Calvinist culture she so despised and the religious quality of her skepticism. Bulstrode was a man of staunch and unwavering piety, yet incapable of distinguishing between "the glory of God" and his own advancement; a man of mechanical decorum, whose "celestial intimacies" failed to register in a pulse of human warmth. Bulstrode was the specter of a soul-centered spirituality that started and ended with his own: a man worthy of the brisker utterances of his name.

Yet Eliot's portrait was more than a mocking caricature. The force of her analysis lay in the subtlety and sincerity of Bulstrode's theological maneuvering. Bulstrode genuinely believed he was serving God as he rigged appointments, manipulated enemies, and concealed the sins of his youth from everybody, including his wife. The inconsistency was furnished by a theological imagination that either spiritualized sin into abstraction, or incarnated it into a convenient litany of avoidable pleasures. Bulstrode piously abstained from excesses of food and wine while enjoying a "vampire's feast" of "mastery" over fellow mortals. He strained gnats and swallowed camels, and his theology justified him all the way. Bulstrode's technical, propositional orthodoxy flattered his egoism, providing the "mould into which he had constrained his immense need of being something important and predominating." Bulstrode's piety insulated him against self-criticism. As Eliot reflected with caustic penetration, "the egoism which enters our theories does not affect their sincerity; rather, the more our egoism is satisfied, the more robust is our belief." Bulstrode had a chilling capacity to pour out "utterances of repentance" while holding to a course of ruthless self-interest. And time only polished the deception: "as age made egoism more eager but less enjoying, his soul became more saturated with the belief that he did everything for God's sake."[131]

The mature Bulstrode was a haunting image of glazed virtue, in which prayer was a sequence of evasions, and ethics a series of navigable constraints through which the darker instincts flowed with impunity: "For Bulstrode shrank from a direct lie with an intensity disproportionate to the number of his more indirect misdeeds. But many of these misdeeds were like the subtle muscular movements which are not taken account of in the consciousness, though they bring about the end that we fix our mind on and desire. And it is only what we are vividly conscious of that we can vividly imagine to be seen by Omniscience." Bulstrode's piety, in other words, had put his conscience to sleep. When his transgressions finally caught up with him, forcing him "to a kind of propitiation which was not simply a doctrinal transaction," the result was humiliation and ruin. The "resurgent threatening past," wrote Eliot with puritanical relish, "was [finally] making a conscience within him," but it was too little too late. As the chicanery and cruelty behind Bulstrode's fortune went public, he was forced into a form of penitence, though his role in the death of the man who exposed him remained a dark secret. There was no happy ending for Bulstrode, no reconciliation, and his cagey, partial repentance was shown to be little more than self-preservation. Arrogance, furnished by piety, had undone him, cutting him off from those who might have arrested his sorry descent. "There is no general doctrine," Eliot reflected with pastoral emphasis, "which is not capable of eating out our morality if unchecked by the deep-seated habit of direct fellow feeling with individual fellow-men."[132]

This sense of the brittleness and inhumanity of religious zeal pointed to another powerful strand of Eliot's criticism, however. Part of Bulstrode's charade was the ability to hide intangible vices behind a puritanism of visible abstinence, and Eliot believed the hypocrisy extended more widely. Her distaste for an evangelical culture that "had cast a certain suspicion as of plague-infection over the few amusements which survived in the provinces"[133] resonated with a body of Victorian literature, of which Gosse's memoir was perhaps the clearest statement. Gosse complained of a spiritual regimen in which Sundays were endured, friends were to be converted, and parents feared. "There was," he recalled with a chilling hunting analogy, "no close time for souls." Gosse's memory of a visit to another boy's house where he discovered, to his humiliation, that he "had not the faintest idea how to 'play,'" captured the essence of his revolt. He "had never learned, had never *heard of* any 'games.'" His indictment of "evangelical religion" centered on its tendency to exchange "all the tender, indulgent affections, all the genial play of life, all the exquisite pleasures and soft resignations of the body" for "what is harsh and void and negative."[134] The *Westminster Review* article on working-class heresies noted a similar perception of Christianity as an "ungenial religion," while Samuel Butler's *The Way of All Flesh* (1903) delivered the definitive blow to a puritanical culture in which a parent's absence always made the air feel "lighter." It is notable that Eliot, often regarded as the symbol of the earnestness rejected by the late Victorian generation, was asking the same questions. If the essay on Cumming revealed the intimacy of intellectual and moral criticism, *Middlemarch* wove the equally significant thread of stifled sensibility.

When the young and beautiful Dorothea married the desiccated clergyman-scholar, Edward Casaubon, disaster duly beckoned. Thinking she was securing a life of infinitely rewarding duty, she instead suffered a schooling in the egoism of austerity. She told herself that "there would be nothing trivial about our lives"; "it would be like marrying Pascal." And so it was. The sacrilege of a honeymoon passing the time in Rome, while her husband toiled in the Vatican archives, presaged a more enduring alienation. Casaubon was a cloud of gloom and condescension; a one-man weather system of misery and unpublished angst; a symbol of diabolical seriousness. From the elegant harpsichord profaned as a place to stack books, to the dusty, sun-starved misery of the rectory, Eliot's portrait was again brutal. Dorothea had walked into a deathly puritanism of intellectual egoism: the sin of self-assertion masked as the saintly toil of scholarship. Casaubon was "present at this great spectacle of life" but never really there. Dorothea's marriage to such a man was something little short of blasphemy: the "imprisonment" of a "blooming full-pulsed youth" in a "chill, colourless, narrowed landscape." This was a protest on behalf of flesh and humanity, but it was also a religious one. Under Casaubon's cold hand, Dorothea's "religious faith" shrunk to a "solitary cry." Casaubon's grave and ghostly intellectualism drained the life out of Dorothea's hopeful piety.[135]

It was through Will Ladislaw, Casaubon's flamboyant cousin whom Dorothea finally married, that the critique of asceticism was driven home. Sensing the fragility of the duty that tied Dorothea to an unloving husband, Ladislaw went on the offensive, accusing her of a "fanaticism of sympathy," of relishing the misery brought on by her "own goodness." "It is of no use to try and take care of all the world," he challenged. "Would you turn all the youth of the world into a tragic chorus, wailing and moralising over misery? I suspect that you have some false belief in the virtues of misery, and want to make your life a martyrdom." To Dorothea's claim that she was not a melancholy creature, Ladislaw responded: "You talk as if you had never known any youth. It is monstrous—as if you had had a vision of Hades in your childhood, like the boy in the legend. You have been brought up in some of those horrible notions that choose the sweetest women to devour—like Minotaurs. And now you will go and be shut up in that stone prison at Lowick: you will be buried alive." This was an early exchange, but events vindicated Ladislaw. Dorothea remained a woman of infectious virtue, "a noble nature, generous in its wishes, ardent in its charity." She had a presence that "changes the lights" for others.[136] But her courtship with Ladislaw felt like a puritan's repentance: a slow and marvelous recognition that the physical world exists; that life can be enjoyed, and love embraced.

Eliot covered the spectrum of the crisis of faith—from the thrust of conscience against orthodoxy, the frisson of German scholarship, to the aesthetic revolt against "ungenial" rigor. She also revealed another aspect of the revolt: its uncertainty. Eliot's sympathetic treatment of a generous, undogmatic clergyman such as "Farebrother," in *Middlemarch*, or her glowing portrait of the Methodist "prophetess," Dinah Morris, in *Adam Bede*, is a reminder not to overstate the finality of the crisis. Eliot could be warm in praise of the kind of Christianity that met her ethical criteria, proving that the moral critique was not a cover for a harder philosophical stance. Like Voltaire, she could be fulsome on the subject of love and forgiveness.[137] Her account of the "strange blending of exultation and sadness" in an old-fashioned Methodist meeting says something about the wider struggle of faith and doubt—a rising and falling which often evoked "the cadence of a hymn."[138] When Eliot described Celia's ambivalence toward her pious sister, Dorothea, as a mixture of "criticism and awe" she said something about the period as a whole. Unbelief could be as uncertain as faith. Criticism always contained a germ of respect—even a flicker of esteem. An urge to correct is in some sense an urge to restore.

Eliot's praise of the piety that can lift people "above the sordid details of their own narrow lives" and suffuse "their souls with the sense of a pitying, loving, infinite Presence, sweet as summer to the houseless needy" was unfeigned.[139] One of her objections to Cumming was the preference for doctrine and proposition over the unfiltered personality of Christ. Men like Cumming, she lamented, rarely speak of a Christ who wept over Jerusalem, and uttered "the sublime prayer, 'Father forgive them'." They have little to say about "the gentler fruits of the Spirit, and the peace of God which passeth understanding." Eliot's contrast between "spiritual communion" with Christ and a mechanical piety more concerned "to fix the date when He shall appear in the sky" is indicative of a Christian fervor that continued to haunt the world of unbelief.[140] It suggests a fact frequently overlooked in histories of the period: that unbelief was not a one-way street. There was a significant Victorian phenomenon of "reconversion," characterized by one historian as a "crisis of doubt."[141] Of the eight national leaders of the secularist movement who took to the stage at a high-profile meeting in 1860, three reconverted to Christianity.[142]

"It is . . . clear," noted the *Westminster Review* article on working-class heresies in 1862, "that many who are driven into unbelief by the old theology cannot contentedly remain there." The author cited the strange history of a Methodist chapel in Yorkshire that came to be known as the "Infidel Chapel," subsequently serving as a meeting place for the radical politics of the "Chartists" in the 1840s, a home for "Owenite Socialists," and then serving as a base for some "Spiritualists." Spiritualism, however, led back to heterodox versions of Christianity. Finally, "a theology half Unitarian and half Swedenborgian gradually grew up, and what they called a 'Free Christian Church' was established."[143] The early twentieth century witnessed a similar pattern of reengagement among British intellectuals, a phenomenon mirrored by a minor "Catholic renaissance" in France. Such reconversions were unusual but by no means exceptional and they often involved minds fully conversant with the challenges of "modern thought."

The weakening hold of Christian orthodoxy was a phenomenon often justified, but rarely driven, by the progress of science and scholarship. One study cited the evolutionary biologist, George Romanes, as "one of the very few men whose loss of faith in the truth of religion can be directly ascribed to the influence of scientific naturalism." But Romanes's "agnosticism" was too "pure" to live with a dogmatic naturalism and he inched his way back to Christian faith. The "lonely mystery of existence" raised questions that science could not answer.[144] Romanes is significant not only for demonstrating the rarity and fragility of the scientific path to unbelief, but for his commentary on the psychology of disenchantment. "Reason," he reflected, with the mathematician and theologian, Blaise Pascal, by his side, "is very far indeed from being the sole guide of judgment that it is usually taken to be—so far indeed, that, save in matters approaching down-right demonstration . . . it is usually hampered by custom, prejudice, dislike, etc. to a degree that would astonish the most sober philosopher could he lay bare to himself all the mental processes whereby the complex act of dissent is eventually determined."[145]

Samuel Butler was similarly dismissive of rationalist postures, complaining that "men strive after fixed immutable arrangements of ideas much as the French strive after a written constitution, and with much the same result."[146] These were virtual paraphrases of Nietzsche's blunt appraisal of the intellectual critique of religion as a phony war: a ritual in which passion hides under the pseudonymous dignity of reason. "What decides against Christianity," he wrote in the *Gay Science* (1882), "is our taste, not our reasons."[147] It disappointed him that moral sensibility so often took precedence over aesthetic and sensual exuberance. He considered "little moralistic females à la Eliot" the arch-exponents of this continuing bondage. But he never claimed that this was an exclusively "English consistency."[148] It was with a sigh of regret that he offered a summary of the age of unbelief as penetrating as Darwin's: "You see what it was that really triumphed over the Christian God: Christian morality itself."[149]

6

The God that Failed

FEUERBACH, MARX, AND THE POLITICS OF SALVATION

Men make their own history, but they do not make it just as they please; they do not make it under circumstances chosen by themselves, but under circumstances directly encountered, given, and transmitted from the past.

—MARX, "The Eighteenth Brumaire of Louis BONAPARTE," 1852

THE LAVISHLY DECORATED Church of the Resurrection in Podgorica, the capital of Montenegro, contains an unusual detail. Within sumptuous frescoes depicting the life of a sacred community is an image of hell, in which Marx, Engels, and the Yugoslav communist leader, Josip Broz Tito, writhe with august desperation in crimson currents of wrath. Bound fast in what looks like a river of blood, the communist icons are finally caught in a stream of hatred they had themselves unleashed. Only their heads are visible. In a further insult, a grey-bearded devil, perching with cruel hands around the body of a child, displays a striking resemblance to Karl Marx.[1] The image has drawn criticism, but it is not the only religious building in the region to breathe judgment on communist leaders, and the gesture reflects a dark reality of twentieth-century history. Communist authorities, operating under a Marxist ideology that condemned faith as counterrevolutionary deception, may have been responsible for the deaths of more religious believers than all other regimes in history. As a spokesman defending the imagery of the Church of the Resurrection pointed out, works by Marx and Engels were compulsory reading during the communist era. Persecution had its proof texts. When Stalin appointed a minister for religious affairs in 1943, he acquired the nickname of *Narkomopium*—"people's commissar for opium"—in macabre allusion to

Marx's most famous put-down.[2] Communism represents the fiercest challenge to religion of the modern era: the twentieth-century's "dominant form of secularism."[3]

More prosaically, perhaps, the structures of thought bequeathed by Marx, including the social interpretation of religion, represent one of the most enduring intellectual legacies of the nineteenth century. Marx may not have conquered the capitalist West, but any student of the social sciences or humanities in the late twentieth century could be forgiven for thinking he had. There was a time when you could not study anything without first demonstrating its relation to "the means of production." While there has been great value in exposing the economic affinities of ancient and august cultures, the study of religion has not always gained. When religious motivation is casually dismissed as "false consciousness" or "social control," insight becomes constraint. If the political legacy of Marxism has been persecution, the intellectual legacy has been a kind of historical color blindness: a persistent bleaching of the spectrum of human motivation. One of the costs has been confusion about the origins of Marxism itself.

Judged by outcomes, and by its own "scientific" claims, Marxism stands as a defiant exception to Nietzsche's dictum about "Christian morality" triumphing over "the Christian God." But judged by origins, and by its animating charisma of protest, Marxism affirms Nietzsche's insight with stunning amplitude. The germ of revolt against religion and spiritually sanctioned capitalism is unmistakably religious. Not for the first time: aggression was born in tempestuous kinship.

By severing ties with "utopian" predecessors, Marx and Engels presented their brand of socialism as a clean, scientific formula, uncontaminated by religious idealism. In mature, theoretical Marxism, questions of morality and justice were regarded as epiphenomenal to economics. Everything was taken care of. Yet it is difficult to read the early documents of the movement, including Marx's unfinished treatise on *Capital*, without sensing a ferocity of moral passion: stories of young children, aged and diminished by the licensed barbarism of the factory system; gangs of undernourished agricultural laborers, drained of health and hope; struggling artisans, thrown onto the street by merciless landlords; a London washerwoman, literally worked to death as she toiled to prepare dresses for a society ball. Marx prefaced the German edition of *Capital* with a biblical allusion: "Should the German reader shrug his shoulders, like a Pharisee, at the conditions of the English industrial and agricultural workers, or optimistically calm himself by thinking, that in Germany things are by far not yet so bad, then I must call out to him: *De te fabula narratur!*" ("It is your story being told!")[4]

The truth is that Marx was both a materialist and a moralist. The claim of this chapter is that his materialism emerged from his moralism. The withering account of history as a tale of greed and gain was an originally religious insight, gleaned above all from Ludwig Feuerbach. Marx's sweeping critique of democracy and "political economy" as the servants of capitalist power was an extension of his critique of religion. And his religious criticism, centering on theology's nefarious habit of massaging power, was part of a tradition of prophetic protest that reached only a superficial terminus in Feuerbach's atheist humanism. Marx once claimed to have found Hegel standing on his head, reading history as mind not matter, insensible to the crunch of events. But having turned Hegel "the right way up," Marx was never quite sure which way to stand himself.

Feuerbach and the Selfish God

The radicalism of socialism lay in disappointment with the broken promises of modernity. Enlightenment, philosophy, liberalism, and the iconic caesura of the French Revolution had each flattered to deceive. Commerce was crueler than feudalism. The age of reform represented only a changing of the guard. As an English radical warned in 1830, "Of all governments, a government of the middle classes is the most grinding and remorseless."[5] Peerless among the critics was Marx, who quickly perceived that without structural change the vaunted liberties of modernity were chimeras. The celebrated comment that history repeats itself, "the first time as tragedy, the second as farce," contained one of the vital seeds of his thought.[6] Without profound reorganization of society and economy, one Napoleon will lead to another—the second only more ridiculous than the first. The power of Marx's indictment rested on his ability to see through the coded rhetoric of liberty, the scandal of words without action. "None of the so-called rights of man," he protested in 1844, "go beyond egoistic man."[7] True freedom would be larger than anything contemplated by the Enlightenment.

For Marx, and a number of Christian socialists, the critique of religion and reason was almost synonymous. There was a deep, shared resentment of theologies and political philosophies that served to extenuate the cruelties of industrialism, counseling submission rather than protest. In *The Poor Sinner's Gospel* (1845), George Weitling, a leading voice of German communism, attacked the "pharisees" of modern Christianity for turning "a gospel of freedom, equality and love [into] a gospel of tyranny, servitude and deception." He situated the fallacy in an absconding theology of heavenly justice, which winks at oppression and leaves the world as it is. "To transfer the goal of Christianity into an ideal region," Weitling complained, was to sanctify injustice. "Poverty and misery wait patiently for the hereafter and serve the interests of others here on earth." "We should not always be looking up at the sky when we talk about the kingdom of God," Weitling urged. He excoriated the kind of technical, priestly theology that serves to "confuse our fellow men and put their spiritual powers to sleep, in order to enjoy the fruits of their physical labors." A "faith" that fails to bear fruit, Weitling warned, "is dead." Judgment would be imminent and decisive.[8]

Marx and Engels ousted Weitling from the leadership of the communist movement in 1846. They considered his methods of propaganda and agitation naïve and dangerous. They rebranded the brotherly fellowship hitherto known as the "League of the Just" with the more imposing nomenclature of the "Communist League." Yet their critique of a spiritually sanctioned industrial system was essentially the same as Weitling's. Religion underwrites economic violence by postponing justice to another age and putting the conscience to sleep. It muzzles the voice of protest. In theoretical Marxism, such ideas were shrouded in a technical language of "ideology" and "false consciousness." After Feuerbach, all mention of "God" and "faith" smacked of reaction and theoretical innocence. Yet there was a direct link between the "scientific" exposure of religion-as-ideology and the biblical, in-house criticism of figures like Weitling, and the link was Feuerbach himself. In the stark assertion that faith without works is dead, Weitling provided a one-line summary of Feuerbach's atheist smart bomb of 1841, *The Essence of Christianity*.

Feuerbach's exposure of both theology and philosophy as smooth and enabling agents of power was the outcome of a very simple intellectual maneuver. It consisted of the challenge that for a God, or an idea, to be considered real, it must possess powers of social influence. If an idea or a faith system cannot interrupt the rhythms of ordinary living, Feuerbach suggests, there is no reason to take it seriously—except to expose it as a sanctifying gloss on already regnant appetites. If a theology or a philosophy consistently fails to change the weather, Feuerbach challenges, it may be no more than a totem or an idol. And it was as such that he was prepared to denominate the Christian God. Feuerbach's assertion that the Christian deity is nothing more than a convenient invention—a projection of the human "ego"—rested on the same sensitivity that excited Weitling and a host of Christian socialists. Feuerbach's humanism, and the Marxist criticism that was forged around it, was another child of conscience.

Feuerbach was born in 1804 in Landshut, Bavaria, where he received a strong Lutheran upbringing, partly to fortify him against the pervasive Catholicism of the region. As a teenager, he demonstrated a deep, scripture-oriented piety, taking private lessons in Hebrew to supplement his studies of the New Testament. He prepared to enter the ministry. During his studies at Heidelberg, however, he encountered, first, rationalist biblical criticism (a "spider's web of sophisms"), and, second, Hegelian philosophy, which entranced him. In 1824 he transferred to Berlin to study under the great man. Feuerbach was initially drawn to philosophy as a way of expressing his religious belief but soon after arriving in Berlin he seems to have lost all affection for theology. His "soul" demanded "truth," "unity," and "decisiveness," and these could not be found within Christianity's "mishmash of freedom and dependence." The unity and dynamism of Hegel's system became Feuerbach's reference point and a weapon for attacking orthodoxy. Hegel provided harmony and symmetry where theology had sown confusion and discord. His philosophy was the "Bethlehem of the new world."[9]

It was not long, however, before the Lutheran came back to bite the philosopher. Feuerbach turned his back on Hegel, rejecting his philosophy as a fog of abstractions, a whitewash of unhappy reality, a system of speculation that "wrenches man out of nature."[10] He began to associate philosophy with arrogance and dereliction of duty, later reflecting that he had to "shake off" the philosopher, to enable "the philosopher to give way to the man."[11] As he subsequently summarized his intellectual journey: "God was my first thought, reason my second, and man my third and last."[12] Although Feuerbach later turned on Luther in spectacular fashion, the earthiness of Lutheran theology helped to furnish his critique of the arrogance of speculation and the treachery of theory. Luther was rare among Western thinkers in the value he placed on ordinary human existence, the sacredness of the mundane. Feuerbach cited Luther in the *Essence of Christianity* on the virtues of a "full belly" and a "merry head," and on the "religious act" of "eating and drinking."[13] More than once Feuerbach described himself as "Luther II".[14] Luther was a vital source of Feuerbach's growing indictment of the flesh-searing dualism of Western philosophy, helping him to see the egoism that can inhere in sacrifice, and the hollowness of intellectual sophistication.

Feuerbach's suspicion was that any impulse to separate "ultimate" reality from lived experience was rooted in selfish desire. We divide mind and spirit from matter because, deep down, it suits us to renounce responsibility for the world and its problems. This was an idea that would soon crash violently upon Christian theology but it surfaced initially as a kind of incarnational protest against the bloodless intellectualism of Western philosophy, and Hegelian thought in particular. Feuerbach lost his faith before he parted company with his philosophical master, but it was from the break with Hegel and the Enlightenment that he gathered some of his most challenging insights for Christian theology. Indeed it was the ability to classify philosophy and theology as two sides of the same coin that gave his ideas such political potency. Words come in many varieties, but they are still only words.

"World neglect" was a harsh charge to level at Hegel, of all people. Hegel's mission had been to overcome precisely this fallacy of Western philosophy, reaching its culmination in Kantian "idealism." Hegel believed that he had grounded reason in reality, tempering the savage zeal of a French Revolution in which reason swept in to destroy whatever stood in its path. Hegel's deeply spiritual concept of reason was one in which truth emerged within the historical process, as a kind of immanent force, rebounding from conflict in a series of dynamic "syntheses." It was an alluring vision, but one that required the wind to blow in the right direction.

When history was on his side, during a period of exciting reform in the 1820s, Hegel's claim that the real is rational and the rational is real gained force. Prussia was accomplishing peacefully what the French Revolution had attempted to achieve with violence. But when reform turned to reaction, Hegel's sails began to flap in the wind. His grand philosophical system began to look like an apology for power. Under the conservative regime of Frederick William IV, a model that counted the Prussian state among the prized manifestations of the Spirit started to creak, and Hegel's followers divided into conservative and radical camps ("Young Hegelians"). The assertion of Feuerbach, preeminent among the radicals, was that claims of "synthesis" and immanent rationality amounted to an exercise in public relations: the philosophical baptism of an unchanged world. You cannot rescue history by simply asserting its rationality. Philosophy was theology, using even longer words. Although scarcely immune to rhetorical exuberance himself, the power of Feuerbach's humanism lay in the capacity to cut through acres of justifying verbiage to expose the inner "secret" of intellectual discourse. If there was clarity there was not always originality: the cry of hypocrisy was an old one.

The Secret of Religion

Feuerbach had written widely on religion and philosophy by the time he wrote the *Essence of Christianity*, finding an inspiring predecessor in "the acute and learned Bayle." Bayle prompted Feuerbach to the insight that a person's purest religiosity may be no more than the expression of his or her "own true essence," an idea for which he had a growing dossier of personal evidence.[15] His criticism emerged organically from a kind of pastoral despair. Feuerbach was like a small-town preacher, maddened by the inertia of his flock. In his *Thoughts on Death and Immortality* (1830), Feuerbach decried a comfortable Christianity that had "clouded" its "light" by becoming "the Spirit of the world." He condemned modern religion as a glorified "life-insurance company," where God functions as "the grease on the squeaky wagon of life." A returning Jesus, Feuerbach suggested, would be perceived as "the Antichrist" by the easy pilgrims of the present.[16] The more spiritual flourishes of the volume were purged from later editions, but this method of demystification-by-jeremiad was the very model of the *Essence of Christianity*.

Feuerbach made no effort to distinguish ethical critique from intellectual exposure. Like Spinoza, weighing miracles in the scales of divine equity, Feuerbach felt that if he could expose the tawdriness of the ethics involved the science could wait. "I do not ask whether this or that, or any miracle can happen or not," he explained in the preface. "I only show what miracle is."[17] Questions of fact or historicity paled against the central claim that a theology will be known by its fruits. The technical, proto-Freudian thesis of "projection" rests on the ethical intuition that a God who exists to furnish my neighbor's needs is probably a conceit of my neighbor's imagination.

Humans differ from animals in their capacity for reflection, Feuerbach explained, and it is from such cords of consciousness that a tapestry of divinity is woven. "We feel awe, reverence, humility, devout admiration, in thinking of a truly great, noble man; we feel ourselves worthless, we sink into nothing, even in the presence of human greatness," Feuerbach ventured, and such sentiments were the raw materials of religion. "Whatever strongly impresses a man, whatever produces an unusual effect on his mind," Feuerbach suggested, "he personifies as a divine being." But the advantage of an invisible God is that we can make of him what we want. In Christian faith, Feuerbach contends, spiritual awe meshes with subtle threads of pragmatism, so that we worship but we also control the projected being. Religion comes to provide the kind of power that is typically elusive in ordinary living. It is an acoustic illusion in which we mistake our own voice for the comforting approbation of a divine bodyguard. "God for me," writes Feuerbach, "this is the consolatory mystery of religion, of Christianity." "Religion is a dream, in which our own conceptions and emotions appear to us as separate existences." Or in the most evocative summary of a Copernican challenge: "Man is the motive principle, the soul of God."[18]

Feuerbach claimed that the first half of the book would be descriptive, rather than polemical. But his aggression was instantly apparent as he portrayed the appetite for divinity as a kind of refracted lust. "Heaven," Feuerbach asserts, "is [the Christian's] treasure-casket," a repository of "self-flattering wishes." God is "a mirror of human vanity and self-complacency." His personality "is nothing else than the projected personality of man." Religion, for Feuerbach, is a money-laundering scheme in which our worst instincts are passed through a series of heavenly transactions before being claimed back as virtue. Under religion's broad and enabling terms, *my* need becomes *God's* demand. Selfish desire is reconceived as fidelity to the divine personality, who turns out to be nothing more than an inflated image of the self. In faith, Feuerbach contends, "Man gives up his personality" before claiming it all back in an "Almighty, infinite, unlimited being" who just happens to be on his side. Such a God, Feuerbach contends, "is the very luxury of egoism." For the man of faith, while superficially "humiliated to the lowest degree, is in truth exalted to the highest."[19] Religion is a game in which we make a show of sacrifice while quietly counting our gains.

This was partly the Lutheran at work on the casuistry of performative religion, and Feuerbach had harsh words for the subtle egoism of the monastery. But such comments faded into insignificance next to his response to the Protestant reaction. The observation that in Luther one finds a theology of flesh and blood lost all innocence for Feuerbach. By the time he wrote the *Essence of Christianity* and the supplementary volume,

The Essence of Faith according to Luther (1844), the Protestant reformer had become the supreme symbol of the religious delusion. "Luther" Feuerbach went so far as to declare, "was the first to let out the secret of the Christian faith." With his swaggering dogmatism and his all-absolving doctrine of faith, Luther had shown "What really motivates the Christian in his belief in God," namely, "Human egoism, or self-love."[20]

Feuerbach's thesis is overwhelmingly dependent on Luther. Quotations run into their hundreds. Feuerbach treads a fine line between denouncing him as a violator of Christian instincts and holding him up as the natural terminus of the faith principle. In search of clear, "irrefragable proof that man in religion contemplates himself as the object of the Divine Being," Feuerbach simply piles up the Protestant evidence. Before venturing an explanation in the Lutheran doctrine of faith, Feuerbach establishes the identity of God and self on little more than the evidence of Luther's exultant rhetoric. Luther claimed that in faith, "we are thus honoured above all creatures, even above the angels, so that we can with truth boast, My own flesh and blood sits at the right hand of God and reigns over all. Such honour has no creature, not even an angel." "We Christians are greater and more than all creatures, not in or by ourselves, but through the gift of God in Christ, against whom the world is nothing, and can do nothing." "We are lords not only of birds, but of all living creatures, and all things are given for our service, and are created only for our sake."[21] For Feuerbach, the rampant egoism of such sentiments disclosed the hidden motor of religious faith. The gloating reformer had let the cat out of the bag. The secret of religion is self.

Feuerbach echoed Spinoza in the view that Judaism had pioneered religion as "narrow-hearted egoism," centering on the conceit that Israel is "dearer and more precious" than other nations. But Christianity had turned the egoism of the nation into the pride of the chosen individual. "Know that God so takes thee unto himself that thy enemies are his enemies," wrote Luther. "It is the Christians for whose sake God spares the whole world. The Father makes his sun to rise on the evil and on the good, and sends rain on the just and on the unjust. Yet this happens only for the sake of the pious and thankful." "He who despises me, despises God." Feuerbach let Luther speak for himself, before adding, with crisp condescension: "Such declarations as these are, I should think, *argumenta ad hominem* for the identity of God and man."[22]

It was in the doctrine of providence—the mutation of an originally innocent idea of God-as-love—that Feuerbach found some of his clearest "evidence" of egoism. A God who delighted in the service of a self-regarding elect was a God who reeked of human presumption. It was again in Luther that Feuerbach fell upon his most excruciating material. Luther had suggested that the miracles of the Old Testament, including the parting of the Red Sea, were performed "for us, who are chosen"; that the whole symphony of creation was a song to the elect. Feuerbach catalogued the material before offering another summary judgment. Following a playground boast from Luther on the impotence of pagan gods next to the majesty of Jehovah, he declared: "Providence is therefore the most undeniable, striking proof, that in religion, in the nature of God himself, man is occupied only with himself, that the mystery of theology is anthropology, that the substance, the content of the infinite being, is the 'finite' being."[23]

Feuerbach's brutal reduction of theology to "anthropology" rests on little more than moral revulsion from the ethical complacency of religion. The seminal charge of an invented deity is "proven" from the roguish servility of Christian theology, as defined by one theologian in particular. As Feuerbach continues, in a passage that captures the ethical passion of his assault:

> Faith in Providence is faith in one's own worth, the faith of man in himself; hence the beneficent consequences of this faith, but hence also false humility, religious arrogance, which, it is true, does not rely on itself, but only because it commits the care of itself to the blessed God. God concerns himself about me; he has in view my happiness, my salvation; he wills that I shall be blest; but that is my will also: thus, my interest is God's interest, my own will is God's will, my own aim is God's aim,—God's love for me is nothing else than my self-love deified. Thus when I believe in Providence, in what do I believe but in the divine reality and significance of my own being?[24]

Luther had described faith as the "Creator of the Godhead," insofar as it turns a hidden God into a mighty friend. Belief was everything: "As thou believest of God, so is He to thee." Feuerbach appreciated Luther's candor: "That God is another being is only illusion, only imagination," he responded. "In declaring that God is for thee, thou declarest that he is thy own being." The magical, all-sufficing language of faith proved that "God is what the soul desires and needs him to be."[25] It was all too easy. " 'As in your heart,' says Luther, 'so is your God,' " noted Feuerbach in the supplementary volume. The suspicious ease of the transaction confirmed to the disillusioned critic that "God is a blank tablet on which there is nothing written but what you yourself have written."[26]

Feuerbach clearly failed in his task of being only a "listener," an observer of the religious illusion. He was preaching a sermon. The tone was urgent, angry, and prophetic. "If, therefore, you would be clear on these subjects," he challenged, with another burst of demystifying outrage, "exchange your mystical, perverted anthropology, which you call theology, for real anthropology." "You yourselves," he continued, "admit that the essence of the pantheistical God is nothing but the essence of Nature. Why, then, will you only see the mote in the eyes of your opponents, and not observe the very obvious beam in your own eyes? . . . Admit that your personal God is nothing else than your own personal nature, that while you believe in and construct your supra- and extra-natural God, you believe in and construct nothing else than the supra- and extra-naturalism of your own self."[27]

Luther dominated the discussion but Feuerbach also quoted Calvin on the suspicious odor of providence, in a later work. The true believer, Calvin had written,

> will not doubt that a special Providence, encompassing every detail, watches over him, permitting nothing that does not redound to his welfare and salvation. Consequently, he will relate everything that happens for the best, in accordance with his heart's desires, to God and regard God alone as its cause, even if he has experienced God's benefaction through the service of man or received help from soulless creatures. For in his heart he will think: Surely it is the Lord who has inclined their souls toward me, in order that they might be the instruments of His benevolence toward me.

Feuerbach could not contain his fury. Here was a passage in which "the entire wretchedness of this theological view is brought home to us"; where the whole chain of sentient life is conceived as a hammock for the elect; where "soulless creatures" wait on the chosen. "But that is in the nature of theology," Feuerbach concluded. "Its personification, the theologian, is an angel in his dealings with God, a devil in his dealings with man."[28]

Feuerbach's critique of the opposite extreme of asceticism was more than a passing concern. He ridiculed the urge to escape "this gross, material, sinful body," and he likened the self-scrutiny of asceticism to the vanity of gazing into a mirror. It was pointless and reprehensible, at the same time. The "unwedded and ascetic" ideal served to "stimulate" the desires it aimed to repress. The "secret enjoyment of sensuality" had been the inevitable reality of monastic life. Feuerbach despised this kind of piety but he admitted that it had produced its saints. It represented a genuine attempt to subject earthly desire to supernatural guidance and discipline. "Protestant morality," on the other hand, "is and was a carnal mingling of the Christian with the man, the natural, political, civil, social man, or whatever else he may be called in distinction from the Christian," Feuerbach censured. "Catholic morality was the *Mater dolorosa*; Protestant morality a comely, fruitful matron."[29]

Where Catholic morality made the two-way conversation of prayer at least temporarily credible, Protestantism shattered the illusion by collapsing human and divine interest into a common, "carnal" morality. Where saintly perseverance gave luster to the illusion of transcendence, making religion for a moment realistic, Protestant indulgence gave the game away. "Protestantism," Feuerbach suggested, "denied the sufferings of Christ as constituting a principle of morality." And by denying that Christians have to live any more admirably than other people, Protestantism divulged the essential egoism of faith. In Feuerbach's breathless takedown: Protestantism was at once the aberration and the essence. It was the scorching emancipation from Christian duty that somehow pointed a finger at the entire Christian faith. "It is," he contended with a vital but precarious link in his argument, the "Christians of the present day [who] decline to know anything more of the sufferings of Christ" who have "first made out what true Christianity is." A religion, he explained, "stands and falls" by its morality. "With a supernatural faith is necessarily associated a supernatural morality." "Protestantism," however, "tore this bond asunder: in faith it affirmed Christianity; in life, in practice, it denied Christianity." It "binds men only in faith, all the rest it leaves free." "Protestantism is," he triumphantly asserted, "the practical negation of Christianity, the practical assertion of the natural man." It proved everything he wished to argue about the human origins of religion. "The necessary practical consequences of the Christian faith," Feuerbach concluded, with his usual blend of horror and glee, "Protestantism has relegated to the other world, to heaven—in other words, has denied them."[30]

Whereas the egoism of the monk is subtle, complex, and essentially honest, the egoism of the Protestant is brazen, unapologetic, and, to Feuerbach, self-damning. Feuerbach did to Lutheran theology what

Luther did to the contritional piety of the middle ages: he reduced it to "carnality," a work of the "flesh." He is almost grateful to Luther for spelling out, in defiant effusions of ethical abandon, what he considers the raw psychology of faith. After a series of assurances from Luther that "Christ did not come on earth to interfere in the government of the Emperor Augustus and teach him how to reign"; "Where worldly government begins, Christianity ends"; and—most unfortunately of all—that "Christ did not come to change the creature," Feuerbach offered his own summary of the Protestant dispensation: "You cannot in life, at least in this life, be Christians, peculiar, superhuman beings, therefore ye ought not to be such." Protestantism "legitimized this negation of Christianity before its still Christian conscience," Feuerbach thundered. We will be "new creatures" in heaven, he added with unrestrained sarcasm, "but here everything remains as of old."[31]

Here was the seed of the Marxist concept of religion as ideology, emerging not as social science but as a theological critique of Feuerbach's own, Lutheran tradition. Of Luther's conscience-salving "chasm" between heaven and earth, Feuerbach claimed, "Catholicism knows nothing. What it denies in heaven, i.e., in faith, it denies also, as far as possible, on earth, i.e., in morality." There was, he ventured, an almost persuasive integrity to a figure like St. Anthony, abandoning his possessions in a literal interpretation of Christ's injunction to sell what you have and give to the poor. "Only thus did he prove his spiritual freedom from the treasures of this world." But such gestures only highlighted the leisured folly of modern religion:

> Such freedom, such truth, is certainly in contradiction with the Christianity of the present day, according, to which the Lord has required only a spiritual freedom, i.e., a freedom which demands no sacrifice, no energy;—an illusory, self-deceptive freedom—a freedom from earthly good, which consists in its possession and enjoyment! For certainly the Lord said, "My yoke is easy." How harsh, how unreasonable would Christianity be if it exacted from man the renunciation of earthly riches! Then assuredly Christianity would not be suited to this world. So far from this, Christianity is in the highest decree practical and judicious; it defers the freeing oneself from the wealth and pleasures of this world to the moment of natural death (monkish mortification is an unchristian suicide);—and allots to our spontaneous activity the acquisition and enjoyment of

> earthly possessions. Genuine Christians do not indeed doubt the truth of the heavenly life,—God forbid! Therein they still agree with the ancient monks; but they await that life patiently, submissive to the will of God, i.e., to their own selfishness, to the agreeable pursuit of worldly enjoyment.[32]

This was the heart of the Protestant problem: a scorching dualism that turns out to be very comfortable in the world. Torn between a theoretical strategy of judging the whole of Christianity through Protestant sins and a more impulsive urge to isolate the Lutheran formula as a scandalous aberration, Feuerbach constantly succumbed to the latter. He cited the medieval mystic, Johannes Tauler, on the impossibility of loving both God and the world, before replying with another exasperated rejoinder: "But they were abstract Christians. And we live now in the age of conciliation. Yes, truly!" He pitted the ethical rigor of *The Imitation of Christ* against the moral amnesia he perceived in Luther. Here, Feuerbach suggested, was a glimpse of "the genuine morality of Catholicism, that morality which the saints attested by their lives, and which was sanctioned even by the Head of the Church, otherwise so worldly." But, he continued,

> I turn away with loathing and contempt from modern Christianity, in which the bride of Christ readily acquiesces in polygamy . . . but yet at the same time—oh! shameful hypocrisy!—swears by the eternal, universally binding irrefragable sacred truth of God's Word. I turn back with reverence to the misconceived truth of the chaste monastic cell, where the soul betrothed to heaven did not allow itself to be wooed into faithlessness by a strange earthly body![33]

It is sometimes unclear whether Feuerbach was writing an atheist manifesto or a religious tract. The contrast between the "genuine morality of Catholicism" and the "shameful hypocrisy" of Protestantism is real and compelling for Feuerbach. A Catholic reader could feel largely vindicated by his prose. So the question arises: Can the entire Christian religion be tethered to Luther's doomed vessel? Does the charge of egoism apply to all theology? Feuerbach's answer is that it does, to varying degrees. His claim is that Christianity contains two original yet competing impulses: love and faith. Lutheran theology represents the mutation of a tension basic to the whole tradition. There is a positive and unifying principle of love in the earliest Christian literature; and there is a divisive, alienating principle of faith, which constantly threatens to sever the bonds of love and unity. Feuerbach's challenge is that love can only triumph over the alienating effects of amoral faith by destroying the illusion of transcendence altogether. It was on this not unchristian ground that Feuerbach pitched his atheist tent.

The Secret of the Secret: The Curse of Faith

Feuerbach's critique of faith has a clear, spatial quality. Love, the primordial and benign impulse of Christianity, is horizontal, immediate, and directed to friend and neighbor alike. Faith is vertical, projected beyond kith and kin to an imaginary being, severed from human responsibility. Faith begins with a certain innocence: a humble reverence for a holy other. But theology turns "the originally involuntary and harmless separation of God from man" into a fixed duality, and it is from this seemingly innocent dualism of God and humankind that the affections of a believer are fatally sundered. For the heavenly deity, though in reality only the echo of the earthly ego, is also the dangerous God. As soon as we think of God as a separate being working from different rules, ethics and humanity become relative values. In the space established between human and "divine" prerogatives, evil runs amok, the irony being that the freedoms granted by this "supernatural" being are only the unshackled desires of the heart. Under the green light of faith, Feuerbach warned, God can become the "image of thy passions, thy revenge, or ambition."[34] The loftier the theology: the more patently human the religion.

Feuerbach's intuitions were less than novel. Castellio said the same thing in his quarrel with Calvin. The shattering contention was that the sins of the untamed God are a direct consequence of Christian faith. Faith is responsible for the enabling canopy of "Christian sophistry," and even the crimes committed beneath it. Once God is separate from humankind, he can assume qualities like "omnipotence" and "omniscience," reducing love to the status of a "predicate." In faith, Feuerbach contends, "God appears to me in another form besides that of love; in the form of omnipotence, of a severe power not bound by love; a power in which, though in a smaller degree, the devils participate." "So long as love is not exalted into a substance, into an essence," he continues, "so long there lurks in the background of love a subject who even without love is something by himself, an unloving monster, a diabolical being, whose personality, separable and actually separated from love, delights in the blood of heretics and unbelievers,—the phantom of religious fanaticism."[35] The claim was that such a deity is the inevitable fruit of Christianity's priority of faith over love. But once again, it is to Protestant sources that Feuerbach turns for damning proof.

In Christian orthodoxy, Feuerbach argued, "Faith has the significance of religion, love only that of morality. This has been declared very decidedly by Protestantism." Under the stern eye of faith, "Love does not alone fill my soul: I leave a place open for my uncharitableness by thinking of God as a subject in distinction from the predicate [of love]." Christianity has advocated love, but it "has not made love free; it has not raised itself to the height of accepting love as absolute." "And," he continues, "it has not given this freedom, nay, cannot give it, because it is a religion,—and hence subjects love to the dominion of faith. Love is only the exoteric, faith the esoteric doctrine of Christianity; love is only the morality, faith the religion of the Christian religion." Faith and love are at war in Christianity, Feuerbach maintained, and orthodoxy has declared only one winner.[36] As he expressed the tension more bluntly in the volume on Luther: "Love is the heart which beats for others, but faith is the heart which only beats for itself."[37]

Luther exulted in the belief "that our justification, salvation, and consolation, lie out of ourselves." This was the foundation of the Christian hope. Feuerbach sensed criminal evasion in the very idea. The upward gaze represented a betrayal of human responsibility, even when the manifestations were subtle and inoffensive. Such was the argument of the final, definitive chapter of the *Essence of Christianity,* on "The Contradiction of Faith and Love." Here, Feuerbach added the crimes of persecution to the moral complacency of Protestantism in his arraignment of religious egoism, and he attempted to diagnose a cause—or at least a mechanism—in Christianity's lurching preference for purity of belief over purity of living. Feuerbach had no time for the darting sophistry that would deny that religion was essentially responsible for the wars of religion. Such scholarship only proved his theme. The theological bromide that "the horrors of Christian religious history" are theoretically separable from Christian faith; and the comforting myth that social evils may be cast "on the shoulders of unbelief, or of misbelief, or of men in general" provided further evidence of the blinding propensities of religious egoism. Feuerbach's contention was that the finest theological minds had been complicit in the barbarities of persecution. Indeed, he challenged: the "very denial of faith that it is itself to blame for the evil in Christianity, is a striking proof that it is really the originator of that evil, because it is a proof of the narrowness, partiality, and intolerance which render it well-disposed only to itself, to its own adherents, but ill-disposed, unjust towards others."[38] Feuerbach never suggested that religion was an exclusive cause of violence. His argument was that religion had provided a vehicle for aggression—so successfully that some of its most pious votaries were entirely ignorant of their real motives as they pursued brutal ambitions in the name of a supernatural God. Religion was thus a masking agent for passions that Feuerbach regarded as anything but transcendent. Indeed it was the sanguinary history of Christianity that convinced Feuerbach, like so many dismayed critics before him, of the human origins of his subject. Violence was the ultimate anthropomorphism—and one that Feuerbach ascribed directly to the encrypted egoism of faith.

Faith was a principle that could pronounce the virtues of heathens "only splendid sins" while passing over the sins of the believer as the prerogatives of the chosen, complained Feuerbach, in a clear allusion to Augustine. It was by faith that Augustine could descend to the "diabolical sophisms" by which he justified "the persecution of heretics." It was by faith that Luther could trivialize the injunction to "Love your enemies" when a point of doctrine was at issue, echoing David in the "hatred" of those who "hate God." But, Feuerbach warned, the faith that "curses," "seeks vengeance," and "destroys" its adversaries is the faith that destroys itself: by exposing its human provenance. It is in the dangerous freedom of faith that Christianity tears up its supernatural credentials, offering not a window on the divine but a mirror to human pride—as Feuerbach asserted in another summary judgment: "Faith gives man a peculiar sense of his own dignity and importance. The believer finds himself distinguished above other men, exalted above the natural man; he knows himself to be a person of distinction, in the possession of peculiar privileges; believers are aristocrats, unbelievers plebeians. God is this distinction and pre-eminence of believers above unbelievers, personified."[39]

Luther once again served as the shining exhibit. "I am proud and exulting on account of my blessedness and the forgiveness of my sins," wrote the reformer, "but through what? Through the glory and pride of another, namely, the Lord Christ." Such "arrogance," Feuerbach adds, proves that the "distinct person" posited by the believer "is simply his own hidden self, his personified, contented desire of happiness." And the tendency of such arrogance to nurture the aggression of persecution sealed the connection. Conflating personal desire "with the honour of God," faith is he claims, "essentially illiberal." It dares to determine what is "Christian" and what is "antichristian," classing "unbelief" as the "cardinal wickedness" (Luther's phrase). "It is," Feuerbach suggests, "essential to faith to condemn, to anathematize," to "sacrifice" human life "to God." "In faith," he concludes, "there lies a *malignant* principle."[40]

Where Spinoza or Voltaire explained hellfire theology as the corruption of religion, good and true, Feuerbach regarded the impulse to damn a fellow mortal as proof that religion is *always* psychology, dressed up as piety. Feuerbach shares their distaste but his conclusions are more radical. He reduces the architecture of divine wrath to the psychology of a domestic quarrel. And like Castellio, three centuries before him, he links intensity of zeal to paucity of charity:

> The Turks exterminate unbelievers with fire and sword, the Christians with the flames of hell. But the fires of the other world blaze forth into this, to glare through the night of unbelief. As the believer already here below anticipates the joys of heaven, so the flames of the abyss must be seen to flash here as a foretaste of the awaiting hell,—at least in the moments when faith attains its highest enthusiasm.

Quoting Luther on the propensity of "God himself" to punish heretics "in this life," "for the benefit of Christendom and the strengthening of faith," Feuerbach delivered another bone-rattling verdict: "The flames of hell are only the flashings of the exterminating vindictive glance which faith casts on unbelievers." "It was faith, not love, not reason, which invented Hell," he added with almost pastoral solicitude. The secret was out. The "luminous fire of discriminating and limiting criticism," as Feuerbach humbly described his project, was doing its work.[41]

Feuerbach admitted that the Bible contained ambiguity, indeed blazing correctives to the persecuting impulse. "Christianity ordains no persecution of heretics, still less conversion by force of arms." But, he countered, "uncharitable actions, hatred of heretics, at once accord and clash with Christianity." "Christian love has not overcome hell," he asserted, "because it has not overcome faith." By dividing its loyalties between God and neighbor, faith nurtures an "abnormal, loveless love." Luther's paradoxes were rooted in the scriptures: "The Bible curses through faith, blesses through love," he suggested. "But the only love it knows is a love founded on faith. Thus here already it is a love which curses, an unreliable love, a love which gives me no guarantee that it will not turn into hatred; for if I do not acknowledge the articles of faith, I am out of the sphere of love, a child of hell, an object of anathema, of the anger of God, to whom the existence of unbelievers is a vexation, a thorn in the eye."[42]

From disquieted love Feuerbach moved to the disabled conscience. A faith-centered or theological Christianity, Feuerbach claimed, smothers the natural springs of virtue, changing "that which is naturally active into the passive." Faith, "being inherently external," enters into competition with the internal rhythms of morality. "Faith left to itself necessarily exalts itself above the laws of natural morality," Feuerbach claimed. It is "separated from morality, from love." Faith can generate "moral actions," he admitted, "but no moral dispositions." In religion, moral rules are often observed, "but they are severed from the inward disposition, the heart, by being represented as the commandments of an external lawgiver, by being placed in the category of arbitrary laws, police regulations. What is done is done not because it is good and right, but because it is commanded by God. The inherent quality of the deed is indifferent; whatever God commands is right." It was, he suggested, natural "morality alone, and by no means faith, that cries out in the conscience of the believer: thy faith is nothing, if it does not make thee good."[43]

How "natural" such sentiments actually were, is open to question. Feuerbach was constantly throwing biblical concepts before the stony priests of faith. His argument consisted of outrage against the perversions of Protestantism, followed by the less certain contention that the bugs in Luther's system were in fact features of the whole. There was a lot of Christianity in Feuerbach's enraged humanism, rarely more palpable than in his discussion of the capacity of faith to destroy the principle of a human species made in the image of God.

Feuerbach acknowledged that Christianity proclaimed the creature good and holy in theory, but the reign of doctrine had emasculated the principle. Christianity's original humanism was decimated by the doctrine of original sin, which turned "the mystery of sexual desire" into a curse and accelerated theology's "hyper-cosmic then anti-cosmic tendency." Human worth was measured in terms of creedal discipline, not intrinsic value, making the unbeliever "an outlaw, a man worthy of extermination." Against every natural instinct, theologians came to regard heretics as something less than creatures made in the image of God. This was the principle that brought "Servetus to the stake" in the ultimate crime of "religious hatred," "the hatred which springs from the nature of unchecked faith." Calvin the man could never have hounded Servetus to his death, Feuerbach suggested. Indeed it was the still-human Calvin who wanted to mitigate the cruelty of the execution. But the man was powerless against the theologian, who delivered savage words of condemnation to the heretic "two hours before his death." Likewise Luther, whose bursting humanity had tragically dissolved into his abrasive theology. It was no good, Feuerbach complained, talking to Luther about the love of neighbor, or the love of enemies. His theology had negotiated both into abstraction. "For the sake of the person I should love them," Luther admitted, "but for the sake of the doctrine I should hate them. And thus I must hate them or hate God, who commands and wills that we should cleave to his word alone."[44]

Finally, Feuerbach trained his sights on Augustine, Christianity's original inverter. Augustine also "distinguishes the man from the enemy of God," Feuerbach noted, urging that we should "hate the ungodliness in the man, but love the humanity in him." "But what, in the eyes of faith, is the man in distinction from faith, man without faith, i.e., without God?" Feuerbach challenged. "Nothing." "It is true that man as man is the image of God," in Augustine's theology. But this divinity pertains only to "God as the Creator of Nature," a secondary, subordinate role. The God of faith is deaf to the plea of humanity. For Augustine and his successors, "the image of this true, essential, Christian God, is only the believer, the Christian." Under this proud and divisive deity, "man is not to be loved for his own sake, but for God's." Faith has destroyed the *imago Dei*. The "unbelieving man," Feuerbach concludes, "has no resemblance to the true God."[45]

This was not to quote Thomas à Kempis against Luther, the Catholic against the Protestant. It was to cite the God of Genesis against the God of theology. But Feuerbach had seen enough. Proud zealots, defending the "honor" of their God, casting their critics into the fires of hell, brought down the whole illusion of airborne, transcendent piety. Feuerbach's harshest contention was that he was not preaching atheism: he was identifying it in the working principles of religious faith. Without a prior sense that love is more admirable than egoism, his criticism would have lacked any kind of leverage. And as he moved from criticism to exhortation, Feuerbach's Christian affinities appeared to deepen. A pure and honest atheism would restore the Christian virtue of love. Such was the challenge of a bruised believer.

"Who Then Is Our Saviour and Redeemer? God or Love?"

Ernest Renan had a saying that you should never believe a German if he tells you he is an atheist.[46] In the land of mysticism, pietism, and idealism, intimations of the divine were the habits of the heart. Feuerbach's atheism was not in doubt but he suggests Renan's point. Feuerbach rejects the Christian God as a violation of qualities that he freely identifies with a pure, pre-theological Christianity. He pleads a human, non-transcendent Christ against the alien constructions of faith and theology. His charge of "egoism" assumes Christian standards of morality. Feuerbach maintained that his quarrel was with the alienating, supernatural elements of Christianity, not its loving or communal aspects: the original esteem for "the species." "Certainly, my work is negative, destructive," he acknowledged, "but, be it observed, only in relation to the unhuman, not to the human elements of religion." "Our relation to religion is," he repeated, "not a merely negative, but a critical one; we only separate the true from the false." "While reducing theology to anthropology," he aimed to "exalt anthropology into theology."[47]

This included a certain plundering of the mangled fuselage of Christian doctrine. For the idea of the Incarnation, where "Love conquers God," where God is seen to renounce "his divine majesty," Feuerbach had stirring praise. He based his model of the triumph of love over faith on the concept, commending atheism as a Christ-like renunciation of supernatural rights:

> Who then is our Saviour and Redeemer? God or Love? Love; for God as God has not saved us, but Love, which transcends the difference between the divine and human personality. As God has renounced himself out of love, so we, out of love, should renounce God; for if we do not sacrifice God to love, we sacrifice love to God, and, in spite of the predicate of love, we have the God—the evil being—of religious fanaticism.[48]

Feuerbach was happy to praise the Bible when it celebrated the goodness of creation and the sacredness of humankind. His "sensualism" was ethical, emerging from a fierce priority of love. While Feuerbach regrets the Christian individualism that separated the person from the species, he is hostile to the "heathenism" that "abolishes the distinction between man and the brute." The philosophical heathenism that could make light of the death of a child as a mere "homunculus," a drop in the ocean of humanity, excites his scorn. Part of the polemic against modern religion was that its spiritual individualism represented a new heathenism, unmindful of the human race as a whole. Under the Lutheran dispensation, Feuerbach protested, "we are half heathens, half Christians." The "Christianity of the present day, which has incorporated with itself the culture of heathenism," he complains, "has preserved only the name and some general positions of Christianity." Whereas original "Christianity," "untravestied by arbitrary speculative interpretation" is "the direct opposite of heathenism." It was humanism.

The earliest Christians understood things like community, love, and suffering, before faith and theology triggered a series of divorces. "Theology," Feuerbach contended, "denies the possibility that God should suffer, but in so doing it denies the truth of religion." "Religion," he urged,

> is the relation of man to his own nature,—therein lies its truth and its power of moral amelioration;—but to his nature not recognised as his own, but regarded as another nature, separate, nay, contra-distinguished from his own: herein lies its untruth, its limitation, its contradiction to reason and morality; herein lies the noxious source of religious fanaticism, the chief metaphysical principle of human sacrifices, in a word, the *prima materia* of all the atrocities, all the horrible scenes, in the tragedy of religious history.[49]

The attempt to distinguish the truth from the untruth of Christianity reaches a climax in the chapter on faith and love. Christianity has sanctioned both "the actions that spring out of love, and the actions that spring from faith without love," Feuerbach repeats. It contains a basic duality, leading to "dogmatic creeds" and "horrible actions," on the one hand, and radiant goodness, on the other. Acts of cruelty at once reflect and "contradict Christianity," he maintains, "because Christianity is not only a religion of faith, but of love also." Humanism would steer the ship back to its holy, pre-theological course. As Feuerbach urged, in a remarkable passage:

> Now, that which reveals the basis, the hidden essence of religion, is Love; that which constitutes its conscious form is Faith. Love identifies man with God and God with man, consequently it identifies man with man; faith separates God from man,

> consequently it separates man from man, for God is nothing else than the idea of the species invested with a mystical form,—the separation of God from man is therefore the separation of man from man, the unloosening of the social bond. By faith religion places itself in contradiction with morality, with reason, with the unsophisticated sense of truth in man; by love, it opposes itself again to this contradiction. Faith isolates God, it makes him a particular, distinct being: love universalises; it makes God a common being, the love of whom is one with the love of man. Faith produces in man an inward disunion, a disunion with himself, and by consequence in outward disunion also; but *love heals the wounds which are made by faith in the heart of man*. Faith makes belief in its God a law: love is freedom,—it condemns not even the atheist, because it is itself atheistic, itself denies, if not theoretically, at least practically, the existence of a particular, individual God, opposed to man. Love has God in itself: faith has God out of itself; it estranges God from man, it makes him an external object.[50]

The theological force of Feuerbach's writing is unmistakable: faith is sin, the rupturing scourge of the person and the species. Love will heal the wounds, shattering the idol of supernaturalism and restoring the divinity of humanity. Faith is "law." Love is "freedom." Love, Feuerbach continues, is the singular foil for spiritual arrogance: "Faith necessarily passes into hatred, hatred into persecution, where the power of faith meets with no contradiction, where it does not find itself in collision with a power foreign to faith, the power of love, of humanity, of the sense of justice. Faith left to itself necessarily exalts itself above the laws of natural morality."

The apostle Paul was an ambivalent figure for Feuerbach, criticized for extolling "the household of faith" above the needs of "all men." But such a criticism only highlights the esteem with which he could write of Christ as the herald of a true, "well-grounded love, safe in its principle, guaranteed, free." "Christ loved men: he wished to bless and unite them all without distinction of sex, race, rank, or nationality. Christ is the love of mankind to itself embodied in an image," Feuerbach urged. "For this reason," he added, "love is pronounced to be the characteristic mark of the disciples." The task was to follow the example without succumbing to the idolatry of the "image"—the invented, inverted Christ of theology. Christ was not the *source* of this love of the species but its "apostle." It was ludicrous to divinize a figure who grasped better than anyone that "Love can only be founded on the unity of the species." As Feuerbach challenged:

> Is Christ the cause of love? Is he not rather the apostle of love? . . . What ennobled Christ was love; whatever qualities he had, he held in fealty to love; he was not the proprietor of love, as he is represented to be in all superstitious conceptions. The idea of love is an independent idea; I do not first deduce it from the life of Christ; on the contrary, I revere that life only because I find it accordant with the law, the idea of love.[51]

Love is "an independent idea"—but one that Feuerbach is very keen to identify with Christ. Indeed he proposes the brave path of atheism as a road to be walked with an ethical, mystical, untheological Christ. More than rhetoric, this is a work of retrieval:

> Christ, as the consciousness of love, is the consciousness of the species. We are all one in Christ. Christ is the consciousness of our identity. He therefore who loves man for the sake of man, who rises to the love of the species, to universal love . . . he is a Christian, is Christ himself. He does what Christ did, what made Christ Christ. Thus, where there arises the consciousness of the species as a species, the idea of humanity as a whole, Christ disappears, without, however, his true nature disappearing . . .[52]

Feuerbach's naturalism is often said to anticipate Nietzsche's revolt against a "castrated, disembodied" Christianity; a religion of negation and denial.[53] This is partly true. But the protest of sensuality is coiled within a more powerful moral, even spiritual, ferment. Feuerbach personified Nietzsche's insight about the Christian God making way for Christian morality. Feuerbach's contempt for a Protestantism "of and for flesh and blood" is fiercer than his disdain for a Catholicism that set itself against the flesh.[54] His fury against Luther's "carnal mingling of the Christian with the man" is hotter than his disdain for ascetic separation, and it is here, in the religious urge to claim the earth while pretending to rise above it, that the Marxist critique of religion as "ideology" germinates. It is this peculiarly Protestant dualism, proclaiming freedom from the theater of life while claiming the best seats in the house, that drives Feuerbach's critique. This was the incriminating odor of egoism, which aroused

Feuerbach's suspicion rather as Luther detected the "stench of philosophy" in medieval theologies of conscience and merit.[55] Sometime around 1830, Feuerbach wrote in his diary that "there is only one evil—egoism; and only one good, it is love."[56] This was the seed of his atheism. He concluded the *Essence of Christianity* with an "Amen" and signed off the appendix with the claim that, far from an evisceration of the Christian religion, his criticism constituted "the liberation of Protestantism, of Christianity in general, from its fundamental contradiction." It was "the reduction of [Christianity] to its truth." Indeed his prophetic atheism was nothing less than "the necessary, irrepressible, irrefragable result of Christianity."[57] Authorial intentionality may have fallen on hard times, but if such was Feuerbach's verdict, who could argue? As Engels later remarked: "He by no means wishes to abolish religion: he wants to perfect it."[58]

"The Premise of All Criticism": Marx's Critique of Religion

> *Dr. Marx will give medieval religion and politics their* coup de grace. *Imagine Rousseau, Voltaire, Holbach, Lessing, Heine and Hegel fused into one person.*
>
> —MOSES HESS

The *Essence of Christianity* electrified the Young Hegelians, crystallizing their hostility to the Protestant establishment and to the moonlighting theology of Hegel. "The spell was broken," Engels recalled. "The 'system' was exploded and cast aside . . . we all became at once Feuerbachians."[59] Engels championed Feuerbach's cause in England. Eliot began work on a translation. And Marx, "the disciple who eclipsed all others," began his journey from the misty regions of idealism to revolutionary historical materialism.[60] Marx hailed Feuerbach as "the true conqueror of the old philosophy," the "only one who has a serious, critical attitude to the Hegelian dialectic," and he praised him for "the unpretentious simplicity" of his style. The fog was lifting. As Marx presumed to address all "speculative theologians and philosophers" in 1842: "there is no other road to truth and freedom for you except the one that leads through the *Feuerbach* [stream of fire]. Feuerbach is the *purgatory* of the present."[61]

In 1844, Marx thanked Feuerbach privately for giving "socialism a philosophical foundation" by affirming "the unity of man with man," "pulled down from the heaven of abstraction to the real earth." He added a note of criticism for the halfway men among the Young Hegelians, who "do not behave like *human beings* who *criticize* but like *critics* who happen to have the misfortune of being human." Such criticism was no more than "a sad and supercilious spiritualism," the afterglow of a now-exploded theology.[62]

Marx had abandoned his legal training to study philosophy, announcing his conversion to Hegelian thought in a rhapsodic letter to his father. But the prospect of an academic career vanished in the tension between the Prussian authorities and the radicalism of the Young Hegelians. When Marx's mentor, Bruno Bauer, lost his university chair for publishing works critical of the New Testament, it was clear that Marx's own career would be outside the "feudal-bureaucratic" establishment. Having completed a doctorate on the Greek philosophers Democritus and Epicurus, Marx turned to the more tradable currency of journalism, announcing his genius in shards of glistening, epigrammatic prose. Like Feuerbach, he scorned the world of philosophy, with its "urge for isolation, for systematic seclusion, for dispassionate self-examination," warming instead to "the quick-witted and alive-to-events newspapers." Yet Marx was never less than an intellectual, all but pioneering an eminently German brand of philosophical politics.

Unlike Feuerbach, Marx had never considered himself a Christian. His father's "conversion" from Judaism to Christianity was a tactical decision prompted by the withdrawal of civil liberties that had been granted during Napoleon's brief control of the Rhineland. When Trier passed into Prussian hands in 1815, Heinrich and his children were baptized but the "Christianity" of the Marx household was a mixture of Rousseau and Voltaire, who supplied bedtime reading to a self-consciously enlightened home. Heinrich's affections were with the French Revolution and the brief liberties enjoyed thereafter, not the counterrevolution of Frederick William III. A raucous rendering of the Marseillaise after a night of heavy drinking nearly cost the otherwise impeccable senior Marx his career. Karl's Enlightenment proclivities accelerated during his university studies and it was the demystifying side of Kantian philosophy that informed his skepticism. Medieval "proofs" for the existence of God were dispatched with the languid ease of a natural athlete. Marx was an atheist by the time he finished his dissertation, complete with defiant epigraphs from Prometheus and Epicurus.

Marx's theoretical atheism was, however, only a bridge to the practical criticism that defined his political philosophy. In the emerging model of ethical and political criticism, technical analysis of the existence of God played little part. The aim was not to debunk so much as to explain, and the power of Feuerbach's analysis was the elegance with which it resolved "the religious world into its secular basis."[63] Armed with this weapon of reduction, the critic could ignore the pyrotechnics on either side of the fence. Religion had been exposed as the cipher of selfish interest. It only remained to apply the same principle to capricious deity of the free market and the silver-tongued chimera of democracy. Marx's intellectual charisma lay in the power to expose and unmask; to disclose the animating "secret" behind a conspiracy of events; to tap at the knees of modernity to reveal the old, animal reflexes beneath the hallowed garment of liberty. He found a method and a model in Feuerbach.

Although Marx did not write very much about religion, he did to Feuerbach something similar to what Voltaire did to Bayle: he turned a profoundly personal stream of criticism into a formula that would define an era. If Feuerbach's conscience was thus externalized into Marx's armored revolutionary philosophy, it continued to burn with indignation. As the twentieth-century philosopher Sergei Bulgakov commented, Marx's religious criticism was "the central nerve of his entire life work."[64] And as Marx himself volunteered: "the criticism of religion is the presupposition of all criticism." The "criticism of earth" begins with the "criticism of heaven." And in a culture where the state serves as "a theologian *ex professo*," the "criticism of politics" has to begin with the "criticism of theology."[65] Marx was at once dismissive of religion and obsessed with it. His materialist project was one of the more remarkable fruits of the accusing conscience.

The image of a heroic, Enlightenment-vanquishing Marx is so enduring that it is easily forgotten that this is exactly where he started. And no history of conscience could fail to note that it was in such a name that his historic work of criticism began. "Ideas which gain a hold on our intelligence, our soul, our conscience," Marx wrote in an early edition of the *Rhineland News*, "are chains from which we cannot tear ourselves loose without tearing our hearts."[66] It was at this point that a starstruck Hess likened Marx to Voltaire. Responding to a new Prussian censorship law in 1842, Marx offered a textbook example of Enlightenment criticism, defending the "moral conscience" against an arbitrary, politically sanctioned "religious conscience." He complained of a new law that "must reject the intellectual heroes of morality, such as Kant, Fichte and Spinoza, as irreligious." He disputed a law that seeks to "protect religion" but "violates the most general principle of all religions, the sanctity and inviolability of the subjective frame of mind. It makes the censor instead of God the judge of the heart."[67]

The more destructive commentary, however, was Marx's discussion of what the new censors actually meant by "religion." Here he deepened the Enlightenment worry about religion corrupting secular power with the more disturbing contention that power is what religion now is: "you want to base the state not on free reason, but on faith, religion being for you the general sanction for what exists." His concern was not that the state was now bowing to zealots. It was that religion was serving as a silent guardian to secular power. Marx almost berates the theocrats for shrinking from their own spiritual commission: "He who wants to ally himself with religion owing to religious feelings must concede it the decisive voice in all questions, or do you perhaps understand by religion the cult of your own unlimited authority and governmental wisdom?"[68]

Marx issued the same charge in his first contribution to the *Rhineland News*, which he edited from October 1842, dismissing the "religion" that was clinging to its place at the high table as "simply a sacred cloak to hide desires that are both very secular and at the same time very imaginary."[69] When a conservative newspaper published a defense of Christianity as the "basis of the state," Marx likened such a religion to "fetishism." It was a mascot, a passenger, a chaplain to unholy "desire." He denied that there had ever been a culture in which Christian values truly reigned. The demand for a Christian state had to be recognized for the power play that it was: "Read St. Augustine's *De civitate Dei*, study the Fathers of the Church and the spirit of Christianity, and then come back and tell us whether the state or the church is the 'Christian state'! Or does not every moment of your practical life brand your theory as a lie?" As he continued, in the tones of a modern Amos:

> Do you consider it wrong to appeal to the courts if you have been cheated? But the apostle writes that it is wrong. If you have been struck on one cheek, do you turn the other also, or do you not rather start an action for assault? But the gospel forbids it. Do you not demand rational right in this world, do you not grumble at the slightest raising of taxes, are you not beside yourself at the least infringement of your personal liberty?

Marx's concern is not the veracity but the practical function of religion, and it is from this ethical angle that he introduces an economic dimension to the discussion: "Are not most of your court cases and most of your civil laws concerned with property?," he challenged. The drift toward an economic theory of religion in a pre-communist Marx is powered by moral reprehension. The ability to expose piety as politics bears the same stamp: "the rule of religion is nothing but the religion of rule," Marx concluded, "the cult of the government's will."[70]

In another article, Marx spoke in Voltairean terms of "the infamy of [the state's] secular aims, for which religion serves as a cloak." It was the task of "criticism" to force the "state that relies on the Bible into a mental derangement" in which this "illusion" finally unravels. He spoke of a necessary collision between the truth of religious motivation and "the sincerity" of religious "consciousness," as if the critic were a prophet, exposing faith as idolatry.[71] Some years later, Marx protested on behalf of a proletariat, still cringing "under the double wings of the Prussian eagle and the Holy Ghost." He castigated a theology that places "compensation for all infamies in heaven, and thereby justif[ies] the continuation of these infamies on earth." This was purest Feuerbach—but with a sharper eye for social justice. Charity was not enough. "The proletariat," he thundered, "needs its courage, its self-confidence, its pride and its sense of independence even more than its bread."[72] Man cannot live on bread alone.

"It is hardly possible to talk about Marx's attitude toward religion," writes one scholar, "without mentioning the connection between his philosophy of history, and of socialism, with the Messianic hope of the Old Testament prophets." "While Christianity, especially since Paul, tended to transform the historical concept of salvation into an 'other-worldly,' purely spiritual one," he explains, millenarian sects tended to protest against such a "divorce" of spiritual and secular values. Enlightenment philosophy and revolutionary Marxism took up their quarrel: "What is common to prophetic, thirteenth-century Christian thought, eighteenth-century enlightenment, and nineteenth-century socialism, is the idea that State (society) and spiritual values cannot be divorced from each other; that politics and moral values are indivisible."[73] This captures the rage for integration that runs from Hegel to Marx. Marx often gives the impression that he would not mind if people actually were religious. But the Feuerbachian intuition that saints are few and far between acquired the status of a dogma. And with this harsh and rugged certainty, Marx turned his thoughts to politics.

The consanguinity of Marx's religious criticism and his political theory was strikingly apparent in his essay "On the Jewish Question," written in 1843. Here, he added a penetrating analysis of democratic liberalism to his critique of the theocratic Prussian state. If European religion was a vestment covering raw and unapologetic power, the American alternative was only a more genial version of the same. Writing in the wake of Alexis de Tocqueville's rhapsodies on a land where the spirit of freedom and the spirit of religion marched in glorious unison, Marx introduced a note of caution. The American miracle was, he suggested, the sanctification of private interest at the expense of real freedom. And God was once more on the side of the winners. In this self-admiring Christian democracy, "Religion has become the spirit of civil society, of the sphere of egoism, of *bellum omnium contra omnes* [the war of all against all]." Europe had nothing to gain by following America in a separation of church and state. Religion is even more inclined to nourish egoism when it is awash in the sanctifying slogans of liberty; when it lives to baptize illusions of equality. "The emancipation of the state from religion," he urged, "is not the emancipation of the real man from religion." The lesson of America was that, "*Political* emancipation itself is not *human* emancipation."[74]

Religion was thus central to Marx's analysis of an authoritarian Prussian state and the democratic experiment of America. But from the very insight that egoism is the soul of religion and politics emerged the limitations of criticism. If there are darker forces at work beneath the extenuating verbiage of theology and democracy, such must be the focus of any program of repair. It is better to address the sin than the propitiating apparatus of what would soon be termed "bourgeois ideology." Communism was at once the continuation and the end of the prophetic-rhetorical line of attack. Words can only take you so far.

In 1843 the Prussian authorities closed down the *Rhineland News* and Marx's career as an editor and a veritable celebrity of Cologne was at an end. He married Jenny Westphal in the summer and they moved in October to Paris, an auspicious destination, described by their collaborator, Arnold Ruge, as "the cradle of Europe, the broad magic kettle in which world history is steaming, and out of which it ever and again bubbles forth anew."[75] It was here that a wave of continent-wide revolutions were triggered in 1848, it was here that Europe's first communist experiment came to brief fruition in 1871, and it was in Paris that Marx himself joined the movement. By the final decade of the century, workers' parties inspired by Marx's communist vision existed in every major European country.[76]

One of the first of the so-called "Paris manuscripts" was a "Critique of Hegel's *Philosophy of Right*," which contained Marx's most famous remarks on religion and an announcement of retirement from religious criticism. Marx wrote to Feuerbach as he prepared the attack on Hegel, assuring him that his "*Philosophy of the Future* and *Essence of Faith* [according to Luther] are . . . of more weight than the whole of contemporary German literature put together."[77] And the homage was unambiguous when he declared, in the opening sentence of the critique of Hegel, that "as far as Germany is concerned, the criticism of religion is essentially complete." Such criticism, Marx averred, was the foundation "of all criticism." But homage turned to dissent as Marx, with fresh concern for the origins of the illusion, injected a degree of sympathy for religious faith. Religion was a symptom, not a cause, and it carried its consolations: "Religious suffering is at the same time an expression of real suffering and a protest against real suffering. Religion is the sigh of the oppressed creature, the heart of a heartless world, and the soul of soulless circumstances. It is the opium of the people."[78]

This was perhaps the first time that he looked at the matter from the point of view of the underdog. Religion reflects suffering, and it is also a protest against it. In his notes on the Reformation, Marx expressed praise for brave spirits such as "the great Sebastian Franck" who spoke "of the Christ in us" and stood up to the "philistine," "thickheaded Luther."[79] Yet a sigh cannot address injustice. And an army does not fight on opium. Religion may be slipping from a status of villain to accomplice, but it still carries a burden of guilt for Marx. Religion does not create inequality but it sanctions and assuages it: tranquilizing instincts of revolt, promising redress in another age. It bathes inequality in a sanctifying glow of permanence. It is striking how firmly, if implicitly, Marx confronted the Lutheran bifurcation of earthly and heavenly justice, with its breezy exhortations to submit to higher powers and await God's timetable of restitution. The brilliance of the opium metaphor was the way in which it reached up and down the spectrum of religious motivation. Religion consoles the oppressed and justifies the oppressors. It eases one person's pain and another person's conscience. But the force of Marx's fury is clearly aimed at the latter, the gospel of unavoidable sin: a theology that lives to affirm the secular order. "Religion," he writes with scathing candor, "is the general theory of this world, its encyclopaedic compendium, its logic in popular form, its spiritual *point d'honneur*, its enthusiasm, its moral sanction, its solemn complement, its universal basis for consolation and justification." It is—in the most damning phrase of all—the "spiritual aroma" of an unjust world. Yet Marx's response to both aspects of the opiate is the same: change the conditions not the air conditioning.

Marx began to express impatience with theoretical, discursive approaches to the problem of inequality. The "struggle against religion" needed to turn into a "struggle against the world" that called spiritual consolations into being. There was continuity here but also a point of departure: "The abolition of religion as the illusory happiness of the people," Marx explained, "is the demand for their real happiness. The demand to give up the illusions about their condition is a demand to give up a condition that requires illusion. The criticism of religion is therefore the germ of the criticism of the vale of tears whose halo is religion." With a metaphor at once reverent and damning of his forebears, Marx added: "Criticism has plucked the imaginary flowers from the chains not so that man may bear the chains without any imagination or comfort, but so that he may throw away the chains and pluck living flowers."[80]

The task of history, Marx asserted, was not to maunder on about religious illusions but "to establish the truth of the here and now." The task of philosophy, now that "the holy form of human self-alienation has been discovered, is to discover self-alienation in its unholy forms."[81] Suddenly Feuerbach, conqueror of Hegel and slayer of metaphysics, was part of the problem. To talk about the fallacies of religion, to preach atheism from the rooftops, was only to thicken the anesthetic of bourgeois chatter. Atheism without action was just more "ideology." In the preface to *The German Ideology* (1845), Marx turned on Feuerbach with a withering analogy:

> Once upon a time a valiant fellow had the idea that men were drowned in water only because they were possessed with the idea of gravity. If they were to knock this notion out of their heads, say by stating it to be a superstition, a religious concept, they would be sublimely proof against any danger from water. His whole life long he fought against the illusion of gravity, of whose harmful results all statistics brought him new and manifold evidence. This valiant fellow was the type of the new revolutionary philosophers in Germany.[82]

And, of course, it was of Feuerbach that Marx coined his most enduring aphorism: "The philosophers have only interpreted the world, in various ways; the point is to change it."[83]

In the authorized version of events, Marx was thus converted from the ersatz theology of philosophy to hardheaded historical materialism: a decision for science over speculation. Ideas, Marx now asserted, "have no history," no independence from the social relations that generate them. The secret of history was found in the rhythms of production and exchange, not the patter of intellectual commentary. Ideology came in many forms, including atheist humanism. "Atheism," Marx primly asserted, "no longer has any meaning."[84] Yet apart from Marx's continuing debt to Feuerbach's method of dissolving ideas into their "secular basis," the claim of emancipation from moralizing philosophy was surely premature. Even as a communist, from late 1843, Marx radiated certainties that had no obvious source in his stark, economistic vision. The harder he protested, the more he seemed to prove it. He was stung by a work that appeared in late 1844, accusing the Young Hegelians of creating a new religion in the service of an imaginary being called "Man." This "human religion," challenged the author, Max Stirner, "is only the last metamorphosis of the Christian religion . . . it separates my essence from me and sets it above me." It perpetuated Christianity's "tearing apart of Man into natural impulse and conscience."[85] But the communist Marx, who attempted to bury conscience in an inexorable historical process, was perhaps the most theological Marx of all.

"Unconscionable Freedom": The Sins of Trade and the Sword of Justice

Marx was first prompted to address economic questions by an essay "On the Essence of Money" by Moses Hess.[86] Combining Feuerbach's humanism with the millenarian ardor of French socialism, Hess argued that money served in modern culture as a materialized "God," stripping humanity of its inherent worth and establishing a new form of "slavery." It turns the world "upside-down." Hess's sense of a true and natural order was set out in a work of 1837 entitled, *The Holy History of Mankind by a disciple of Spinoza*, and his economic analysis is best described in terms of a theology of sin. Love, Hess argued, was the natural impulse of humanity. But only a handful of exceptional individuals, including Jesus Christ and Spinoza, had grasped this. The working pattern of the world was "egoism." Egoism had been sanctified by an evasive, servile Christianity of "the letter" and incarnated in money. Hess's essay was the first attempt to apply Feuerbach's idea of religious alienation to economic and social life, and it was a major influence on Marx.[87]

For Hess, the rebellious son of a wealthy manufacturer, millenarian communism was the only hope for the restoration of nature's original order: the "unity of nature and spirit." This was the final stage of history, which had been inaugurated by Spinoza but was yet to reach fulfillment. In such an age, Hess urged in the essay on money, love will return from "heaven" to "earth." "We will no longer vainly seek our life outside and above us."[88] The Christian doctrine of heaven and the all-dividing god of money were two expressions of the same fallacy. Both located happiness, joy, and human fulfillment beyond ordinary life, conniving at injustice and corruption. Hess applied Feuerbach's critique of the transcendent God to the cruel deity of money, though his central vision predated Feuerbach's masterwork. In *The Holy History*, Hess challenged Christians not to "find offence in" a terrestrial interpretation of "the Kingdom of God," prefacing one of his chapters with the words of the Lord's Prayer: "Thy kingdom come. Thy will be done in earth, as it is in heaven." His *Communist Confession of Faith* (1844) urged that "we shall experience this heaven on earth when we no longer live in self-seeking and hate but in love, in a unified human species, in the communist society." "Once we unite and live in communism," he continued, "hell will no longer be on earth and heaven will no longer be beyond this world; everything which has been presented to us by Christianity in prophecy and phantasy is about to be wholly realized in the true human society according to the eternal laws of love and reason."[89]

If this was one of the foundations of an economic worldview, it is no wonder that theological terminology continued to haunt the project. Hess wrote of the "estrangement" caused by money's blind and implacable reign. He wrote of a "bondage" that reduced human worth to "numbers," forcing people to "sell" themselves to an insensible market. It was precisely such ideas that dominated Marx's "Economic and Philosophical Manuscripts," some of the most important of his early works, written in the summer of 1844.[90] Among them, the passage on "Alienated Labour" stands as one of the most penetrating discussions of modern working relations ever written. Marx wrote of a condition that divided a person from their deepest essence, "mortifying" mind and body in equal measure: a condition in which the worker's life "belongs to another." In the licensed slavery of the market economy, the worker experiences "the loss of himself," he "feels himself an animal."[91]

Marx likened the process to religious servitude, in which a person pours their purest service into "an alien" deity, and he continued to draw on theological language in pursuit of a solution. The term he used to describe the "alienation" of the worker was the word Luther had used to describe Christ "emptying himself" to assume the condition of a slave, based on a passage in Paul's letter to the Philippians. As one scholar writes, Marx's ability to attach a promise of emancipation to such language of alienation "recaptured much of the drama attached to the original Lutheran reading of Christ."[92] With little knowledge of working people or the realities of industrial life, Marx commissioned the proletariat as the bearer of an awesome historical promise: "the revolutionary class, the class that holds the future in its hands."[93] The idea of a cosmic "antithesis" to capitalism's "thesis" was also, of course, Hegelian. But it was no less theological for that. Marx continued to liken the market to an untamed deity, tearing up a holy order. And he conceived communism as a kind of practical secularism, offering freedom from the unfeeling God of heaven and the crushing god of industry: "The religion of the workers has no God," he once wrote, "because it seeks to restore the divinity of man."[94]

In his essay "On Money," Marx echoed Hess's tone of pious outrage, as well as many of the same ideas. Indeed, one scholar notes, the parallels between the two texts are "enough to justify the statement that Marx copied Hess's ideas at this stage."[95] The essay opened with a quotation from Goethe and two longer excerpts from Shakespeare on the "confounding," "distorting," overturning "divinity" of wealth. Money, Marx contended, turns everything into its "opposite." "It changes fidelity into infidelity, love into hate, hate into love, virtue into vice, vice into virtue, slave into master, master into slave, stupidity into intelligence and intelligence into stupidity." Money, he continued, destroys "individuality," twisting and confusing human judgment: "I am ugly, but I can buy myself the most beautiful women. Consequently I am not ugly, for the effect of ugliness, its power of repulsion, is annulled by money." And more than merely taste and intellect, money corrupts the holy ground of conscience: "I am a wicked, dishonest man without conscience or intellect, but money is honoured and so also is its possessor. Money is the highest good and so its possessor is good. Money relieves me of the trouble of being dishonest; so I am presumed to be honest." "He who can buy courage," Marx continued, "is courageous though he be a coward." As society's "existing and self-affirming concept of value," Marx concluded, money "confounds and exchanges all things." It creates an "inverted world," molding human beings in its own, distorted image. Marx was again drawing analogies between a "perverting power" that "appears as the enemy of man" and the transcendent Christian God. He was condemning both as sin. Money was "the visible god-head" of a confused and corrupted social order. It was "the true agent both of separation and of union, the galvano-chemical power of society."[96] Marx penned these fulminations before he had any familiarity with industrial conditions or a clear grasp of the political economy that so ennobled the god of money. But he was, in 1844, a moralist, not an economist, and it was from the moral critique of religion, politics, and finally the economy that he conjured a revolutionary philosophy.

The second vital influence on Marx's conversion to communism was an essay by Friedrich Engels, "Outlines of a Critique of Political Economy." Engels was the son of a cotton magnate, writing with first-hand knowledge of factory conditions in Manchester, and like Hess, with the energizing guilt of a second-generation capitalist—a kind of Protestant ethic in reverse. He drew on socialist and political critiques of the factory system, including the ideas of Robert Owen and the "Chartists," both of whom claimed to represent "a true and genuine Christianity" of equality. Engels, who had lost his evangelical faith reading David Strauss, brought a biblical ardor to his writing, echoing the anxiety of Thomas Carlyle about a society held together by a "cash nexus." He built upon Christian critiques of economic barbarism offered by socialists such as John Watts. With a theological vigor no less keen than Hess's, Engels eviscerated Adam Smith's gospel of free trade as a creed of destruction and estrangement. Far from signaling a shift from religious criticism to economics, Engels suggested the inseparability of secularism and communism. The gospel of trade was rooted in a theology of judgment and just deserts. Both had to go.

With free-market apologists like Thomas Chalmers clearly in view, Engels condemned the "Malthusian theory" of "Christian economics" as nothing "but the economic expression of the religious dogma of the contradiction of spirit and nature." "Political economy" was a theology of judgment masquerading as a science. It tried to dignify the sins of greed and selfish gain by normalizing suffering and inequality as the natural state of a fallen world. Engels offered a weary tribute to the "Catholic candour" of the old "Mercantile System," which made no attempt to "conceal the immoral nature of trade." This older doctrine of competition, he suggested, "openly paraded its mean avarice." "But when the economic

Luther, Adam Smith, criticised past economics," Engels noted sarcastically, "morality began to claim its eternal right." "Protestant hypocrisy took the place of Catholic candour," and avarice was clothed as virtue. "And this hypocritical way of misusing morality for immoral purposes," raged Engels, "is the pride of the free-trade system."

> "Have we not overthrown the barbarism of the monopolies?" exclaim the hypocrites. "Have we not carried civilisation to distant parts of the world? Have we not brought about the fraternisation of the peoples, and reduced the number of wars?" Yes, all this you have done—but how! You have destroyed the small monopolies so that the one great basic monopoly, property, may function the more freely and unrestrictedly. You have civilised the ends of the earth to win new terrain for the deployment of your vile avarice. You have brought about the fraternisation of the peoples—but the fraternity is the fraternity of thieves. You have reduced the number of wars—to earn all the bigger profits in peace, to intensify to the utmost the enmity between individuals, the ignominious war of competition!

"When," he challenged the priests of political economy, "have you done anything out of pure humanity . . .? When have you been moral without being interested, without harbouring at the back of your mind immoral, egoistical motives?"[97]

Engels excoriated the punitive and much-theologized English "Poor Law" of 1834, a symbol of the free trade mania and the cult of "Christian economics." Under this new and "liberal" law, poverty had become a "crime" and debt a grossly stigmatized sin—grimly expiated in nasty, prison-like workhouses, where families were separated and the "morality" of commerce coldly enforced. "It is true," Engels noted, "that this theory ill conforms with the Bible's doctrine of the perfection of God and of His creation; but," he added in mordant deference to the new science, " 'it is a poor refutation to enlist the Bible against facts.' " "Am I to go on any longer," he wondered, "elaborating this vile, infamous theory, this hideous blasphemy against nature and mankind? Am I to pursue its consequences any further? Here at last we have the immorality of the economist brought to its highest pitch. What are all the wars and horrors of the monopoly system compared with this theory! And it is just this theory which is the keystone of the liberal system of free trade."[98]

"Avarice," "blasphemy," "hypocrisy," and the enduring complaint of "egoism"—such were the provocations of the communist millennium. Stirner's charge of recycled theology may have prompted some hasty self-editing but the Communist Manifesto (1848) preserved the blistering idiom. As one scholar has noted, the foundation document of European communism strikes an uncertain blow for disenchanted, scientific materialism.[99] With its dark "Specters" and hidden "Powers," and the promise of a coming warfare between the forces of the Bourgeoisie and the Proletariat, "directly facing each other" like Israel and the Philistines in the Old Testament, the Manifesto crackles with cosmic righteousness. For the bourgeoisie, "like the sorcerer, who is no longer able to control the powers of the nether world whom he has called up by his spells," the only advice was to "tremble." In a passage worthy of Carlyle or any of the spiritual judges of "the dismal science" of political economy, Marx and Engels counted the cost of the commercial age:

> The bourgeoisie, wherever it has got the upper hand, has put an end to all feudal, patriarchal, idyllic relations. It has pitilessly torn asunder the motley feudal ties that bound man to his "natural superiors," and has left remaining no other nexus between man and man than naked self-interest, than callous "cash payment." It has drowned the most heavenly ecstasies of religious fervour, of chivalrous enthusiasm, of philistine sentimentalism, in the icy water of egotistical calculation. It has resolved personal worth into exchange value, and in place of the numberless and indefeasible chartered freedoms, has set up that single, *unconscionable* freedom—Free Trade.

As they continue:

> The bourgeoisie has stripped of its halo every occupation hitherto honoured and looked up to with reverent awe. It has converted the physician, the lawyer, the priest, the poet, the man of science, into its paid wage labourers.

Finally:

> The bourgeoisie has torn away from the family its sentimental veil, and has reduced the family relation to a mere money relation.

These are hardly tones of celebration. "All that is solid melts into air," the passage continues, "all that is holy is profaned, and man is at last compelled to face with sober senses, his real conditions of life, and his relations with his kind." There is a necessary demystification here—the facing of life's real conditions—but the indignation remains theological. Capital is a violent scourge of a once-holy order: "it creates a world after its own image."[100]

The insight that "law, morality, religion" are, to the bourgeois exploiter, a tapestry of prejudices "behind which lurk in ambush just as many bourgeois interests" is one that presupposes morality of its own. Materialism remains an ethical judgment. "The selfish misconception that induces you to transform into eternal laws of nature and of reason, the social forms springing from your present mode of production," they challenge, "you share with every ruling class that has preceded you." Even the pious symbol of the "bourgeois family," they contend, represents hypocrisy and egoism. The "bourgeois" preaches the sacredness of the family, while cheerfully separating other people's families in pursuit of his needs. And, under the priestly rubric of respectability, he treats his own wife as "a mere instrument of production." "The bourgeois clap-trap about the family and education, about the hallowed co-relation of parent and child," they continue, "becomes all the more disgusting, the more, by the action of Modern Industry, all family ties among the proletarians are torn asunder, and their children transformed into simple articles of commerce and instruments of labour."[101]

When Marx gravitated toward radical philosophy in Berlin in the summer of 1837, the first set of lectures he attended was on the prophet Isaiah. "Criticism," he then believed, was prophetic work, breaking out of the cloistered holiness of the monk to the public ministry of the philosopher: "what was inner light has become consuming flame," Marx wrote with menacing delight.[102] It was an ominous metaphor. There can be no doubt that the raging conscience was part of the fuel in Marx's machine. He shudders at the indignities of the industrial system, and he expects readers to do the same. His ongoing critique of theologies of justification and enablement shimmers with biblical passion. In making "a world after its own image," the bourgeoisie stands accused of overturning an original, sacred goodness. Engels's protest against the economy's "blasphemy against nature and mankind" is undimmed in the Manifesto. Yet it has assumed a new and threatening form. The revolutionary conscience points outward, not inward. It is externalized into a process, an event, a moment of necessary violence. "The weapon of criticism," Marx wrote as early as 1844, "cannot supplant the criticism of weapons."[103] Words cannot create a revolution. Marx cannot be held responsible for atrocities committed in his name, but there is a startling clarity in the Manifesto, a frightening division between real and parasitic human agency, that simply demands violence. By incarnating conscience in a revolutionary process, Marx also incarcerated it, damning critics with a ferocity that rivaled any of his forebears. The final tribute to a sectarian pedigree was sectarianism itself.

Marx never outgrew the prophetic idiom. He continued to read history, economics, and science through the appraisive lens of justice. His definitive egalitarian slogan, "From each according to his ability, to each according to his needs!"[104] has been persuasively traced to a passage in the Acts of the Apostles, which describes the first Christians sharing all things "in common," "as every man had need."[105] People make their own history, but with materials "given, and transmitted from the past"—to paraphrase a principle that Marx found easier to identify in others than himself.[106] When he finally read the *Origin of Species* in 1862, Marx expressed his disappointment with a scientific document that reeked of bourgeois prejudice: "It is remarkable," he wrote to Engels, "how Darwin recognizes among beasts and plants his English society with its division of labor, competition, opening of new markets, 'inventions' and Malthusian 'struggle for existence.'" Just as Hegel theologized bourgeois society as a "spiritual" kingdom, Marx complained, "in Darwin the animal kingdom appears as bourgeois."[107] The frustration was that a subjective theory, lending itself to arrant political exploitation, acquired the impregnable status of "science." But Marx's doctrines of determinism and a coming revolution were no less the fruit of extraneous impulses, of ideas external to the subject matter. *Capital*, Marx's crowning treatise on political economy, continued the policy of searing exposure, offering a grisly inventory of industrial sin modeled in part on Dante's *Inferno*.[108] "Nowadays," Marx reflected, in sardonic affirmation of his own journey, "atheism itself is *culpa levis* [a small sin], as compared with criticism of existing property relations."[109] But he never doubted that the god of property and the God of delayed justice were linked.

Marx was dismissive of the soulless, "mechanical" sociology of the Positivists, accusing them of elevating data above consciousness among the levers of historical change. The rejoinder might be that his theory was all soul, all consciousness: the promise of a higher destiny with the details to follow. Certainly, Marx never ceased to be a Hegelian, reading history as conflict and redemption. He was never a Christian, and the brusqueness of his appropriations suggests an alienation cooler and more distant Feuerbach's. He was a prophet, not a saint. Yet his biting dependence on Judeo-Christian expectations reveals the folly of a binary model of "secularization." Modernity is a war of religious ideas, not a war on them. Like almost every figure quoted in this study, Marx criticized Christian cultures for not being Christian enough. Secularization was an accusation before it was an aspiration. Like most of his prophetic forebears, Marx was reaching for something higher—even if it took him into a crude and ultimately destructive demonology of religious belief. And within that dark and unyielding demonology, there were moments of praise. In an age credited with the "invention" of childhood, Marx was willing to give Christianity its due. As his daughter Eleanor said after her father's death: "Again and again I heard him say: 'Despite everything, we can forgive Christianity much, for it has taught to love children.' "[110] As Bayle always said: "everything has two faces."[111]

Conclusion

IN AUGUSTINE'S SHADOW

. . . the Christian religion is the religion of criticism and freedom.

—FEUERBACH, *The Essence of Christianity*, 1841

IN AUGUST 1672, Johan de Witt, statesman and former Grand Pensionary of Holland, was murdered with his brother in the streets of The Hague. Their bodies were hung up for public derision and organs were removed and kept for display by the masterminds of an affair that shocked one portion of the Dutch Republic and provoked deafening silence from another. The motives were political, but the "Orangist" faction that lay behind the attack was allied with the "orthodox Calvinist Voetian wing" of the Dutch Reformed Church, together representing the fanaticism that had inspired Spinoza's *Theological-Political Treatise*.[1] This time, Spinoza's Latin was more concise. He made a large placard bearing the words, *Ultimi Barbarorum* ("The most extreme of barbarians"), and prepared to display it at the site of the murder. Spinoza's landlord had to lock him in the house to prevent him going through with a protest that may have cost him his life.

Sometimes intellectual history is more complicated than it needs to be. European doubt was a series of commentaries on incidents such as this. It emerged from an essentially moral intuition that a dangerous God cannot be real—cannot be the real God. The tendency to associate unbelief with what a Victorian writer termed an "outbreak of reckless speculative intelligence" represents the convergence of two mistaken schools of thought.[2] It reflects the urge of secularism to build a narrative of objective, scientific reason triumphing over ignorance and superstition. And it reflects a tendency of theologians and religious communities to look for causes of alienation outside their own traditions. If Darwin serves as a master cause in popular apologetics, the secular rationality of a godless Enlightenment plays a similar role for several schools of theology. I have often wondered what Pierre Bayle would make of the bullish apologias of modern Christian scholarship—including the notion that the "Wars of Religion" were not really "religious," but a "myth" conjured by a hostile "secular ideology";[3] or the idea that the "burning" of heretics in the sixteenth century was "inevitable" and should not be judged with "hindsight attained this side of the Enlightenment."[4] Scholarly defenses of "the efficiency of mass execution" may now be rare, but such approaches reflect a wider theological instinct to look indulgently on native religious traditions and to treat the Enlightenment as some sort of foreign visitation, an intellectual ambush.

The burning of heretics was not "inevitable" in the sixteenth century, and it was the embattled Christians who said so who arguably created the Enlightenment. The "reason" with which the Enlightenment assailed a persecuting religious culture was neither secular nor primarily intellectual. It was the direct heir to the "inner light" of spiritualist Christianity, rooted in the exalted terminology of the first chapter of John's Gospel. In Kantian terms, it was "practical" not "pure" reason that set the decisive "limits" of modern religion: that eternal law "inscribed in the heart of all human beings."[5] Somewhere between George Fox and Immanuel Kant, there was a certain outgrowing of supernatural services, a dispensing with "grace," a dismantling of the religious "scaffolding," but the outcome consistently resists the clarity and finality of "secularization." When a theologian interrogated a Quaker on the "dark and fleshly reason that you call the light,"[6] he assumed rights of discernment that are no scholar's to claim. One writer suggested that Voltaire's awkwardly resilient piety would have been unnecessary in the age of Darwin and "our new goddess, Evolution."[7] But everything we know about Voltaire and the Victorian "crisis of faith" would dispute such an idea. The smoking gun of science never fired. Even the "luminous fire" of German atheism was rooted in fierce Christian conviction. The haunting phrase used by the war poet, Wilfred Owen, in a letter to his mother, could apply to many of these studies of disenchantment: "I am more and more Christian as I walk the unchristian ways of Christendom."[8]

Time and again, the religion rejected was an expression of what Jean Delumeau has termed "Augustinism," a "type" of Christianity "that spoke more of the Passion of the Savior than of His Resurrection, more of sin than of pardon, of the Judge than of the Father, of Hell than of Paradise."[9] The dominant emotion was fear. Calvinism clearly drives the process in the English and Dutch nurseries of Enlightenment, and the Victorian crisis of faith, but Voltaire's enraged "anti-Jansenism" reveals the same collision of values. As late as the nineteenth century, the "diabolical sophisms" with which Augustine had justified the persecution of heretics were inspiring Feuerbach to agitated contempt. One of the most powerful, indeed moving, moments in *The Essence of Christianity* is the passage in which Feuerbach interrogates Augustine on what remains of "the image of God" under a theology of doom, destruction, and selective redemption, before concluding: "Nothing."[10]

The very predestinarian theology that brought a young, pre-evangelical Luther "to the very depth and abyss of despair, so that I wished I had never been created a man,"[11] brought others—under a Protestant theology theoretically continuous with his—to genuinely suicidal torments. The Augustinian psychology of terror that provoked the Reformation arguably destroyed it. Where Luther found refuge in the crucified Christ, others found it in a "celestial," ahistorical Jesus, or in the weary hope that the nightmare of looming judgment was only that. The fact that Luther's example of conscientious revolt, indeed his very doctrine of conscience, was foundational to the culture of dissent confirms the sense of an internal drama. Fear of "a God who instead of sharing and aiding our human sympathies, is directly in collision with them," in George Eliot's phrase, was the fuel of unbelief.[12] But the motor was the dynamic, enlarged conscience that divided Latin Christendom in 1521 and continued to hold its successors to rigorous account.

What distinguished a modern critic, like Eliot, from a medieval victim of Augustinian agonies was active and articulate resources of resistance. In rejecting a crushing, predestinarian scheme of theology, Eliot remained very much the defiant evangelical, confident of God's ultimate mercy and of the superiority of a pure heart to a mechanical, spoken orthodoxy. Like Feuerbach, Castellio, Bayle, and many others, Eliot's unbelief revealed a potent chemistry of discernment. It knew what a religion ought to look like. It retained a title of ownership even as it left the building. The tendency of such discernment to destroy, rather than merely correct, was perhaps a tribute to the intellectual ambition of orthodoxy. The power and precision of a theological system such as Calvinism made it vulnerable to wholesale critique. To the degree that a harsh and alienating orthodoxy was bonded to the pages of the Bible, the Bible shared its fate.

No better summary of the process can be found than in the twelfth chapter of Spinoza's *Theological-Political Treatise*, where he accuses his Dutch Reformed adversaries of destroying the sacred vessel of scripture. The more closely a text is linked to injustice, Spinoza warned, the more precarious it becomes. When the Bible becomes a battleground and the church a place of "ceaseless learned controversy," dissent becomes an obligation.[13] There is a degree to which some people were forced into doubt.

It would, however, undersell "conscience" to characterize it as a primarily emotive reaction to the violence of orthodoxy and the arrogance of precision. Coiled within the protest, from Castellio to Feuerbach, was a plea on behalf of the integrity of creation and the dignity of the human person. This is why language of secularization is ultimately so misplaced. It is arguably in the atheist humanism of Feuerbach that moral revolt is at its most theological, as he excoriates Christianity's "hyper-cosmic" and "anti-cosmic tendency" as a kind of blasphemy.[14] "The attitude of the anti-theologian Feuerbach," wrote Karl Barth, "was more theological than that of many theologians."[15] Here too, Augustinian ideas framed the debate. Original sin continued to offend a biblical esteem for the natural world, and the "not yet" of Augustinian eschatology struck many as a scandalous evasion of social responsibility. Socialism was above all a quest for integration: a rage against theologies that divided what was meant to be whole.

Finally, it is important not to exaggerate either the terrors of "Augustinism" or the generality of aggressive unbelief—even in the late modern era. Delumeau painted a dark picture of an age of "sin and fear" in medieval and early modern Europe, but if Augustine ruled seminary and pulpit, the pews often belonged to his benighted adversary. One reason not everyone reached Bayle-like conclusions about the corruption of theology was that lived religion moved to different rhythms. "Our common people," the English Puritan, William Perkins, once complained, "bolster themselves in their blind ways by a presumption that God is all of mercy, and that if they do their true intent, serve God, say their prayers, deal justly, and do as they would be done unto, they shall certainly be saved." This "vulgar religion," or "country divinity," was, he scoffed, a rank heresy of works.[16] Yet there was mercy in presumption and salvation in vulgarity. Such "rustic Pelagianism"—in one historian's evocative phrase—could act as a brake on sectarian energies.[17] At a time when Europe was being decimated by wars of religion, small communities of Christians often revealed high levels of tolerance and mutual empathy, anticipating the "tolerationist" philosophies of later times.[18] And away from the set pieces of intellectual combat, the worlds of piety and criticism, religion and philosophy, often overlapped. Voltaire took the sacrament; Spinoza discussed sermons with his "peaceful and pious" Lutheran landlady. Social practice confuses the clear lines of intellectual history and tempers its severity.

Great individuals, Eliot suggested in the concluding pages of *Middlemarch,* deserve their place, but any true history must acknowledge the "unhistoric acts" of those who lived "a hidden life, and rest in unvisited tombs."[19] Diarmaid MacCulloch tells the story of Katharina Schutz, wife of the German reformer Matthias Zell, who had a "kindly attitude towards radical spirits and a brusque contempt for male intolerance." When the rigid Lutheran ministers of Strasbourg refused to officiate at the funerals of two sisters who had been inclined to spiritualist heresies, Katharina, "indignant at this bigotry," took it upon herself "to preach sermons and officiate at the burials of these well-deserving women. She was old and ill herself: on both occasions she had to be carried to the graveside from her sickbed."[20] How many such events slipped under the radars of clerical officialdom will never be known. But the fact that skepticism remains a vigorous tradition rather than a universal consensus may reflect an enduring dissonance between ideas and practice, orthodoxy and piety. Religion is more than theology, and the past is more than a rolling sequence of controversy. The judgments of history would be sterner were it not for the quiet, invisible acts of those who elude its drama.

Notes

INTRODUCTION

1. Randall H. Balmer, *Encyclopedia of Evangelicalism* (Louisville, KY: Westminster John Knox Press, 2002), 283, 516; June M. Benowitz, *Encyclopedia of American Women and Religion* (Santa Barbara, CA: ABC-CLIO, 1998), 73.
2. Hugh McLeod, "The Two Americas: Religion and Secularity in the Seventies," in *Yliopisto, Kirkko Ja Yhteiskunta*, ed. Antti Laine and Aappo Laitinen (Helsinki: Finnish Society for Church History, 2011), 200–14. I quote from an unpaginated copy kindly sent by the author.
3. Joel Spring, *Political Agendas for Education: From Change We Can Believe In to Putting America First* (New York: Routledge, 2010), 110.
4. David E. Rosenbaum, "Of 'Secular Humanism' and Its Slide into Law," *New York Times*, February 22, 1985, http://www.nytimes.com/1985/02/22/us/of-secular-humanism-and-its-slide-into-law.html.
5. Francis A. Schaeffer, *How Should We Then Live? The Rise and Decline of Western Thought and Culture* (Old Tappan, NJ: F. H. Revell, 1976).
6. "Francis Schaeffer, A Christian Manifesto," http://www.peopleforlife.org/francis.html.
7. Frank Schaeffer, *Crazy for God: How I Grew Up as One of the Elect, Helped Found the Religious Right, and Lived to Take All (or Almost All) of It Back* (Boston, MA: Da Capo Press, 2008), 314.
8. For a more detailed discussion of links between secularization theory and sectarian criteria of religious purity, see my article, "'Cause Is Not Quite What It Used to Be': The Return of Secularisation." *The English Historical Review* CXXVII, no. 525 (March 1, 2012): 377–400. A recent example of secularization-as-confessional-lament would be, Brad S. Gregory, *The Unintended Reformation: How a Religious Revolution Secularized Society*

(Cambridge, MA: Belknap, 2012). I acknowledge that my own doctoral work may fall into this category, but I would maintain that there is a difference between applying the term secularization to a specific tradition or a given institution, such as the YMCA, and applying the concept to an entire society or Western culture as a whole. The latter is more problematic. I do now think it is better to drop the term altogether, however, since it carries too much freight.

9. Martin Luther King Jr., "Letter from Birmingham Jail," in *The Radical King*, ed. Cornel West (Boston, MA: Beacon Press, 2015), 141, 140, 142, 141, 142.
10. "Billy Graham Urges Restraint in Sit-Ins," *New York Times*, April 18, 1963; Billy Graham, quoted in Michael O. Emerson and Christian Smith, *Divided by Faith: Evangelical Religion and the Problem of Race in America* (New York: Oxford University Press, 2000), 47.
11. Max Weber, *From Max Weber: Essays in Sociology*, ed. C. Wright Mills and H. H. Gerth (New York: Oxford, 1946), 155.
12. Christopher Hill, *The World Turned Upside down: Radical Ideas during the English Revolution* (Harmondsworth: Penguin, 1978), 231.
13. Charles Taylor, *A Secular Age* (Cambridge, MA: Belknap, 2007).
14. A fine discussion of the "intellectualist position" can be found in Frank M. Turner, "The Victorian Crisis of Faith and the Faith That Was Lost," in *Victorian Faith in Crisis: Essays on Continuity and Change in Nineteenth-Century Religious Belief*, ed. Richard J. Helmstadter (Stanford, CA: Stanford University Press, 1990), 9, 32, 36. For a more substantial critique of Taylor along these lines, see Jon Butler, "Disquieted History in *A Secular Age*," in *Varieties of Secularism in a Secular Age*, ed. Michael Warner, Jonathan VanAntwerpen, and Craig J. Calhoun (Cambridge, MA: Harvard University Press, 2010).
15. Jean Delumeau, *Sin and Fear: The Emergence of a Western Guilt Culture, 13th–18th Centuries* (New York: St. Martin's Press, 1990); *Catholicism between Luther and Voltaire: A New View of the Counter-Reformation* (Philadelphia, PA: Westminster Press, 1977), 230–31.
16. Butler, "Disquieted History in *A Secular Age*," 205.
17. Diarmaid MacCulloch, *A History of Christianity: The First Three Thousand Years* (London: Allen Lane, 2009), 915.

CHAPTER 1

1. Heiko A. Oberman, *Luther: Man between God and the Devil* (New Haven, CT: Yale University Press, 1989), 125.
2. Friedrich Nietzsche, *The Gay Science: With a Prelude in German Rhymes and an Appendix of Songs*, ed. Bernard Williams and Josefine Nauckhoff (Cambridge: Cambridge University Press, 2001), 34.
3. Jean Delumeau, *Sin and Fear: The Emergence of a Western Guilt Culture, 13th–18th Centuries* (New York: St. Martin's Press, 1990).

4. Krister Stendahl, "The Apostle Paul and the Introspective Conscience of the West," *Harvard Theological Review* 56, no. 3 (July 1, 1963): 199–215.
5. Heiko A. Oberman, *The Dawn of the Reformation: Essays in Late Medieval and Early Reformation Thought* (Grand Rapids, MI: Eerdmans, 1986), 150.
6. Oberman, *Dawn*, 140.
7. Thomas à Kempis, *The Imitation of Christ* (Leipzig: Bernhard Tauchnitz, 1877), 29.
8. Steven E. Ozment, *Mysticism and Dissent: Religious Ideology and Social Protest in the Sixteenth Century* (New Haven, CT: Yale University Press, 1973), 19–20.
9. Johannes Tauler, *Johannes Tauler, Sermons* (Mahwah, NJ: Paulist Press, 1985), 15.
10. Steven E. Ozment, *Homo Spiritualis: A Comparative Study of the Anthropology of Johannes Tauler, Jean Gerson and Martin Luther (1509–16) in the Context of Their Theological Thought* (Leiden: Brill, 1969), 62.
11. Ozment, *Mysticism*, 11.
12. George Forell, "Luther and Conscience," *Journal of Lutheran Ethics* 2, no. 1 (January 2002), http://www.elca.org/JLE/Articles/991?_ga=1.202045841.141729377.142720426.
13. Oberman, *Luther*, 181.
14. Ozment, *Homo Spiritualis*, 191.
15. Michael G. Baylor, *Action and Person: Conscience in Late Scholasticism and the Young Luther* (Leiden: Brill, 1977), 13.
16. Berndt Hamm, *The Early Luther: Stages in a Reformation Reorientation* (Grand Rapids, MI: Eerdmans, 2014), 32.
17. Ozment, *Homo Spiritualis*, 2.
18. Markus Wriedt, "Luther's Theology," in *The Cambridge Companion to Martin Luther*, ed. Donald K. McKim (Cambridge: Cambridge University Press, 2003), 90.
19. Martin Luther, "Martin Luther's 95 Theses," http://www.gutenberg.org/cache/epub/274/pg274.html.
20. Hamm, *The Early Luther*, 175.
21. Owen Chadwick, *The Reformation* (New York: Penguin Books, 1990), 50, 55.
22. Patrick Collinson, *The Reformation: A History* (London: Random House, 2006), 53.
23. Oberman, *Luther*, 203.
24. Martin Luther, *Selected Political Writings* (Philadelphia, PA: Fortress Press, 1974), 49, 43, 46.
25. Martin Luther, *Martin Luther: Selections from His Writing* (New York: Knopf, 2011), 304, 306.
26. Denis R. Janz, *Reformation Reader* (Philadelphia, PA: Fortress Press, 2008), 383.
27. Roland H. Bainton, "Introduction," in *CH*, 45, 49.
28. Oberman, *Luther*, 258–59.

29. Bainton, "Introduction," 44–45.
30. Oberman, *Luther*, 254.
31. Roland H. Bainton, "The Development and Consistency of Luther's Attitude to Religious Liberty," *Harvard Theological Review* 22, no. 2 (April 1, 1929): 115, 117.
32. *CH*, 149–50.
33. *CH*, 151.
34. Oberman, *Luther*, 129.
35. Oberman, *Luther*, 276.
36. Martin E. Marty, *Martin Luther* (New York: Penguin, 2004), 181.
37. Oberman, *Luther*, 298.
38. Karl Marx, *Karl Marx: Selected Writings* (Oxford: Oxford University Press, 2000), 77.
39. Quoted in Hans R. Guggisberg, *Sebastian Castellio, 1515–1563: Humanist and Defender of Religious Toleration in a Confessional Age*, trans. Bruce Gordon (Aldershot: Ashgate, 2002), 71.
40. Oberman, *Luther*, 224.
41. Marty, *Luther*, 85.
42. Susan Schreiner, *Are You Alone Wise?* (New York: Oxford University Press, 2010), 73–74.
43. Baylor, *Action and Person*, 226.
44. Oberman, *Luther*, 129.
45. Forell, "Luther and Conscience."
46. Oberman, *Luther*, 291.
47. Jane E. Strohl, "Luther's Spiritual Journey," in *The Cambridge Companion to Martin Luther*, ed. Donald K. McKim (Cambridge: Cambridge University Press, 2003), 157.
48. Schreiner, *Are You Alone Wise*, 296.
49. Martin Luther, *Commentary on the Sermon on the Mount*, trans. Charles A. Hay (Philadelphia, PA: Lutheran Publication Society, 1892), 116, 117.
50. Luther, *Commentary on the Sermon on the Mount*, 117, 119, 118, 27, viii.
51. Martin Luther, *Commentary on the Epistle to The Galatians*, trans. Theodore Graebner (Grand Rapids, MI: Zondervan, 1949), chapter 4, verse 5, http://www.gutenberg.org/files/1549/1549-h/1549-h.htm.
52. Luther, *Galatians*, chapter 5, verse 10.
53. Luther, *Galatians*, chapter 4, verse 7.
54. Luther, *Galatians*, chapter 4, verse 30; chapter 5, verse 10.
55. Luther, *Galatians*, chapter 5, verse 9.
56. Luther, *Galatians*, chapter 5, verse 12.
57. Luther, *Galatians*, chapter 5, verses 13, 15.
58. Luther, *Galatians*, chapter 5, verse 16.
59. Luther, *Galatians*, chapter 5, verse 12.

60. For a perceptive discussion of the theological vulnerability of German State Lutheranism to National Socialism, in contrast to the Reformed Protestant tradition of Karl Barth, see Diarmaid MacCulloch, *A History of Christianity: The First Three Thousand Years* (London: Allen Lane, 2009), 941–44.
61. Martin Luther, "Against the Robbing and Murdering Hordes of Peasants," in *Martin Luther, Documents of Modern History*, ed. E. G. Rupp and Benjamin Drewery (London: Edward Arnold, 1970), 121, 122, 123.
62. Diarmaid MacCulloch, *Reformation: Europe's House Divided 1490–1700* (London: Penguin, 2004), 160.
63. Luther, "Robbing," 123.
64. Luther, "Robbing," 123.
65. Luther, "Robbing," 124.
66. MacCulloch, *Reformation*, 160.
67. David M. Whitford, "Luther's Political Encounters," in *The Cambridge Companion to Martin Luther*, ed. Donald K. McKim (Cambridge: Cambridge University Press, 2003), 186.
68. Marty, *Luther*, 98.
69. Nicholas P. Miller, *The Religious Roots of the First Amendment* (New York: Oxford University Press, 2012), 24.
70. Bainton, "Luther's Attitude to Religious Liberty," 120.
71. Miller, *Religious Roots of the First Amendment*, 17–18.
72. Bainton, "Luther's Attitude to Religious Liberty," 109, 121.

CHAPTER 2

1. Barbara S. Tinsley, *Pierre Bayle's Reformation: Conscience and Criticism on the Eve of the Enlightenment* (Selinsgrove, PA: Susquehanna University Press, 2001), 162.
2. Steven E. Ozment, *Mysticism and Dissent: Religious Ideology and Social Protest in the Sixteenth Century* (New Haven, CT: Yale University Press, 1973), 71.
3. Ozment, *Mysticism*, 96.
4. Ozment, *Mysticism*, 105.
5. Ozment, *Mysticism*, 104.
6. Ozment, *Mysticism*, 108.
7. Ozment, *Mysticism*, 114.
8. "Denck, Hans (ca. 1500–1527)" http://www.gameo.org/encyclopedia/contents/D4485.html.
9. Ozment, *Mysticism*, 122, 27.
10. Walter Nigg, *The Heretics* (New York: Knopf, 1962), 320.
11. Ozment, *Mysticism*, 126, 132.

12. Hans Denck, "Concerning the Law of God," in *The Spiritual Legacy of Hans Denck: Including the German Text as Established by Georg Baring and Walter Fellman*, ed. Clarence Bauman (Leiden: Brill, 1991), 137, 135, 149.
13. Harry Loewen, *Luther and the Radicals: Another Look at Some Aspects of the Struggle between Luther and the Radical Reformers* (Waterloo, ON: Wilfrid Laurier University Press, 1974), 113.
14. George H. Williams, *The Radical Reformation*, 3rd ed. (Kirksville, MO: Truman State University Press, 2000), 1249.
15. Williams, *Radical Reformation*, 397.
16. Ozment, *Mysticism*, 163.
17. Patrick Marshall Hayden-Roy, *The Inner Word and the Outer World: A Biography of Sebastian Franck* (New York: Peter Lang, 1994), 14.
18. Hayden-Roy, *Inner Word*, 37.
19. Hayden-Roy, *Inner Word*, 41.
20. Hayden-Roy, *Inner Word*, 184.
21. Robert W. Brenning, "The Ethical Hermeneutic of Sebastian Franck, 1499–1542," Ph.D. thesis, Temple University Microfilms, 1978, 55.
22. *CH*, 195.
23. *CH*, 192–93.
24. *CH*, 191–92.
25. *CH*, 191.
26. George H. Williams, *Spiritual and Anabaptist Writers: Documents Illustrative of the Radical Reformation* (Louisville, KY: Westminster John Knox Press, 1957), 151.
27. Williams, *Spiritual and Anabaptist Writers*, 151, 148.
28. Sebastian Franck, *280 Paradoxes or Wondrous Sayings* (New York: Edwin Mellen Press, 1986), 480.
29. Ozment, *Mysticism*, 141.
30. Martin Luther, *Martin Luther: Selections from His Writing* (New York: Knopf, 2011), 83.
31. Williams, *Spiritual and Anabaptist Writers*, 160.
32. James Buckley, Frederick Christian Bauerschmidt, and Trent Pomplun, *The Blackwell Companion to Catholicism* (Oxford: Blackwell, 2010), 70.
33. Franck, *Paradoxes*, 7.
34. Rufus Jones, *Spiritual Reformers in the Sixteenth and Seventeenth Centuries* (London: Macmillan, 1914), 61.
35. Franck, *Paradoxes*, 6.
36. Franck, *Paradoxes*, 8.
37. Williams, *Spiritual and Anabaptist Writers*, 159.
38. Franck, *Paradoxes*, 416.
39. Williams, *Spiritual and Anabaptist Writers*, 158, 159.
40. Franck, *Paradoxes*, 12–13.

41. Williams, *Spiritual and Anabaptist Writers*, 154.
42. Williams, *Spiritual and Anabaptist Writers*, 156.
43. Hans J. Hillerbrand, *A Fellowship of Discontent* (New York: Harper & Row, 1967), 57, 55.
44. Franck, *Paradoxes*, 426.
45. Franck, *Paradoxes*, 193, 66.
46. Franck, *Paradoxes*, 426.
47. Franck, *Paradoxes*, 11, 10.
48. *CH*, 97.
49. Franck, *Paradoxes*, 63.
50. Franck, *Paradoxes*, 53.
51. Hayden-Roy, *Inner Word*, 165.
52. Jones, *Spiritual Reformers*, 52.
53. *CH*, 202; Roland H. Bainton, *Hunted Heretic: The Life and Death of Michael Servetus, 1511–1553* (Providence, RI: Blackstone Editions, 2005), 210.
54. Brad S. Gregory, *The Unintended Reformation: How a Religious Revolution Secularized Society* (Cambridge, MA: Belknap, 2012), 41.
55. Bainton, *Hunted*, 209, 116.
56. Alister E. McGrath, *Reformation Thought: An Introduction*, 3rd ed. (Oxford: Blackwell, 1991), 82.
57. Williams, *Radical Reformation*, 947.
58. Bruce Gordon, *Calvin* (New Haven, CT: Yale University Press, 2011), 146.
59. Diarmaid MacCulloch, *Reformation: Europe's House Divided 1490–1700* (London: Penguin, 2004), 246.
60. Gordon, *Calvin*, 146.
61. John Calvin, *Institutes of the Christian Religion*, ed. John T. McNeill, trans. Ford L. Battles (Philadelphia, PA: Westminster Press, 1960), 551.
62. Richard H. Popkin, *The History of Scepticism: From Savonarola to Bayle* (Oxford: Oxford University Press, 2003), 11.
63. Roland H. Bainton, *Sebastian Castellio, Champion of Religious Liberty, 1515–1563* (Leiden: Brill, 1951), 31.
64. John Stachniewski, *The Persecutory Imagination: English Puritanism and the Literature of Religious Despair* (New York: Oxford University Press, 1991), 80.
65. Calvin, *Institutes of the Christian Religion*, 402.
66. Roland H. Bainton, "Introduction," in *CH*, 1935, 73.
67. Bainton, *Hunted*, 116.
68. John Marshall, *John Locke, Toleration and Early Enlightenment Culture* (Cambridge: Cambridge University Press, 2006), 325.
69. Bainton, "Introduction," 74.
70. Bainton, *Hunted*, 97.
71. Bainton, *Hunted*, 211–12.
72. Bainton, *Hunted*, 194.

73. Bainton, *Hunted*, 147.
74. Bainton, *Hunted*, 138.
75. Williams, *Radical Reformation*, 945, 944.
76. Hans R. Guggisberg, *Sebastian Castellio, 1515–1563: Humanist and Defender of Religious Toleration in a Confessional Age*, trans. Bruce Gordon (Aldershot: Ashgate, 2002), 76.
77. Which I will quote thematically rather than chronologically, from Bainton's combined edition of Castellio's major works.
78. Guggisberg, *Castellio*, 21, 22.
79. Guggisberg, *Castellio*, 71.
80. Roland H. Bainton, *The Travail of Religious Liberty: Nine Biographical Studies* (Philadelphia, PA: Westminster Press, 1951), 105.
81. *CH*, 127.
82. *CH*, 121–23, 219.
83. *CH*, 253, 285, 134.
84. Marshall, *John Locke*, 323.
85. *CH*, 261.
86. *CH*, 307.
87. *CH*, 125.
88. *CH*, 133.
89. *CH*, 276–77, 268.
90. Guggisberg, *Castellio*, 117.
91. *CH*, 217, 218, 259.
92. *CH*, 220–21.
93. *CH*, 221–22, 213.
94. *CH*, 129.
95. *CH*, 224, 272, 285.
96. *CH*, 230.
97. *CH*, 236, 246, 279, 280.
98. *CH*, 279–80.
99. *CH*, 287, 279, 276, 275.
100. *CH*, 283.
101. *CH*, 267.
102. *CH*, 282, 279.
103. *CH*, 290, 292, 305.
104. *CH*, 292.
105. Guggisberg, *Castellio*, 218.
106. *CH*, 292.
107. *CH*, 296.
108. *CH*, 305.
109. Ozment, *Mysticism*, 197.
110. Guggisberg, *Castellio*, 229.

111. Ozment, *Mysticism*, 198.
112. Gordon, *Calvin*, 146.
113. Guggisberg, *Castellio*, 199.
114. Guggisberg, *Castellio*, 205.
115. Malcolm Smith, *Montaigne and Religious Freedom: The Dawn of Pluralism* (Geneva: Librairie Droz, 1991), 128.
116. *CH*, 295.
117. Ozment, *Mysticism*, 240.

CHAPTER 3

1. Steven Nadler, *A Book Forged in Hell: Spinoza's Scandalous Treatise and the Birth of the Secular Age* (Princeton, NJ: Princeton University Press, 2011), 8–9.
2. Matthew Stewart, *The Courtier and the Heretic: Leibniz, Spinoza, and the Fate of God in the Modern World* (New York: Norton, 2007), 37.
3. Jonathan I. Israel, *Radical Enlightenment: Philosophy and the Making of Modernity, 1650–1750* (New York: Oxford University Press, 2002), 159.
4. Yirmiyahu Yovel, *Spinoza and Other Heretics: The Adventures of Immanence* (Princeton, NJ: Princeton University Press, 1992), 51.
5. Israel, *Radical Enlightenment*, 159, 715, 718, 7.
6. Israel, *Radical Enlightenment*, 7.
7. Stewart, *Courtier*, 107.
8. Nadler, *Forged*, 231, 13.
9. Leo Strauss, *Spinoza's Critique of Religion* (Chicago, IL: University of Chicago Press, 1997).
10. Richard Mason, *The God of Spinoza: A Philosophical Study* (Cambridge: Cambridge University Press, 1997), 179.
11. Yirmiyahu Yovel, *Spinoza and Other Heretics: The Marrano of Reason* (Princeton, NJ: Princeton University Press, 1992), 173.
12. Jonathan I. Israel, *Enlightenment Contested: Philosophy, Modernity, and the Emancipation of Man, 1670–1752* (New York: Oxford University Press, 2008), 123.
13. Leszek Kolakowski, *The Two Eyes of Spinoza & Other Essays on Philosophers*, trans. Zbigniew Janowski (South Bend, IN: St. Augustine's Press, 2004), 88.
14. Benedict de Spinoza, *The Chief Works of Benedict de Spinoza: On the Improvement of the Understanding, the Ethics Correspondence* (New York: Dover, 1955), 277.
15. I am grateful to Clare Carlisle for this important point. See the discussion in the *Ethics*. Spinoza, *Chief Works*, 201.
16. Travis L. Frampton, *Spinoza and the Rise of Historical Criticism of the Bible* (London: T & T Clark, 2006), 166.
17. Diarmaid MacCulloch, *Reformation: Europe's House Divided, 1490–1700* (London: Penguin, 2004), 374–76.

18. John Coffey, *John Goodwin and the Puritan Revolution: Religion and Intellectual Change in Seventeenth-Century England* (Woodbridge: Boydell, 2008), 38.
19. John Marshall, *John Locke, Toleration and Early Enlightenment Culture* (Cambridge: Cambridge University Press, 2006), 365.
20. Hans R. Guggisberg, *Sebastian Castellio, 1515–1563: Humanist and Defender of Religious Toleration in a Confessional Age*, trans. Bruce Gordon (Aldershot: Ashgate, 2002), 238.
21. Quoted in Marshall, *John Locke*, 348, 349.
22. Richard H. Popkin, "The Religious Background of Seventeenth-Century Philosophy," in *The Cambridge History of Seventeenth-Century Philosophy*, vol. 1, ed. Daniel Garber and Michael Ayers (Cambridge: Cambridge University Press, 1998), 13.
23. Gerrit Voogt, " 'Anyone Who Can Read May Be a Preacher': Sixteenth-Century Roots of the Collegiants," in *The Formation of Clerical and Confessional Identities in Early Modern Europe*, ed. Wim Janse and Barbara Pitkin (Leiden: Brill, 2006), 414.
24. H. Bonger and Gerrit Voogt, *The Life and Work of Dirck Volkertszoon Coornhert* (Amsterdam: Rodopi, 2004), 302.
25. Gerrit Voogt, *Constraint on Trial: Dirck Volckertsz Coornhert and Religious Freedom* (Kirksville, MO: Truman State University Press, 2000), 52–53; Andrew C. Fix, *Prophecy and Reason: The Dutch Collegiants in the Early Enlightenment* (Princeton, NJ: Princeton University Press, 1991).
26. Andrew Fix, "Angels, Devils, and Evil Spirits in Seventeenth-Century Thought: Balthasar Bekker and the Collegiants," *Journal of the History of Ideas* 50, no. 4 (October 1, 1989): 529–30.
27. Fix, *Prophecy and Reason*.
28. Fix, *Prophecy and Reason*, 10.
29. 1 Thessalonians 5:20–21.
30. Fix, *Prophecy and Reason*, 191.
31. Kolakowski, *Two Eyes*, 82.
32. Fix, *Prophecy and Reason*, 199.
33. Dominique Colas, quoted in MacCulloch, *Reformation*, 373.
34. *TTP*, 178.
35. Fix, *Prophecy and Reason*, 200.
36. Fix, *Prophecy and Reason*, 198.
37. Fix, *Prophecy and Reason*, 192.
38. Anon., *The Light upon the Candlestick Serving for Observation of the Principal Things in the Book Called, The Mysteries of the Kingdom of God, &c., against Several Professors* (London: Printed for Robert Wilson, 1663), 3, 1, 11.
39. Anon., *The Light upon the Candlestick*, 4–5, 9.
40. Nicholas McDowell, *The English Radical Imagination* (Oxford: Oxford University Press, 2003), 164.

41. Gerrard Winstanley, *The Complete Works of Gerrard Winstanley*, ed. Thomas N. Corns, Ann Hughes, and David Loewenstein (New York: Oxford University Press, 2009), 2:5.
42. John Stachniewski, *The Persecutory Imagination: English Puritanism and the Literature of Religious Despair* (New York: Oxford University Press, 1991), 42, 50.
43. Stachniewski, *Persecutory Imagination*, 49, 50, 47.
44. Alec Ryrie, *Being Protestant in Reformation Britain* (Oxford: Oxford University Press, 2013), 12.
45. *Westminster Confession of Faith*, chapter 3, Of God's Eternal Decree, http://www.reformed.org/documents/wcf_with_proofs/index.html.
46. Stachniewski, *Persecutory Imagination*, 48.
47. John Donne, *The Collected Poems of John Donne* (Ware: Wordsworth Editions, 1994), 255.
48. John Stachniewski, "John Donne: The Despair of the 'Holy Sonnets,'" *English Literary History* 48, no. 4 (December 1, 1981): 686, 687, 694.
49. Stachniewski, *Persecutory Imagination*, 50, 53.
50. Jean Delumeau, *Sin and Fear: The Emergence of a Western Guilt Culture, 13th–18th Centuries* (New York: St. Martin's Press, 1990), ix; J. B. Bamborough, "Burton, Robert (1577–1640)," in *ODNB*.
51. Delumeau, *Sin and Fear*, ix.
52. Delumeau, *Sin and Fear*, 246, 176, 169.
53. Christopher Hill, *The World Turned Upside Down: Radical Ideas during the English Revolution* (Harmondsworth: Penguin, 1978), 173.
54. Hill, *World Turned*, 239, 237.
55. David Wootton, quoted in McDowell, *Radical Imagination*, 50.
56. McDowell, *Radical Imagination*, 57.
57. McDowell, *Radical Imagination*, 57.
58. McDowell, *Radical Imagination*, 58, 62, 66–67.
59. Barbara Taft, "Walwyn, William (bap. 1600, D. 1681)," in *ODNB*.
60. Taft, "Walwyn."
61. Hill, *World Turned*, 394.
62. Thomas Hobbes, *Leviathan; or, The Matter, Form and Power of a Commonwealth, Ecclesiastical and Civil* (London: Routledge, 1886), 273.
63. Hill, *World Turned*, 173.
64. Hobbes, *Leviathan*, 272, 267.
65. McDowell, *Radical Imagination*, 172.
66. The Saints Paradice (1648), Winstanley, *Complete Works*, 1:313–14.
67. Truth Lifting up his Head (1648), quoted in David Loewenstein, "Gerrard Winstanley and the Diggers," in *The Oxford Handbook of Literature and the English Revolution*, ed. Laura Lunger Knoppers (Oxford: Oxford University Press, 2012), DOI: 10.1093/oxfordhb/9780199560608.013.0018.
68. Winstanley, *Complete Works*, 1:419.

69. Winstanley, *Complete Works*, 2:345.
70. Winstanley, *Complete Works*, 1:419, 419–20, 410.
71. Winstanley, *Complete Works*, 2:200.
72. Hill, *World Turned*, 226, 262.
73. Hill, *World Turned*, 263.
74. Hill, *World Turned*, 141–42.
75. Hilary Hinds, "'And the Lord's Power Was over All': Calvinist Anxiety, Sacred Confidence, and George Fox's Journal," *English Literary History* (2008): 841.
76. Hinds, "'And the Lord's Power Was over All'," 864.
77. George Fox, *Journal of George Fox* (London: Friends' Tract Association, 1891), 512.
78. McDowell, *Radical Imagination*, 142.
79. Richard H. Popkin, "Spinoza and Samuel Fisher," *Philosophia* 15, no. 3 (December 1985): 229.
80. Frampton, *Spinoza*, 219.
81. Frampton, *Spinoza*, 220.
82. Popkin, "Spinoza and Samuel Fisher," 229, 230.
83. McDowell, *Radical Imagination*, 166.
84. Frampton, *Spinoza*, 221.
85. Hill, *World Turned*, 267.
86. Hill, *World Turned*, 260–1.
87. McDowell, *Radical Imagination*, 166.
88. McDowell, *Radical Imagination*, 180.
89. Richard H. Popkin and Michael A. Signer, *Spinoza's Earliest Publication?: The Hebrew Translation of Margaret Fell's A Loving Salutation to the Seed of Abraham Among the Jews, Wherever They Are Scattered up and down Upon the Face of the Earth* (Assen, The Netherlands: Van Gorcum, 1987), 1–12.
90. Steven Nadler, *Spinoza: A Life* (Cambridge: Cambridge University Press, 2001), 160.
91. Popkin and Signer, *Spinoza's Earliest Publication*, 1.
92. Richard H. Popkin, *Spinoza* (Oxford: Oneworld, 2004), 11.
93. Popkin and Signer, *Spinoza's Earliest Publication*, 12.
94. Richard H. Popkin, *The Third Force in Seventeenth-Century Thought* (Leiden: Brill, 1992), 356.
95. Spinoza, *Chief Works*, 260.
96. Although my emphasis is stronger, I acknowledge a particular debt to Graeme Hunter, *Radical Protestantism in Spinoza's Thought* (Aldershot: Ashgate, 2005).
97. Benedict de Spinoza, *The Collected Works of Spinoza*, ed. E. M. Curley (Princeton, NJ: Princeton University Press, 1984), 128.
98. Spinoza, *Collected Works*, 130, 134, 128, 139, 140.
99. Spinoza, *Collected Works*, 265.
100. Nadler, *Forged*, 44.

101. Hunter, *Radical Protestantism*, 70–71; Susan James, *Spinoza on Philosophy, Religion, and Politics* (Oxford: Oxford University Press, 2012), 203–5.
102. Brad Gregory, Introduction, Benedict de Spinoza, Samuel Shirley, and Brad S. Gregory, *Tractatus Theologico-Politicus* (Leiden: Brill, 1991).
103. Nadler, *Forged*, 47.
104. Popkin, *The Third Force in Seventeenth-Century Thought*, 166.
105. *TTP*, 234.
106. *TTP*, 7.
107. *TTP*, 7.
108. *TTP*, 7, 8.
109. *TTP*, 8.
110. *TTP*, 181.
111. Christopher Hill, *Antichrist in Seventeenth-Century England* (Oxford: Oxford University Press, 1971).
112. A point well made by Nadler, *Forged*, 175, and discussion on page 259.
113. Jonathan I. Israel, "Introduction," in *TTP*, xvii.
114. Israel, *Radical Enlightenment*, 218.
115. *TTP*, 16.
116. *TTP*, 102.
117. *TTP*, 93.
118. *TTP*, 53.
119. *TTP*, 182.
120. *TTP*, 88.
121. *TTP*, 52, 43.
122. *TTP*, 54.
123. Spinoza, *Collected Works*, 53, 62.
124. Spinoza, *Collected Works*, 76.
125. Hans Boersma, *Heavenly Participation: The Weaving of a Sacramental Tapestry* (Grand Rapids, MI: Eerdmans, 2011), 76.
126. Spinoza, *Chief Works*, 77.
127. Spinoza, *Chief Works*, 219, 242.
128. Spinoza, *Chief Works*, 223–24.
129. *TTP*, 83.
130. *TTP*, 87, 83.
131. *TTP*, 82.
132. Benedict de Spinoza, *The Principles of Descartes' Philosophy* (Chicago, IL: Open Court, 1905), 161.
133. *TTP*, 52.
134. *TTP*, 96.
135. *TTP*, 89.
136. *TTP*, 88.
137. *TTP*, 160.

138. *TTP*, 96.
139. Here I have translated "ad Dei cultum" as "to the worship of God" rather than using the pejorative term "cult" that appears in the Cambridge translation, which I do not think is the sense Spinoza intended.
140. *TTP*, 96.
141. *TTP*, 81.
142. *TTP*, 234.
143. Frampton, *Spinoza*, 216, 217.
144. *TTP*, 170.
145. *TTP*, 164.
146. *TTP*, 168.
147. *TTP*, 173.
148. *TTP*, 174.
149. *TTP*, 38–39.
150. *TTP*, 25.
151. *TTP*, 24.
152. *TTP*, 40.
153. *TTP*, 145.
154. Parallels between Spinoza's hermeneutics and Luther's notion of the "living voice" of scripture have been noted by Hunter, *Radical Protestantism*, 76.
155. *TTP*, 191.
156. *TTP*, 78, 64.
157. *TTP*, 173, 115.
158. *TTP*, 114.
159. *TTP*, 180–81.
160. *TTP*, 183.
161. *TTP*, 182.
162. *TTP*, 165.
163. *TTP*, 165, 166.
164. *TTP*, 97, 97–98.
165. *TTP*, 80.
166. *TTP*, 166.
167. *TTP*, 67.
168. *TTP*, 64.
169. *TTP*, 59.
170. *TTP*, 66.
171. Spinoza, *Chief Works*, 232.
172. *TTP*, 64.
173. *TTP*, 53.
174. *TTP*, 177.
175. *TTP*, 14.
176. Annotation 34, *TTP*, 272.

177. *TTP*, 78.
178. *TTP*, 156, 157.
179. *TTP*, 160.
180. Spinoza, *Chief Works*, 238.
181. *TTP*, 18.
182. *TTP*, 157.
183. *TTP*, 19.
184. *TTP*, 63.
185. *TTP*, 64, emphasis in original.
186. *TTP*, 69–70.
187. *TTP*, 103.
188. Ehrenfried Walther von Tschirnhaus, quoted in Israel, "Introduction," xviii.
189. Spinoza, *Chief Works*, 303.
190. Spinoza, *Chief Works*, 299.
191. Spinoza, *Chief Works*, 416.
192. Spinoza, *Chief Works*, 304.
193. Spinoza, *Chief Works*, 307.
194. Spinoza, *Chief Works*, 294.
195. Spinoza, *Chief Works*, 368.
196. Spinoza, *Chief Works*, 233.
197. As argued by Colerus, an early biographer, and by many subsequent scholars, especially Bayle. Michael J. Buckley, *At the Origins of Modern Atheism* (New Haven, CT: Yale University Press, 1987), 11.
198. Clare Carlisle, "Spinoza On Eternal Life," *American Catholic Philosophical Quarterly* 89, no. 1 (2015): 84.
199. Carlisle, "Spinoza On Eternal Life," 95.
200. Spinoza, *Chief Works*, 341–42.
201. Spinoza, *Chief Works*, 298.
202. *TTP*, 185.
203. *Gangraena* (1646), quoted in Marshall, *John Locke*, 334.
204. Hill, *World Turned*, 385.

CHAPTER 4

1. E. P. Thompson, *The Making of the English Working Class* (London: Penguin, 1980), 12.
2. Alasdair C. MacIntyre, *After Virtue: A Study in Moral Theory*, 2nd ed. (London: Duckworth, 1985), 69–70.
3. Gordon E. Michalson, *Kant and the Problem of God* (Oxford: Blackwell, 1999); David S. Pacini, *Through Narcissus' Glass Darkly: The Modern Religion of Conscience*, 1st ed. (New York: Fordham University Press, 2008).

4. Immanuel Kant, *Religion within the Boundaries of Mere Reason and Other Writings*, ed. Allen W. Wood and George Di Giovanni (Cambridge: Cambridge University Press, 1998), 157, 33.
5. Kant, *Religion*, 157, xxii, xxxi.
6. Kant, *Religion*, 158, 162, 169, 186, 188, 168, 170.
7. Pacini, *Through Narcissus' Glass Darkly*, 19.
8. Søren Kierkegaard, *Kierkegaard's Writings*, vol. 6: *Fear and Trembling/Repetition* (Princeton, NJ: Princeton University Press, 2013), 117.
9. Owen Chadwick, *The Secularization of the European Mind in the Nineteenth Century* (Cambridge: Cambridge University Press, 1977), 148.
10. Voltaire, *The Ignorant Philosopher* (London: S. Bladon, 1767).
11. MacIntyre, *After Virtue*, 60.
12. Chadwick, *Secularization*, 148.
13. David Beeson and Nicholas Cronk, "Voltaire: Philosopher or Philosophe?" in *The Cambridge Companion to Voltaire*, ed. Nicholas Cronk (Cambridge: Cambridge University Press, 2009), 62.
14. Carl L. Becker, *The Heavenly City of the Eighteenth-Century Philosophers*, 2nd ed. (London: Yale University Press, 2003), 57.
15. Voltaire, *Letters on England* (London: Penguin, 1980), 63.
16. John Locke, *An Essay Concerning Human Understanding* (London, 1760), 63, 65, 64–65.
17. D. W. Bebbington, *Evangelicalism in Modern Britain: A History from the 1730s to the 1980s* (London: Unwin Hyman, 1989), 49.
18. Voltaire, *The Sage and the Atheist: Including the Adventures of a Young Englishman* (New York: P. Eckler, 1921), 127.
19. Christopher Hill, *The Century of Revolution, 1603–1714* (London: Routledge, 2002), 303.
20. Hill, *Century of Revolution*, 303.
21. Anthony Pagden, *The Enlightenment: And Why It Still Matters* (New York: Random House, 2013), 10.
22. Elisabeth Labrousse, *Bayle* (Oxford: Oxford University Press, 1983), 61.
23. H. T. Mason, *Pierre Bayle and Voltaire* (Oxford: Oxford University Press, 1963), 3.
24. *WV*, 6/iv:172; 10/i:16; Peter Gay, *The Enlightenment: The Rise of Modern Paganism* (New York: Norton, 1995), 295.
25. Richard H. Popkin, *The History of Scepticism: From Savonarola to Bayle* (Oxford: Oxford University Press, 2003), 301.
26. Labrousse, *Bayle*, 46.
27. *General Criticism of Monsieur Maimbourg's History of Calvinism* (1682).
28. Labrousse, *Bayle*, 27.
29. Pierre Bayle, *Various Thoughts on the Occasion of a Comet* (Albany, NY: State University of New York Press, 2000), 203.

30. Margaret Jacob, "The Enlightenment Critique of Christianity," in *Enlightenment, Reawakening, and Revolution, 1660–1815*, ed. Stewart J. Brown and Timothy Tackett (Cambridge: Cambridge University Press, 2006), 267.
31. Labrousse, *Bayle*, 47.
32. Pierre Bayle, *A Philosophical Commentary on These Words of the Gospel, Luke 14.23: "Compel Them to Come In, That My House May Be Full"* (Indianapolis, IN: Liberty Fund, 2005), 35.
33. Bayle, *Philosophical Commentary*, xix.
34. Bayle, *Philosophical Commentary*, 64.
35. Bayle, *Philosophical Commentary*, 83.
36. Bayle, *Philosophical Commentary*, 101, 102, 64, 156, 102.
37. Labrousse, *Bayle*, 85.
38. Bayle, *Philosophical Commentary*, 69. Emphasis added.
39. Bayle, *Philosophical Commentary*, 68, 69, 70–71.
40. Labrousse, *Bayle*, 57.
41. Labrousse, *Bayle*, 88.
42. Walter Rex, *Essays on Pierre Bayle and Religious Controversy* (The Hague: Martinus Nijhoff, 1965), 203ff. I am grateful to John Coffey for alerting me to this reference.
43. *WV*, 6/iv:173, 174.
44. Pierre Bayle, *A General Dictionary, Historical and Critical* (London: G. Strahan, 1734), 537.
45. Voltaire, *Toleration and Other Essays*, trans. Joseph McCabe (New York: G. P. Putnam, 1912), 261; I am grateful for this observation to Mason, *Pierre Bayle and Voltaire*, 55.
46. Craig D. Atwood, *Community of the Cross: Moravian Piety in Colonial Bethlehem* (University Park, PA: Penn State University Press, 2004), 52.
47. Becker, *Heavenly City*, 45, 83.
48. Peter Gay quoted in Johnson Kent Wright's Foreword to Becker, *Heavenly City*, ix.
49. Baron D'Holbach, *The System of Nature* (Sioux Falls, SD: NuVision, 2007), 158.
50. I am again grateful to John Coffey for this reference.
51. Quoted in Karen Pagani, "Forgiveness and the Age of Reason: Fénelon, Voltaire, Rousseau and Stael," Ph.D. diss., University of Chicago, 2008, 36.
52. Norman Hampson, *The Enlightenment* (London: Penguin, 1990), 188.
53. D'Holbach, *The System of Nature*, 160, 270.
54. Becker, *Heavenly City*, 36–37.
55. John Morley, "A Biographical Critique of Voltaire," *WV*, 21:235.
56. Gay, *The Enlightenment*, 197.
57. Roger Pearson, *Voltaire Almighty: A Life in Pursuit of Freedom* (London: Bloomsbury, 2005), 379.
58. S. J. Barnett, *The Enlightenment and Religion: The Myths of Modernity* (Manchester: Manchester University Press, 2003), 99.

59. Jonathan I. Israel, *Enlightenment Contested: Philosophy, Modernity, and the Emancipation of Man, 1670–1752* (New York: Oxford University Press, 2008), 104.
60. Israel, *Enlightenment Contested,* 102.
61. John Toland, *Christianity Not Mysterious: Or, A Treatise Shewing, That There Is Nothing in the Gospel Contrary to Reason, nor above It. To Which Is Added, An Apology for Mr. Toland* (London, 1702), xxvi, xxvii–xxviii.
62. Norman L. Torrey, *Voltaire and the English Deists* (New Haven, CT: Yale University Press, 1930), 130–31.
63. Nicholas McDowell, *The English Radical Imagination* (Oxford: Oxford University Press, 2003), 140.
64. Beeson and Cronk, "Voltaire," 49.
65. Beeson and Cronk, "Voltaire," 50.
66. René Pomeau, *La Religion de Voltaire,* 2nd ed. (Paris: Nizet, 1969), 28.
67. Pomeau, *La Religion de Voltaire,* 48, 50.
68. A point also made in Pearson, *Voltaire Almighty,* 31.
69. *WV,* 11/ii:186, 181.
70. Pagani, "Forgiveness and the Age of Reason," 140.
71. Pomeau, *La Religion de Voltaire,* 64.
72. Pagani, "Forgiveness and the Age of Reason," 281.
73. Pomeau, *La Religion de Voltaire,* 365.
74. *WV,* 10/ii:26, 24, 32, 33.
75. *WV,* 5:5.
76. *WV,* 8/ii:10.
77. Voltaire, *Oeuvres de Voltaire,* ed. Adrien Jean Quentin Beuchot (Paris: Lefèvre, 1832), 57:249.
78. Voltaire, *Treatise on Tolerance,* ed. Simon Harvey (Cambridge: Cambridge University Press, 2000), 100.
79. *WV,* 6/iv:118.
80. Voltaire, *Candide* (New York: Dover Publications, 1991), 1.
81. *WV,* 9/i:47.
82. Voltaire, *Zadig; Or, the Book of Fate. An Oriental History, Translated from the French Original of Mr. Voltaire.* (London: J. Brindley, 1749), 108.
83. Voltaire, *Candide,* 60.
84. Voltaire, *Candide,* 85.
85. Voltaire, *Voltaire in His Letters: Being a Selection from His Correspondence,* trans. S. G. Tallentyre (New York: G. P. Putnam, 1919), 48, xi.
86. Gay, *The Enlightenment,* 180.
87. Voltaire, *Candide,* 69.
88. Gay, *The Enlightenment,* 141.
89. Voltaire, *Candide,* 53.
90. Voltaire, *Candide,* 86, 87.

91. Mason, *Pierre Bayle and Voltaire,* 27.
92. Bayle, *Philosophical Commentary,* 67.
93. Graham Gargett, "Voltaire and the Bible," in *The Cambridge Companion to Voltaire,* ed. Nicholas Cronk (Cambridge: Cambridge University Press, 2009), 199.
94. Pomeau, *La Religion de Voltaire,* 370.
95. *WV,* 6/iv:5–8.
96. Pearson, *Voltaire Almighty,* 50.
97. *WV,* 3/i:100.
98. *WV,* 11/ii:150, 148.
99. *WV,* 10/ii:221.
100. Voltaire, *The Works of Voltaire: Romances,* trans. William F. Fleming (New York: E. R. Du Mont, 1901), 156.
101. Mason, *Pierre Bayle and Voltaire,* 60.
102. Voltaire, *Oeuvres de Voltaire,* 12:15–17.
103. Voltaire, *Oeuvres de Voltaire,* 12:17–19.
104. Voltaire, *Oeuvres de Voltaire,* 12:20.
105. Matthew 9:13. English Standard Version.
106. Voltaire, *Letters on England,* 120–25, 131.
107. Voltaire, *Letters on England,* 130, 124.
108. *WV,* 6/iv:118–26.
109. Voltaire, *Toleration and Other Essays,* 91.
110. Voltaire, *Treatise on Tolerance,* 90.
111. Voltaire, *Toleration and Other Essays,* 122.
112. Pagani, "Forgiveness and the Age of Reason," 237.
113. *WV,* 6/iv:123.
114. Pearson, *Voltaire Almighty,* 296.
115. *WV,* 6/iv:63.
116. Voltaire, *Candide,* 9.
117. *WV,* 4/ii:239, 239–40.
118. Voltaire, *The Henriad,* trans. Charles L. S. Jones (Mobile, AL: S. Smith, 1834), 44, 151, 157, 155.
119. Voltaire, *Henriad,* 286, 183, 218, 221.
120. Voltaire, *Selections from Voltaire: With Explanatory Comment upon his Life and Works,* ed. George R. Havens (New York: Appleton-Century-Crofts, 1969), 99.
121. *WV,* 9/i:5–7, 7–8, 9.
122. *WV,* 9/i:60.
123. *WV,* 9/i:40, 61.
124. *WV,* 9/i:59, 62.
125. Pearson, *Voltaire Almighty,* 134.
126. *WV,* 9/i:4.
127. *WV,* 9/i:22.
128. *WV,* 9/i:11, 50, 11.

129. Beeson and Cronk, "Voltaire," 48.
130. *WV*, 9/i:19.
131. *WV*, 5/iii:315, 317, 315, 311.
132. Voltaire, *The Sage and the Atheist*, 151.
133. *WV*, 5/iii:226.
134. For the connection between Fénelon, Guyon, and the Quakers, see Pagani, "Forgiveness and the Age of Reason," 309.
135. Voltaire, *Letters on England*, 23, 26.
136. Voltaire, *Letters on England*, 34.
137. *WV*, 4/ii:165, 166, 170.
138. Pomeau, *La Religion de Voltaire*, 137.
139. Voltaire, *The Sage and the Atheist*, 117.
140. Voltaire, *The Sage and the Atheist*, 125, 152.
141. Voltaire, *The Sage and the Atheist*, 127.
142. Voltaire, *The Sage and the Atheist*, 130, 131.
143. Voltaire, *The Sage and the Atheist*, 114, 116, 117.
144. Voltaire, *The Sage and the Atheist*, 132, 141, 143, 140.
145. Voltaire, *The Sage and the Atheist*, 140, 143, 144, 145, 147, 148.
146. See, for example, the discussion on "Candide: The Epicurean as Stoic," in Gay, *The Enlightenment*, 197ff.
147. Gay, *The Enlightenment*, 8, 51.
148. Theodore Besterman, *Voltaire* (London: Longman, 1969), 232.
149. Becker, *Heavenly City*, 43.
150. Gay, *The Enlightenment*, 190.
151. "A Biographical Critique of Voltaire" *WV*, 21:248–49.
152. William J. Baker, *Sports in the Western World* (Totowa, NJ: Rowman and Littlefield, 1988), 36.
153. Ludwig Feuerbach, *The Essence of Christianity*, trans. George Eliot, 2nd ed. (London: John Chapman, 1854), 150.
154. Hannah Arendt, *The Human Condition*, 2nd ed. (Chicago, IL: University of Chicago Press, 2013), 238.
155. Voltaire, *Toleration and Other Essays*, 262.
156. Clifton Cherpack, "Voltaire's 'Histoire de Jenni': A Synthetic Creed," *Modern Philology* 54, no. 1 (August 1, 1956): 32.
157. Voltaire, *Toleration and Other Essays*, 182, 179.
158. Voltaire, *Toleration and Other Essays*, 96.
159. Voltaire, *Dialogues Philosophiques* (Paris, 1929), 232, 233, http://fr.wikisource.org/wiki/Dialogues_philosophiques.
160. Pomeau, *La Religion de Voltaire*, 378.
161. Voltaire, *Oeuvres Complètes de Voltaire*, ed. Louis Moland, vol. 28 (Paris: Garnier, 1877), 208.

162. Voltaire, *Oeuvres complètes de Voltaire*, ed. Louis Moland, vol. 27 (Paris: Garnier, 1879), 123.
163. Voltaire, *Oeuvres complètes*, 27:230.
164. Voltaire, *Voltaire in His Letters*, 196.
165. Voltaire, *Oeuvres complètes de Voltaire: Mélanges, 1879–1880*, ed. Louis Moland (Paris: Garnier, 1879), 68–69.
166. Voltaire, *Treatise on Tolerance*, 94.
167. Voltaire, *Treatise on Tolerance*, 66, 67.
168. Voltaire, *Toleration and Other Essays*, 124.
169. Voltaire, *Treatise on Tolerance*, 67.
170. Jacques Derrida, *Acts of Religion* (London: Routledge, 2013), 59–60.
171. I quote from the more modern translation found in Micheline Ishay, *The Human Rights Reader: Major Political Essays, Speeches, and Documents from Ancient Times to the Present* (Abingdon: Taylor & Francis, 2007), 99–100.
172. Ishay, *Human Rights Reader*, 101–2.
173. Pomeau, *La Religion de Voltaire*, 395.
174. Voltaire, *Voltaire in His Letters*, 198.
175. Voltaire, *Toleration and Other Essays*, 233–34.
176. Davidson, *Voltaire*, 320.
177. *WV*, 21:233.
178. Voltaire, *Treatise on Tolerance*, 3.
179. Davidson, *Voltaire*, 350.
180. Pearson, *Voltaire Almighty*, 152.
181. Davidson, *Voltaire*, 405.
182. Davidson, *Voltaire*, 410.
183. Davidson, *Voltaire*, 402.
184. Davidson, *Voltaire*, 340.
185. Chadwick, *Secularization*, 160.
186. Chadwick, *Secularization*, 159.
187. Pagani, "Forgiveness and the Age of Reason," 314.

CHAPTER 5

1. George M. Marsden, *Fundamentalism and American Culture*, 2nd ed. (New York: Oxford University Press, 2006), 4.
2. Sigmund Freud, *A General Introduction to Psychoanalysis*, trans. G. Stanley Hall (New York: Horace Liveright, 1920), 247.
3. Stanley Kramer, *Inherit the Wind* (MGM, 1960), http://www.amazon.com/Inherit-Wind-Spencer-Tracy/dp/B000IZXRRA/. Quotation at 1 hour, 10 minutes and 40 seconds.
4. L. De Camp Sprague, *The Great Monkey Trial* (New York: Doubleday, 1968), 6–7.

5. Howard R. Murphy, "The Ethical Revolt against Christian Orthodoxy in Early Victorian England," *American Historical Review* 60, no. 4 (July 1955): 800–817; Susan Budd, "The Loss of Faith: Reasons for Unbelief among Members of the Secular Movement in England, 1850–1950," *Past & Present*, no. 36 (April 1967): 106–25; Edward Royle, *Victorian Infidels: The Origins of the British Secularist Movement, 1791–1866* (Manchester: Manchester University Press, 1974); Josef L. Altholz, "The Warfare of Conscience with Theology," in *Religion in Victorian Britain*, vol. 4: *Interpretations*, ed. Gerald Parsons (Manchester: Manchester University Press, 1988), 150–69; Michael Bartholomew, "The Moral Critique of Christian Orthodoxy," in *Religion in Victorian Britain*, vol. 2: *Controversies*, ed. Gerald Parsons and James Richard Moore (Manchester: Manchester University Press, 1988), 166–90; Frank M. Turner, "The Victorian Crisis of Faith and the Faith That Was Lost," in *Victorian Faith in Crisis: Essays on Continuity and Change in Nineteenth-Century Religious Belief*, ed. Richard J. Helmstadter (Stanford, CA: Stanford University Press, 1990), 9–38.
6. Charles Raven quoted in Frank M. Turner, "The Victorian Conflict between Science and Religion: A Professional Dimension," *Isis* 69, no. 3 (September 1978): 356.
7. Charles Darwin, *The Autobiography of Charles Darwin, 1809–1882. With Original Omissions Restored*, ed. Nora Barlow (London: Collins, 1958), 120.
8. Frank M. Turner, *Between Science and Religion: The Reaction to Scientific Naturalism in Late Victorian England* (New Haven: Yale University Press, 1974), 25.
9. Steven D. Hales, *This Is Philosophy: An Introduction* (Malden, MA: Wiley-Blackwell, 2012), 155.
10. Frank M. Turner, "Victorian Scientific Naturalism and Thomas Carlyle," *Victorian Studies* 18, no. 3 (March 1, 1975): 325–43.
11. Norman Hampson, *The Enlightenment* (London: Penguin, 1990), 81.
12. Robert M. Young, *Darwin's Metaphor: Nature's Place in Victorian Culture* (Cambridge: Cambridge University Press, 1985), 94.
13. Charles Darwin, *The Origin of Species by Means of Natural Selection, or the Preservation of Favoured Races in the Struggle for Life* (London: John Murray, 1859), 490.
14. Letter to J. D. Hooker, July 13th, 1856. Charles Darwin, *More Letters of Charles Darwin*, ed. Francis Darwin (London: John Murray, 1903), 94.
15. Young, *Darwin's Metaphor*, 106.
16. Charles Darwin, *The Life and Letters of Charles Darwin: Including an Autobiographical Chapter*, ed. Francis Darwin, 2nd ed. (London: Murray, 1887), 287–88.
17. Nick Spencer, *Darwin and God* (London: SPCK, 2009), 110.
18. Edmund Gosse, *Father and Son: A Study of Two Temperaments*, new ed. (London: Penguin Classics, 1989), 230, 241, 248.

19. Young, *Darwin's Metaphor*, 119.
20. Jonathan Conlin, *Evolution and the Victorians: Science, Culture and Politics in Darwin's Britain* (New York: Bloomsbury, 2014), 204.
21. Conlin, *Evolution and the Victorians*, 13.
22. Gosse, *Father and Son*, 139.
23. Boyd Hilton, *A Mad, Bad and Dangerous People?: England, 1783–1846* (Oxford: Clarendon Press, 2006), 454.
24. Adrian Desmond, "Huxley, Thomas Henry (1825–1895)," in *ODNB*.
25. Desmond, "Huxley."
26. Thomas Henry Huxley, "Darwin on the Origin of Species," *Westminster Review* 17, no. 2 (April 1860): 556.
27. Thomas Henry Huxley, *Essays upon Some Controverted Questions* (New York : D. Appleton and Co., 1893), 17.
28. John Morley, *Recollections* (London: Macmillan, 1917), 90.
29. Timothy Larsen, *A People of One Book* (New York: Oxford University Press, 2011), 201.
30. Turner, "The Victorian Conflict between Science and Religion," 370.
31. Adrian Desmond, "Huxley, Thomas Henry (1825–1895)," in *ODNB*.
32. Huxley, *Essays*, 453–54.
33. Robin Gilmour, *The Victorian Period: Intellectual and Cultural Context, 1830–90* (London: Longman, 1994), 78.
34. D. W. Bebbington, "The Secularization of British Universities since the Mid-Nineteenth Century," in *Secularization of the Academy*, ed. George M. Marsden (New York: Oxford University Press, 1992), 259.
35. Larsen, *A People of One Book*, 202.
36. Desmond, "Huxley."
37. Bernard Lightman, "Interpreting Agnosticism as a Nonconformist Sect: T. H. Huxley's 'New Reformation,'" in *Science and Dissent in England, 1688–1945*, ed. Paul Wood (Aldershot: Ashgate, 2004), 197–214.
38. Turner, "Victorian Scientific Naturalism and Thomas Carlyle," 333–34.
39. Huxley, *Essays*, 320.
40. Thomas Henry Huxley, "The School Boards: What They Can Do, and What They May Do," *Contemporary Review* 16 (1871): 12–13.
41. Huxley, *Essays*, 39, 289, 321, 159, 40, 287–88.
42. Thomas Henry Huxley, *Collected Essays: Science and Hebrew Tradition* (New York: D. Appleton, 1894), 161–62.
43. Larsen, *A People of One Book*, 215.
44. Huxley, *Essays*, 283, 179, 171, 289.
45. Larsen, *A People of One Book*, 195.
46. Larsen, *A People of One Book*, 209, 196, 207.
47. Huxley, *Essays*, 72.
48. Larsen, *A People of One Book*, 199.

49. Turner, "Victorian Scientific Naturalism and Thomas Carlyle," 341.
50. Huxley quoted the Latin original: "Per Deum intelligo ens absolute infinitum, hoc est substantiam constantem infinitis attributis."
51. Huxley, *Essays*, 179.
52. John Tyndall, *Address Delivered before the British Association Assembled at Belfast, With Additions* (London: Longmans, Green and Company, 1874), 57–58.
53. Tyndall, *Belfast Address*, 55.
54. Tyndall, *Belfast Address*, 12, 15, 20, 58–59.
55. Tyndall, *Belfast Address*, 60, 62, 65.
56. Bernard Lightman, "Does the History of Science and Religion Change Depending on the Narrator? Some Atheist and Agnostic Perspectives," *Science & Christian Belief* 24, no. 2 (October 2012): 159.
57. Lightman, "History of Science," 158–59.
58. Hugh McLeod, *Secularisation in Western Europe* (Basingstoke: Palgrave Macmillan, 2000), 155.
59. Turner, *Between Science and Religion*, 10.
60. To borrow a phrase applied by Christopher Hill to some of the seventeenth-century radicals discussed in chapter 3. *The World Turned Upside down: Radical Ideas During the English Revolution* (Harmondsworth: Penguin, 1978), 183.
61. Beatrice Webb, *My Apprenticeship* (Harmondsworth: Penguin Books, 1938), 153.
62. Jose Harris, "Mill, John Stuart (1806–1873)," in *ODNB*.
63. John Stuart Mill and Mary Taylor, *The Letters of John Stuart Mill* (London: Longman, 1910), 362.
64. Young, *Darwin's Metaphor*, 126ff.
65. Max Weber, *From Max Weber: Essays in Sociology*, ed. C. Wright Mills and H. H. Gerth (New York: Oxford, 1946), 155.
66. "The Religious Heresies of the Working Classes," *Westminster Review* 21, no. 1 (January 1862): 67.
67. Royle, *Victorian Infidels*, 108.
68. Budd, "Loss of Faith," 125, 122, 112, 125, 112.
69. George Jacob Holyoake, *English Secularism: A Confession of Belief* (Chicago, IL: Open Court Publishing Company, 1896), 76.
70. Holyoake, *English Secularism*, 59.
71. George Eliot, *The Essays of George Eliot*, ed. Nathan Sheppard (New York: Funk & Wagnalls, 2009), 250.
72. John Hedley Brooke, "Darwin and Victorian Christianity," in *The Cambridge Companion to Darwin*, ed. Jonathan Hodge and Gregory Radick, 2nd ed. (Cambridge: Cambridge University Press, 2009), 209.
73. Thomas Chalmers, *The Expulsive Power of a New Affection* (London: Hatchard & Co, 1861).

74. "Evangelical Religion Contrasted With Its Rivals Ancient and Modern," *Evangelical Magazine*, January 1889, 3.
75. John Walsh, " 'Methodism' and the Origins of English-Speaking Evangelicalism," in *Evangelicalism: Comparative Studies of Popular Protestantism in North America, the British Isles and Beyond, 1700–1990*, ed. Mark A. Noll, David W. Bebbington, and George A. Rawlyk (Oxford: Oxford University Press, 1994), 30, 27.
76. George Eliot, *Scenes of Clerical Life* (Chicago, IL: Belford, Clarke, 1887), 522.
77. Dominic Erdozain, *The Problem of Pleasure: Sport, Recreation and the Crisis of Victorian Religion* (Woodbridge: Boydell, 2010).
78. Spencer, *Darwin and God*, 63.
79. David Hempton, *Evangelical Disenchantment: Nine Portraits of Faith and Doubt*, 1st ed. (New Haven, CT: Yale University Press, 2008), 44.
80. Maurice Cowling, *Religion and Public Doctrine in Modern England*, vol. 2: *Assaults* (Cambridge: Cambridge University Press, 1985), 118–19.
81. Francis William Newman, *Phases of Faith; or, Passages from the History of My Creed*, 2nd ed. (London: Trubner and Co., 1874), 1.
82. Hempton, *Evangelical Disenchantment*, 43.
83. Newman, *Phases*, 16.
84. Newman, *Phases*, 26, 30, 34.
85. Newman, *Phases*, 34, 36, 37.
86. Newman, *Phases*, 38, 42.
87. Newman, *Phases*, 62, 43, 44.
88. Newman, *Phases*, 44, 48.
89. Newman, *Phases*, 48, 60.
90. Newman, *Phases*, 60, 62, 67, 68, 138, 56–57.
91. Hempton, *Evangelical Disenchantment*, 64.
92. Hempton, *Evangelical Disenchantment*, 59–61, 65.
93. James Anthony Froude, *The Nemesis of Faith* (London: Chapman, 1849), 17, 19.
94. A. F. Pollard, "Froude, James Anthony (1818–1894)," in *ODNB*.
95. Edward Royle, "Holyoake, George Jacob (1817–1906)," in *ODNB*.
96. George Jacob Holyoake, *The Trial of Theism* (London: Holyoake & Co., 1858), 115.
97. James R. Moore, *Religion in Victorian Britain*, vol. 3: *Sources* (Manchester: Manchester University Press, 1988), 351.
98. Joseph McCabe, *Life and Letters of George Jacob Holyoake* (London: Watts, 1908), 9.
99. Holyoake, *The Trial of Theism*, 115, 112–13.
100. Brooke, "Darwin and Victorian Christianity," 211.
101. Darwin, *More Letters of Charles Darwin*, 39.
102. Turner, *Between Science and Religion*, 100.
103. Turner, *Between Science and Religion*, 89.
104. Charles H. Smith, "Wallace, Alfred Russel (1823–1913)," in *ODNB*.

105. Alfred Russel Wallace, *My Life: A Record of Events and Opinions* (London: Chapman & Hall, 1905), 88–89.
106. Charles H. Smith and George Beccaloni, *Natural Selection and Beyond: The Intellectual Legacy of Alfred Russel Wallace: The Intellectual Legacy of Alfred Russel Wallace* (Oxford: Oxford University Press, 2008), 343.
107. Darwin, *The Autobiography of Charles Darwin, 1809–1882. With Original Omissions Restored*, 86–87.
108. Darwin, *The Life and Letters of Charles Darwin*, 311–12.
109. James R. Moore, "The Crisis of Faith: Reformation versus Revolution," in *Religion in Victorian Britain*, vol. 2: *Controversies*, ed. Gerald Parsons and James R. Moore (Manchester: Manchester University Press, 1988), 224.
110. Altholz, "The Warfare of Conscience with Theology," 157.
111. Altholz, "The Warfare of Conscience with Theology," 157.
112. Bartholomew, "The Moral Critique of Christian Orthodoxy," 168.
113. Altholz, "The Warfare of Conscience with Theology," 157.
114. "The Religious Education of Children," *Westminster Review* 48, no. 2 (October 1875): 382, 385.
115. "The Religious Education of Children," 383.
116. See the forthcoming dissertation on MacDonald by John de Jong, doctoral candidate at King's College London.
117. Webb, *My Apprenticeship*, 124.
118. "The Religious Heresies of the Working Classes," 73.
119. "The Folly of Abuse," *Birmingham Pulpit*, July 22, 1871, 3.
120. A. L. Moore, *Lectures and Papers on the History of the Reformation in England and on the Continent* (London: Keegan Paul, 1890), 515–16.
121. "Men of the Day No. 16," *Vanity Fair*, December 10, 1870, 236.
122. "The Approachableness of Jesus," A Sermon Delivered on Sunday Evening, May 3rd, 1868, http://www.spurgeon.org/lk15_1.htm.
123. Friedrich Nietzsche, *The Portable Nietzsche* (New York: Viking Press, 1968), 515.
124. Murphy, "Ethical Revolt," 813.
125. Murphy, "Ethical Revolt," 814.
126. Turner, "The Victorian Crisis of Faith and the Faith That Was Lost," 28.
127. George Eliot, *Middlemarch* (London: Penguin, 1994), 16.
128. George Eliot, "Evangelical Teaching: Dr. Cumming," *Westminster Review* 64, no. 126 (October 1855): 444.
129. Eliot, "Evangelical Teaching," 447, 453.
130. Eliot, "Evangelical Teaching," 455, 462, 461, 454, 455.
131. Eliot, *Middlemarch*, 172, 151, 591, 500, 589.
132. Eliot, *Middlemarch*, 654, 592, 591.
133. Eliot, *Middlemarch*, 156.
134. Gosse, *Father and Son*, 167, 138, 248.
135. Eliot, *Middlemarch*, 271, 265–66.

136. Eliot, *Middlemarch*, 213, 214, 724.
137. Hempton, *Evangelical Disenchantment*, 21.
138. Hempton, *Evangelical Disenchantment*, 21.
139. Hempton, *Evangelical Disenchantment*, 23.
140. Eliot, "Evangelical Teaching," 439, 455.
141. Timothy Larsen, *Crisis of Doubt: Honest Faith in Nineteenth-Century England* (Oxford: Oxford University Press, 2006).
142. Timothy Larsen, "The Regaining of Faith: Reconversions among Popular Radicals in Mid-Victorian England," *Church History* 70, no. 3 (September 2001): 542.
143. "The Religious Heresies of the Working Classes," 89–90.
144. Turner, *Between Science and Religion*, 143–44; for more on Romanes and "his religious journey," see J. David Pleins, *In Praise of Darwin: George Romanes and the Evolution of a Darwinian Believer* (New York: Bloomsbury, 2014).
145. George John Romanes, *Thoughts on Religion* (Chicago, IL: Open Court, 1898), 145.
146. Turner, *Between Science and Religion*, 180.
147. Friedrich Nietzsche, *The Gay Science: With a Prelude in German Rhymes and an Appendix of Songs*, ed. Bernard Williams and Josefine Nauckhoff (Cambridge: Cambridge University Press, 2001), 123.
148. Nietzsche, *The Portable Nietzsche*, 515.
149. Friedrich Nietzsche, *The Nietzsche Reader*, ed. Keith Ansell-Pearson and Duncan Large (Oxford: Blackwell, 2006), 372.

CHAPTER 6

1. "Church Depicts Marx and Tito in Hell," *BBC*, January 31, 2014, http://www.bbc.co.uk/news/world-europe-25993584.
2. Michael Bourdeaux, *Opium of the People: The Christian Religion in the U.S.S.R.* (London: Faber and Faber, 1965), 62.
3. Denis Janz, *World Christianity and Marxism* (New York: Oxford University Press, 1998), 3–4.
4. Jonathan Sperber, *Karl Marx: A Nineteenth-Century Life* (New York: Liveright, 2013), 437.
5. Bronterre O'Brien, quoted in Eric J. Evans, *The Forging of the Modern State: Early Industrial Britain, 1783–1870* (London: Routledge, 2014), 273.
6. Karl Marx, *Karl Marx: Selected Writings* (Oxford: Oxford University Press, 2000), 329.
7. Marx, *Selected Writings*, 61.
8. Wilhelm Weitling, *The Poor Sinner's Gospel*, trans. Dinah Livingstone (London: Sheed & Ward, 1969), 121–22, 115, 196.

9. James A. Massey, introduction in Ludwig Feuerbach, *Thoughts on Death and Immortality: From the Papers of a Thinker, along with an Appendix of Theological-Satirical Epigrams* (Berkeley: University of California Press, 1980), xviii–xix.
10. Christy Flanagan, "The Paradox of Feuerbach: Luther and Religious Naturalism," Ph.D. diss., Florida State, 2009, 178, http://diginole.lib.fsu.edu/etd/4443.
11. Van Austin Harvey, *Feuerbach and the Interpretation of Religion* (New York: Cambridge University Press, 1995), 151.
12. Henri de Lubac, *The Drama of Atheist Humanism* (San Francisco, CA: Ignatius Press, 1995), 30.
13. Ludwig Feuerbach, *The Essence of Christianity*, trans. George Eliot, 2nd ed. (London: John Chapman, 1854), 274.
14. Flanagan, "The Paradox of Feuerbach," 21, 23, 3.
15. Marx W. Wartofsky, *Feuerbach* (Cambridge: Cambridge University Press, 1977), 113.
16. Feuerbach, *Thoughts*, 235, 197, 201.
17. Feuerbach, *Essence*, 276, xiv.
18. Feuerbach, *Essence*, 275, 21, 298, 203, 298.
19. Feuerbach, *Essence*, 167, 218, 224, 26–27, 29.
20. Ludwig Feuerbach, *The Essence of Faith According to Luther* (New York: Harper & Row, 1967), 18, 47, 50.
21. Feuerbach, *Essence*, 56, 57, 294, 297.
22. Feuerbach, *Essence*, 294, 295.
23. Feuerbach, *Essence*, 303, 151.
24. Feuerbach, *Essence*, 104.
25. Feuerbach, *Essence*, 126, 144.
26. Feuerbach, *Luther*, 107.
27. Feuerbach, *Essence*, viii, 106–7.
28. Harvey, *Feuerbach and the Interpretation of Religion*, 213–14.
29. Feuerbach, *Essence*, 161, 169, 313, 138.
30. Feuerbach, *Essence*, 287, 288, 328, 329.
31. Feuerbach, *Essence*, 329.
32. Feuerbach, *Essence*, 330, 162–63.
33. Feuerbach, *Essence*, 163, 330, 163.
34. Feuerbach, *Essence*, 198, 200.
35. Feuerbach, *Essence*, 51–52.
36. Feuerbach, *Essence*, 327, 262, 261.
37. Feuerbach, *Luther*, 100.
38. Feuerbach, *Essence*, 327, 255–56.
39. Feuerbach, *Essence*, 142, 262, 325, 247–48.
40. Feuerbach, *Essence*, 248, 320.

41. Feuerbach, *Essence,* 251, 253, 255, 292.
42. Feuerbach, *Essence,* 251, 263.
43. Feuerbach, *Essence,* 287, 246, 258–59, 244, 207, 260.
44. Feuerbach, *Essence,* 308, 306, 321, 322, 324–25.
45. Feuerbach, *Essence,* 325.
46. Owen Chadwick, *The Secularization of the European Mind in the Nineteenth Century* (Cambridge: Cambridge University Press, 1977), 54.
47. Feuerbach, *Essence,* ix, 267, xi.
48. Feuerbach, *Essence,* 52.
49. Feuerbach, *Essence,* 329, 150, 53–54, 196.
50. Feuerbach, *Essence,* 261, 245.
51. Feuerbach, *Essence,* 257–58, 264.
52. Feuerbach, *Essence,* 266.
53. Harvey, *Feuerbach and the Interpretation of Religion,* 226.
54. Feuerbach, *Essence,* 338.
55. Steven E. Ozment, *Homo Spiritualis: A Comparative Study of the Anthropology of Johannes Tauler, Jean Gerson and Martin Luther (1509–16) in the Context of Their Theological Thought* (Leiden: Brill, 1969), 208.
56. Harvey, *Feuerbach and the Interpretation of Religion,* 175.
57. Feuerbach, *Essence,* 340.
58. Friedrich Engels, *Ludwig Feuerbach & the Outcome of Classical German Philosophy* (New York: International Publishers, 1941), 33.
59. Karl Marx and Friedrich Engels, *Karl Marx and Frederick Engels: Selected Works in One Volume* (New York: International Publishers, 1968), 603.
60. Lubac, *The Drama of Atheist Humanism,* 35.
61. Karl Marx, *On Religion* (New York: McGraw-Hill, 1974), 33.
62. Marx, *On Religion,* 236, 237.
63. Marx, *Selected Writings,* 172.
64. Sergei Nikolaevich Bulgakov, *Karl Marx as a Religious Type: His Relation to the Religion of Anthropotheism of L. Feuerbach,* ed. Virgil R. Lang, trans. Luba Barna (Belmont, MA: Norland, 1980), 19.
65. Marx, *Selected Writings,* 72; Karl Marx and Friedrich Engels, *Collected Works* (London: Lawrence and Wishart, 1975), 3:150.
66. McLellan, *The Young Hegelians and Karl Marx,* 146.
67. Marx and Engels, *Collected Works,* 1:121.
68. Marx and Engels, *Collected Works,* 1:117–18.
69. Marx, *Selected Writings,* 22.
70. Marx and Engels, *Collected Works,* 1:191, 198, 199.
71. Marx and Engels, *Collected Works,* 1975, 3:158.
72. Karl Marx and Friedrich Engels, *Collected Works* (London: Lawrence and Wishart, 1976), 6:230, 231.
73. Erich Fromm, *Marx's Concept of Man* (New York: Ungar, 1961), 95–96.

74. Marx and Engels, *Collected Works*, 1975, 3:155, 160.
75. Sperber, *Marx*, 116.
76. Gareth Stedman Jones, "The Young Hegelians, Marx and Engels," in *The Cambridge History of Nineteenth-Century Political Thought*, ed. Gareth Stedman Jones and Gregory Claeys (Cambridge: Cambridge University Press, 2011), 590.
77. Marx, *Selected Writings*, 122.
78. Marx, *Selected Writings*, 71, 72.
79. Marx, *On Religion*, 156–57.
80. Marx, *Selected Writings*, 71–72.
81. Marx, *Selected Writings*, 72.
82. Marx, *Selected Writings*, 176.
83. Marx, *Selected Writings*, 173.
84. Denys Turner, "Religion," in *The Cambridge Companion to Marx*, ed. Terrell Carver and Terrell Carver (Cambridge: Cambridge University Press, 1991), 336.
85. Gareth Stedman Jones, "Introduction," in *The Communist Manifesto* (London: Penguin, 2002), 140–41.
86. Stedman Jones, "Introduction," 114.
87. McLellan, *The Young Hegelians and Karl Marx*, 155.
88. Moses Hess, "The Essence of Money," trans. Adam Buick, *Rheinische Jarhrbücher Zur Gesellschaftlichen Reform*, 1845, https://www.marxists.org/archive/hess/1845/essence-money.htm.
89. Moses Hess, *The Holy History of Mankind and Other Writings*, ed. Shlomo Avineri (Cambridge: Cambridge University Press, 2004), 5, 21, 40, 45, 49, 126.
90. First published in 1927 and also known as the "Paris manuscripts."
91. Marx, *Selected Writings*, 88–89.
92. Stedman Jones, "Introduction," 136.
93. Karl Marx and Friedrich Engels, *The Communist Manifesto*, ed. Gareth Stedman Jones (London: Penguin, 2002), 231.
94. Lubac, *The Drama of Atheist Humanism*, 41.
95. McLellan, *The Young Hegelians and Karl Marx*, 158.
96. Marx, *Selected Writings*, 118–19.
97. Marx and Engels, *Collected Works*, 1975, 3:439, 422, 423.
98. Marx and Engels, *Collected Works*, 1975, 3:437.
99. Wendy Brown, "The Sacred, the Secular, and the Profane: Charles Taylor and Karl Marx," in *Varieties of Secularism in a Secular Age*, ed. Michael Warner, Jonathan VanAntwerpen, and Craig J. Calhoun (Cambridge, MA: Harvard University Press, 2010), 83–104.
100. Marx and Engels, *Communist Manifesto*, 225, 258, 222, 223, 224, emphasis added.
101. Marx and Engels, *Communist Manifesto*, 232, 239, 239–40.
102. Stedman Jones, "Introduction," 94, 95.
103. Marx, *Selected Writings*, 77.

104. Marx, *Selected Writings*, 615.
105. Acts 2:44–45. I am grateful to the novelist Marilynne Robinson for sharing this insight and reference during a conversation at Emory University, March 19, 2015.
106. Marx, *Selected Writings*, 329.
107. Sperber, *Marx*, 394.
108. William Clare Roberts, "Marx in Hell: The Critique of Political Economy as Katabasis," *Critical Sociology* 31, nos. 1–2 (January 1, 2005): 39–55.
109. Marx, *Selected Writings*, 455.
110. Marx, *On Religion*, xxvii.
111. Quoted in Paul Hazard, *The European Mind, 1680–1715* (London: Hollis & Carter, 1953), 139.

CONCLUSION

1. Jonathan I. Israel, "Religious Toleration and Radical Philosophy in the Later Dutch Golden Age (1668–1710)," in *Calvinism and Religious Toleration in the Dutch Golden Age*, ed. R. Po-Chia Hsia and Henk Van Nierop (Cambridge: Cambridge University Press, 2002), 151.
2. John Morley, "A Biographical Critique of Voltaire," in *WV*, 21:203.
3. William T. Cavanaugh, "The 'Wars of Religion' and Other Fairy Tales," *ABC Religion and Ethics*, February 3, 2012, http://www.abc.net.au/religion/articles/2012/02/03/3422519.htm; William T. Cavanaugh, *The Myth of Religious Violence: Secular Ideology and the Roots of Modern Conflict* (New York: Oxford University Press, 2009).
4. Eamon Duffy, *Fires of Faith: Catholic England under Mary Tudor* (New Haven, CT: Yale University Press, 2009), 7, 79.
5. Immanuel Kant, *Religion within the Boundaries of Mere Reason and Other Writings*, ed. Allen W. Wood and George Di Giovanni (Cambridge: Cambridge University Press, 1998), 157.
6. Andrew C. Fix, *Prophecy and Reason: The Dutch Collegiants in the Early Enlightenment* (Princeton, NJ: Princeton University Press, 1991), 198.
7. Joseph McCabe, "Introduction," in Voltaire, *Toleration and Other Essays*, trans. Joseph McCabe (New York: G. P. Putnam, 1912), iv.
8. Wilfred Owen, *Collected Letters* (Oxford: Oxford University Press, 1967), 461.
9. Jean Delumeau, *Sin and Fear: The Emergence of a Western Guilt Culture, 13th–18th Centuries* (New York: St. Martin's Press, 1990), 557.
10. Feuerbach, *Essence*, 325.
11. Berndt Hamm, *The Early Luther: Stages in a Reformation Reorientation* (Grand Rapids, MI: Eerdmans, 2014), 32.
12. George Eliot, "Evangelical Teaching: Dr. Cumming," *Westminster Review* 64, no. 126 (October 1855): 461.

13. *TTP*, 173.
14. Feuerbach, *Essence*, 306.
15. Karl Barth, "Introduction," in Ludwig Feuerbach, *The Essence of Christianity*, trans. George Eliot (New York: Harper, 1957), x.
16. Keith Thomas, *The Ends of Life: Roads to Fulfillment in Early Modern England* (New York: Oxford University Press, 2009), 233.
17. *The Elizabethan Puritan Movement* (Oxford: Oxford University Press, 1990), 37.
18. Benjamin J. Kaplan, *Divided by Faith: Religious Conflict and the Practice of Toleration in Early Modern Europe* (Cambridge, MA: Harvard University Press, 2007).
19. George Eliot, *Middlemarch* (London: Penguin, 1994), 795.
20. Diarmaid MacCulloch, *Reformation: Europe's House Divided 1490–1700* (London: Penguin, 2004), 182.

References

PRIMARY SOURCES

Anon. *The Light upon the Candlestick Serving for Observation of the Principal Things in the Book Called, The Mysteries of the Kingdom of God, &c., against Several Professors*. London: Printed for Robert Wilson, 1663.

Bayle, Pierre. *A General Dictionary, Historical and Critical*. London: G. Strahan, 1734.

———. *A Philosophical Commentary on These Words of the Gospel, Luke 14.23: "Compel Them to Come In, That My House May Be Full."* Indianapolis, IN: Liberty Fund, 2005.

———. *Various Thoughts on the Occasion of a Comet*. Albany: State University of New York Press, 2000.

Calvin, John. *Institutes of the Christian Religion*. Edited by John T. McNeill. Translated by Ford L. Battles. Philadelphia, PA: Westminster Press, 1960.

Castellio, Sebastian. *Concerning Heretics; Whether They Are to Be Persecuted and How They Are to Be Treated; a Collection of the Opinions of Learned Men, Both Ancient and Modern; an Anonymous Work Attributed to Sebastian Castellio, together with Excerpts from Other Works of Sebastian Castellio and David Joris on Religious Liberty*. Edited by Roland H. Bainton. Records of Civilization, Sources and Studies, no. 22. New York: Columbia University Press, 1935.

Chalmers, Thomas. *The Expulsive Power of a New Affection*. London: Hatchard & Co, 1861.

Darwin, Charles. *The Autobiography of Charles Darwin, 1809–1882. With Original Omissions Restored*. Edited by Nora Barlow. London: Collins, 1958.

———. *The Life and Letters of Charles Darwin: Including an Autobiographical Chapter*. Edited by Francis Darwin. 2nd ed. London: Murray, 1887.

———. *More Letters of Charles Darwin*. Edited by Francis Darwin. London: John Murray, 1903.

———. *The Origin of Species by Means of Natural Selection, or the Preservation of Favoured Races in the Struggle for Life*. London: John Murray, 1859.

Denck, Hans. "Concerning the Law of God." In *The Spiritual Legacy of Hans Denck: Including the German Text as Established by Georg Baring and Walter Fellman*. Edited by Clarence Bauman. Leiden: Brill, 1991.

D'Holbach, Baron. *The System of Nature*. Sioux Falls, SD: NuVision, 2007.

Donne, John. *The Collected Poems of John Donne*. Ware: Wordsworth Editions, 1994.

Eliot, George. *The Essays of George Eliot*. Edited by Nathan Sheppard. New York: Funk & Wagnalls, 2009.

———. "Evangelical Teaching: Dr. Cumming." *Westminster Review* 64, no. 126 (October 1855): 436–62.

———. *Middlemarch*. London: Penguin, 1994.

———. *Scenes of Clerical Life*. Chicago: Belford, Clarke, 1887.

Engels, Friedrich. *Ludwig Feuerbach & the Outcome of Classical German Philosophy*. New York: International Publishers, 1941.

Feuerbach, Ludwig. *The Essence of Christianity*. Translated by George Eliot. 2nd ed. London: John Chapman, 1854.

———. *The Essence of Christianity*. Translated by George Eliot. New York: Harper, 1957.

———. *The Essence of Faith According to Luther*. New York: Harper & Row, 1967.

———. *Thoughts on Death and Immortality: From the Papers of a Thinker, along with an Appendix of Theological-Satirical Epigrams*. Berkeley: University of California Press, 1980.

Fox, George. *Journal of George Fox*. London: Friends' Tract Association, 1891.

Franck, Sebastian. *280 Paradoxes or Wondrous Sayings*. New York: Edwin Mellen Press, 1986.

Freud, Sigmund. *A General Introduction to Psychoanalysis*. Translated by G. Stanley Hall. New York: Horace Liveright, 1920.

Froude, James Anthony. *The Nemesis of Faith*. London: Chapman, 1849.

Gosse, Edmund. *Father and Son: A Study of Two Temperaments*. New ed. London: Penguin Classics, 1989.

Hess, Moses. "The Essence of Money." Translated by Adam Buick. *Rheinische Jarhrbücher Zur Gesellschaftlichen Reform*, 1845. https://www.marxists.org/archive/hess/1845/essence-money.htm.

———. *The Holy History of Mankind and Other Writings*. Edited by Shlomo Avineri. Cambridge: Cambridge University Press, 2004.

Hobbes, Thomas. *Leviathan; Or, The Matter, Form and Power of a Commonwealth, Ecclesiastical and Civil*. London: Routledge, 1886.

Holyoake, George Jacob. *English Secularism: A Confession of Belief*. Chicago, IL: Open Court Publishing Company, 1896.

———. *The Trial of Theism*. London: Holyoake & Co., 1858.

Huxley, Thomas Henry. *Collected Essays: Science and Hebrew Tradition*. New York: D. Appleton, 1894.

———. “Darwin on the Origin of Species.” *Westminster Review* 17, no. 2 (April 1860): 541–70.

———. *Essays upon Some Controverted Questions*. New York : D. Appleton and Co., 1893.

———. “The School Boards: What They Can Do, and What They May Do.” *Contemporary Review* 16 (1871).

Kant, Immanuel. *Religion within the Boundaries of Mere Reason and Other Writings*. Edited by Allen W. Wood and George Di Giovanni. Cambridge: Cambridge University Press, 1998.

Kempis, Thomas à. *The Imitation of Christ*. Leipzig: Bernhard Tauchnitz, 1877.

Kierkegaard, Søren. *Kierkegaard's Writings. Vol. 6: Fear and Trembling/Repetition*. Princeton, NJ: Princeton University Press, 2013.

King, Martin Luther, Jr. ‘Letter from Birmingham Jail’ In *The Radical King*, edited by Cornel West, 127–145. Boston, MA: Beacon Press, 2015.

Locke, John. *An Essay Concerning Human Understanding*. London, 1760.

Luther, Martin. “Against the Robbing and Murdering Hordes of Peasants.” In *Martin Luther, Documents of Modern History*. Edited by E. G. Rupp and Benjamin Drewery. London: Edward Arnold, 1970.

———. *Commentary on the Epistle to the Galatians*. Translated by Theodore Graebner. Grand Rapids, MI: Zondervan, 1949. http://www.gutenberg.org/files/1549/1549-h/1549-h.htm.

———. *Commentary on the Sermon on the Mount*. Translated by Charles A. Hay. Philadelphia: Lutheran Publication Society, 1892.

———. “Martin Luther's 95 Theses.” http://www.gutenberg.org/cache/epub/274/pg274.html.

———. *Martin Luther: Selections from His Writing*. New York: Knopf, 2011.

———. *Selected Political Writings*. Philadelphia: Fortress Press, 1974.

Marx, Karl. *Karl Marx: Selected Writings*. Oxford: Oxford University Press, 2000.

———. *On Religion*. New York: McGraw-Hill, 1974.

Marx, Karl, and Friedrich Engels. *Collected Works*. vols. 1–6. London: Lawrence and Wishart, 1975–1976.

———. *The Communist Manifesto*. Edited by Gareth Stedman Jones. London: Penguin, 2002.

———. *Karl Marx and Frederick Engels: Selected Works in One Volume*. New York: International Publishers, 1968.

McCabe, Joseph. *Life and Letters of George Jacob Holyoake*. London: Watts, 1908.

Mill, John Stuart, and Mary Taylor. *The Letters of John Stuart Mill*. London: Longman, 1910.

Moore, A. L. *Lectures and Papers on the History of the Reformation in England and on the Continent*. London: Keegan Paul, 1890.

Newman, Francis William. *Phases of Faith; Or, Passages from the History of My Creed*. 2nd ed. London: Trubner and Co., 1874.

Nietzsche, Friedrich. *The Gay Science: With a Prelude in German Rhymes and an Appendix of Songs*. Edited by Bernard Williams and Josefine Nauckhoff. Cambridge: Cambridge University Press, 2001.

———. *The Nietzsche Reader*. Edited by Keith Ansell-Pearson and Duncan Large. Oxford: Blackwell, 2006.

———. *The Portable Nietzsche*. New York: Viking Press, 1968.

Owen, Wilfred. *Collected Letters*. Oxford: Oxford University Press, 1967.

Romanes, George John. *Thoughts on Religion*. Chicago, IL: Open Court, 1898.

Schaeffer, Francis A. *How Should We Then Live? The Rise and Decline of Western Thought and Culture*. Old Tappan, NJ: F. H. Revell, 1976.

Schaeffer, Frank. *Crazy for God: How I Grew Up as One of the Elect, Helped Found the Religious Right, and Lived to Take All (or Almost All) of It Back*. Boston: Da Capo Press, 2008.

Spinoza, Benedict de. *The Chief Works of Benedict de Spinoza: On the Improvement of the Understanding, the Ethics Correspondence*. New York: Dover, 1955.

———. *The Collected Works of Spinoza*. Edited by E. M. Curley. Princeton, NJ: Princeton University Press, 1984.

———. *The Principles of Descartes' Philosophy*. Chicago: Open court, 1905.

———. *Theological-Political Treatise*. Edited by Jonathan I. Israel. Translated by Michael Silverthorne and Jonathan I. Israel. Cambridge: Cambridge University Press, 2007.

Tauler, Johannes. *Johannes Tauler, Sermons*. Mahwah, NJ: Paulist Press, 1985.

Toland, John. *Christianity Not Mysterious: Or, A Treatise Shewing, That There Is Nothing in the Gospel Contrary to Reason, nor above It. To Which Is Added, An Apology for Mr. Toland*. London, 1702.

Tyndall, John. *Address Delivered Before the British Association Assembled at Belfast, With Additions*. London: Longmans, Green and Company, 1874.

Voltaire. *Candide*. New York: Dover Publications, 1991.

———. *Dialogues Philosophiques*. Paris: À l'enseigne du pot cassé, 1929. http://fr.wikisource.org/wiki/Dialogues_philosophiques.

———. *The Henriad*. Translated by Charles L. S. Jones. Mobile, AL: S. Smith, 1834.

———. *The Ignorant Philosopher*. London: S. Bladon, 1767.

———. *Letters on England*. London: Penguin, 1980.

———. *Oeuvres Complètes de Voltaire*. Edited by Louis Moland. Vol. 28. Paris: Garnier, 1877.

———. *Oeuvres complètes de Voltaire*. Edited by Louis Moland. Vol. 27. Paris: Garnier, 1879.

———. *Oeuvres complètes de Voltaire: Mélanges, 1879–1880*. Edited by Louis Moland. Paris: Garnier, 1879.

———. *Oeuvres de Voltaire*. Edited by Adrien Jean Quentin Beuchot. Paris: Lefèvre, 1832.

———. *The Sage and the Atheist: Including the Adventures of a Young Englishman.* New York: P. Eckler, 1921.

———. *Selections from Voltaire: With Explanatory Comment upon his Life and Works.* Edited by George R. Havens. New York: Appleton-Century-Crofts, 1969.

———. *Toleration and Other Essays.* Translated by Joseph McCabe. New York: G. P. Putnam, 1912.

———. *Treatise on Tolerance.* Edited by Simon Harvey. Cambridge: Cambridge University Press, 2000.

———. *Voltaire in His Letters: Being a Selection from His Correspondence.* Translated by S. G. Tallentyre. New York: G. P. Putnam, 1919.

———. *The Works of Voltaire: A Contemporary Version.* A Critique and Biography by John Morley, notes by Tobias Smollett, translated by William F. Fleming. 21 vols. New York: E. R. DuMont, 1901.

———. *The Works of Voltaire: Romances.* Translated by William F. Fleming. New York: E. R. Du Mont, 1901.

———. *Zadig; Or, the Book of Fate. An Oriental History, Translated from the French Original of Mr. Voltaire.* London: J. Brindley, 1749.

Wallace, Alfred Russel. *My Life: A Record of Events and Opinions.* London: Chapman & Hall, 1905.

Webb, Beatrice. *My Apprenticeship.* Harmondsworth: Penguin Books, 1938.

Weber, Max. *From Max Weber: Essays in Sociology.* Edited by C. Wright Mills and H. H. Gerth. New York: Oxford, 1946.

Weitling, Wilhelm. *The Poor Sinner's Gospel.* Translated by Dinah Livingstone. London: Sheed & Ward, 1969.

Westminster Confession of Faith. http://www.reformed.org/documents/wcf_with_proofs/index.html.

Winstanley, Gerrard. *The Complete Works of Gerrard Winstanley.* Edited by Thomas N. Corns, Ann Hughes, and David Loewenstein. New York: Oxford University Press, 2009.

SECONDARY SOURCES

Altholz, Josef L. "The Warfare of Conscience with Theology." In *Religion in Victorian Britain, vol. 4: Interpretations,* edited by Gerald Parsons, 150–69. Manchester: Manchester University Press, 1988.

Arendt, Hannah. *The Human Condition.* 2nd ed. Chicago, IL: University of Chicago Press, 2013.

Atwood, Craig D. *Community of the Cross: Moravian Piety in Colonial Bethlehem.* University Park, PA: Penn State University Press, 2004.

Bainton, Roland H. "The Development and Consistency of Luther's Attitude to Religious Liberty." *Harvard Theological Review* 22, no. 2 (April 1, 1929): 107–49.

Bainton, Roland H.. *Hunted Heretic: The Life and Death of Michael Servetus, 1511–1553*. Providence, RI: Blackstone Editions, 2005.

———. *Sebastian Castellio, Champion of Religious Liberty, 1515–1563*. Leiden: Brill, 1951.

———. *The Travail of Religious Liberty: Nine Biographical Studies*. Philadelphia, PA: Westminster Press, 1951.

Baker, William J. *Sports in the Western World*. Totowa, NJ: Rowman and Littlefield, 1988.

Balmer, Randall H. *Encyclopedia of Evangelicalism*. Louisville, KY: Westminster John Knox Press, 2002.

Barnett, S. J. *The Enlightenment and Religion: The Myths of Modernity*. Manchester: Manchester University Press, 2003.

Bartholomew, Michael. "The Moral Critique of Christian Orthodoxy." In *Religion in Victorian Britain, vol. 2: Controversies*, edited by Gerald Parsons and James Richard Moore, 166–90. Manchester: Manchester University Press, 1988.

Barton, Ruth. "John Tyndall, Pantheist: A Rereading of the Belfast Address." *Osiris* 3 (January 1, 1987): 111–34.

Baylor, Michael G. *Action and Person: Conscience in Late Scholasticism and the Young Luther*. Leiden: Brill, 1977.

Bebbington, D. W. *Evangelicalism in Modern Britain: A History from the 1730s to the 1980s*. London: Unwin Hyman, 1989.

———. "The Secularization of British Universities since the Mid-Nineteenth Century." In *Secularization of the Academy*, edited by George M. Marsden, 259–77. New York: Oxford University Press, 1992.

Becker, Carl L. *The Heavenly City of the Eighteenth-Century Philosophers*. 2nd ed. London: Yale University Press, 2003.

Beeson, David, and Nicholas Cronk. "Voltaire: Philosopher or Philosophe?" In *The Cambridge Companion to Voltaire*, edited by Nicholas Cronk, 47–64. Cambridge: Cambridge University Press, 2009.

Benowitz, June M. *Encyclopedia of American Women and Religion*. Santa Barbara, CA: ABC-CLIO, 1998.

Besterman, Theodore. *Voltaire*. London: Longman, 1969.

Boersma, Hans. *Heavenly Participation: The Weaving of a Sacramental Tapestry*. Grand Rapids, MI: Eerdmans, 2011.

Bonger, H., and Gerrit Voogt. *The Life and Work of Dirck Volkertszoon Coornhert*. Amsterdam: Rodopi, 2004.

Bourdeaux, Michael. *Opium of the People: The Christian Religion in the U.S.S.R.* London: Faber and Faber, 1965.

Brenning, Robert W. "The Ethical Hermeneutic of Sebastian Franck, 1499–1542." Ph.D. diss., Temple University Microfilms, 1978.

Brooke, John Hedley. "Darwin and Victorian Christianity." In *The Cambridge Companion to Darwin*, edited by Jonathan Hodge and Gregory Radick, 2nd ed., 197–218. Cambridge: Cambridge University Press, 2009.

Brown, Wendy. "The Sacred, the Secular, and the Profane: Charles Taylor and Karl Marx." In *Varieties of Secularism in a Secular Age*, edited by Michael Warner, Jonathan VanAntwerpen, and Craig J. Calhoun, 83–104. Cambridge, MA: Harvard University Press, 2010.

Buckley, James, Frederick Christian Bauerschmidt, and Trent Pomplun. *The Blackwell Companion to Catholicism*. Oxford: Blackwell, 2010.

Buckley, Michael J. *At the Origins of Modern Atheism*. New Haven, CT: Yale University Press, 1987.

Budd, Susan. "The Loss of Faith. Reasons for Unbelief among Members of the Secular Movement in England, 1850–1950." *Past & Present*, no. 36 (April 1967): 106–25.

Bulgakov, Sergei Nikolaevich. *Karl Marx as a Religious Type: His Relation to the Religion of Anthropotheism of L. Feuerbach*. Edited by Virgil R. Lang. Translated by Luba Barna. Belmont, MA: Norland, 1980.

Butler, Jon. "Disquieted History in a Secular Age." In *Varieties of Secularism in a Secular Age*, edited by Michael Warner, Jonathan VanAntwerpen, and Craig J. Calhoun, 193–216. Cambridge, MA: Harvard University Press, 2010.

Carlisle, Clare. "Spinoza On Eternal Life." *American Catholic Philosophical Quarterly* 89, no. 1 (2015): 69–96.

Cavanaugh, William T. *The Myth of Religious Violence: Secular Ideology and the Roots of Modern Conflict*. New York: Oxford University Press, 2009.

Chadwick, Owen. *The Reformation*. New York: Penguin Books, 1990.

———. *The Secularization of the European Mind in the Nineteenth Century*. Cambridge: Cambridge University Press, 1977.

Cherpack, Clifton. "Voltaire's 'Histoire de Jenni': A Synthetic Creed." *Modern Philology* 54, no. 1 (August 1, 1956): 26–32.

Coffey, John. *John Goodwin and the Puritan Revolution: Religion and Intellectual Change in Seventeenth-Century England*. Woodbridge: Boydell, 2008.

Collinson, Patrick. *The Elizabethan Puritan Movement*. Oxford: Oxford University Press, 1990.

———. *The Reformation: A History*. London: Random House, 2006.

Conlin, Jonathan. *Evolution and the Victorians: Science, Culture and Politics in Darwin's Britain*. New York: Bloomsbury, 2014.

Cowling, Maurice. *Religion and Public Doctrine in Modern England. Vol. 2: Assaults*. Cambridge: Cambridge University Press, 1985.

Davidson, Ian. *Voltaire: A Life*. London: Profile Books, 2010.

Delumeau, Jean. *Sin and Fear: The Emergence of a Western Guilt Culture, 13th–18th Centuries*. New York: St. Martin's Press, 1990.

———. *Sin and Fear: The Emergence of a Western Guilt Culture, 13th–18th Centuries*. New York: St. Martin's Press, 1990.

Derrida, Jacques. *Acts of Religion*. London: Routledge, 2013.

Desmond, Adrian. "Huxley, Thomas Henry (1825–1895)." In *ODNB*.

Duffy, Eamon. *Fires of Faith: Catholic England under Mary Tudor*. New Haven, CT: Yale University Press, 2009.

Emerson, Michael O., and Christian Smith. *Divided by Faith: Evangelical Religion and the Problem of Race in America.* New York: Oxford University Press, 2000.

Erdozain, Dominic. "'Cause Is Not Quite What It Used to Be': The Return of Secularisation." *The English Historical Review* CXXVII, no. 525 (March 1, 2012): 377–400.

———. *The Problem of Pleasure: Sport, Recreation and the Crisis of Victorian Religion.* Woodbridge: Boydell, 2010.

Evans, Eric J. *The Forging of the Modern State: Early Industrial Britain, 1783–1870.* London: Routledge, 2014.

Fix, Andrew. "Angels, Devils, and Evil Spirits in Seventeenth-Century Thought: Balthasar Bekker and the Collegiants." *Journal of the History of Ideas* 50, no. 4 (October 1, 1989): 527–47.

———. *Prophecy and Reason: The Dutch Collegiants in the Early Enlightenment.* Princeton, NJ: Princeton University Press, 1991.

Flanagan, Christy. "The Paradox of Feuerbach: Luther and Religious Naturalism." Ph.D. diss., Florida State, 2009. http://diginole.lib.fsu.edu/etd/4443.

Forell, George. "Luther and Conscience." *Journal of Lutheran Ethics* 2, no. 1 (January 2002). http://www.elca.org/JLE/Articles/991?_ga=1.202045841.141729377.1427204265.

Frampton, Travis L. *Spinoza and the Rise of Historical Criticism of the Bible.* London: T & T Clark, 2006.

Fromm, Erich. *Marx's Concept of Man.* New York: Ungar, 1961.

Gargett, Graham. "Voltaire and the Bible." In *The Cambridge Companion to Voltaire,* edited by Nicholas Cronk, 193–204. Cambridge: Cambridge University Press, 2009.

Gay, Peter. *The Enlightenment: The Rise of Modern Paganism.* New York: Norton, 1995.

Gilmour, Robin. *The Victorian Period: Intellectual and Cultural Context, 1830–90.* London: Longman, 1994.

Gordon, Bruce. *Calvin.* New Haven, CT: Yale University Press, 2011.

Gregory, Brad S. *The Unintended Reformation: How a Religious Revolution Secularized Society.* Cambridge, MA: Belknap, 2012.

Guggisberg, Hans R. *Sebastian Castellio, 1515–1563: Humanist and Defender of Religious Toleration in a Confessional Age.* Translated by Bruce Gordon. Aldershot: Ashgate, 2002.

Hales, Steven D. *This Is Philosophy: An Introduction.* Malden, MA: Wiley-Blackwell, 2012.

Hamm, Berndt. *The Early Luther: Stages in a Reformation Reorientation.* Grand Rapids, MI: Eerdmans, 2014.

Hampson, Norman. *The Enlightenment.* London: Penguin, 1990.

Harris, Jose. "Mill, John Stuart (1806–1873)." In *ODNB.*

Harvey, Van Austin. *Feuerbach and the Interpretation of Religion.* New York: Cambridge University Press, 1995.

Hayden-Roy, Patrick Marshall. *The Inner Word and the Outer World: A Biography of Sebastian Franck*. New York: Peter Lang, 1994.

Hazard, Paul. *The European Mind, 1680–1715*. London: Hollis & Carter, 1953.

Hempton, David. *Evangelical Disenchantment: Nine Portraits of Faith and Doubt*. 1st ed. New Haven, CT: Yale University Press, 2008.

Hill, Christopher. *Antichrist in Seventeenth-Century England*. Oxford: Oxford University Press, 1971.

———. *The Century of Revolution, 1603–1714*. London: Routledge, 2002.

———. *The World Turned Upside down: Radical Ideas during the English Revolution*. Harmondsworth: Penguin, 1978.

Hillerbrand, Hans J. *A Fellowship of Discontent*. New York: Harper & Row, 1967.

Hilton, Boyd. *A Mad, Bad and Dangerous People?: England 1783–1846*. Oxford: Clarendon Press, 2006.

Hinds, Hilary. "'And the Lord's Power Was over All': Calvinist Anxiety, Sacred Confidence, and George Fox's Journal." *English Literary History*, 2008, 841–70.

Hunter, Graeme. *Radical Protestantism in Spinoza's Thought*. Aldershot: Ashgate, 2005.

Ishay, Micheline. *The Human Rights Reader: Major Political Essays, Speeches, and Documents from Ancient Times to the Present*. Abingdon: Taylor & Francis, 2007.

Israel, Jonathan I. *Enlightenment Contested: Philosophy, Modernity, and the Emancipation of Man, 1670–1752*. New York: Oxford University Press, 2008.

———. *Radical Enlightenment: Philosophy and the Making of Modernity, 1650–1750*. New York: Oxford University Press, 2002.

———. "Religious Toleration and Radical Philosophy in the Later Dutch Golden Age (1668–1710)." In *Calvinism and Religious Toleration in the Dutch Golden Age*, edited by R. Po-Chia Hsia and Henk Van Nierop, 148–58. Cambridge: Cambridge University Press, 2002.

Jacob, Margaret. "The Enlightenment Critique of Christianity." In *Enlightenment, Reawakening, and Revolution, 1660–1815*, edited by Stewart J. Brown and Timothy Tackett, 265–82. Cambridge: Cambridge University Press, 2006.

James, Susan. *Spinoza on Philosophy, Religion, and Politics*. Oxford: Oxford University Press, 2012.

Janz, Denis. *World Christianity and Marxism*. New York: Oxford University Press, 1998.

Janz, Denis R. *Reformation Reader*. Philadelphia, PA: Fortress Press, 2008.

Jones, Rufus. *Spiritual Reformers in the Sixteenth and Seventeenth Centuries*. London: Macmillan, 1914.

Kaplan, Benjamin J. *Divided by Faith: Religious Conflict and the Practice of Toleration in Early Modern Europe*. Cambridge, MA: Harvard University Press, 2007.

Kolakowski, Leszek. *The Two Eyes of Spinoza & Other Essays on Philosophers*. Translated by Zbigniew Janowski. South Bend, IN: St. Augustine's Press, 2004.

Labrousse, Elisabeth. *Bayle*. Oxford: Oxford University Press, 1983.

Larsen, Timothy. *A People of One Book*. New York: Oxford University Press, 2011.

Larsen, Timothy. *Crisis of Doubt: Honest Faith in Nineteenth-Century England.* Oxford: Oxford University Press, 2006.

———. "The Regaining of Faith: Reconversions among Popular Radicals in Mid-Victorian England." *Church History* 70, no. 3 (September 2001): 527–43.

Lightman, Bernard. "Does the History of Science and Religion Change Depending on the Narrator? Some Atheist and Agnostic Perspectives." *Science & Christian Belief* 24, no. 2 (October 2012): 149–68.

———. "Interpreting Agnosticism as a Nonconformist Sect: T. H. Huxley's 'New Reformation.'" In *Science and Dissent in England, 1688–1945*, edited by Paul Wood, 197–214. Aldershot: Ashgate, 2004.

Loewen, Harry. *Luther and the Radicals: Another Look at Some Aspects of the Struggle between Luther and the Radical Reformers.* Waterloo, ON: Wilfrid Laurier University Press, 1974.

Loewenstein, David. "Gerrard Winstanley and the Diggers." In *The Oxford Handbook of Literature and the English Revolution*, edited by Laura Lunger Knoppers. Oxford: Oxford University Press, 2012. DOI: 10.1093/oxfordhb/9780199560608.013.0018.

Lubac, Henri de. *The Drama of Atheist Humanism.* San Francisco, CA: Ignatius Press, 1995.

MacCulloch, Diarmaid. *A History of Christianity: The First Three Thousand Years.* London: Allen Lane, 2009.

———. *Reformation: Europe's House Divided, 1490–1700.* London: Penguin, 2004.

MacIntyre, Alasdair C. *After Virtue: A Study in Moral Theory.* 2nd ed. London: Duckworth, 1985.

Marsden, George M. *Fundamentalism and American Culture.* 2nd ed. New York: Oxford University Press, 2006.

Marshall, John. *John Locke, Toleration and Early Enlightenment Culture.* Cambridge: Cambridge University Press, 2006.

Marty, Martin E. *Martin Luther.* New York: Penguin, 2004.

Mason, H. T. *Pierre Bayle and Voltaire.* Oxford: Oxford University Press, 1963.

Mason, Richard. *The God of Spinoza: A Philosophical Study.* Cambridge: Cambridge University Press, 1997.

McDowell, Nicholas. *The English Radical Imagination.* Oxford: Oxford University Press, 2003.

McGrath, Alister E. *Reformation Thought: An Introduction.* 3rd ed. Oxford: Blackwell, 1991.

McLellan, David. *The Young Hegelians and Karl Marx.* London: Macmillan, 1969.

McLeod, Hugh. *Secularisation in Western Europe.* Basingstoke: Palgrave Macmillan, 2000.

———. "The Two Americas: Religion and Secularity in the Seventies." In *Yliopisto, Kirkko Ja Yhteiskunta*, edited by Antti Laine and Aappo Laitinen, 200–214. Helsinki: Finnish Society for Church History, 2011.

Michalson, Gordon E. *Kant and the Problem of God.* Oxford: Blackwell, 1999.

Miller, Nicholas P. *The Religious Roots of the First Amendment.* New York: Oxford University Press, 2012.

Moore, James R. "The Crisis of Faith: Reformation versus Revolution." In *Religion in Victorian Britain, vol. 2: Controversies,* edited by Gerald Parsons and James R Moore, 220–37. Manchester: Manchester University Press, 1988.

———. *Religion in Victorian Britain. Vol. 3: Sources.* Manchester: Manchester University Press, 1988.

Murphy, Howard R. "The Ethical Revolt against Christian Orthodoxy in Early Victorian England." *American Historical Review* 60, no. 4 (July 1955): 800–817.

Nadler, Steven. *A Book Forged in Hell: Spinoza's Scandalous Treatise and the Birth of the Secular Age.* Princeton, NJ: Princeton University Press, 2011.

———. *Spinoza: A Life.* Cambridge: Cambridge University Press, 2001.

Nigg, Walter. *The Heretics.* New York: Knopf, 1962.

Oberman, Heiko A. *The Dawn of the Reformation: Essays in Late Medieval and Early Reformation Thought.* Grand Rapids, MI: Eerdmans, 1986.

———. *Luther: Man between God and the Devil.* New Haven, CT: Yale University Press, 1989.

Ozment, Steven E. *Homo Spiritualis: A Comparative Study of the Anthropology of Johannes Tauler, Jean Gerson and Martin Luther (1509–16) in the Context of Their Theological Thought.* Leiden: Brill, 1969.

———. *Mysticism and Dissent: Religious Ideology and Social Protest in the Sixteenth Century.* New Haven, CT: Yale University Press, 1973.

Pacini, David S. *Through Narcissus' Glass Darkly : The Modern Religion of Conscience.* 1st ed. New York: Fordham University Press, 2008.

Pagani, Karen. "Forgiveness and the Age of Reason: Fenelon, Voltaire, Rousseau and Stael." Ph.D. diss., University of Chicago, 2008.

Pagden, Anthony. *The Enlightenment: And Why It Still Matters.* New York: Random House, 2013.

Pearson, Roger. *Voltaire Almighty: A Life in Pursuit of Freedom.* London: Bloomsbury, 2005.

Pleins, J. David. *In Praise of Darwin: George Romanes and the Evolution of a Darwinian Believer.* New York: Bloomsbury, 2014.

Pomeau, René. *La Religion de Voltaire.* 2nd ed. Paris: Nizet, 1969.

Popkin, Richard H. *The History of Scepticism: From Savonarola to Bayle.* Oxford: Oxford University Press, 2003.

———. "The Religious Background of Seventeenth-Century Philosophy." In *The Cambridge History of Seventeenth-Century Philosophy,* edited by Daniel Garber and Michael Ayers, Vol. 1. Cambridge: Cambridge University Press, 1998.

———. *Spinoza.* Oxford: Oneworld, 2004.

———. "Spinoza and Samuel Fisher." *Philosophia* 15, no. 3 (December 1985): 219–36.

Popkin, Richard H. *The Third Force in Seventeenth-Century Thought*. Leiden: Brill, 1992.

Popkin, Richard H., and Michael A. Signer. *Spinoza's Earliest Publication?: The Hebrew Translation of Margaret Fell's A Loving Salutation to the Seed of Abraham Among the Jews, Wherever They Are Scattered up and down Upon the Face of the Earth*. Assen, The Netherlands: Van Gorcum, 1987.

Rex, Walter. *Essays on Pierre Bayle and Religious Controversy*. The Hague: Martinus Nijhoff, 1965.

Roberts, William Clare. "Marx in Hell: The Critique of Political Economy as Katabasis." *Critical Sociology* 31, nos. 1–2 (January 1, 2005): 39–55.

Royle, Edward. *Victorian Infidels: The Origins of the British Secularist Movement, 1791–1866*. Manchester: Manchester University Press, 1974.

Ryrie, Alec. *Being Protestant in Reformation Britain*. Oxford: Oxford University Press, 2013.

Schreiner, Susan. *Are You Alone Wise?* New York: Oxford University Press, 2010.

Smith, Charles H., and George Beccaloni. *Natural Selection and Beyond: The Intellectual Legacy of Alfred Russel Wallace: The Intellectual Legacy of Alfred Russel Wallace*. Oxford: Oxford University Press, 2008.

Smith, Malcolm. *Montaigne and Religious Freedom: The Dawn of Pluralism*. Geneva: Librairie Droz, 1991.

Spencer, Nick. *Darwin and God*. London: SPCK, 2009.

Sperber, Jonathan. *Karl Marx: A Nineteenth-Century Life*. New York: Liveright, 2013.

Sprague, L. De Camp. *The Great Monkey Trial*. New York: Doubleday, 1968.

Spring, Joel. *Political Agendas for Education: From Change We Can Believe In to Putting America First*. New York: Routledge, 2010.

Stachniewski, John. "John Donne: The Despair of the 'Holy Sonnets.'" *English Literary History* 48, no. 4 (December 1, 1981): 677–705.

———. *The Persecutory Imagination: English Puritanism and the Literature of Religious Despair*. New York: Oxford University Press, 1991.

Stedman Jones, Gareth. "The Young Hegelians, Marx and Engels." In *The Cambridge History of Nineteenth-Century Political Thought*, edited by Gareth Stedman Jones and Gregory Claeys, 556–600. Cambridge: Cambridge University Press, 2011.

Stendahl, Krister. "The Apostle Paul and the Introspective Conscience of the West." *Harvard Theological Review* 56, no. 3 (July 1, 1963): 199–215.

Stewart, Matthew. *The Courtier and the Heretic: Leibniz, Spinoza, and the Fate of God in the Modern World*. New York: Norton, 2007.

Strauss, Leo. *Spinoza's Critique of Religion*. Chicago: University of Chicago Press, 1997.

Strohl, Jane E. "Luther's Spiritual Journey." In *The Cambridge Companion to Martin Luther*, edited by Donald K. McKim, 149–64. Cambridge: Cambridge University Press, 2003.

Taft, Barbara. "Walwyn, William (bap. 1600, D. 1681)." In *ODNB*.

Taylor, Charles. *A Secular Age*. Cambridge, MA: Belknap, 2007.

Thomas, Keith. *The Ends of Life: Roads to Fulfillment in Early Modern England*. New York: Oxford University Press, 2009.

Thompson, E. P. *The Making of the English Working Class*. London: Penguin, 1980.

Tinsley, Barbara S. *Pierre Bayle's Reformation: Conscience and Criticism on the Eve of the Enlightenment*. Selinsgrove, PA: Susquehanna University Press, 2001.

Torrey, Norman L. *Voltaire and the English Deists*. New Haven, CT: Yale University Press, 1930.

Turner, Denys. "Religion." In *The Cambridge Companion to Marx*, edited by Terrell Carver and Terrell Carver, 320–38. Cambridge: Cambridge University Press, 1991.

Turner, Frank M. *Between Science and Religion: The Reaction to Scientific Naturalism in Late Victorian England*. New Haven, CT: Yale University Press, 1974.

———. "The Victorian Conflict between Science and Religion: A Professional Dimension." *Isis* 69, no. 3 (September 1978): 356–76.

———. "The Victorian Crisis of Faith and the Faith That Was Lost." In *Victorian Faith in Crisis: Essays on Continuity and Change in Nineteenth-Century Religious Belief*, edited by Richard J. Helmstadter, 9–38. Stanford, CA: Stanford University Press, 1990.

———. "Victorian Scientific Naturalism and Thomas Carlyle." *Victorian Studies* 18, no. 3 (March 1, 1975): 325–43.

Voogt, Gerrit. "'Anyone Who Can Read May Be a Preacher': Sixteenth-Century Roots of the Collegiants." In *The Formation of Clerical and Confessional Identities in Early Modern Europe*, edited by Wim Janse and Barbara Pitkin, 409–24. Leiden: Brill, 2006.

———. *Constraint on Trial: Dirck Volckertsz Coornhert and Religious Freedom*. Kirksville, MO: Truman State University Press, 2000.

Walsh, John. "'Methodism' and the Origins of English Speaking Evangelicalism." In *Evangelicalism: Comparative Studies of Popular Protestantism in North America, the British Isles and Beyond, 1700–1990*, edited by Mark A. Noll, David W. Bebbington, and George A. Rawlyk, 19–37. Oxford: Oxford University Press, 1994.

Wartofsky, Marx W. *Feuerbach*. Cambridge: Cambridge University Press, 1977.

Whitford, David M. "Luther's Political Encounters." In *The Cambridge Companion to Martin Luther*, edited by Donald K. McKim, 179–91. Cambridge: Cambridge University Press, 2003.

Williams, George H. *The Radical Reformation*. 3rd ed. Kirksville, MO: Truman State University Press, 2000.

———. *Spiritual and Anabaptist Writers: Documents Illustrative of the Radical Reformation*. Louisville, KY: Westminster John Knox Press, 1957.

Wriedt, Markus. "Luther's Theology." In *The Cambridge Companion to Martin Luther*, edited by Donald K. McKim, 86–119. Cambridge: Cambridge University Press, 2003.

Young, Robert M. *Darwin's Metaphor: Nature's Place in Victorian Culture*. Cambridge: Cambridge University Press, 1985.

Yovel, Yirmiyahu. *Spinoza and Other Heretics: The Adventures of Immanence*. Princeton, NJ: Princeton University Press, 1992.

———. *Spinoza and Other Heretics: The Marrano of Reason*. Princeton, NJ: Princeton University Press, 1992.

Index